Self-Study
Teacher Research

D0162086

This book is dedicated to all my family and especially to our newest members, Theodore, Lucia, and Rohan, to my dear sisters Irene and Alexandra and to those who have been like sisters to me, and to my brothers John, Nicos, and Andre. With special thanks to my brother John who paved the way for all six of us as first-generation college graduates with the courage and perseverance of our parents and grandparents.

In Loving Memory of My Mother, Magdalena Theodora Savvas Pantelides

Self-Study
Teacher Research

Improving Your Practice Through Collaborative Inquiry

Anastasia P. Samaras

George Mason University

Los Angeles | London | New Delhi
Singapore | Washington DC

Copyright © 2011 by SAGE Publications, Inc.

All rights reserved. No part of this book may be reproduced or utilized in any form or by any means, electronic or mechanical, including photocopying, recording, or by any information storage and retrieval system, without permission in writing from the publisher.

For information:

SAGE Publications, Inc.
2455 Teller Road
Thousand Oaks, California 91320
E-mail: order@sagepub.com

SAGE Publications Ltd.
1 Oliver's Yard
55 City Road, London EC1Y 1SP
United Kingdom

SAGE Publications India Pvt. Ltd.
B 1/I 1 Mohan Cooperative Industrial Area
Mathura Road, New Delhi 110 044
India

SAGE Publications Asia-Pacific Pte. Ltd.
33 Pekin Street #02-01
Far East Square
Singapore 048763

Printed in the United States of America

Library of Congress Cataloging-in-Publication Data

Samaras, Anastasia P. (Anastasia Pantelides), 1950-
Self-study teacher research: improving your practice through collaborative inquiry/Anastasia Samaras.
    p. cm.
Includes bibliographical references and index.
ISBN 978-1-4129-7207-9 (pbk.)

  1. Action research in education. 2. Teachers—Training of. 3. Group work in education. I. Title.

LB1028.24.S36 2011
370.71′1—dc22   2009047312

This book is printed on acid-free paper.

10   11   12   13   14   10   9   8   7   6   5   4   3   2   1

Acquisitions Editor:	Diane McDaniel
Editorial Assistant:	Ashley Conlon
Production Editor:	Brittany Bauhaus
Copy Editor:	Melinda Masson
Typesetter:	C&M Digitals (P) Ltd.
Proofreader:	Sally Jaskold
Indexer:	Holly Day
Cover Designer:	Candice Harman
Marketing Manager:	Dory Schrader

Brief Contents

Detailed Contents

PART II. Your Self-Study Project

6   Design

7   Protect

8   Organize Data   158

9   Collect Data   173

Preface

A PREFACE WORTH READING

I see this task now as motivating. I am getting my hands dirty learning, playing, and transforming who I am. I was so afraid of making mistakes. Now I am afraid if I don't try enough.

—Diana P. Ortiz (2008),
Doctoral Candidate, George Mason University

Photo 0.1   Get Your Hands Dirty

GET YOUR HANDS DIRTY!

Many years ago I taught preschoolers and observed how much they learned by getting their hands dirty. My advanced studies involved learning about early childhood education, human development, curriculum and instruction, and teacher education. I find myself smiling when I reminisce on teaching young children. I watched 3-year-olds energetically fill their paper cups of dirt, carefully plant their seeds, happily water and talk to their sprouting plants, and eagerly watch their plants grow over time. They also enthusiastically dug their hands into finger paint, shaving cream, clay, and mud as they played with and shared their ideas with classmates. With busy hands, they traced and painted, designed and cut, and placed and glued fabric, yarn, and buttons on their self-portraits, which were posted in hallways and on home refrigerators. With excitement, they shared the castles they designed in the outside sandbox and the chalk art they sketched on school sidewalks.

I also observed my own three children tirelessly constructing new designs in the makeshift sandbox where our deck was planned. As children, we relish getting our hands dirty in order to explore and learn. And then we grow up. As we get older, we often forget how much we learned by playing with our ideas and sharing those ideas with colleagues of muddying up our hands, making mistakes, and enjoying the process of learning and coming to know the world through our engagement in it.

I would like to begin this writing by inviting you to "get your hands dirty." Come into my university classroom where I teach people just like you who want to learn about self-study teacher research and how to use it in their classrooms. Dig in and join us in the doing of self-study research!

Imagine for a moment you are sitting in our classroom filled with people just like you who are curious about their teaching. You may be a student taking a teacher education course at a community college, a beginning teacher in a college program, or a graduate student completing a capstone teacher research course. You may be completing your internship or student teaching experience and working with a mentor. You may be a preservice or an inservice teacher; a teacher relatively new to the profession or a veteran; or an early childhood, elementary, or secondary school teacher. Regardless of your experience, expertise, teaching context, and discipline, I'll take you through a beginning activity that will introduce you to the self-study research methodology. The activity is an inquiry that applies to you wherever you are in your program of studies or teaching career. You'll be invited to partake in various self-study activities throughout the book because it will give you practice. The inquiries with colleagues are designed to help you build your research project—your castle in the sand. So let's start doing self-study while we're talking about how to do it.

BOOK OVERVIEW

This book is responding to the burgeoning interest of teachers seeking a guide to conduct self-study research and teacher educators searching for a textbook to more comprehensibly and systematically teach it. Zeichner (1999) wrote that "the birth of the self-study in teacher education movement around 1990 has been probably the single most significant development ever in the field of teacher education research" (p. 8). Self-study research has come of age, and an accessible and comprehensive textbook is greatly needed. You will be introduced to the Self-Study School: its foundations, its culture, and the community of teacher educators who seeded and developed it to be one of the most productive special interest groups, Self-Study of Teacher Education Practices (S-STEP) of the American Educational Research Association (AERA).

A major goal of self-study teacher research is for teachers like you to gain a tacit knowledge about their teaching as they seek to improve and assess their teaching, its impact on their students' learning, and its contribution to the knowledge base of teaching. Self-study entails a teacher's personal inquiry supported and critiqued by colleagues. Self-study involves you in an open, reflective, and systematic investigation of an issue you want to study in your own classroom. This textbook offers you a framework to do just that. You will find a framework of the self-study research process, or how to conduct your own self-study research project.

The book integrates my learning and my many years of teaching and research experiences to offer you a useful textbook and resource. This writing integrates my belief that teacher and school improvement begins with you. From my own teaching, I have come to recognize that students need a guiding framework for organizing a manageable research study as they gain an overview of how it can be done. Along with other teacher educators, I am all too familiar with students asking for clearer guidelines, checkpoints, and the necessary details on how to successfully complete their research projects. My students tell me they appreciate having some structure for their report with a suggested headings template. They are pleased with the Self-Study Research Project Planner and the sample timeline because they can gauge the work needed and fit it accordingly in their own project and schedules. On the other hand, students are reminded that teacher research is not just a series of steps to be completed for a final required class project or for a grade they will receive. Instead, they are asked to consider what self-study research contributes to their current and continuous learning as a teacher and what it can mean to their practice.

If we think in terms of backward design planning (McTighe & Wiggins, 2005), or given the educative outcomes of learning (Wiggins, 1998) about self-study teacher research, the following learner outcomes apply:

- Students will be able to demonstrate their understanding of the self-study methodology by applying it in a self-study teacher research project.
- Students will catalogue and present the process of research through a Critical Friends Portfolio charting and documenting their individual and collective learning.
- Students will be able to present a self-assessment and critical friend assessment of how their self-study teacher research project aligns with self-study methodological components.

Each chapter is designed to move you systematically toward your final self-study research project. I open each chapter with an overview of what the chapter includes followed by a short personal anecdote related to the chapter topic.

The book is designed in two parts: Part I, "The 6 Ws of Self-Study Research," introduces you to self-study (i.e., the *what*, *why*, *where*, *when*, *who*, and *how* of self-study). In Part II, "Your Self-Study Project," you will find the research tools, techniques, and activities to help you plan, enact, and assess your research project.

In Chapter 1, "Understanding Self-Study Research," you will be introduced to self-study research, what self-study is, and what it is not. The chapter places the discussion of self-study within its usefulness to your personal and professional accountability as a teacher and with particular emphasis on the need for teachers to be able to apply and assess what they learn as they work toward improving learning and education reform.

Chapter 2, "Overview of the Self-Study Research Process," presents what your research project encompasses with descriptions of each research component. Within this chapter you will also find an example of a self-study project so you have an idea of the research components.

Chapter 3, "The Self-Study Learning Community," provides a discussion of the culture of the self-study community and self-study as a paradigm shift and earlier paradigms that influenced its emergence as a new research methodology. Included is a timeline of important events in the outgrowth of the Self-Study School placed within a discussion of the development and formalization of the self-study community. This chapter is offered to highlight how current practices and the culture of self-study flow from this historical background while also noting that the community has continuously reshaped and developed the Self-Study School.

Chapter 4, "The Self-Study Methodology," describes the characteristics of self-study research that inform the Five Foci, or the methodological components of self-study. These Five Foci are the cornerstone of the broadly defined standards of self-study and provide a gauge for you to assess the quality and validity of your self-study research project.

Chapter 5, "Self-Study Methods," introduces six self-study methods and invites you to consider exploring them and especially the developmental portfolio self-study method, creating a Critical Friends Portfolio. You will also be given an overview of a Critical Friends Portfolio. Other self-study methods presented here include personal history self-study method, living educational theory, collective self-study method, arts-based self-study method, and memory work self-study method.

Chapter 6, "Design," offers you a framework to develop your self-study research project using a seven-element design framework. You will be prompted to think about your inquiry while also placing your inquiry within a strong theoretical and conceptual foundation informed through a literature review. This chapter revisits the self-study methodological components of personal situated inquiry, critical collaborative inquiry, and planning for improving learning.

Chapter 7, "Protect," includes standards of research ethics as noted by professional organizations and asks you to seriously contemplate what it means to be an ethical researcher. It includes the role that your critical friend plays in guiding you toward that objective. This chapter revisits the self-study methodological component of critical collaborative inquiry essential for the discussion and review of the ethics of your research.

Chapter 8, "Organize Data," offers guidelines on organizing and effectively managing your data set, which is essential for transparency for documentation. A template is provided to guide you through your data collection (i.e., the data you will collect before, during, and after your study).

Chapter 9, "Collect Data," focuses on your work in enacting your study and methods for collecting data generated from your pedagogical strategies. This chapter revisits the self-study methodological component of the need for a transparent and systematic research process with detail about how the data were collected and shared with critical friends through research memos.

Chapter 10, "Analyze Data," is where you learn about techniques for analyzing qualitative data. This chapter revisits the self-study methodological component of the need for a transparent and systematic research process (i.e., documenting a data audit trail, providing detail about how data were analyzed, and establishing trustworthiness with critical friends).

Chapter 11, "Assess Research Quality," offers a discussion about the multiplicity of your data sources in your research design. Issues of transparency, validation and trustworthiness, reliability, and generalizability are addressed in this chapter. A detailed outline and rubric is provided for your self-assessment and critical friend assessment of your research project.

Chapter 12, "Write," offers guidelines for writing and editing research findings with a special section on developing a polished abstract.

Chapter 13, "Present and Publish," highlights the self-study methodological component of knowledge generation and presentation (i.e., the need for self-study teacher researchers to make their work public for review and critique through writing and publishing). A special section for submitting and presenting your self-study research is included. This chapter revisits the self-study methodological component of knowledge generation through presenting.

The "Closing Remarks" at the end of Chapter 13 provide a place for you to look back, consider, and celebrate what you have learned about self-study teacher research. It is also a place for you to reflect on your visions and plans for improving education, and your continued professional development goals for the work ahead.

NOTE TO USERS

The book chapters do not have to be read in order. I suggest you skim through the text before reading it. For example, Chapter 3, "The Self-Study Learning Community," offers an interesting discussion of the outgrowth and history of self-study, but you may decide to skim it at first and move directly to conducting your self-study. Please do read ahead in Chapter 12 about writing so you can be sure to establish a writing routine from the beginning of your research. I find that my students like to first have an idea and overview of what is involved in completing a self-study project. Therefore, I briefly share the Self-Study Research Project Planner in Chapter 2 while I'm also introducing self-study and then provide the detail in Part II. You will find some notes in some chapters suggesting you look ahead.

Also, the critical friend inquiries are invitations that you may elect to do depending on your time. For example, if you are using this textbook for a one-semester-long course, then you will not be able to complete all of the inquiries. So, please use the book as it works for your needs and within your time frame.

UNIQUE BOOK FEATURES

Self-Study Research Guideposts

You will find the *ski flag* for each self-study research guidepost.

I watched our grandson Rohan learn to ski. He first learned to navigate the clearly marked-off "bunny slope" with his parents carefully guiding him along the way. There were flags and safety cones highlighting the path. The next winter, I watched him ride the chairlift with his parents and learn to ski down another clearly marked-off slope. His skiing continues to be facilitated by the guideposts made available to him. Novice and experienced skiers, as well as researchers, benefit from clearly marked guideposts. Indeed, Anne Freese and I wrote, "We see the need for some agreed upon methodological components," some "brighter guide-posts" (Samaras & Freese, 2009, p. 13). With this need in mind, I have designed *Self-Study Research Guideposts* interconnected to the self-study methodological components.

The methodological components are introduced within activities in a graduated manner with increasing detail to scaffold your understanding and application of each one. Self-study scholars have offered descriptions of the self-study methodology, which has been refined over time through its enactment. Their work has been essential to my own understanding of self-study and is embedded throughout this text. The practice and research conducted by self-study colleagues has allowed me to learn self-study. Their work made this book possible, and I am deeply indebted to the self-study community. Now, I share what I learned from others with you. It is my hope that these self-study research guideposts are useful to you and are responsive to refining and improving the quality of self-study research. The goal of the guideposts is to help guide your way along an accessible, safe, and enjoyable path as you develop, refine, and assess your research project according to the self-study methodological components.

The book is also interspersed with tables, charts, and visuals to help you see the big picture and stay organized. The organizers are designed to help you construct an understanding of both the details and the process of conducting self-study research.

Reflections

There are places throughout the text where it is recommend that you pause to reflect. You will find prompts encouraging you to take time to do just that.

Critical Friend Inquiries

You will find the *hand icon* for each critical friend inquiry.

This book is uniquely designed to introduce you to learning about and practicing self-study teacher research. Self-study teacher research is presented in a reader-friendly way with interactive activities that you can practice with your critical friend. Student examples are also provided. You are encouraged to keep your critical friend inquiries in a Critical

Friends Portfolio to experience the full potential of the role of collaborative inquiry in self-study research. You will find invitations for critical collaborative inquiries to build your portfolio—a "developmental portfolio self-study method" (Samaras & Freese, 2006, p. 69) designed as a manageable approach to help you build your research project over time. Throughout the text, you will find critical friend inquiries designed to help you frame and build your research project. Many of those inquiries engage you informally in other self-study methods. You may choose the inquiries you want to try.

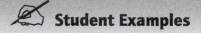 **Student Examples**

You will find the *writing hand icon* for each example from student and/or teacher work.

I have found that more than anything else, students want examples of what I am talking about and ask, "But what's it look like?" Therefore, I asked students if I could include some of their work. They have generously shared their work as examples throughout the textbook. The textbook offers examples of self-study research, which demonstrate the practical connections among self-study research in classrooms, teachers' professional growth, and their students' learning with anecdotal evidence and examples from teaching and research. Also included in this textbook are exemplar sections of self-study research projects conducted by teachers as well as other practitioners. Their examples highlight the broad applicability of self-study research in educational reform efforts and the possibilities of this cutting-edge paradigm across disciplines. You will find examples of self-study research and various self-study methods.

Please note that the student examples are presented to give you an idea of what self-study can look like. They are not presented as "the" model or something you should try to match. I encourage you to let your own ideas propel you forward and use the student examples as a way to see self-study with a broad lens. I understand it may be easier to want to mock the example, but that usually makes it more difficult.

Advice From a Self-Study Scholar

You will find the *hand with star icon* for some stellar advice offered by self-study scholars!

This book includes advice from experienced self-study scholars working in the United States and internationally. They offer firsthand suggestions about conducting self-study research.

 Key Ideas

You will find the *page brief icon* for the presentation of key ideas at the end of each chapter.

The key ideas of each chapter are summarized at the end of each chapter to assist you in thinking through what you read. These key ideas help reinforce what you read. They can also be easily retrieved at any point when you want to look back at the key ideas in a chapter.

Key Terms

The book includes **key terms** in bold throughout the text. Those terms are defined in a glossary at the end of the book.

Self-Study Web Site and Your Self-Study Resource Center

A companion student study Web site is available for easy access to key features included in the textbook. The study site includes the following resources:

Chapter Summaries

Your Self-Study Research Planner

Your Self-Study Project Timeline

Your Critical Friends Portfolio

Self-Study Guideposts

Self-Study Scholar Advice

Self-Study Resource Center

Resource A: Topic-Based Self-Study Research

Resource B: Self-Study Books

Resource C: Castle Conferences

Resource D: Related Web sites

Resource E: The Cultural Inquiry Process

Resource F: Formatting Your Research Report

Resource G: Writing and Publishing Resources

Resource H: Presentation and Publication Outlets

Resource I: Qualitative Research Sources

Integrative and Interactive Text Components

This textbook integrates three distinctive yet integrated components to assist you in learning about self-study and conducting a self-study research project:

1. Purpose-Driven Research

2. A Critical Friends Portfolio

3. Five Foci: Methodological Components of Self-Study Research

Purpose-Driven Research

I have always found that students appreciate working on something that matters to them and to their students. Purpose does matter. Your professional goals for improving your practice and your students' learning especially matter. Consider what you want for your teaching at the end of your project. *Self-Study Teacher Research* was designed to guide and support you as you conduct and assess classroom-based research with attention to the role you play in that process and inside of that research. It is teacher research in the first person that empowers you to make the needed changes you recognize in your own classroom.

The self-study research methodology, developed by self-study teacher educators, has immediate applicability and usefulness to classroom teachers. In this textbook, you are provided detailed steps in conducting self-study research while you are encouraged to think deeply about not only the "how," but the "why" of self-study. That "why" is essential for your ongoing self-study research and professional development and does not stop after you finish reading this book. Embrace what matters to you and to your students. Your passion and purpose will carry you through the challenges that teacher researchers face because it makes a difference you care about and recognize as important.

A Critical Friends Portfolio

Teaching can be a lonely craft, and so can teacher research. But it does not need to be. Self-study teacher research requires that you work with colleagues as critical friends to gain their perspectives, support, and review. You are invited to develop a **Critical Friends Portfolio** or a specifically designed pedagogical approach to provide opportunities for you to learn from and about your teaching. It entails an anthology of your work and engagement in a series of inquiries with peer interchange. All inquiries have been implemented and generated from field-tested teaching and research experiences. The inquiries help make the overall research process more manageable and are useful to writing the final research project. You choose which inquiries you complete.

Five Foci Framework: Methodological Components of Self-Study Research

Unique and immediately applicable, this textbook includes a **Five Foci Framework**, or the methodological components of self-study research that have been gleaned, extended, and refined from the work of self-study scholars. The Five Foci are woven and revisited throughout the chapters and are particularly important toward your self-assessment and critical friend assessment of addressing the quality of your self-study research project.

The Five Foci are in essence also guideposts. They are not "standards," which have the potential of destroying what self-study is or to align it with other traditional research methodologies (Zeichner, 2009). Instead, the foci are offered as a definitional framework for your own assessment of how you are addressing what self-study scholars to date have identified as key components of self-study practice. Self-study methodological components will initially appear in the beginning chapters. Then we will cycle back and revisit each methodological component in subsequent chapters with examples and a fuller discussion.

USES OF THE BOOK

Teachers, Schools, and Other Practitioners

The primary audience for *Self-Study Teacher Research* is teachers and teaching teams and teacher education students including preservice and inservice teachers in undergraduate, graduate, and advanced programs of study. This textbook would be valuable to school reform teams as teachers in schools are searching for resources that will assist them in making sense of their practices. The self-assessment guidelines and Critical Friends Portfolio could play a critical role in the development of teacher-initiated and school-based performance measures, which encourage teachers to create portfolios and complete self-assessments of their professional teaching practices. It would be quite useful to school and state professional development teacher leaders and coordinators who offer teachers opportunities to work collaboratively in professional development workshops although generated from teachers' inquiries and interests. The book would be of interest to those involved in the many levels and venues of school education because of its applicability to other practitioner-based contexts such as principals, administrators, counselors, reading specialists, program evaluators, research methodologists, policy analysts, and community workers. Other practitioner-based programs that require research-based internships such as counselors and health practitioners would also find this book useful.

Teacher Educators

The textbook is not limited to just one phase in the continuum of teacher development (i.e., initial teacher certification). Rather, it can be used by teacher educators who work in a range of teacher education programs in community colleges and universities with preservice teachers and practicing classroom teachers and graduate and doctoral students. This textbook has much appeal as a course textbook or as supplemental text for other preservice and inservice teacher education courses (e.g., Introduction to Teaching, Education Methods, Education Research, Cooperative Learning, and Advanced Seminars in Teacher Education, Scholarship, and Early Childhood, Elementary, and Secondary Education). Additionally, this textbook is useful in a doctoral-level course in advanced research methods in self-study research methodology. The textbook would also be useful as a supplementary text for courses in qualitative research, research on teacher education, arts-based research, the study of teaching, and ways of knowing.

Faculty Study Groups

This book would be valuable to faculty study groups since faculty are also interested in improving their professional practice and programs and generating research about them.

Universities that promote faculty development would find this book useful. It is applicable to new and/or experienced faculty across disciplines since the book addresses a method to improve the scholarship of teaching, which is not specific to a discipline. The landscape in achieving "teaching excellence" has shifted with a growing attention to the quality of university teaching in terms of annual merit reviews, promotion, and tenure. University programs and colleges may find this book useful when they plan and reshape their accreditation reviews, which are actually called a self-study. Professional organizations, like the National Council for Accreditation of Teacher Education (NCATE), ask faculty to self-assess their programs: their progress and areas for improvement. As Pinnegar and Erickson (2009) argue, NCATE site visits could also include a "Parallel Cycle of Self-Study" for research conducted by teacher educators (p. 156).

✉ A PERSONAL NOTE TO READERS

I bring to this book over a decade of experience as a public school secondary education teacher and a preschool teacher with an appreciation and respect for the daily challenges teachers face. I also bring over two decades of teaching and researching in higher education and working in schools with teachers and administrators. Nonetheless, I am a continuous learner. Consequently, this writing is my current understanding of self-study and is not offered or suggested as the only way to go about the craft of studying your practice. As teachers, we are a professional community that continues to learn from our *doing* or practicing of self-study with open and honest conversations about what we still do not understand. I have come to recognize that it was in the practicing of self-study with others that I was best able to understand its nature and impact. With invitations from self-study colleagues to present and write about my practice of self-study, I began to appreciate the essentialness in generating and sharing our collective work in self-study research, which is what I see as a major thrust for our sustainability and continued growth as a professional organization. Indeed, a textbook on self-study research would not be possible without the decades of work of my self-study colleagues and those who have served as leaders. Therefore, you will find their work cited throughout the book, which has been foundational to the Self-Study School. Although we come from different institutions and countries and have different research questions, we are a community that continues to learn from our practice and our differing perspectives and with a deep respect for each other's work.

In writing this text, I bring a full and rich "story of self with critical friends" that has impacted my learning with colleagues and students. I write to offer our collective work in self-study scholarship. Serving as a coeditor of the "Castle" proceedings with Clare Kosnik and Anne Freese (Kosnik, Freese, & Samaras, 2002a) and our subsequent books along with Clive Beck (Kosnik, Beck, Freese, & Samaras, 2006; Samaras, Freese, Kosnik, & Beck, 2008) generated educative conversations with a diversity of self-study scholars. Thorough discussions with Anne in our attempt to articulate the *what, when, who, how,* and very important *why* of self-study in a primer (Samaras & Freese, 2006) gave us insight into the past and future possibilities of self-study research (Samaras & Freese, 2009).

Critical to my professional development has been the dialogue and questions raised about teaching practice with a diversity of students and self-study colleagues both from the United States and internationally. My years of teaching education students and doctoral students learning self-study research (e.g., *The Mason Group* [Breslin et al., 2008; Mittapalli & Samaras, 2008; Samaras et al., 2008]), as well as the self-study of my teaching (e.g., Samaras, 2002; Samaras et al., 2007), have helped me come to a reframed understanding of the complexity of teaching and researching about self-study and its value to practitioners other than teachers. You will find their work cited throughout the book.

I have fond memories of self-study colleagues and their intellectually stimulating conference sessions as well as our teatime, social gatherings, and outings at the Castle Conference. Deliberations and explorations with Hafdís Guðjónsdóttir, Mary Dalmau, and many others on the outgrowth of the Self-Study School from a sociocultural perspective highlight our commitment to studying our own practice as a professional community (Samaras, Guðjónsdóttir, & Dalmau, 2009). I am intrigued at the possibilities ahead as we continue to learn and support each other's efforts, and I am passionate about continuing to be a part of that developing and collective story. My hope is that you find this book useful as you work to be a contributor to the collective story of self-study as we strive to improve education and schooling by continuously studying our practice.

I ask that you give yourself permission and time to learn and appreciate the process of self-study teacher research. Enjoy the curiosities you have about your research. Do not see them as a burden because you do not have a final answer. You do not have to figure out your research all at once or feel you do not know it all. Teachers are always learning and exploring changes to make things better for their students. The process of learning to teach never ends. Our self-efficacy comes from our efforts and commitment in wanting to know more about our practice. It also comes from the support we receive along the way. Now let's go try to do something to improve learning!

You can contact me at asamaras@gmu.edu. Your comments are most welcomed and always valued and appreciated. My Web site is http://mason.gmu.edu/ ~ asamaras/.

Enjoy the self-study research process.

Acknowledgments

I did not write this book alone. The groundbreaking work of my self-study colleagues laid the foundation for this wiring. My teaching about self-study research would not be possible without the volumes of self-study research conducted by the self-study community, and I am deeply indebted and grateful to each of them. I sincerely thank my students who were willing to share their work with you. Indeed, they have also been collaborators in this writing, and you will find their work cited throughout the book. Their work made this textbook practical. The examples from their classrooms and practitioner contexts make self-study research come alive. Because I had taught them, their work is aligned with the self-study research framework I use to teach and now present to you. They, in turn, taught me a great deal and have been my very best teachers. Along with my colleagues, they reviewed drafts, offered ideas, and were a major part of helping me write this textbook. I very much appreciate the contributions of my colleagues and students:

Mary Adams-Legge

LaKesha Anderson

Kathleen McNamara Brown

Sarah J. Craig

Maria I. Cuevas

Mary C. Dalmau

Patricia Demitry

Stacy Dumaresq

Janet Jakusz Favero

Linda May Fitzgerald

Kelli Frattini

Anne R. Freese

Sally Galman

Hafdís Guðjónsdóttir

Julia B. Hiles

Jeanmarie Infranco

Evelyn Jacob

Arvinder Kaur Johri

Jeffrey Kaplan

Darwin A. Kiel

Julian Kitchen

Fred A. Korthagen

Clare Kosnik

Cynthia A. Lassonde

John Loughran

Mieke Lunenberg

Joseph A. Maxwell

Mary Jane McIlwain

Jennifer R. McMurrer

Irene Pantelides Meehan

James W. Mercer

Pat Mitchell

Kavita Mittapalli

Jennifer A. M. O'Looney

Diana Patricia Ortiz

Bernadine Pearson

Stefinee Pinnegar

Tamie Pratt-Fartro

Jason K. Ritter

Corey Sell

Martin Shaw

Amos O. Simms-Smith

Amy Smith

Jennifer Soehnlin

Patience Sowa

Deborah Tidwell

Dawn Renee Wilcox

Deanna (Breslin) Kelley Winstead

Rosanne C. Zwart

Additionally, my longtime friend and self-study colleague, Anne Freese, coordinated the sharing of Andrea M. Aiona's and Annemarie Ratke's exemplary self-study projects with you. My thanks to Andrea and Annemarie for their willingness to share their work with you. Ken Lawson shared his expertise on school division reviews.

I would also like to thank the following reviewers for their critique and suggestions in my writing of this book:

Betty Bisplinghoff, *University of Georgia*

Cheryl Craig, *University of Houston*

Pamela Jewett, *University of South Carolina*

Jeffrey Kaplan, *University of Central Florida*

Wendy Mann, *George Mason University*

Kavita Mittapalli, *George Mason University*

Sandra Sanford, *George Mason University*

Melanie Shoffner, *Purdue University*

Kevin Wheatley, *Cleveland State University*

Anna Wilson, *Chapman University*

My deep appreciation to SAGE Publications: to Steve Wainwright, senior acquisitions editor, for his support and confidence in my scholarship and his keen insights that teachers will benefit from the cutting-edge self-study research methodology; to Diane McDaniel, senior acquisitions editor, for her superb guidance in shaping early drafts into a polished and published book and obtaining volumes of invaluable feedback from external reviewers; to Ashley Conlon, editorial assistant for education, for her excellent administrative coordination; and to the outstanding editorial team at SAGE for helping bring the textbook to fruition.

Finally, I would like to thank my husband, Ted; my children, Constantine, Lucas, and Athena; and my daughters-in-law, Gabriella and Amelia, for their love and support in this writing project.

List of Tables

The 6 Ws of Self-Study Research

PART

I

> *I keep six honest serving-men*
> *(They taught me all I knew);*
> *Their names are What and Why and When*
> *And How and Where and Who.*
>
> —Rudyard Kipling, *The Elephant Child* (1902)

Part I introduces you to the basics of self-study teacher research. It is framed in Kipling's model of the 6 Ws, also known as the Five Ws and one H, which was an early model of journalist writing: Who? Why? What? Where? When? and How? Chapter 1, "Understanding Self-Study Research," mainly provides a discussion of the *what* and *why* of self-study. Chapter 2, "Overview of the Self-Study Research Process," charts what your research project entails and provides a suggested timeline of *how* you might approach it. Chapter 3, "The Self-Study Learning Community," provides a discussion of the *when, how, where,* and *who.* Chapter 4, "The Self-Study Methodology," provides a discussion of the *why* and *how* of self-study.

Chapter 5, "Self-Study Methods," presents a description and examples of self-study methods you may decide to employ for your current and future research projects. Throughout these chapters, you will find invitations to participate in critical friend inquiries.

But please do not mistake Part I as a series of facts about self-study. This 6W introduction to self-study research is more than a list of information. The 6 Ws are used to help you make sense of your research project, the complex and very interesting story of self-study, the beginnings and development of the Self-Study School, and the research methodology that emerged out of the work of self-study teacher educators and some of the self-study research methods they developed. Experience critical friend inquiries as you begin to frame your question, and set a foundation for your self-study research project, which you will launch in Part II.

Understanding Self-Study Research

What and Why

To my surprise, of all the projects I have worked on to date, my self-study research project has been the most practical. . . . The insights I gained about myself, my colleagues, and the position have helped me enormously. Self-study forced me to think outside the box in new ways, and it changed my way of thinking, despite myself.

—Mary Adams-Legge (2006), *English Teacher and Department Chair, Frederick County Public Schools, Virginia*

CHAPTER DESCRIPTION

This first chapter introduces you to self-study teacher research and immediately prompts you to consider its usefulness to your practice. You will have an opportunity to play with your wonderments, to ponder and sketch out what may become your research question. You will also share your unrefined ideas with a peer. In that way, you will learn about self-study while gaining an overview of the research process. You will be introduced to what self-study is and what it is not. Then the discussion moves to the very important question of "Why conduct self-study research?" which includes personal professional accountability, applicability, and reforming in the first person with critical friends. Self-study teacher research puts you at the center of an inquiry you choose.

◆ Reading this chapter will provide an opportunity for you to gain a basic understanding of what self-study is, what it is not, what it entails, and how it broadly benefits students, teachers, and education more generally.

Self-study has always been a part of my teaching although I did not call it self-study. I remember my early years of teaching junior high school students in the early '70s. After a day of teaching, I would come home and reflect deeply and silently about my role in classroom events, how my teaching philosophy played out in my actual practice, the problems I encountered, and what part of myself I brought to students' learning. I welcomed conversations with my teacher colleague, Kathy Lawson, whom I talked with about ideas to improve my teaching. I had not been taught to study my teaching in any teacher education methods course. It just seemed to be what I did. Now, after four decades of teaching and researching in a wide variety of education settings, I still have an insatiable passion toward self-study teacher research. I still enjoy personal inquiry and spend enormous amounts of energy thinking about and talking about my teaching with colleagues. I find self-study to be a challenging, yet emancipating, process because it allows me to better understand who I am as a teacher and who my students are as learners.

A Self-Study Teacher Researcher *Can!*

✓ I can design a study driven from my questions situated in my particular context.
✓ I can work in an intellectually safe and highly supportive collaborative inquiry community with critical friends.
✓ I can question the status quo of my teaching in order to improve and impact learning for myself and for my students.
✓ I can study my practice through employing a transparent, open, reflective, and systematic research process.
✓ I can hold a disposition of openness to outside views, questions, and critique.
✓ I can use various self-study methods to study my practice.
✓ I can contribute to the knowledge base of teaching as a knower and not just a receiver of knowledge.
✓ I can generate and share knowledge that can be useful to other teachers and educators.

With these privileges comes ethical responsibility, which you will read about in Chapter 7.

You might be wondering if self-study research and collaborative inquiry are an oxymoron. Now, this may surprise you, but self-study research actually requires that you work with someone else: a critical friend. Granted, the word *self-study* doesn't sound like it is collaborative, but actually this research necessitates collaboration (LaBoskey, 2004a). That is right. First, teacher inquiry begins with you. The power of your personal narrative to define the parameters of your own classroom inquiry must be at the forefront of your academic thinking and professional development. You are a generator of knowledge who can learn about your teaching and about your students' learning by studying your own classroom. Despite any frustrations you might have in trying to change the educational system, the one thing you know you can try to improve and change is yourself. And yet, that change requires support and constructive critique.

The Beatles' famous 1967 song, "With a Little Help From My Friends," reminds us of how our lives, relationships, and work are interconnected. **Self-study research** builds on the necessity of a relationship between individual and collective cognition in teachers' professional development and the power of dialogue in building a learning community of engaged scholarship (Lave & Wenger, 1991; Pinnegar & Hamilton, 2009; Samaras, Freese, Kosnik, & Beck, 2008; Vygotsky, 1978). Thus the textbook's subtitle, *Improving Your Practice Through Collaborative Inquiry.* As teachers raise their own questions generated from their practice, critical friends serve to mediate, provoke, and support new understandings. Self-study requires working with a *critical friend*, which is a term used widely by self-study scholars. McNiff and Whitehead (2006) note that it is "a term coined by Kemmis and McTaggart (1988) to denote a person who will listen to a researcher's account of practice and critique the thinking behind the account" (p. 256). Although related, "critical friends" in self-study research are not the same as Critical Friends Groups (CFG) established by the Annenberg Institute for School Reform in 1994 and with the CFG training coordinated by the National School Reform Faculty since the summer of 2000 (http://www.nsrfharmony.org/index.html).

Critical friends are trusted colleagues who seek support and validation of their research to gain new perspectives in understanding and reframing of their interpretations. Critical friends also "nurture a community of intellectual and emotional caring" (Pine, 2009, p. 236) through their commitment to inquiry and ongoing support throughout the research process. We will talk more about critical collaborative inquiry throughout this text, but for now, try your hand at Critical Friend Inquiry 1.1 as an exercise to practice sharing your personal insights for feedback and critical review from a colleague (Loughran & Northfield, 1998).

CRITICAL FRIEND INQUIRY 1.1

Self-study research allows you to openly ask questions about your teaching practice. It is a research process that allows you to choose your own research question about something that captures your attention and needs your attention in your classroom. Self-study allows you to enact research inside your classroom while you receive support and direction from your peers. It allows you to plan, enact, and assess your efforts and examine the impact of your efforts on your students' learning.

What questions have you been asking yourself lately about your teaching? What teaching issues or tensions do you find yourself thinking about and talking about constantly with your colleagues? What do you want to better understand? Is there something you wish was different? Do not worry that your ideas are not polished. These are sketches and not final research questions.

First, like artists, take pen or computer in hand and sketch out what you wonder about in your practice. Write your first initial thoughts. Be curious about your teaching. Reflect on a problem that might initiate a study, but as Loughran (2004) illuminates, a "problem in this case is not a negative term . . . [but] linked to the notion of a curious or puzzling situation or dilemma, tension, issue, or concern. It is something that causes one to stop and pay more careful attention to a given situation" (p. 25).

I wonder about_____because _____.

Take a moment to jot down your initial and very raw responses to the three short questions in this activity. Find a critical friend who is also interested in working with you on your research project. To be highly effective, "both members should be partners in the self-study . . . prepared to share, on an equal basis" to avoid an unbalanced status of researcher and critique (Schuck & Segal, 2002, p. 100).

1. What do you wonder about in your teaching practice? I wonder about _____because _____.

2. Why is this issue important to you? What experiences and perspectives brought you to ask this question?

3. Who would benefit from addressing this question (e.g., you, your students, your school, a school division, society at large)?

Below is a student example.

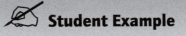 **Student Example**

ESOL Teacher

Here's an example of a teacher's pondering drawn from his personal history and education-related life experiences.

What do you wonder about in your teaching practice?

I wonder about what role I can play as a Hispanic teacher in helping Hispanic students survive and understand biology.

Why this issue or question?

This question is important to me because of my background as a Hispanic and the fact that I was an ESL [English as a Second Language] student for a brief period of time.

Who would benefit from addressing this question?

Many would benefit from addressing this question: ESOL [English for Speakers of Other Languages] teachers, students, parents, and other teachers. I want to work to improve ESOL students' weak performance in school.

Source: Student Work (2008). *Improving ESOL instruction based on my one-on-one instruction.* Paper submitted to the Secondary Education Program, Graduate School of Education, College of Education and Human Development, George Mason University in partial fulfillment of the requirements for the degree of Master of Education.

1.1 Advice From a Self-Study Scholar
Openness and Collaboration

Establishing a team of critical friends is an important first step for self-study teachers. Critical friends are important to self-study because self-study calls for openness and collaboration. Openness means making your classroom teaching public and sharing your work and ideas with colleagues and students. Openness is crucial to improving your teaching, but it also leaves you vulnerable and open to critique. Trust, then, becomes a vital element in establishing and sustaining a team of critical friends. Finding and choosing colleagues who are honest, supportive, collaborative, and committed to the goals of self-study is vital in the process of helping you consider and gain insight into your work.

Patience A. Sowa
Zayed University, United Arab Emirates

Next, share your wonderment with a peer whom you may decide to continue to work with as your critical friend.

Present what you wrote and ask each other for clarifications. What did you inquire about? Why are you curious about this question? Who would benefit from addressing this question? Take notes on the responses and comments you receive and further questions that are generated from your discussion. As in all the critical friend work, reverse roles and repeat the activity again with your critical friend's research. One of the first and key steps in the self-study research process is establishing and sustaining your critical friend team.

Establishing Your Critical Friend Team

Create a Working Structure.

Create a working structure for critique and support. Critical friends are tasked with two principle roles: to offer critique and to provide support (Breslin et al., 2008). Discuss and agree on your working structure. Establish ground rules with critical friends and revisit and reclarify them often. Openly share what is working and what is not working in your critical friend inquiries. Discuss and negotiate any problematic issues early and regularly. Practice professional ethics. Honor confidentiality about each other's work. The accessibility and reliability of your critical friends will help ease anxiety for participants. Agree on a structure for how and when the feedback will be posted, such as through regularly scheduled meetings, progress reports, and/or memos. You might decide to use an Internet group forum space or a wiki to post, respond, and store each other's memos. While sharing electronically allows for

(Continued)

(Continued)

documents to be easily shared and recorded, "a critical friendship may be more successful and mutually satisfying when it includes face-to-face interaction as well" (Schuck & Russell, 2005, p. 120).

Take a Critical Approach.

Take a critical approach to each other's research. It is critical to have friends in research, but critical friends are not critical in their approach with each other. Be clear and open about your responsibilities and commitment to each other in the mutual task of developing, enacting, and assessing your self-study research. Use active listening (i.e., listening for each other without judgment and without personal agendas). Critical friend work is not a blaming game about your teaching or a diatribe about your students' deficits in learning. Rather, its purpose is "to examine the possibilities and limitations of pedagogy" (Wade, Fauske, & Thompson, 2008, p. 414). The role of a critical friend is pivotal to the developmental process of self-study research. Check in regularly with each other and talk about "the level of critical commentary with which each feels comfortable" (Schuck & Russell, 2005, p. 120).

Embrace Alternative Perspectives.

Embrace alternative perspectives for improving the quality of your research. Critical friends serve to support each other's efforts while encouraging each other to be open to change in the changing world of teaching. Critical friends serve as validators who provide feedback, help shape research, and work as a validation team to provide feedback on the quality and legitimacy of claims as they "scrutinize your progress report and evidence" (McNiff & Whitehead, 2005, p. 11). Asking questions about data, interpretations, analysis, and assertions, critical friends are a valuable source in the research process and for "confirming and disconfirming evidence for our understandings and assertions for action" (Pinnegar & Hamilton, 2009, p. 15).

Acknowledge the Complexity of Collaboration.

Collaboration is a complex process. According to John-Steiner (2000), collaboration is "charged both cognitively and emotionally" (p. 124), and in productive working relationships "making oneself known and heard is central to emotional survival and growth" (p. 146). Optimal feedback includes both cognitive and emotional support (Breslin et al., 2008; Samaras et al., 2007). There are differences in how people approach and work in a critical friend team, but utmost is the need for honesty, openness, and transparency of any problems that are surfacing. Trust is not a given but is a privilege developed over time with a mutual commitment to each other's work. As Klein, Riordian, Schwartz, and Sotirhos (2008) state in their work as critical friends in a dissertation support group, "people need to believe they can both meet their own needs and others' needs; in particular, we found it was essential to care for the ideas of other members" (p. 128). A class community of critical friends suggests that it is important to "enter the community with an open mind, honoring each other's individual strengths and valuing each other's contributions" (Samaras et al., 2008, p. 145).

Congratulations!

What you just accomplished is the first component of the self-study teacher research process; you initiated the beginnings of a personal situated inquiry. Research is not something that some teachers do. Research is what all teachers do. It is a logical extension of your teaching. You conduct research informally every single day of your teaching life when you wonder and try something new and assess how it worked or how it did not work. You are not trying to prove something. You are trying to understand something. Your classroom is a living laboratory for your personal understanding of your development, work, and growth as a teacher. Picture the internal monologue that is occurring in your head when you teach. Learning to follow through and engage in that monologue and hear your voice and your students' voices inside your classroom is empowering. Teaching thinking, action, and self-study about that action is research. Consider how research is "an ongoing process of discovery that leads the researcher to focus on the complex interactions that occur during the learning and teaching process" (Samaras & Freese, 2006, p. 83).

WHAT IS SELF-STUDY TEACHER RESEARCH?

One of the first questions my students ask me when I talk about self-study is "What *is* self-study research?" It sounds like an analytical study that is all about you. It is easy to get stuck on asking what self-study is, but the really important question is "Why self-study for teachers?" Nonetheless, we will begin with "what" self-study is and is not to help you understand the "why" of it. And so, we begin with these two questions: What is self-study teacher research? What is not self-study teacher research? Let's get started.

I have had many incredible discussions about self-study research with my self-study colleagues. For over a decade, we have read volumes of literature about self-study, listened attentively to each other's conference presentations, and read each other's writings, all the while acknowledging the multiple and multifaceted nature of self-study. With colleagues, I have coedited books and self-study conference proceedings (Kosnik, Beck, Freese, & Samaras, 2006; Samaras, Freese, Kosnik, & Beck, 2008; Kosnik, Freese, & Samaras, 2002a). In a primer on self-study of teaching (Samaras & Freese, 2006), Anne Freese and I came to the conclusion that we as a community of self-study scholars have struggled to capture a definition of self-study although there has been more agreement about why self-study is important and what it entails (i.e., its characteristics and methodological components).

Let's start with considering what self-study *is* and what it *is not*, which will be useful for framing your self-study teacher research project and checking for possible research design pitfalls. The Five Foci Framework presented throughout this textbook provides a manageable format for you to understand and apply self-study in a high-quality self-study teacher research project. The framework has been gleaned, refined, and extended from almost two decades of work by self-study scholars, particularly from the work of Barnes (1998), LaBoskey (2004a), Loughran and Northfield (1998), and Samaras and Freese (2006). The framework outlines the methodological components of self-study.

Accordingly, self-study research is:

1. Personal situated inquiry

2. Critical collaborative inquiry

3. Improved learning

4. A transparent and systematic research process

5. Knowledge generation and presentation

In his efforts to understand self-study, one of my students brilliantly articulated and connected these Five Foci.

I believe self-study to be a *personal*, *systematic* inquiry *situated* within one's own teaching context that requires *critical and collaborative reflection* in order to *generate knowledge*, as well as *inform the broader educational field* (Sell, 2009a).

You will find a full discussion of these methodological components in a later chapter. They are briefly presented here by way of introduction.

Self-study is a personal situated inquiry.

Self-study draws directly from teachers' personal experience, which is situated within their classroom. Self-study teachers can initiate their own research question generated from observations of their classroom. The tensions you choose to examine are opportunities for professional growth and learning (Berry, 2007). Self-study gives you the opportunity to examine your lived practice and whether or not there is a **living contradiction,** or a contradiction between what you say you believe and what you actually do in practice (Whitehead, 1989). Examining the realities created by this gap leads to new understandings of personal theory making. The questions you pose can also be positive ones (LaBoskey, 2004a). You can choose from various self-study methods to inquire into beliefs and action in practice, explore who you are as a teacher, and self-assess your teaching. You have the opportunity to consider the role culture and history play in your theories and practices to assess its impact on your teaching.

Self-study is critical collaborative inquiry.

Self-study requires critical collaborative inquiry. It is personal and interpersonal with learning, thinking, and knowing arising through collaboration and the appropriating of feedback from others. It is the community that helps extend an individual's understanding. Critical friends encourage and solicit respectful questioning and divergent views to obtain alternative perspectives and work to help validate the quality and legitimacy of each other's claims.

Self-study is improved learning.

Self-study is for improved learning or the "so what" of what we do as teachers. As teachers study their teaching, they work to understand and improve their work as professionals, impact students' learning, inform education and school programs, influence policy decisions, and reform education. Sometimes students ask, "What if my research does not work or result in my hoped-for outcome?" In your research efforts, you are learning what works and what does not work and the consequences of the changes you enact. You are improving your learning about your teaching as a teacher and its impact on students' learning. That is progress and research.

Self-study is a transparent and systematic research process.

Self-study is a transparent and systematic research process requiring an open, honest, and clear description of the spiral of questioning, framing, revisiting of data, and reframing of a researcher's interpretations. Self-study necessitates a disposition of openness to outside views, questions, and critique. Self-study teachers strive to make their practice explicit to themselves and to others. The transparency of the research process is enhanced through the review of critical friends who ask probing questions and offer alternative perspectives and interpretations.

Self-study is knowledge generation and presentation.

Self-study research contributes broadly to the knowledge base of personal, professional, program, and school development. Making the study public allows it to be available for review and critique. It contributes to the accumulation of pedagogical, content, and issue-based knowledge and serves to build validation across related work.

The Five Foci presented in the textbook provide a definitional framework that describes the process of self-study research first introduced here and then integrated throughout the book. It is in response to an important call by some of the founders of self-study research who wrote, "To promote self-study research, researchers could endeavor to: Work toward maintaining the integrity of self-study research through explicit adherence to methodological standards (broadly defined)" (Cole & Knowles, 1998, p. 51).

WHAT SELF-STUDY TEACHER RESEARCH IS NOT

Next, let's look at what self-study is *not* and some research design pitfalls of self-study research.

- Self-study is *not* about you studying others' personal inquiries.
- Self-study is *not* all about you and only about you.
- Self-study is *not* conducted alone.
- Self-study research is *not* merely reflection.
- Self-study is *not* only about personal knowledge.

Self-study research is not about you studying others' personal inquiries.

After reviewing a manuscript where the researcher incorrectly criticized and reported on the actions of teachers, I was reminded why the field needs self-study research. Self-study is not about studying others' inquiries. You are the researcher and also the teacher. Your position is inside, not outside, the research. While it is essential to be aware that your position as teacher does not cause you to misread or misguide your students' feedback, your position also gives you the unique opportunity to use yourself as an instrument of the research and to make explicit the tacit assumptions about your practice (Mason, 2002). Your research and analysis will help explain your role in the research and its impact on your learning and your participants' learning with data to support both. A description of your context is essential for others to draw from your experience to envision your classroom and learn from your research efforts.

Self-study research is not about you and only about you.

Self-study is not just about you and only about you. It is what you can do for your students and education. That cause is bigger than you and one that as teachers we understand and embrace fully and daily in our practice. Self-study is not narcissism. Self-study is not a psychoanalytic study of you, your childhood, and your past.

> [The] invitation of a self-study (to see if the case for me is also the case for you) is not to be made passively but actively. In this respect the self-researcher is claiming that their story is not only *not* a fiction, it is not a simple psychotherapeutic confessional either. They are actively inviting the reader to see them, or their experience as they have investigated it, as "a case" of something. For most self-studiers, it seems, to claim a study as research, they are under some obligation not

just to tell the story but also to actively locate it in some more general issue, debate, problem or theoretical context that is more rather than less likely to be of interest to someone else. . . . It is not research because it is "by me, for me"; it is research because it is self-consciously "by me, for us." (Ham & Kane, 2004, p. 117)

Bullough and Pinnegar (2001) explain that self-study is about you in relation to your practice and the others who share your practice setting:

Quality self-study research requires that the researcher negotiate a particularly sensitive balance between biography and history. While self-study researchers acknowledge the role of the self in the research project . . . such study does not focus on the self per se but on the space between self and the practice engaged in. There is always a tension between those two elements, self and the arena of practice, between self in relation to practice and the others who share the practice setting. (p. 15)

Bullough and Pinnegar (2001) further assert that self-study is not about making yourself look like a hero or a huge success in your research. Frankly, it is more valuable if you are willing to explain what you learned and what you might do differently. On the other hand, self-study is not equal to self-criticism. The gaze is neither entirely inward nor outward "but on the space between the self and the practice engaged in" (Bullough & Pinnegar, 2001, p. 15). When studying oneself, "If gaze is always outward, then the most valuable resource one has as a researcher, namely oneself as instrument, is denied" (Mason, 2002, p. 174). In the process of studying your teaching, you gain entry into understanding your own learning in order to teach your students better. As you develop as a professional, your ultimate goal is to positively impact your students' learning.

Self-study research is not conducted alone.

Granted, the terminology of self-study suggests that self-study research is about the self. It is about the self, but it is not conducted alone. Indeed the nature of self-study is paradoxical on many levels (Loughran & Northfield, 1998). Paradoxically, self-study is *individual and collective* (Samaras & Freese, 2006). It is about your questions that you share with others. Quality self-study research involves peer review with mutual benefits. It is about having and being a critical friend. I explain to my students that the "getting is in the giving," or as Schuck and Russell (2005) surmise, "A critical friendship works in two directions. It is not solely for the person whose teaching is being studied; the critical friend also expects benefits" (p. 119).

Self-study entails an ongoing dialogue about your research with others to better understand it for yourself. Yet another paradox is that self-study is *personal and interpersonal* (Samaras & Freese, 2006). Your work on an interpersonal, or social, plane promotes your understanding on an intrapersonal, or personal, plane (Vygotsky, 1981). In essence, critical friends are invaluable because "learning, thinking, and knowing arise through collaboration and reappropriating feedback from others" (Samaras, 2002, p. 80). Critical friends serve as validators who provide feedback while you are shaping your research. They also serve as your **validation team** to provide feedback on the quality and legitimacy of your claims as they "scrutinize your progress report and evidence" (McNiff & Whitehead, 2005, p. 11). Thus another paradox is that self-study is *private and public* (Samaras & Freese, 2006).

Self-study research is not merely reflection.

While self-study "facilitates both inductive and deductive inquiry . . . like any systematic inquiry, self-study must be grounded in the extant literature to ensure it is not merely personal reflection" (Louie, Drevdahl, Purdy, & Stackman, 2003, p. 161). Self-study is a "recognized discipline" of scholars "creating democratic communities of practice committed to a scholarship of educational enquiry" (McNiff & Whitehead, 2006, p. 18). It is cautious and legitimate research that involves conducting a systematic and high-quality research project that is shared for critique and appraisal. Loughran (2007a) states, "Quality self-study is evident when it demonstrates . . . that it is disciplined and systematic inquiry [and] values professional learning as a research outcome" (p. 19). Self-study research has rigor, high quality, and peer review for critique and appraisal. Teacher educators work to promote self-study as a habit of mind for teachers (Lassonde & Strub, 2009). Self-study moves beyond narrative analysis and telling a story to producing new knowledge (Loughran, 2008).

As in any high-quality research, self-study researchers need to (a) clearly identify the problem or focus; (b) provide a detailed description of the situated practice; (c) explain the self-study method and why it was chosen; (d) describe the multiple data sources; (e) provide a clear explanation of any alternative forms of data employed such as artistic representation (Feldman, 2003; Mittapalli & Samaras, 2008); (f) establish trustworthiness (Hamilton & Pinnegar, 2000); (g) include a thorough and transparent data trail; and (h) offer a discussion of the findings to themselves, to others, and to the field.

Self-study is not only about personal knowledge.

Self-study research contributes to personal knowledge *and* to the knowledge base of teaching and education. Self-study research is for your personal and professional development. But self-study also provides the opportunity for you to contribute to the knowledge base of teaching. Teachers are contributors of knowledge. They are doers and knowers about the world of teaching who make decisions every minute of their teaching day. Teachers constantly encounter and resolve dilemmas that require continuous "in flight" assessments and decisions made through their observing the situation, educational beliefs, and collecting and analyzing data (Borko, Cone, Atwood Russo, & Shavelson, 1979). According to Schwab (1973), teaching dilemmas revolve around students, subject matter, the teacher, and the social milieu. When a teacher examines his or her role in the dilemma, it moves the conversation and study from what others are doing to what the teacher does with others. A self-study allows the teacher to consider the impact he or she makes on students' learning. It also provides an opportunity for the teacher to share what he or she learned so other teachers might gain insights about their related research.

WHY CONDUCT SELF-STUDY TEACHER RESEARCH?

Self-study teacher research is an empowering research methodology for teachers that holds much promise for educational reform. Teacher research is not a new phenomenon, but self-study "places individual researchers at the centre of their own enquiries. . . . The individual 'I' is always seen to exist in company with other individual 'I's,' and each asks, 'How do I hold myself accountable to myself and to you?'" (McNiff & Whitehead, 2006, p. 11). First, self-study offers you a new way to think about your professional accountability (i.e., a self-assessment of your professional development). That is, as a professional, you are accountable to yourself and to your students. Second, self-study research has instant applicability to your teaching and your students' learning. You can actually use the research findings immediately. Third, self-study as a new school of thought enables you as a teacher to reform in the first person. Self-study research demands that it is not only acceptable to include your viewpoint but actually essential to do so. Furthermore, the improvements you and other teachers enact multiply the possibilities of change on a larger scale. Let's look at these three "whys" of self-study research: personal professional accountability, applicability, and reforming in the first person with critical friends.

1. Personal Professional Accountability

As a teacher, you are accountable to your students' learning. That is a major and serious responsibility. Self-study involves a self-reflective stance in concert with self-responsibility as well as a responsibility to others. As teachers conduct self-study research projects, they are reminded about the important role they play, and *can* play, in addressing performance measures and improving the educational system. This does not mean that there should be no outside accountability. It does, however, bring to mind that change that is demanded by others is less powerful, less meaningful, and less sustainable than change that is self-initiated and self-motivated.

As a former secondary education social studies teacher, I have vivid memories of being evaluated by others, staying up late to prepare the observed lesson at the cost of other lessons, and meeting a set of ever-changing standards. One of the key ingredients in sustaining and revitalizing the teaching profession is professional accountability—one's own accountability rather than accountability demanded by others, rewarded by others, and punished by others. That personal professional accountability is developed with the support and interchange of school and university learning communities. It does take a village to build a community of mutually caring and developing teacher professionals. School districts and teacher unions, and ultimately students and their families, would benefit from a peer review process initiated by teachers instead of playing "gotcha" through outside-only review.

Additionally, school districts would save money in the long run from litigations in teacher dismissal and turnover.

In the teacher education programs where I have taught, I have observed how teachers are tempted to zero in on meeting mandated standards for their classrooms and professional portfolios at the cost of assessing their own role and practices in meeting those standards. The need for demonstrating teacher impact on student learning has increasingly gained the attention of schools and universities in a time of performance-based reform. Teachers' instructional roles are "increasingly regulated and monitored through assessment and data analysis expectations" (Valli & Buese, 2007, p. 551) and with serious negative consequences in teacher-student relationships, pedagogy, and teacher stress. One can easily argue that national and state teacher evaluation standards are a necessary and important component of teachers' professional development. And yet, the assessment of teachers does not need to rely only on evaluation by others. It does not have to create a system of competition; it has to create one of cooperation toward improving students' learning.

While teachers need to address specific mandated standards and performance-based assessment measures for student learning, the inclusion of their own professional assessment is an essential pathway toward making a difference in their students' learning. Clarke and Erickson (2004b) offer a strong argument for why self-study as a form of teacher inquiry is a part of the process of impacting students' learning:

> We are claiming that student learning is a critical aspect of all teachers' practice and as such represents an important focus of their work as educators. However, without inquiry, one's teaching practice becomes perfunctory and routinised. When teachers cease to be inquisitive about their practice, their practice ceases to be professional. This is an important distinction for us; as argued earlier, "inquiry is a defining feature of professional practice," and distinguishes professional practice from labour or technical work. (p. 203)

Teacher voices need to be visible and their personal agency high in terms of having the opportunity to ask their own questions and challenge themselves as they struggle to frame and reframe their very practice. When educators propose a personal and situated inquiry and take ownership, recognition, and responsibility to undertake that inquiry in a supportive and guided forum, professional development is enhanced and fears involving the change reduced (Smith, 2003). In the age of accountability, self-study research offers teachers a conduit to document their teaching according to the professional accountability they set for themselves as teachers, in general and/or specific to their subject and grade level.

Self-study scholars argue that accountability begins with the self. Lighthall (2004) presents a powerful argument for professional accountability and writes:

> Humans do not like to be forced. They resist whenever and wherever the force comes from those who take little account of the local complexities, local values, local resources, local situation, denying or ignoring the realities that make up the situation in which any and all improvements will or will not take place, the

situation of this teacher, this student, this set of resources, in this school, with this administration, these students, and this community. The s-step enterprise stands in stark contrast to imposed forms of accountability, starting as it does with individuals who are intent on improving their own actions and practices, and who have empirical methods to further that commitment. (p. 233)

Self-study of teaching practices begins to build the muscle for professional development as a lifelong process. It reminds us that some of the hardest and most important work is working on oneself. Self-study can build teacher efficacy by encouraging teachers to be agents of their own learning and reform initiatives while collaborating with professional colleagues to improve their daily and long-term work with students (Samaras & Freese, 2006). As professionals, teachers learn to recognize the abilities they have to question, reflect, and take action in practice. Consequently, teachers gain self-efficacy and confidence in their abilities to promote students' learning through self-study research.

What teachers discover is that their greatest contributions to the educational system begin with their questions. When teachers across the United States and around the world each have the opportunity to ask their questions and assess their own practice, the impact for students is multiplied. Teachers need a means to be motivated to assess their practice, and that process must include outside interpretations (i.e., self-study teacher research). Teachers and schools will benefit when teachers ask their own questions about their own practice. Self-study research lays the groundwork for teachers' better-informed educational actions and decisions. Those individual and collaborative efforts in investigating pedagogy will have far-reaching implications for school change within and across schools.

1.2 Advice From a Self-Study Scholar
Personal Professional Accountability

In many instances, the catalyst for self-study is similar to a problem in relation to reflective practice. Being confronted by a problem (curious or puzzling situation) can cause one to stop and look again at taken-for-granted aspects of practice. Jack Whitehead (1989) described this as being a living contradiction, and in terms of personal professional accountability, it seems to me that a central issue for self-study is being sensitive to, or actively seeking to find, instances of being a living contradiction in our teaching. As Tom Russell (e.g., Russell, 2002) has highlighted many times, the way we teach has much more influence than what we say. Therefore, if we are to genuinely be scholars of teaching, we need to be able to demonstrate that we learn through the challenges created by our own actions in our practice. In that way, self-study is an important touchstone to personal professional accountability.

John Loughran
Monash University, Australia

What's in It for You?

Self-study research offers teachers like you the professional tools to study their classroom strategies and actions for change *and* also who they are as teachers. Teacher research is clearly related to teacher instruction. You are researching your instruction to improve students' learning. The pedagogies and strategies you plan, enact, and assess move you toward that improvement. The process of self-study research offers you an opportunity to ask what difference you make in your students' learning. As a teacher, you have a professional and ethical commitment to help students learn. Your peers are essential in that process of your personal professional accountability. They serve to support your efforts and can challenge your assumptions and interpretations. Self-study research is an excellent forum for demonstrating the value of peer review and the impact of working with colleagues. Learning to pose questions, search for your own answers, and be agents of your own learning in collaboration with critical friends will provide you with systematic collegial support for accountability in your practice. You might ask:

"What am I curious or puzzled about in my teaching?"

"How can I be a researcher of my teaching in order to impact my students' learning and my professional development?"

"Does my actual teaching align with my teaching philosophy?"

"What role does my culture play in my theories about teaching and learning?"

"How can I work collaboratively with colleagues to frame my study, to validate my findings, to improve my practice, and to make a difference in my students' learning?"

"How can I help develop a network of professional support with other self-study teachers?"

"How will my self-study research contribute to the knowledge base about teaching and learning?"

Perhaps you are both teacher and school leader. Self-study scholarship is not limited to teachers. A high school English teacher and department chair posed questions related to her professional accountability:

Does my role as the mother of a special education student help or hinder my ability to help colleagues? What traits do I have the most trouble balancing? Do my colleagues hold the same perception of these roles as problems or benefits? How do my colleagues view the role of department chair? Which hats, such as liaison, mentor, diplomat, or advocate, make the most difference to my colleagues? Finally, are/were these concerns for other department chairs as well? (Samaras et al., 2007, p. 476)

Examining what works and what does not work in your teaching plays a significant role in defining yourself as a teacher and learner (i.e., your teacher identity). As a teacher and school leader, you can make a commitment to change yourself instead of feeling you must respond to another new educational fad. Lindsey, Robins, and Terrell (2003) note the importance of cultural proficiency—of being aware of your own culture and values and their effect on your practice and your interactions with others. Looking inward introspectively is an essential step to looking outward so that your actions are not just something to do but something to reflect deeply about and to examine. Change begins from the inside out. That professional work begins and belongs with you. When you are encouraged to pose questions about your own practice, you collect convincing evidence of the realities of your classroom and the possibilities for change. You come to recognize that learning is a continuous process for yourself and your students.

2. Applicability

Self-study brings the envisioning process for educational reform beyond the rhetoric to a reality where teachers work to study and apply their reframed knowing directly to their own teaching practices. Loughran (2007b) asserts that "one immediate value of self-study is in the way it can inform and almost immediately influence practice" (p. xv). The simple truth is that students are interested in self-study research because by doing self-study, they recognize that it is valuable and useful to their practice. Teachers deserve research that is practical and directly applicable to their classrooms and educational reform efforts.

Self-study research has proven quite useful to teacher educators and students as they seek to improve their practice and enhance their personal, professional, and program development (Kosnik, Beck, Freese, & Samaras, 2006). Collaboration is becoming more common in teacher education programs and in schools where teachers are assigned to teacher teams by grade or discipline. Schools are increasingly working to build learning communities of practice through grassroots efforts and ones that are sustained over time. That groundwork is rooted in the direct work of teachers working with a critical friend to deliberate the dilemmas of teaching practice collectively and with mutual benefit. Schools will profit from the applications of critical friend inquiries as teachers begin to experience the sense of agency that comes through collegial teamwork, review, and a shared recognition of the complexities of teaching.

What's in It for You?

Self-study research can contribute to your professional development because it allows you to apply changes that you believe in. As a teacher, you have the right to ask your own questions, particularly for school reform efforts toward making informed educational decisions and actions. Valli and Buese (2007) found that "teachers are motivated to enact changes they believe in" (p. 553). Accordingly, teachers are more likely to reject changes that are not part of their personal knowledge.

You are encouraged to build a sustainable learning community that is generated directly from your classroom needs and personal motivation instead of "top down" initiatives. As Cuban (1993) has noted, "The knowledge, beliefs, and attitudes that teachers have, then, shape what they choose to do in their classroom and explain the core of instructional practices that have endured over time" (p. 256).

3. Reforming in the First Person With Critical Friends

Successful reform efforts are grounded in the work of participants (Mitchell & Mitchell, 2008), and in this case, those participants are teachers. Teachers can, and will, benefit from challenging the doubts they have and constructing new understandings about their practice instead of being receivers of knowledge constructed by others. Teachers benefit when they understand themselves and their teaching as shaped by the social, cultural, and political influences in their lives and when they recognize how they have shaped and can shape education. Teachers need opportunities "to think critically and challenge ideas of how power and control are constructed in the world and mapped onto them" (Schulte, 2002, p. 101). Reforming in the first person with critical collaborative inquiry allows teachers to develop and direct their professional development in learning communities that support and extend that development (Samaras, Freese, Kosnik, & Beck, 2008). Teachers must see themselves as learners and be given opportunities to work together as they engage in meaningful discussions about reform related to student learning (Hinde, 2003). Teachers should be encouraged to be clinical researchers in the laboratory of their own classrooms.

Lighthall (2004), in his meta-analysis of self-study research, declares, "It is no accident that reform is one of s-step's major features" (p. 224). Teaching is, after all, a political act. Self-study teacher educators have been committed to modeling what they believe. They embrace teaching "not just as a pedagogical task, but also a 'social-pedagogical task'" (LaBoskey, 2004a, p. 830) with moral, ethical, and political aims. They have studied their role in working for social justice in their teaching and teacher education programs (Brown, 2004; Griffiths, 2002; Hamilton, 2002; LaBoskey, 2009; Schulte, 2004). Self-study allows teachers to begin the reforming process by examining their own classrooms, programs, and institutions. They work to authenticate their practice through the explorations. Often the questions they raise are ones that challenge their own ways of doing things. In turn that questioning is set within a larger context of needed change in other classrooms.

Broadly, self-study comes under the conceptual umbrella of practitioner-based research, which has taken many forms (e.g., the teacher-as-researcher movement, reflective practitioner research, action research, narrative inquiry, and praxis inquiry) (Cochran-Smith & Lytle, 2004). Practitioner research is "a promising line of research [that] involves questions related to pedagogical approaches designed to help people learn from their own practice" (Grossman, 2005, p. 452). Unlike other forms of practitioner-based research, self-study teacher researchers study their role within the research as they inquire within themselves to ask the taken-for-granted questions about their practice. The research is not only about their practice but researched from the first person instead of an onlooker. They are the change they seek in their field. Considering the tasks of teaching and schooling, Cochran-Smith and Lytle (1996) argue that in "every classroom where teachers are learners and all learners are teachers, there is a radical, but quiet, kind of school reform in process" (p. 110).

Addressing action research as a form of practitioner research related to self-study, McNiff, Lomax, and Whitehead (2003) claim that action research "place[s] the 'I' at the centre of enquiry processes . . . as a form of self-study or first-person enquiry" (p. 9). They eloquently articulate their position in supporting such social research that fits the "I" in the research of action and influence:

The emphasis on the living person "I" shows how individuals can take responsibility for improving and sustaining themselves, and the world they are in. "I" have the capacity to influence the process of social change in this way, because "I" can influence others in my immediate context, who in turn can influence others in their contexts. The circles of influence are potentially without limit. Collectively, individuals can generate world-wide change. (p. 20)

The field of self-study has grown dramatically and distinctively from other forms of practitioner research in the past decades. Educators are eager to better understand what self-study is and what value it holds for education. A major goal in writing this textbook was a way to bring the value of self-study as a conduit for educational reform directly to you as teachers. Your research is the most powerful thrust for this work.

What's in It for You?

The work you do to improve learning is an improvement for social justice as your efforts are to improve learning for all children (LaBoskey, 2004a). That important work is accomplished with the support and critique of your colleagues. In that regard, you are an educational reformer, reforming in the first person and with others. Bodone, Guðjónsdóttir, and Dalmau (2004) clearly explain the collaborative nature and reform in self-study research:

Self-study research is situated within the discourses of the social construction of knowledge, reflective practice and action for social change. The strong presence of collaboration in the practice of self-study of teacher education is a natural response to this ethical and theoretical location. (p. 742)

Self-study is individual and communal. Essential to your self-study is the collective work you will do with critical friends with mutual and communal benefits in receiving multiple levels of dialogue and points of view. You are constantly prompted to reach away from your way of knowing.

We will return to these three *whys* of self-study again as we come full circle at the end of the textbook. In the meantime, keep them in mind as you learn about self-study teacher research throughout this book. Begin to ask yourself, "How do I hold myself accountable to my students?" "What is the value in applying self-study in my practice?" "In what ways might I reform in the first person to impact student learning?"

KEY IDEAS

- Self-study begins with your wonderments about your practice.
- Self-study can be defined through the Five Foci, a definitional framework of self-study methodological components.

- Self-study research is:
  1. Personal situated inquiry
  2. Critical collaborative inquiry
  3. Improved learning
  4. A transparent and systematic research process
  5. Knowledge generation and presentation

- Self-study research is not:
  1. About you studying others' personal inquiries
  2. Just about you
  3. Conducted alone
  4. Merely reflection
  5. Only about personal knowledge

- Three *whys* of self-study research were presented in this chapter:
  1. Personal professional development
  2. Applicability
  3. Reforming in the first person with critical friends

Overview of the Self-Study Research Process

What and How

My goal is to help others gain the kind of knowledge that has helped me in understanding a broad range of science concepts to gain an understanding of the natural world. More importantly, understanding the personal experiences that have enabled me to more quickly grasp the importance of science concepts from well-rounded, well-framed scientific contexts will help me guide students in becoming more aware of the role science will play in their futures.

—Dawn Renee Wilcox (2006), *Science Coordinator,*
Spotsylvania County Public Schools, Virginia

CHAPTER DESCRIPTION

In this chapter, you will gain an overview of the self-study process by reviewing the self-study project planner, which includes components of your final research report. Your attention is brought to the recursive nature of self-study research while also acknowledging that teachers need to have a project planner to move toward the goal of improving practice and students' learning. A suggested timeline also provides a structure for your scholarly project and highlights the many and often overlapping components of conducting a quality self-study research project. A student self-study research exemplar is provided in brief, highlighting project research components.

✦ Reading this chapter will provide you with a framework for your entire study. It allows you to see the big picture before you begin.

A self-study research project planner helps you envision where you are headed. As my yoga teacher explained, consider that like a surfer, the direction you look is where you will go. So look out to your eventual landing—your shore, your professional goal. Your forward-looking gaze gives you balance and propels you toward that goal. It's natural to lose your balance here and there, so be gentle with yourself and the process of learning and developing as a self-study teacher scholar.

Self-study teachers conduct research in their classrooms. That is what you are about to do. You will engage in a process that begins with your questions and curiosities about your practice. Those curiosities will emerge from your observations of your classroom and your dialogue with peers. Research involves designing a study, carefully reviewing the research ethics of your study, collecting data, analyzing the data, and writing and presenting your findings. Each of these components is enriched and supported from collaborative inquiries. Please note that although a planner is offered to give you an overview of your project, self-study is not a linear process. Research is discovery, and discoveries most often involve moving back and forth in a search to understand something yet uncovered. Be patient with yourself and that wonderful process of learning.

Self-study research is recursive. Nonetheless, having a tentative planner serves to document where you are in the process and organizes and stores the insights you gained along the way. We are all busy teachers with busy schedules. So let's embrace the power of getting organized and glancing at what's ahead. You might want to also look ahead at headings and subheadings of your research project, which are presented in detail in Chapter 12.

Organize your project using a self-study research planner (see Table 2.1). Paying attention to what you will do, how you will do it, and when you will do it will assist you in successfully completing a major project. Make note of each component and plan accordingly. Chart your progress using a personal timeline with a feasible schedule for accomplishing each step. Be purposeful, although flexible, in meeting your own deadlines with time to write, receive peer feedback, and rewrite a polished final report. Update your progress weekly and share it with your critical friend and instructor.

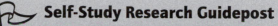

Self-Study Research Guidepost

SELF-STUDY RESEARCH PROJECT PLANNER

Inquire with critical friends throughout entire process.

Table 2.1   Self-Study Research Project Planner

	Research Component	Description of Research Component	Suggested Timeline
BEFORE ENACTMENT	• **DESIGN** • **PROTECT**	*Introduction, Research Question, Conceptual Framework*	
1	Author your research question.	A thoughtful, personal, and manageable inquiry situated in your context to improve your practice and to impact learning for yourself and others.	Weeks 1–2
2	Establish your critical friend team.	Peer support and review of your research process including analysis with multiple perspectives, addressing interpretations of findings, and working toward trustworthiness and validation of your findings.	Week 1 and ongoing through study
3	Observe your classroom.	Observations of your teaching, classroom, and students' learning that give you pause and suggest an area worthy of study and research.	Week 1 and ongoing through study
4	Articulate rationale and proposal.	A clear articulation of what you are asking, what you are trying to do, and with whom, how, and why.	Weeks 2–4
5	Frame your question within literature.	A comprehensive review of the literature related to your topic with relevance to your research design and usefulness to extending knowledge of the field; identification of common topics to design conceptual framework; an integrated mapping of the theories and phenomena that frame and shape your study and are informed by the literature reviewed.	Weeks 2–4 and ongoing through study
6	Align your question with self-study method.	Research procedures and techniques useful in providing data specific to your study's purpose (e.g., developmental portfolio, personal history self-study method, living educational theory, collective self-study method, arts-based self-study method, memory work self-study method).	Weeks 3–4

(Continued)

Table 2.1 (Continued)

	Research Component	Description of Research Component	Suggested Timeline
7	Plan purposeful pedagogies.	An inquiry and plan that is purposeful and manageable; includes maintaining a project timeline; involves taking an ethical approach throughout your project assessing the ethics of your pedagogical strategies on participants; assess the ethics of your pedagogical strategies, data collecting, and data reporting.	Weeks 3–4
DURING ENACTMENT	• **ORGANIZE** • **COLLECT** • **ANALYZE** • **ASSESS RESEARCH QUALITY**	*Method and Validation*	
8	Describe your context.	A detailed description of the research context including the immediate and broader environment (e.g., school community, school, and your classroom).	Weeks 2–3
9	Describe your participants.	A detailed description of the research participants with demographic information.	Weeks 2–3
10	Describe your data sources generated from your pedagogical strategies.	A detailed description of the multiple data sources you collect to help you understand the underlying problem and to assess the impact of your research; includes detail about your planned pedagogical strategies.	Weeks 4–8
11	Explain your data analysis and interpretation to critical friends for validation.	A detailed and transparent data trail describing the analysis process in specific detail used to make meaning of your data and formulate preliminary and concluding interpretations; requires alignment of analysis and interpretation with research question and theoretical framework; presented to critical friends for dialogue, critique, and validation.	Weeks 7–9
AFTER ENACTMENT	• **WRITE** • **PRESENT**	*Findings, Discussion, and Implications*	
12	Write your findings	Research report drafts reviewed by critical friends and finalized into a formal polished final report; includes relevance of findings to national professional standards (e.g., in the United States: INTASC	Weeks 8–10

	Research Component	Description of Research Component	Suggested Timeline
		http://www.ccsso.org/content/pdfs/corestrd .pdf; National Board for Professional Teaching Standards, http://www.nbpts.org/; and professional standards such as those available from http://www.naeyc.org/, http://nsta.org/, http://www.ncss.org/, http://nctm.org/, and http://www.ncte.org/).	Weeks 8–10
13	Write your discussion: Impact on Students.	A discussion and explanation of what the findings or results mean and the impact on students within the context of the study.	Weeks 9–10
	Write your discussion: Impact on Teacher Researcher.	A discussion of the impact of research on your understanding and reframing of teaching; includes a self-assessment of how the self-study methodological components were addressed.	Weeks 9–10
	Write your discussion: Impact on Education Field.	A discussion and explanation of what the findings or results mean for the broader field and possible areas for further study.	Weeks 9–10
14	Write limitations.	Include the limitations that you and your critical friends identified in your dialogic validity activity.	Weeks 9–10
15	Include references.	Include all citations in text.	Week 10
16	Insert appendixes.	Include data that will help the reader better understand your research but perhaps is not needed within the body of your report.	Week 11
17	Write an abstract.	A single, articulate, concise paragraph of no more than 150 words that describes project purpose, context, method, key findings, and significance; note that the abstract is placed at the beginning of your report, yet it cannot be fully written until the end of your project when you have findings.	Weeks 9–12
18	Present and share your research.	An opportunity for you to make your research public through presentation to a larger audience for critique and appraisal.	Week 12 and beyond

The suggested timeline in Table 2.2 is an excellent organizing tool that you can adapt for your project. You will ultimately need to determine a feasible schedule that works best for you.

SELF-STUDY RESEARCH PROJECT TIMELINE

Inquire with critical friends throughout the entire process.

Table 2.2   Self-Study Research Project Timeline

	1	2	3	4	5	6	7	8	9	10	11	Dated notes	✓
BEFORE ENACTMENT													
Design and Protect													
Author your research question.	▲	▲										e.g., How can I create a class learning community? 09/01	✓
Establish your critical friend team.	▲	▲										e.g., Anne, Clare, Clive, and I agreed to work as a critical friend team 09/05	✓
Observe your classroom.												e.g., Something I notice often that perplexes me is . . . 09/06	✓
Articulate rationale.													
Frame question within literature and review and beginnings of your conceptual framework.													
Assess research ethics of study.													
Write research proposal.													
Describe context: community, school, and your classroom.													

	1	2	3	4	5	6	7	8	9	10	11	Dated notes	✓
Describe participants.													
Plan purposeful pedagogies.													
DURING ENACTMENT													
Organize, Collect, Analyze, and Assess Research Quality													
Enact study.													
Describe data sources.													
Explain data analysis.													
Validate with critical friends.													
AFTER ENACTMENT													
Write and Present													
Discussion: Impact on Participants.													
Discussion: Impact on Teacher.													
Discussion: Impact on Education Field.													
Write limitations.													
Include references.													
Insert appendixes.													
Write abstract.													
Complete final project.													
Present													

✎ Student Example: Project Timeline

Patricia Demitry (2009), *English Teacher*

Below is a timeline Patricia created using a bulleted format rather than a chart. You will find a brief of her project at the end of this chapter. Note that she conducted a literature review to help her refine her question and pedagogies. She understands that research is a process of discovery and takes effort. You may also find that although you choose a research question, it most often is refined later. Furthermore, as you inquire, receive feedback, and make decisions based on new ideas about your question, your research question and ideas for change may shift. Notice that Patricia writes that "the research continues to be something I shape and experiment with each day. I used the following timeline to organize my data during the research process. These dates encompass the set amount of time where data was collected, though the research continues to be something I shape and experiment with every day."

Literature Review:

- I did a preliminary gathering of research on struggling male adolescent readers before deciding on the exact question for my discussion. Completed on 2/28/2009
- Created a focused research question. Completed on 3/1/2009
- Finished gathering literature with a focus on motivating the struggling male adolescent reader. Completed on 3/12/2009

Methods:

- Based on the review of literature, and development of problem, several pedagogies are available to combat failure among male adolescents and are used to support research. Completed on 3/19/2009

Plan of Action:

- Using strategies and practices researched in the literature to combat decreasing grades and interest level in males. Completed on 4/1/2009

Data Collection:

- Collected qualitative and quantitative data based on research methods. Completed on 4/10/2009

Enactment:

- Presurvey linked to reading habits. Collected on 3/25/2009
- Initial average of adolescent males' grade point average. Gathered on 3/25/2009
- Begin journal log on 3/1/2009

- Introduce independent reading as supplementary material at beginning of unit on 3/27/2009
- Kinesthetic lesson plan on 3/30/2009
- Game-based lesson plan/posting of work on 4/3/2009
- Computer-based reading on 4/7/2009 and 4/9/2009
- Postcalculation of adolescent males' grade point average on 4/10/2009
- Postsurveys completed after each new research method on 3/27, 3/30, 4/3, 4/7, & 4/9.

Data Analysis and Findings:

- Data analysis began on 3/25/2009 and continued until 4/10/2009
- Findings: 4/10/2009

My students always appreciate seeing an example early in the semester to get a general overview of what the research project entails. See if you can find the research components listed in the planner in this **exemplar** brief, or "concrete problem-solutions that students encounter from the start of their scientific education" (Kuhn, 1996, p. 187) or "concrete models of research practice" (Mishler, 1990, p. 415). Patricia's work is presented briefly here and does not exactly match the suggested report headings presented in Chapter 12. You will continue to find segments of her project interspersed throughout the book. Likewise, you will also find segments of Amy Smith's self-study research project interspersed throughout the book and then presented in a brief in Appendix A. These two examples are provided to help you gain a fuller picture of what a project entails and the major research components.

SELF-STUDY TEACHER RESEARCH EXEMPLAR BRIEF

Frustrated and Flunking: The Adolescent Male Struggle With Reading in the Curriculum

Abbreviated Version

Patricia Demitry (2009), *English Teacher*

Abstract

This study investigates the impact of motivational instruction and technology on curriculum-based texts for the struggling male adolescent reader. Over a 15-week period, a select group of 11th-grade males were taught with a variety of instructional practices aimed at increasing comprehension and alleviating their observed frustration during the reading process. Data collection included Likert scale surveys, calculated grade point averages, a kinesthetic lesson plan, a computer-based lesson plan, independent reading, and reflective teacher-researcher logs. The findings indicated a positive impact between movement-based lessons coupled with technology and an increase in students' motivation and reading comprehension.

Further studies could include investigating the impact of these pedagogical strategies for female student participants as well as ESL (English as a Second Language) students.

> Notice how the abstract includes the main purpose of the research, the method of data collection employed, the key findings, the major conclusions and implications, and overall what the researcher did and what was discovered.

I am an English teacher, and while my passion for education and literature has developed since college, I struggled as a high school teacher to find relevance in the texts being studied. This is my first year teaching, and I am surprised at the markedly different experience I am encountering on the other side of the desk. I am no longer a student but responsible for the transmittance of information, assessment, and curriculum development. It became evident as early as September that my 11th-grade male students struggled intensely with mastery of the English language, both reading and writing. I knew, as an educator, it was my job to make the curriculum relevant and engaging, but I was struggling alongside these young men to find new activities and lessons that peaked their interest and fostered a sense of responsibility. My goal was to take my observations and understanding of the curriculum and focus on my struggling male readers who dreaded the prospect of English. I rethought my lesson plans and researched techniques specifically geared toward teaching boys literacy.

Significance of Problem on a Personal Level

My research comprises boys in the 11th grade; however, it is their inability to connect with course curriculum that challenges me, not necessarily the reluctance to read overall. Being in the classroom has afforded me experience with several tactics to combat anxious or bored readers. I have tried literature circles, audio books, movie versions, partner plays, reading out loud, silent reading time, and so on. Many of my 11th-grade boys "appear" to be reading but in actuality find the idea of reading repulsive or threatening. If I gave my students the choice to either read for 30 minutes in class from a magazine or start on a novel that would be due for homework, every single male in the room would reach for *Sports Illustrated*. It isn't the reading that remains a problem; it is the curriculum and how best to reach the target audience (i.e., young adolescent males).

Broader Educational Significance of the Problem

My male students, on average, perform at a lower grade level than my female students. Using grade point averages as a measuring tool, it is statistically evident in my classroom that males are performing at a significantly decreased performance level. I attribute this lack of performance to a struggle with the curriculum. If I can transform the curriculum into a variety of lessons that achieve maximum participation and understanding from my male students, then there should be a rise in academic performance exemplified in the average letter grade for each participant. The tools I am creating could be used across the curriculum, and I would be anxious to start a program within my school to alleviate the stigma between boys and reading.

> In her introduction and rationale section, Patricia presents a case for the personal significance of this study as well as the broader educational significance of this work. She notes the experiences, perspectives, and goals that influenced and shaped her interest in this research topic.

Statement of Research Problem and Question

Research Problem

Since September, I have observed that my adolescent male students struggle with reading—not just any reading, but reading that is a requirement in the curriculum. The behavior exhibited by the majority of the mainstream males includes inattention, seeming laziness, lack of comprehension, and a general distaste for the reading material. I want to combat this disconnect with the curriculum and improve performance-based grades.

Research Question

How can I change my instructional pedagogies to help struggling male adolescents in reading?

> Patricia explains the research problem within the context of her observations and her professional goal as a teacher. She presents a clear and specific research question that is meaningful and purposeful for improving her practice to impact learning for herself and her students.

Wonderings and Questions

- Is it all reading my students are struggling with, or just the curriculum?
- Is it a matter of making the material more exciting?
- Can the struggling reader be combated with differentiation? If the curriculum can't be changed, how do I help my male students understand the material and improve the learning process?
- Should secondary material be used to ramp up their interest in often bland and irrelevant texts found in the curriculum?
- Is the presentation of the American literature curriculum off-putting and difficult to understand?
- If I provide my students with copious activities in the classroom to stimulate their reading experience, how do I combat their lack of participation with text at home?
- Are there similar cases of male adolescents struggling to read? Is it just reading in general that is problematic, or is it reading that occurs within the educational curriculum?

I ask students to include their wonderings and questions, which sometimes shift to become the main research question or subquestions useful to articulate as they plan pedagogies and collect research to understand the particulars and sometimes underlying issues. Students recognize that although they can not answer all the subquestions, they may inform their study and provide questions for their continued research.

Review of the Literature

The Issue

My research focused on male adolescent students' underachievement in reading and the various strategies being employed to bridge the educational gap causing a result of failure and frustration. Adolescent males bring a different mental and physical energy to the classroom. Many English educators have a streamlined, organized, multifaceted approach to teaching and "view the natural assets that boys bring to learning—impulsivity, single-task focus, spatial-kinesthetic learning, and physical aggression—as problems" (King & Gurian, 2006, p. 57). The lack of attention to male-oriented differentiation is causing a serious rift between boys and reading. Through my research I discovered that most males refuse to pick up a book outside of the classroom and find the rigors of literacy stupid and pointless: "The gender issue is relevant to classroom learning in more ways than one. Increasingly in the United States, young boys are saying that school is stupid and they don't like to read" (Sax, 2007, p. 42). Interestingly, this sentiment is not affected by socioeconomic conditions; rather boys of all ages and ethnicities are struggling with reading and choose to be "BURNED AT THE STAKE [rather] than read a book!" (Sax, 2007, p. 42). There are numerous articles latent with research on the differences between boys and girls related to reading. There appears to be a perpetuating cycle or self-fulfilling process, where educators accept that boys will never succeed at reading: "This long, well-documented history of underachievement has helped contribute to an entrenched perception—indeed, an expectation—that many boys simply will not become thoughtful, accomplished readers" (Brozo, 2006, p. 71). My purpose in researching this problem was a concerted effort to step outside of the stigma that links boys and a failure to read and use the research to alter my pedagogy and ultimately improve the environment in my classroom.

What Now?

The research illuminated an important question in my report: Are boys struggling to read or merely unmotivated? After surveying my male students, it became evident that they had the ability to read and comprehend but hated the process and neglected to engage in the text. Through my literature review, I discovered numerous tactics educators may employ within the classroom to combat disinterest and boredom in males' reading. (Patricia continues to describe the strategies and cites the related research that supports success in their application.)

Patricia uses an interactive style in conducting her literature as she weaves her thinking about the problem with support she locates through her literature review. Her pedagogies are informed by the literature she reviewed.

Method

Context

Description of the Setting

All names have been changed to protect the privacy of participants and the community. Asheville High School is located in Northern Virginia. The demographic breakdown of Asheville is as follows: 21.8% Asian, 5.7% Black, 0.6% American Indian, 8.9% Latino, and 59.4% White. There are slightly more males at 51.8% than females at 48.2%. The total student population at Asheville High is 2,776. Approximately 11% of the population is on free or reduced lunch.

Asheville High is a 4-year study program, housing Grades 9 through 12. The school is separated into four subschools, with assistant principals presiding over sections of students and the various academic departments. Asheville runs on a block schedule, with three 90-minute periods each day, with alternating "A" and "B" days. Asheville, last year, implemented a new form of enrichment during the school day in the form of LS, or Learning Seminars. This 90-minute block on "A" days is used for remediation and enrichment between students and teachers. Also new to Asheville are 50-minute periods at the beginning of each Friday called PLC, or Professional Learning Communities. These sessions are used as collaborative sessions between team teachers to share lesson plans, test scores, and learning strategies.

Asheville is a fiercely proud school boasting colors of green and gold in banners across the school. The sports program is rife with young athletes in a variety of sports The SGA, or student government association, prides itself on student-centered pep rallies, educational presentations, and exciting dances. Asheville also has an award-winning newspaper, yearbook, drama team, literary magazine, and debate team.

> This context section allows us to "see" Patricia's school and community and place her study within that context.

Description of Participants

The participants in this research project come from my two sections of English 11. I am focusing only on my male adolescent readers; therefore the research concerns 25 boys. Due to the specific nature of my research, girls were eliminated from the data collection. I teach one set of males during the midmorning period from 9:00 a.m. to 10:30 a.m. I teach another class of males at the end of the day from 12:50 p.m. to 2:05 p.m. The adolescent males in this study are between 16 and 17 years of age and originate from varying ethnicities and with a range of learning performance rates. In this study, 2% of the males have an IEP, or Individualized Education Plan, for individuals with disabilities.

Description of the Classroom Setting

My classroom is plastered with quotations from literary giants such as Hemingway, Wilde, Franklin, and Shakespeare. My bulletin board houses a white envelope labeled "exit tickets," which students drop off on their way out the door, as well as bell schedules and a Standards of Learning (SOL) countdown. My desks are arranged in an unconventional double U, with seats pointed to the front. I was inspired by stadium seating and Socratic seminar forums, and I am the only English teacher on my hall to experiment in this way. I do not showcase my students' work on the wall and have instead opted for a natural setting, with photos of nature meant to inspire and spur creativity. As a personal touch, I mounted small biographies of each of my students in diamond pendants on the side wall, for students to learn more about each other and feel a sense of ownership in the classroom. I wanted to create a warm, inspiring, and safe environment that my students would treasure.

> Again here in this participants section, Patricia offers us rich details that invite us into her teaching and help us "see" her classroom and her teaching philosophy.

Data Collection

Initial Grade Calculations

It was important to calculate an average grade for the male adolescents in my study. My objective was to test my new pedagogies in a concrete and visual manner. I wanted to use the current grade point averages as an initial calculation to examine for either a negative or a positive correlation at the conclusion of my research.

Presurvey

My data collection included a presurvey to decipher the reading habits of male adolescents in my classroom. I administered the survey to every student in my 11th-grade periods, and while they were anonymous, I did have the students specify their gender. For this study I disregarded female participants and only included the male results in my data collection. The presurvey focused on male reading habits, both inside and outside of the classroom, as well as personal reading preferences.

Independent Reading

I came across a variety of programs and groups supporting free-choice, independent readings for adolescent boys. Studies show that boys will read, if the literature focuses on masculine-dominated topics. General reading, however, was not the focus of my research problem. Therefore, I used this information as a tool for transforming my own plan for creating lessons. The idea behind independent reading is a deeper appreciation for literature and a personal connection with the text. Using this method, I created a new way of introducing a text that fosters connections to the outside world, as well as incorporating student choice. This anticipation guide disregards the typical mundane series of questions in favor of a student-led quest.

Kinesthetic Lesson Plan

The idea here is movement, movement, movement. Using a foundation of research that supports tapping into the physical dexterity of males, I created a lesson that employs activity and engagement. The idea here is to get males out of their seats and use activity to elevate comprehension, erase frustration, and eliminate the negative stigma surrounding reading. Lessons include dramatizations and student-created videos. My idea was that by developing a community of readers, there will no longer be a self-fulfilling prophecy of failure in my male students: "I can't do it" or "I just don't get it." Now, reading isn't personal or private; it is something to be shared. Here, I have linked the idea of movement and community. I experimented with activity and gender-specific communities, in hopes of achieving greater comprehension and engagement with the English curriculum.

Computer-Based Reading Tools

If males hate reading and have trouble comprehending a text, then I wanted to change the medium through which they read. There is a positive influence between males and technology; therefore I wanted to introduce literature through computers. I created new lessons that prompted my students to experience a text through computer-based books. The experience is interactive and may be completed either in the classroom with lab carts or at home using personal computers. Similarly, I created online study guides and mini quizzes to accompany the technological experience and to determine if males comprehend literature when it is introduced through this new medium.

Postcalculation of Grade Point Average

After careful research and planning, I implemented several strategies in my classroom to combat the male adolescent struggle with reading. I began the project by documenting the male class average of my students to discern if there was a positive reaction to my new pedagogical practices, and I calculated a post average.

Mini Surveys

In order to gauge the success of my lessons, I provided my students with mini surveys. Each survey had the same number of questions and was modeled after the Likert scale with five questions. Using the same survey in a repetitive fashion tested each student's perspective of each lesson. The surveys were also useful for reflection as I learned what motivated my struggling males and worked to alleviate their concerns with comprehension. The surveys were anonymous except for a gender-specific question, and due to the nature of my research, I disregarded female responses in my data.

Researcher Log

A major component of my research consisted of my ongoing process and documentation of self-reflection. I kept a journal of my progress as an educator as I began building lesson plans, sorting through research, and ultimately adopting a new pedagogy. This log helped me reflect on the reactions of my male students after implementing a new lesson, find areas of improvement, and tweak my practices. I could see my growth through this process, as well as continually notice and become aware of the specifically male sentiment within my classroom in conjunction with reading.

Implement and Evaluate Solution Strategies

The males in this study were unaware of their singular involvement in my research. I carefully included all of my students in every activity, survey, and discussion; however, my data collection was exclusively focused on male participants. Using a calculated average from male students as a preliminary marker, I graphically organized the breakdown of grades that would be used to chart any progress made over the observation period. The presurvey focused mainly on reading habits in my male students. I tailored my lesson plans based on research and their candid responses. My observations during the research, planning, and implementation stages were closely monitored in my daily log. Documenting the effectiveness of my lessons occurred through postactivity surveys from all male adolescents as well as noticing the level of engagement and comprehension.

> Examine how Patricia provided a detailed description of the data she collected, the pedagogical strategies she enacted, and the multiple data sources generated from the strategies to help her understand the underlying problem and assess the impact of her research.

Data Analysis

Initial Grade Calculations

I began my research by examining the grade point averages of male adolescents in two periods of English II. I placed the averages on a graphing chart to document each male student and his corresponding grade before implementation of strategies occurred. The averages revealed a wide variability of performance from 95 % to 11 % illustrating a gross disconnect between performance and comprehension.

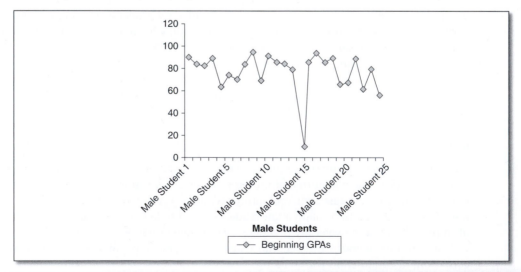

Note: GPAs are calculated in percentages.

Presurvey

After tallying grades, I surveyed my male students on their reading habits both in and out of the classroom. The survey included questions like "How many hours a week do you read?" and "Do you read for pleasure?" followed by "What type of reading material do you prefer?" While results varied on these questions, a concerning pattern emerged.

"How many hours a week do you read?"

Hours read per week	0–1 hour	1–2 hours	2–3 hours	3–4 hours	5 hours and beyond
Male participants	16	4	0	1	4

"Do you read for pleasure?"

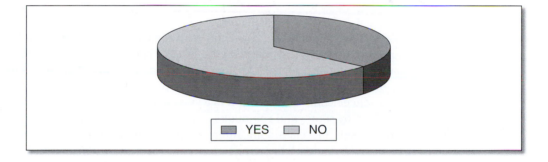

"What type of reading material do you prefer?"

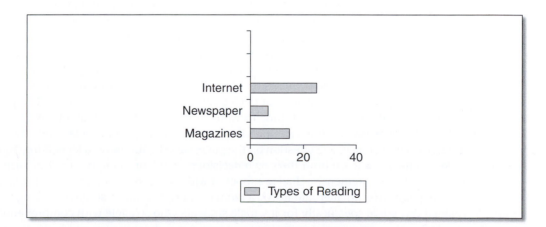

"What type of literature do you like?"

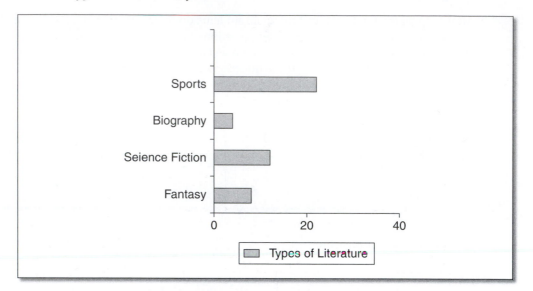

Shockingly, 72 % of male students surveyed only read a maximum of one hour per week. Similarly, but not surprisingly, 70 % of males do not read for pleasure. When questioned on the types of reading material preferred, the majority of males responded with Internet sources and magazines. The favored literary genre for surveyed males was sports by a landslide, followed by science fiction and fantasy. While I was not surprised to discover my male adolescent students enjoy sports and computers, I was deeply concerned with the lack of reading occurring outside the classroom. After compiling the data and consulting my research I began formulating new lessons to increase male students' interests in reading, to heighten their motivation, and to increase their comprehension of curriculum-based texts.

Independent Reading

The initial survey of my male students suggested a small amount of reading, both required and independent reading, both inside and outside of the classroom. I designed an independent reading lesson to bridge the gap between outdated curriculum and male adolescents' interest. The theory behind independent study is to make a personal connection with a text, thereby increasing comprehension through freedom of choice. Learning through reading is facilitated when males take ownership of the text; therefore I introduced a unit on *The Catcher in the Rye* by requiring student choice through an anticipation guide. The guide posed questions about themes the students would uncover in the curriculum-based novel; however, they were asked to find examples in magazines, newspaper articles, and novels of their choice. For instance, one question on the guide stated, "You have to let children make mistakes so they can learn from their own decisions." Students were required to form an opinion about this statement but had to support it with a current example from a magazine or newspaper article, an alternate novel, a radio transcript, a movie script, or a song lyric. I designed this guide specifically for my male students who struggle with comprehending curriculum because the texts are often outdated and disconnected from their interests. The discussion that ensued from this anticipation guide was positive and engaging. Male students, employing types of reading they enjoy, found examples from popular culture to pose arguments about the statements on the guide. I observed that without knowing it, my male students who usually struggle with these preunit questions found clarity and safety in their own reading materials. When I surveyed my male students at the conclusion of the lesson I had mixed reviews. Almost all of my male students disliked the amount of work associated with the guide, but as a teacher, I observed a raised level of consciousness and understanding concerning the themes. There was 100% participation, and my male students were eager to share their sports article, lyric, or newspaper clipping. I was encouraged by this activity and will use it again because it masterfully connects the important concepts and themes of curriculum-based texts with student choice and young adult literature. Using a two-question 5-point Likert scale I compiled male reactions to the lesson.

"I liked this activity."

1-Strongly Disagree	2-Disagree	3-Undecided	4-Agree	5-Strongly Agree
3	14	1	4	3

"I have a better understanding of the class reading/discussion after this activity."

1-Strongly Disagree	2-Disagree	3-Undecided	4-Agree	5-Strongly Agree
2	4	5	10	4

Corresponding with my observations, male students disliked the activity but admitted to a better understanding of the text, themes, and discussion, ultimately leading to greater comprehension of the curriculum throughout the unit.

Kinesthetic Lesson Plan

Receiving positive results for comprehension during the independent reading activity but failure in positive engagement, my goal during this lesson was to excite the struggling male readers through movement and activity. The lesson I created linked the curriculum being studied, *The Catcher in the Rye*, and positive reinforcement. Using video cameras, students were separated into groups and asked to perform scenes from the novel. Creating their own videos, students were responsible for turning the narrative into a script, assigning roles, staging their videos, shooting the film, and splicing the scenes. At the conclusion of the lesson, we made popcorn and viewed each group's movie. Observing my students, paying special attention to the males, I viewed an engagement with the technology as well as the novel. Particularly interesting, the struggling male readers were flipping through the text, furiously rewriting the narrative, and laughing with their peers. This activity simultaneously created a community of learners engaged in a common goal, while leading to mastery of the content. I was anxious to survey my students at the conclusion of this activity, because my observations were extremely positive. Using the same two questions, carefully surveying the lesson and not my students' ability to answer a questionnaire, I diagrammed their interest and engagement with the activity.

"I liked this activity."

1-Strongly Disagree	2-Disagree	3-Undecided	4-Agree	5-Strongly Agree
0	3	0	10	12

"I have a better understanding of the class reading/discussion after this activity."

1-Strongly Disagree	2-Disagree	3-Undecided	4-Agree	5-Strongly Agree
0	0	6	15	4

I was pleased to see the results of this survey aligning with my observations of the lesson. The male students polled overwhelmingly that they enjoyed the activity, which was also discernible through the high energy, laughter, and overall enjoyment of the video-making process. More impressive was the 76% tally of male students who felt the activity improved their comprehension of the text. I will use this activity for every core text in the curriculum because it embraces the masculine personalities in my classroom and encourages collaboration among my students, further aiding my struggling males and turning a seemingly dull text into an exciting piece of film study.

Computer-Based Reading Tools

Introducing technology into my classroom as well as my unit was an attempt to make reading more approachable. When surveyed, my male students admitted to reading Internet sources often; however, few read for more than one hour a week. Linking computers and reading was an effort to erase the stigma surrounding literature and update its relevance. I began by finding chapters of *The Catcher in the Rye* online and linking them to a student-run discussion board on Blackboard. In the classroom, using a mobile laptop cart, each student had a computer and access to the site. Students would be assigned three chapters of reading for homework, and I would allow time for completion of one chapter in class. On Blackboard, students would follow the link for the chapter, read an attached snippet of the novel, and then answer questions about the reading using a discussion thread. Each student would be responsible for answering all questions and responding to at least three threads from his or her classmates. At home, students would complete the remaining two chapters or reading assignment online and corresponding questions. Similarly, I designed reading quizzes on *The Catcher in the Rye* to serve as review, and these were easily accessed from the Blackboard site. Males who struggle with reading could sit comfortably at the computer, look at the answer choices, and find out immediately if they were on the right track. I had students complete these quizzes in the classroom, but I observed an immediate behavioral change when I switched from paper-based assessment to computer-based assessment. There were fewer groans, no sleeping, and better quiz grades. My struggling male readers were the first to grab their laptop, sign on, and get started. This medium really transformed the way my male students viewed reading, and I saw the greatest improvement in my study during these lessons. I surveyed my students after introducing this technique, collecting data only from the males, and calculated their responses below.

"I liked this activity."

1-Strongly Disagree	2-Disagree	3-Undecided	4-Agree	5-Strongly Agree
0	0	5	16	4

"I have a better understanding of the class reading/discussion after this activity."

1-Strongly Disagree	2-Disagree	3-Undecided	4-Agree	5-Strongly Agree
0	0	3	15	7

The results showed that 80% of male students surveyed liked using the computers to read and to respond to questions about the curriculum-based text being studied. An exciting 88% of male students had a better understanding of the novel at the conclusion of the activity. These numbers align with the increase in quiz scores, as males who struggled with content received instantaneous results on the computer when answering a question correctly or incorrectly. This active gauge of their understanding helped males remedy their mistakes, encouraged them to ask questions, and promoted self-reflection about their reading practices. Using computers and literature is time consuming; however, in the future I want to turn an entire reading unit into a technological experience, as well as incorporate at least one computer-based element into every core novel studied.

Postcalculation of Male Grade Point Averages

At the conclusion of my research I examined the grade point averages of the initial 25 males included in my study. I placed the newly calculated averages against the old, to create a visual representation of the data.

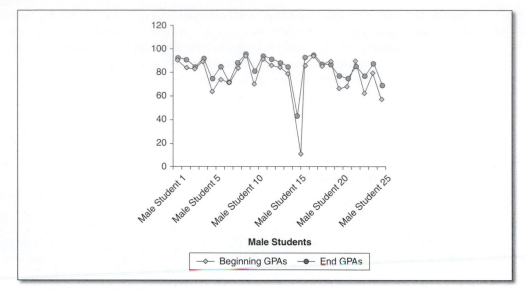

Note: GPAs are calculated in percentages.

The data show an increase in grade point averages in my course from the beginning of the study to the end, illustrating a greater comprehension of the material. I was excited, as an educator, to see the grades rise, but I was equally as impressed with the positive engagement my struggling male students had with the text. Enjoyment of the text is inextricably linked to better performance, and the males in my study excelled in both arenas.

Researcher Log

Keeping a daily log of observations and reactions to classroom activities and lessons was an excellent way for me to reflect on successes and failures in my struggling male students. Similarly, I have noted further areas that need improvement in these lessons, which will benefit my new group of students next year. My log documented my observations of an increase in engagement with reading, which are also supported by the data shown in the above charts. Overall, my researcher log was a reflective space that captured my thinking about the behaviors witnessed in my classroom. I enjoyed the process of making connections among what I was seeing in their work, what I was hearing in their discussions, and what I was calculating in their grade point averages.

Role of a Critical Friend

Critical friends are an important aspect of self-study. As a critical friend, I found the process of editing extremely insightful. I could see the holes in my critical friends' research, which also allowed me to better examine my own data with an analytical eye. Sharing ideas, formulating questions, and communicating on a weekly basis make the relationship current and influential. In the future, I would like to expand my circle to include several critical friends. Similarly, my critical friend works within the same field of study, and I would like to have other disciplines providing feedback on my work and research.

In this section, Patricia provides a detailed and transparent data trail describing her data analysis. She includes data displays and the procedures she used to make meaning of her data and formulate preliminary and concluding interpretations. She offers a discussion of the role of critical friend in the research process.

Findings

Student Choice

Through data analyzed about the new pedagogies as presented above and personal reflection written in my log, I have found several pertinent ways to increase motivation and reading comprehension in struggling male adolescents. At the beginning of my research and implementation process, I found reluctance on the part of male students as new lessons increased the amount of writing associated with reading. While my activity promoting student choice connected the students to popular culture, it demanded attention and only proved effective if students completed the work. Male students reported that they did not appreciate the work. However, the activity linked themes in a curriculum-based text with similar themes found by the student in popular young adult literature. I observed, throughout the course of the unit, that students were aware of the themes, made connections to the novel, and referred back to this guide continuously. In the future, I would like to alter this assignment because it only proved effective if students participated.

Motivation Through Action

Observing my students during the kinesthetic lesson plan, it was clear that their motivation was undeniably linked to comprehension and their comprehension was linked to their academic success. By creating lesson plans that increased movement and utilized previously admonished male behaviors, I was able to promote action and understanding in my classroom. I witnessed all participants answering questions, using the text, and excitedly arguing about themes, symbols, and characters. Similarly, there was a marked success when I introduced video cameras into my classroom and encouraged the students to use dramatization in their understanding of a novel. Here, students responded in their surveys with an overwhelming appreciation for the lesson and attributed the activity to an increase in comprehension and understanding of the text. In a way, I used the energy and psychological differences in males as a proponent for learning. Reading should be engaging, and I have learned that a seemingly boring curriculum-based text can function as a portal to active participation, and capturing a struggling reader's attention facilitates successful comprehension and test scores.

Computer-Based Tools

Introducing technology into my classroom is not a new phenomenon; however, using it as a source of reading comprehension did not present itself until the completion of my research. The lower-achieving male readers in my class struggle with the process of reading, both inside and outside of the classroom. In lieu of attempting the reading, the majority of my male students prefer taking a zero, progressively dropping their grade point averages. To alleviate the anxiety and apprehension that accompanies reading, I introduced literature on a computer. During this lesson I observed my male students engaging with the text, using class time to complete work, and behaving with focused intent. Reading no longer became an isolated function, but instead the males were a community of learners, sharing and discussing using online quizzes and communication threads. Every male student in this study completed his homework, scored above a 64% on all the quizzes, and participated in the online discussion board. Using the computer to facilitate a variety of readers and learning styles caused an increase in participation and comprehension. I attribute the success of my struggling male students to the launch of a curriculum-based text on the computer.

> In this findings section, Patricia provides a discussion and explanation of her interpretations of her data analysis with evidence for her claims. She presents the themes identified through her analysis.

Discussion and Implications

The implications of this study are dual-fold. First, it is necessary for educators to understand the learning differences between boys and girls. Second, this study seeks to acknowledge these differences and promote awareness in classrooms. Adolescent males process information often in a manner contradictory to the pace and style of female-run classrooms and struggle to make sense of outdated and lengthy curriculum. Understanding their behavior and creating lessons that promote their natural energies give struggling males a chance for success. If, as educators, we make ourselves aware of these differences, embrace the behavior, and begin changing our pedagogies, there will be an increase in male comprehension and motivation.

Within the lessons, there was a small matter of time management, because computer-based tools take an enormous amount of time to prepare and execute. Similarly, many of the activities that utilize movement take at least half a class period, if not an entire block. Similarly, access to computer labs may be a challenge; therefore preparation on behalf of the educator becomes essential. Another complication would be employing excellent classroom management skills before attempting new pedagogies. These activities are easily managed when definitive rules are posted for students; however, it is imperative to set ground rules for students before they begin the lesson.

Impact on Participants

My struggling male readers found great success during this research study, and I documented a positive impact between activities that promoted movement and technology and an increase in comprehension and motivation. Each male student improved within one facet of this study, and I was encouraged by the level of discourse being produced by previously shy and frustrated boys. Through my observations, I noted an increased level of excitement, participation, and understanding. All of my male students appreciated a classroom atmosphere that fostered a competitive spirit as well as a connecting of curriculum to popular songs, articles, and novels.

Impact on Teacher

This study has provided me with a new way of looking at my students. Before I began, the frustrations of my male students were reflected in my own teaching practices. I took personal offense to their lack of attention and felt resentment over their lack of participation and subsequent low grades. Over the course of this study, I have realized that research within the educational field provides insight, teaching tools, and an invaluable community of professionals dealing with the same disappointments. Using research and collaboration, previous notions of teaching may be dispelled in favor of new techniques. I embraced the transition in my pedagogy and will continue to further my studies in an effort to continually enhance the learning experience for my students.

My daily log, while not expansive, lent great resources to my research. Becoming an active observer in my own classroom made me notice and study my own teaching practices and ultimately allowed me to grasp the connection between males and reading comprehension.

Using research and my critical friend, I expounded on the topic until I had solidified a meaningful study to conduct with my students. Through active lesson planning, student choice, competition, and technology-based tools, I wanted to change the way my adolescent boys view reading. While reading and planning, my initial questioning underwent several transformations. Initially, I was going to study all of my students, but then I concentrated solely on my male students. Similarly, I began questioning if it was reading in general or texts in the curriculum that caused my students' frustration. After closely viewing their study habits, I concluded that material within the curriculum, and the way I approached the texts, needed to undergo a change. I would like to present my findings to my department and encourage other teachers to approach lesson planning with a strict eye toward gender differentiation.

Impact on Education Field

Although there is a growing amount of literature present on reading and adolescent males, my study further supports that antiquated classroom settings will not facilitate engagement or success for struggling male readers. Researchers are proving discernible differences between the way boys and girls learn. My study, with concrete data, further supports the notion that males excel when presented with activities that challenge their natural behavior and foster a community of learning that includes student choice and technology. As educators, if we become informed of the disparity between students, not merely differentiation between types of learner but between genders as well, there can be an increase in success and comprehension.

In this section on discussion and implications, Patricia provides a discussion of the impact on her research, on her students, on her teaching, and on her understanding and reframing of teaching. She discusses what her study offers the broader realm of education and her specific topic of male adolescent readers.

Limitations

My study was limited to my own classroom setting, grade of teaching, and population of a selective sampling of 25 male students. In the future, I hope to expand my knowledge and include girls in my study, learning how to improve collaboration and increase reading comprehension. On a personal note, I encountered my own limitation as I began researching this topic. As an educator, I had to completely abandon my previous notions of teaching and lesson planning and embrace new pedagogical ideas, specifically geared toward a mind-set very different from my own. Eliminating biases and focusing solely on the adolescent males in my classroom was a difficult experience, and in the future I would be interested in collecting data on female literacy. I opened myself completely to new methods of teaching adolescent males and saw the fallacy of my own practices.

> It is obvious that Patricia has acknowledged the limitations of her research including her own biases and learning and that self-study teacher research improved her practice and her students' learning.

References (Cited in the Brief)

Brozo, W. (2006). Bridges to literacy for boys. *Educational Leadership, 64*(1), 71–74.

King, K., & Gurian, M. (2006). Teaching to the minds of boys. *Educational Leadership, 64*(1), 56–61.

Sax, L. (2007). The boy problem. *School Library Journal, 53*(9), 40–43.

Sokal, L., & Katz, H. (2008). Effects of technology and male teachers on boys' reading. *Australian Journal of Education, 52*(1), 82–94.

KEY IDEAS

- Self-study teacher research involves you in designing a study, carefully reviewing the research ethics of your study, collecting data, analyzing data, and writing and presenting your findings.
- A Self-Study Research Project Planner highlights the specific and the overlapping research components that highlight the recursive nature of self-study research.
- A Self-Study Research Project Timeline is a tool for charting your progress and sharing it with critical friends throughout the research process.
- An example of self-study research gives you a general overview of what a research project entails.

The Self-Study Learning Community

When and How and Where and Who

What does it mean to join the self-study community?
is it a sudden jolt to assumptions galore
that stealthily hold your better sensibilities
is it a shift in center of gravity
that now brings you to the edge and contrarily makes you the center
is it asking how to begin the process of questioning
the ugly, the utterly ugly, and the profound
is it the exposure of vulnerabilities
that were never conquered for they were never acknowledged
it is some of this, all of this, and more
because it involves taking a stance with others,
in a critical but supportive environment,
to ask questions others gloss over as they rush to study others

—Arvinder Kaur Johri, *Doctoral Candidate, George Mason University*, and
Jason K. Ritter, *Duquesne University* (2009)

CHAPTER DESCRIPTION

In this chapter, you will find a discussion about the beginnings of the self-study community, how the Self-Study School evolved, how it was influenced by other scholarship, and how it became formalized. Placed within the larger spectrum of practitioner inquiry research, you will learn that although self-study scholars were influenced by earlier paradigms, self-study became a unique paradigm of its own. You will read about how its members worked to shape and reshape self-study as a new school of thought and action. You will learn how self-study scholars supported each other's work through critical collaborative inquiry as they worked to refine the methodology of self-study and respond to critique. As in earlier chapters, you will continue to learn about the research that has been conducted by self-study scholars while you begin to think about the research question you want to pose for your own self-study research.

✦ Reading this chapter will provide an opportunity for you to acquire an understanding of the foundations of self-study and what propelled it to grow and remain a vibrant research community today.

> I value the self-study community, which is at the core of my being as a teacher educator. I have always been interested in how people learn with each other and what role I played in that process. What I didn't realize when I joined the Self-Study of Teacher Education Practices (S-STEP) special interest group (SIG) over a decade ago was how much I could learn from others when I immersed myself into the community of self-study. S-STEP members generously invited me to join them and embraced me while I stumbled and tried to figure it all out. I went to the edge. No one judged. Colleagues encouraged me to write and offered their constructive and honest review as critical friends. It was the dialogue, openness, and innovative nature of our work that kept me coming back for more. S-STEP is like no other SIG in terms of how we have encouraged each other's inquiries to advance and impact the scholarship of teacher education.

CULTURE OF THE SELF-STUDY LEARNING COMMUNITY

What is the culture of the self-study community? What this group of scholars considers as important in its research tells us a great deal about its values. The goals, tasks, and behavior of a group, on both an individual and a collective level, help describe the group's culture, or the ways its members go about doing their work and how the things they value get embedded into that process. It tells us about *how* self-study scholars go about their research. What thoughts, images, and emotions come to mind when you think about the self-study research culture? Do you see a group of scholars only from the United States? Do you see people who come from similar institutions working in similar programs? Do you see a group of like-minded individuals working on similar topics and projects and from the same discipline? Do you see a group using a singular method or theory? Actually, none of these apply.

Diverse and Unified

Without a doubt, the culture of self-study research is diverse in multiple ways, and yet it is also unified. S-STEP includes members from all over the world and from a diversity of institutions that vary in mission and programs offered; some members have been involved with the organization from its conception, and some are relative newcomers. Membership in the professional organization reflects various racial, cultural, language, and gender perspectives, as well as disciplinary bases, educational levels, practice, and theoretical perspectives.

Self-study includes practitioners "at all levels of the educational enterprise" (Clarke & Erickson, 2004a, p. 55). Furthermore, self-study scholars are not bound to any one specific theory. That is, self-study researchers come from various theoretical orientations and study a variety of research topics. Self-study scholars come from a diversity of disciplines and experiences.

Self-study is not limited to teachers. Although self-study research grew out of the work of teacher educators, it has expanded to include practitioners such as administrators, librarians, occupational therapists, psychotherapists, counselors, and community educators working for social justice and educational reform (e.g., Allender, 2004; Manke, 2004; Wilcox, Watson, & Paterson, 2004). This extension of self-study of teachers to other practitioners is known as **self-studyship** (Samaras & Freese, 2006). Self-study scholars are unified by their practice in using self-study rather than by a discipline, topic, or context.

How did the current practices of self-study scholars develop from the work of the self-study community? It is important to place the development of the Self-Study School in the context of what was taking place in the field of teacher education research. Why self-study research and why now? What was happening in teacher research? Why was the ground fertile for the Self-Study School of thought to emerge as a new paradigm? Why did researchers believe that self-study was necessary for their practice and educational reform? Why were they as Loughran and Northfield (1998) report willing to question existing frames of reference in their teaching? Why were researchers willing to risk identifying with a new methodology that might hurt their chances for tenure and promotion because of its novelty? Why were teacher educators willing to express the political nature of their work so openly?

You are asked to go back in time and sit in a lyceum among self-study scholars. Listen to how they struggle to define the *how* and *why* of self-study. Read about how collectively, and over time, they began to clarify and articulate methodological components of self-study. Learn about the magnetism of self-study teacher research and how it attracted and unified a diverse group of scholars from around the world in the common purpose of questioning their practice in order to improve their students' learning (see Photo 3.1).

The Self-Study School is "a popular research movement which began in the early 1990s by teacher educators studying their practice and through member research, presentation, and publication was formalized and came of age a decade later" (Samaras & Freese, 2006, p. 38).

What is a school of thought? Step into a museum for a moment and find the works of the impressionists of the 19th century. Study the visible brushstrokes and open composition. In the works, you may find people in day-to-day practices often in natural settings and with objects seen in real, not studio, light. The representations are not idealized; the finish is not smooth. The artists broke with earlier and rigid standards of the Academy and the School of Fine Arts. Their work, criticized for its unfinished nature and often not accepted by juried salons, was later presented at their own exhibition in 1874. What gifts they left us as they changed our viewpoint of what art could also include.

Photo 3.1   The Self-Study School of Thought

PARADIGM SHIFT

As is characteristic of a school of thought and shaping of a discipline's way of knowing research, or what Kuhn (1996) calls a **paradigm**, the development of the Self-Study School was a confluence of many influences, and yet with two essential characteristics. Kuhn (1996) explains that scientists in attempting "to define the legitimate problems and methods of a research field for succeeding generations of practitioners . . . were able to do so because . . . their achievement was sufficiently unprecedented to attract an enduring group of adherents away from competing modes of scientific activity" (p. 10). In that respect, teacher educators found like-minded scholars who were beginning to see the need and value in examining their own teaching practice and the possibilities for educational reform when they did so. They began to notice what they were doing in their own practice. They were willing to discuss their teaching publically with other teacher educators so they might learn from each other. Loughran (2004) explains, "Researchers involved in reflective practice were also questioning teacher education practices and they added to the groundswell that further pushed forward the ideas beginning to take shape around self-study" (p. 15).

Nonetheless, the beginning of a paradigm is raw and underdeveloped and does not easily emerge. Kuhn (1996) surmises that a second condition for new methods of research to emerge is that, concurrently to the condition of dissatisfaction with the current methods available, the new method "was sufficiently open-ended to leave all sorts of problems for the redefined group of practitioners to resolve" (p. 10). Indeed the self-study community has shaped, and will continue to shape, the future of self-study research (Dalmau & Guðjónsdóttir, 2008).

This is not to suggest that the Self-Study School is the dominant paradigm in teacher education. Kuhn (1996) noted, unlike the natural sciences, the social sciences are not dominated by a single dominant paradigm. More useful than claiming one paradigm is better than another is "how paradigms exhibit confluence and where and how they exhibit differences, controversies, and contradictions" (Lincoln & Guba, 2000, p. 164). Self-study exists alongside other research methodologies in teacher education, which fall within the genre of qualitative research (Pinnegar & Hamilton, 2009). Shulman (1986a) adds that "the coexistence of competing schools of thought is a natural and quite mature state" (p. 5). The landscape in teacher education was influential in the outgrowth of self-study.

INFLUENCE, CONFLUENCE, AND DIVERGENCE

Practitioner Inquiry

Self-study scholars were influenced largely by the paradigms of their earlier teacher research work in teacher inquiry, reflective practice, and action research. Collectively this work has been called practitioner inquiry, the research conducted by those who are practicing professionals working in the field and "the conceptual umbrella to describe many forms of practitioner-based study of teaching and teacher education" (Cochran-Smith & Lytle, 2004, p. 602). Similarly, Grossman (2005) uses the conceptual umbrella of practitioner research when reviewing a set of related studies where "prospective teachers are required to study and analyze some aspect of their classroom practice" (p. 445). Self-study also comes under that umbrella as do other forms of practitioner inquiry such as teacher inquiry, teacher-as-researcher, reflective practice, and action research, albeit each has its distinct set of outcomes and characteristics. Grossman (2005) notes that forms of practitioner research vary in nature and the "types of outcomes they might choose to study" (p. 445).

There were international movements of practitioner research calling for the teacher as researcher in Great Britain in the 1960s connected with the work of Stenhouse (1985) and Elliott (1991). There was a participatory action research movement in Toronto and Australia. In Canada, Connelly and Clandinin's work (1990) in narrative inquiry also emphasized the teacher as a curriculum maker and helped make explicit teacher educators' professional knowledge through the power of their stories. For more extensive detail on the many forms of practitioner research, see Anderson, Herr, and Nihlen (2007); Cochran-Smith and Lytle (2004); and Zeichner and Noffke (2001). Three movements—teacher inquiry, reflective practice, and action research—are presented next as they are commonly recognized as influencing self-study research (Samaras & Freese, 2006). These are not inclusive of all practitioner research or presented in order of their outgrowth since there was overlap, but they do demonstrate that practitioner research was coming of age. Reading this history will help you grasp the underpinnings of self-study research.

Teacher Inquiry

In the late 1970s research included teachers' thinking (Clark & Yinger, 1979) and decision making (Borko, Cone, Atwood Russo, & Shavelson, 1979). Cognitive science was beginning to be used to examine teachers' thought processes and classroom problems. Nonetheless, the scientific understandings were interpreted by outsiders or what Lowe (1982) considered second-degree constructs and what Kincheloe (1991) describes as "outsider constructs of the insider" (p. 28). Various forms of teacher research were evident in the 20th century, but "it was during the 1980s that teacher research gained new standing because of its potential to lessen the divide between theory and practice, on the one hand, and contribute needed insider perspectives to the knowledge base about teaching and learning" (Cochran-Smith & Lytle, 2004, p. 603). Researchers drew on Dewey's (1938) work, which emphasized that inquiry should lead to practical solutions with individuals motivated to learn through their passions and applications in actual practice. Samaras and Freese (2006) explain that "before the late 1980s, classroom teachers neither viewed themselves as inquirers into their teaching and their students' learning nor did they think about problematizing their experiences . . . Instead, teachers viewed research as academic-oriented and as something that was done by the experts outside of the classroom" (p. 25). This notion of the teacher as a knower and not just a receiver of knowledge propelled the work of self-study. Hamilton and Pinnegar (1998) also assert that "most of our knowledge about developing as teachers has not been grounded in practice or personal experience. The emergence of self-study and teacher research has shifted this trend" (p. 236).

There was much discussion on how theory connected to practice. Qualitative research was slowly becoming more commonplace to provide "thick" or rich descriptions of the context, culture, and institutional factors embedded in educational dilemmas. Tom (1992) explains that few teacher education programs promoted teacher inquiry, and in the late 1980s there was an "explosion of interest" in preparing teachers to be reflective (p. viii). During an American Educational Research Association symposium on inquiry-oriented teacher education, Tom (1992) noticed an "accelerating involvement by teacher educators in inquiry-oriented teaching, now commonly called reflective teaching, a label change, probably attributable to Schön's influential book published in 1983" (pp. vii–viii).

Reflective Practice

Recall in the discussion of what self-study is not that self-study is more than mere reflection. Reflective practice is also more than mere reflection and greatly influenced the outgrowth of self-study research, although there are differences. Loughran and Northfield (1998) assert that "reflection is a personal process of thinking, refining, reframing and developing actions. Self-study takes these processes and makes them public, thus leading to another series of processes that need to reside outside the individual" (p. 15). Self-study, in part, is an extension of the notion of reflection (Dewey, 1933; Schön, 1983, 1987), but self-study "pushes the virtues of reflection further" (Loughran, 2004, p. 25) by requiring dialogue, public critique, and presentation from the researcher's personal reflection. Self-study employs a validation group to gain perspectives on the analysis and a forum to make the research public for review and critique.

In reflective practitioner research, reflection is at the center of professional practice where teachers question dilemmas inherent in their practice and from multiple perspectives (Ciriello, Valli, & Taylor, 1992). In self-study research, reflection is one research technique that self-study teachers use as they select from a variety of self-study methods. For example, a self-study researcher who painted a self-portrait using the arts-based self-study method was prompted to reflect deeply about her practice, but it was the dialogue with others that led to insights about her professional development (Mittapalli & Samaras, 2008). Data about the self-study researcher role and communication with colleagues are essential sources that take the reflection beyond the individual. In self-study research, teachers reflect on what they will do and how they will act upon their classroom dilemmas, while they also articulate their reframed practice to colleagues. They question and investigate their role in a renewed process of knowing.

Self-study for me grew out of my work at The Catholic University of America (CUA). I applied the CUA Reflective Teacher Model in my teaching—a sophisticated teacher preparation framework conceptually based in deliberative reflection and drawn from the work of Schwab's (1973) commonplaces, van Manen's (1977) reflective levels, and Berlak and Berlak's (1981) dilemmas of practice. And yet, although the CUA model was influential in my thinking about self-study, I felt something was missing in the model for me as a teacher educator. For that reason I adapted the CUA model to include a component where teacher educators, including myself, could practice what they preached (i.e., studying one's practice in order to improve it) (see Samaras, 2002).

Many other self-study scholars came to self-study through their work in reflective practice in teacher education programs (Clift, Houston, & Pugach, 1990; Freese, 1999; LaBoskey, 1991; Russell & Munby, 1992; Zeichner, 1995). Russell and Korthagen (1995), two leaders in the self-study movement, wrote, "We hope that *Teachers Who Teach Teachers: Reflections on Teacher Education* will help to sustain the growth and activities of that [S-STEP] organization" (p. x). Their hope became a reality. Included in the Russell and Korthagen (1995) book is the work of Cole and Knowles (1995) in life history and personal history self-study influenced from the work of Bullough, Knowles, and Crow (1991) and Goodson (1980–1981) and still present in self-study research (Russell, 2009). The work of self-study leaders paved the way for other teacher educators to ask themselves a very basic, and yet not always asked, question: "How can I improve my teaching practice?" Self-study encouraged "teacher educators to understand their work, question what might be possible in their practice, and then move to create such practice" (Hamilton & Pinnegar, 1998, p. 241).

Action Research

Action research is another form of practitioner inquiry whereby teachers study their own practice. In the 1980s, Stenhouse's idea for action research for teachers took root and became integrated into teacher education programs. Anderson, Herr, and Nihlen (2007) explain that action research's early beginnings date back to the late 19th and early 20th centuries. It began as a theory of action for problem-solving issues in work contexts developed by Lewin (1946) and is different in its current form. Anderson et al. further note that action research was advanced by Corey (1953) for classroom teachers but not sustained due to the criticism it received in a **positivist,** or scientifically based, research approach, which Freeman, deMarrais, Preissle, Roulston, and St. Pierre (2007) argue is still problematic for qualitative researchers today. A positivist approach ignores the subjective experience and seeks an objective explanation of phenomena. Knowledge is based on natural phenomena that can be observed, measured, and verified. Zeichner and Noffke (2001) note the teacher research tradition was spurred by the work by Stenhouse (1985) and Elliot (1991). Teacher educators became more critical about the dictates of tradition and the importance of reform through participation for curriculum planning reform and with an action research cycle format (Kemmis, 1982; Kemmis & McTaggart, 1988). The spiral of action research includes (a) identifying a focus for something you want to study and improve, (b) developing and implementing a plan of action, (c) collecting and analyzing data, and (d) reflecting on findings and making changes.

Mills (2007) identifies Kemmis and McTaggart's (1988) work as critical action research, or "emancipatory action research because of its goal of liberation through knowledge gathering" (p. 6). The work of Zeichner and his students at the University of Wisconsin–Madison (Zeichner & Melnick, 1996) is a notable exemplar of critical action research. Critical action research is distinguished from practical action research or a "how to" approach (Mills, 2007). Critical action research draws from critical theory, and like self-study it is considered **postmodern** in its orientation and actions taken. Postmodernists question that there is a single truth to guide one's research (Samaras & Freese, 2006). In teacher research, "truth is relative, conditional, and situational, and . . . always the outgrowth of previous experience" (Mills, 2007, p. 6). As postmodernists, self-study scholars examine their practical inquiries with the assumption there is no one way of knowing or final truth to educational research (Hamilton & Pinnegar, 1998) as they work toward social justice. Furthermore, Cochran-Smith and Lytle (2004) write that according to the work of Bullough and Pinnegar (2001) and Cole and Knowles (2000), "self-study works from the postmodernist assumption that it is never possible to divorce the 'self' from either the research process or from educational practice" (p. 607).

Whereas much of the early action research focused on classroom teachers, the action researchers who joined the self-study movement were beginning to question their own practice as teacher educators (Loughran, 2004; Zeichner & Noffke, 2001). Hamilton and Pinnegar (1998) remark that many action researchers "have come to their interests in self-study through their work in action research" (p. 237). Some began to question why they were not practicing the action research they taught and generating theories based in their practice. Whitehead (1989) speaks of a **living educational theory** or the descriptions and explanations and personal theory making produced from practitioners' accounts of their learning and practice. Teaching is based not in propositional theories but in teachers' reconceptualization of practice and with practical implications (McNiff, Lomax, & Whitehead, 2003; McNiff & Whitehead, 2006).

Differences Between Action Research and Self-Study

One of the questions students often ask is "What is the difference between self-study and action research?" Keeping in mind that numerous self-study scholars came to self-study research from action research, it makes sense that there are similarities and yet differences. Self-study, although related to action research, has distinguishing differences (Feldman, Paugh, & Mills, 2004) and distinctive methodological components as presented in this text and elsewhere (LaBoskey, 2004a). In both self-study and action research, the researcher inquires into problems related to one's practice to improve one's teaching (Feldman et al., 2004). However, as Feldman et al. (2004) explain, a major distinction in the research methodologies is in the change that occurs. In action research, the goal of the "action" is for a change in the classroom. In self-study research, the "self" is the focus of the study with the goal of leading to a reframed understanding of one's role in order to impact students' learning. Self-study researchers are a resource for their research and "problematize their selves in their practice situations" to improve their practice (Feldman et al., 2004, p. 971). And yet, self-study focuses on improvement on both the personal and the professional level.

Another defining difference between self-study and action research is that self-study researchers continuously reframe their understanding of practice through their research and knowledge production using and inventing multiple methods to arrive at new understandings; that is, there is no one way of conducting self-study research. Furthermore, the questions asked by self-study scholars are most often framed in an orientation and parallel to **critical pedagogy**, or as Kincheloe (2005) explains the work of teachers "grounded on a social and educational vision of justice and equality" (p. 6). Self-study "is designed to lead to the reconceptualization of the role of the teacher" (Samaras & Freese, 2006, p. 29) despite, and within, the constraints of the politics and practices of schooling. Other differences are that self-study necessitates collaboration and dialogue between the researcher and critical friends to reach new understandings. The research is made public for review and critique.

In each of the teacher research paradigms presented above, teachers had gained prominence as makers of knowledge and not just receivers of it. But what seemed to be largely missing in the earlier paradigms was the personalization of learning about one's teaching with a focus on the self in relation to others as well as how the teacher, not just the students, changed. Those differences appeared to have greatly influenced the self-study movement. Self-study scholars articulated guidelines and methodological components that further distinguished self-study from earlier forms of practitioner inquiry and continue to do so (LaBoskey, 2004a).

Advice From a Self-Study Scholar

Self-Study as a Way of Being: Living as a Teacher-Researcher

A teacher-researcher is someone who consciously commits to improving and researching practice. As I begin the academic year, I establish conditions that will support self-study of teacher education practices.

- I apply to the university's research ethics board for approval to conduct research in my teacher education classes. For courses I teach on a regular basis, I now simply ask for an extension of ongoing studies of practice.

(Continued)

(Continued)

- I identify two or three possible themes for self-study during the year.
- I keep a teacher education journal in which I reflect on my practices as a teacher educator.
- I save evidence of my teacher education practices, including student work and feedback.
- I meet regularly with critical friends in a self-study group to discuss and support each other's work.
- At the end of the year, I write about my teacher education practices using that year's experiences or research data from previous years.

Julian Kitchen
Brock University, Canada

Practicing Self-Study

Increasingly researchers, whose work was largely based in earlier forms of practitioner inquiry, began to practice self-study and publish their self-study research (Bullough & Gitlin, 1995; Korthagen, 1995; Loughran, 1996; Russell & Korthagen, 1995). Many moved from their earlier work as reflective practitioners and action researchers to self-study, which provided a method for them to solve problems the older paradigms did not afford them. Loughran (2004) notes that self-study allowed teacher educators to gain a better understanding of the intersections of their personal histories of learning, their cultures, and their professional practices; develop a self-understanding personally and professionally by examining their own practice with colleagues; and consider how they could reframe their practice.

A distinguishing facet of self-study is that scholars explain that they want to "walk the talk" and practice self-study as a habit of mind in their own work (Guilfoyle, Hamilton, Pinnegar, & Placier, 1998). Although teacher educators had taught the use of reflection and action research in their education courses in the 1980s, it was not until the early 1990s that teacher educators began practicing what they were preaching—to reflect on, inquire into, and study their own practice (Cochran-Smith & Lytle, 1993; Loughran, 2004). Yet there was a risk in undertaking self-study, particularly for untenured faculty who faced the challenge of the academy not understanding self-study as legitimate research or teaching as scholarship. For example, "Self-study in using the Vygotskian approach became strained by my entrance into full-time academic work, although I struggled desperately to align the exploration of my teaching and research—not a popular notion at a research institution" (Samaras, 1998, p. 58). Cole and Knowles (1998) surmised, "Thus, the more important question is not about how or whether self-study is research, but rather how it can be openly practiced by teacher educators without fear of reprisal from the academic community" (p. 50). Over time and with much work, self-study scholars have become the change they wanted to see in their students and began to rethink their work as they modeled and tested their work as teacher educators (Samaras, Hicks, & Garvey Berger, 2004).

Loughran (2004) asserts, though, that self-study scholars have to be confident, yet vulnerable, and willing to take risks by immersing themselves in the doing of self-study with the support of the self-study community. Researchers' "conversion experience," as Kuhn

(1996, p. 150) notes, cannot be forced. Neither does their allegiance shift individually. Instead it is "the sort of community that always sooner or later re-forms as a single group" (p. 153) with reception through "specialized journals, the foundation of specialists' societies, and the claim for a special place in the curriculum" (p. 19).

Looking back, Samaras and Freese (2006, 2009) note that the paradigm shift occurred with a formalization and legitimacy of self-study as the result of a number of factors: (a) a self-study professional biannual conference in 1996, which continues to date; (b) an extensive two-volume international handbook on self-study published in 2004; (c) a scholarly refereed journal devoted to self-study research launched in 2005; and (d) numerous publications by self-study scholars with books and articles in top-tier teacher education journals devoted to self-study research.

IMPORTANT EVENTS IN OUTGROWTH OF SELF-STUDY SCHOOL

1992 →	1993 →	1996 →	2004 →	2005 →	Present Day
AERA Self-Study Symposium	**S-STEP Established**	**The Castle Conference**	**Self-Study International Handbook**	**Self-Study Professional Journal**	**Scholarship of Self-Study**

1992: AERA Self-Study Symposium

It was 1992 when a small group of thoughtful and committed teacher educators gathered to present in a symposium, titled "Holding Up the Mirror: Teacher Educators Reflect on Their Own Teaching," at the Annual Meeting of the American Educational Research Association (AERA). That symposium launched a discussion of the self-study of teaching practices, which remains with us today. Members of a group known as the Arizona Group presented their papers (Guilfoyle, 1992; Hamilton, 1992; Pinnegar, 1992; Placier, 1992) about tensions in their new role as teacher educators. Also presenting was Russell (1992), a seasoned teacher educator, who questioned his practice of teaching about high school physics. Korthagen, serving as the symposium discussant, offered critique and raised reasonable concern. He asked if other scholars would view self-study as legitimate research especially because "formal" research was more evidenced-based (Korthagen, 1995). AERA continues to serve as an invaluable forum in gathering self-study scholars and for those interested in learning about self-study research.

1993: S-STEP Established

From those first symposium conversations set in a climate ripe for change, a new professional special interest group was seeded. It would even be awarded its own descriptor in AERA (Loughran, 2004). As Hamilton and Pinnegar (1998) later reported, "The **Self-Study of Teacher Education Practices** Special Interest Group **[S-STEP]** began in 1993 with a rush of excitement and enthusiasm. Teacher educators studying their own practice seemed quite unique, and yet timely, as they generated practical inquiry to substantiate their formal theorizing" (p. 235). S-STEP members attended each other's conference sessions and gathered to socialize at the AERA meetings. They interacted at the SIGs' unique business meetings, which were listed in the program as "A Business Meeting Like No Other Business Meeting" (AERA, 2001). S-STEP changed the paradigm of business meetings where members were asked to get up out of their seats, draw their ideas on large sheets of paper posted around the room, and share their thinking about teacher research. The SIGs' activities were welcoming and supportive in nature, which can be an anomaly at a large-scale conference. It's easy to feel anonymous at AERA, which "attracted record-breaking attendance of more than 16,000 participants and exhibitors" (*Educational Researcher,* 2008, p. 220). S-STEP members networked and began publishing and presenting together. The annual business meetings and SIG-sponsored social were forums for dialogue, networking, and professional development. Emerging rapidly and "quickly becoming one of the largest special interest groups of the [AERA] Association" (Korthagen, 1995, p. 99), S-STEP grew into a community of scholars committed to developing a new conceptual framework for teacher education research and one that would push the boundaries of the status quo (Samaras et al., 2004), reaching a membership of nearly 300 in 2009.

1996: The Castle Conference

In 1996, Tom Russell took the leadership in orchestrating a professional forum for self-study scholars, other than the AERA conference, at the first biannual **International Conference on the Self-Study of Teacher Education Practices** at the Queen's University International Study Centre at Herstmonceux Castle in East Sussex, England. The **Castle Conference**, termed affectionately due to its presence at an English castle, is a professional venue that brings together self-study teacher educators from a wide range of countries from both research-intensive and teaching-focused universities and marked the beginning of a unique and important forum for self-study scholars (Heston, Tidwell, & Fitzgerald, 2008). The intimate gathering draws about 80 to 100 participants with opportunities for engagement and substantial and extended dialogue over the course of 4 days with a common dorm and eating space to extend conversations that may begin in sessions. Self-study scholars continue their biannual pilgrimage to East Sussex, and newcomers continue to join them.

S-STEP members have served as program chairs and editors of the refereed Castle proceedings (Cole & Finley, 1998; Fitzgerald, Heston, & Tidwell, 2006; Heston, Tidwell, East, & Fitzgerald, 2008; Kosnik, Freese, & Samaras, 2002a; Loughran & Russell, 2000; Richards & Russell, 1996; and Tidwell, Fitzgerald, & Heston, 2004). Alternating leadership roles, in the last three conference editorships, the University of Northern Iowa team has refined and developed the review process for proceeding proposals (Heston, Tidwell, & Fitzgerald, 2008). In that process, they facilitated what they call the *Castle Way,* a community of critical friends.

> When we talk about the *Castle Way,* we refer to those aspects of the conference (both intentional and serendipitous) that help to create a genuine community of scholars. These aspects include creating supportive structures, inviting the community in, including the community throughout the process, making a conscious effort to be open and inclusive to diverse approaches to study, working

to establish collegial friendships, modeling the combination of critique and support, working to create new networks, and making current networks more widely accessible to others. (Heston, Tidwell, & Fitzgerald, 2008, pp. 172–173)

Many self-study scholars, including myself, benefited from the scaffolding that the Castle editors and proposal reviewers provided to refine proposals. Along with the AERA conference, the biannual Castle Conference promoted and sustained the ongoing work of S-STEP. Lighthall (2004) surmises that "the s-step enterprise would not have emerged in anything like its present form without the formation of the S-STEP group, without AERA as a parent organization fostering such groups, and without the Castle Conferences" (p. 235).

2004: Self-Study International Handbook

The International Handbook of Self Study of Teaching and Teacher Education Practices edited by Loughran, Hamilton, LaBoskey, and Russell (2004) is a comprehensive compilation of self-study research conducted by researchers from all over the world. This two-volume handbook contains 61 chapters, edited by some of the early leaders in self-study teacher research and written by chapter authors from many different countries including the United States, Canada, the Netherlands, Belgium, Iceland, Australia, United Kingdom, and New Zealand. It is "the most definitive and expansive collection of self-study research written to date" (Samaras & Freese, 2006, p. 35). The handbook has provided a foundation for the field by exploring the evolving definitions, purposes, and methodology of self-study and how self-study scholarship has developed over the years. The handbook describes self-study as an important movement for teacher educators that developed out of scholars articulating their tacit knowledge as teachers and "people [who] are intimately familiar with two worlds: the world of scientific research on education and the world of practice" (Korthagen, 1995, p. 100). In his handbook chapter, Lighthall (2004) identifies the "fundamental features and approaches of the s-step enterprise" (p. 193) by examining the Castle proceedings papers and the types of self-studies conducted. The most frequent features in order of frequency included (a) collaboration between author(s) and others; (b) self-study of practices with a focus on individual practice and/or teacher education program with student feedback; (c) a specific method for improving self-study or improving professional practices; (d) autobiography including narrative of author's own life experiences; (e) reform of program, profession, or institution; and (f) evidence of theory, conceptualization, or framing of a subject matter. This wide array of topics identified by Lighthall highlights that the handbook documents the extensive research conducted by self-study scholars in a range of teaching and teacher education contexts. Self-study scholars have articulated in their research *and* practice the nature and development of self-study and its contributions to the professional knowledge base for teaching.

2005: Self-Study Professional Journal

Studying Teacher Education: A Journal of Self-Study of Teacher Education Practices, published by Routledge, launched its first volume in 2005. Whereas the handbook compiles conceptual reviews of the nature, development, knowledge base, methods, and applications of self-study in teacher education programs, the journal makes available the ongoing work of self-study scholars. The journal further adds to the formalization of the Self-Study School. One of the dilemmas for any scholar is finding an appropriate and welcoming outlet that is a good fit for one's research. The journal provides a forum for self-study scholars to publically share their self-study research after it undergoes a thorough review by colleagues in a rigorous review process. This internationally refereed journal, edited by Loughran and Russell, includes an editorial board and an international advisory board. The journal is devoted to "self-study research, design and practice; the knowledge base of teaching and teaching about teaching; enhanced understandings of learning to teach; the nature of teacher education; and the professional development of teachers and teacher educators." The journal seeks "to create opportunities for teachers and teacher educators to publish empirical and conceptual research that advances our understanding of the complex work of teaching and teacher education." (See http://www.tandf.co.uk/journals/titles/17425964.asp.)

Present-Day Scholarship of Self-Study

New paradigms emerge through a recognized need by reform leaders and with contributions by its members who discuss, publish, present, and critique each other's work, as they work to formalize a new area of research and thinking (Kuhn, 1996). There has been an explosion of self-study scholarship over the last decade with self-study scholars publishing largely in teacher education and qualitative journals. Quite impressively, the publications highlight how self-study research contributes to the knowledge base of reforming in the first person. Coedited books were generated from the proceedings of the Castle Conferences. A steady stream of self-study books have been written since the 1990s. You will note that self-study scholars have been extremely collaborative in their work. They have supported each other's efforts in an intellectually safe and supportive learning community to improve their practice by making it explicit to themselves and others; that is, critical collaborative inquiry is a self-study methodological component.

Journal Articles

Self-study scholars continue to publish in an array of top-tier educational journals, not only in their own self-study journal but in cross-disciplinary qualitative journals as well. The publications have helped increase awareness and understanding of self-study research and are being recognized by people outside the self-study field (e.g., Bullough & Pinnegar, 2001; Dinkelman, 2003; Feldman, 2003; Freese, 1999; Hamilton & Pinnegar, 2000; Loughran, 2007a; Louie, Drevdahl, Purdy, & Stackman, 2003; Mittapalli & Samaras, 2008; Munby & Russell, 1994).

Edited Books Generated From Castle Conferences

Castle Conference editors, in addition to the published proceedings, have published edited books with topics that found their first audiences at the Castle Conference (Hamilton, Pinnegar, Russell, Loughran, & LaBoskey, 1998; Kosnik, Beck, Freese, & Samaras, 2006; Tidwell & Fitzgerald, 2006; Tidwell, Heston, & Fitzgerald, 2009).

Books

Self-study scholars have published a plethora of books about various self-study topics (see the accompanying book Web site).

CRITIQUE AND SUSTAINABILITY

Self-study has come of age, and as Zeichner (1999) predicted "the birth of the self-study in teacher education movement around 1990 has been probably the single most significant development ever in the field of teacher education research" (p. 8). Nonetheless, its evolution was not without criticism. First of all, it was a major shift in thinking to consider that teachers and teacher educators could research their own practice (Zeichner & Noffke, 2001) especially in an era of "evidence-based" and scientifically based reform.

As with other forms of practitioner inquiry, self-study research met criticisms from inside and outside of the practitioner inquiry movement. Cochran-Smith and Lytle (2004) present a series of five important critiques that have been made about practitioner inquiry in general. They address *the knowledge critique* or whose knowledge and what kinds of knowledge (practical or formal) should count in research. There has also been *a methods critique,* or concerns about data interpretation as defined in one's own words instead of from the more traditional method of data interpreted by others as well as issues of quality and validity. Related to the methods critique is *the science critique*, which calls for effectiveness, impact, and accountability through research-based practice. *The political critique* is another concern and calls into question if all research is, or should be, political in purpose in order to challenge the status quo and bring about positive social change. Last, *the personal/professional critique* raises concern that the personal knowledge does not generate knowledge for the field at large and that if it centers on the self only, it is narcissistic and solipsistic. Self-study scholars have responded to each critique. As self-study scholars responded to the criticisms, they were creating guidelines that refined the scholarship of self-study and claiming its position as legitimate research and as a genre of qualitative research.

Addressing the critique about knowledge, LaBoskey (2006) and Loughran (2004, 2007a) argue that in order to make bold claims and assertions about the impact of self-study and that it contributes to a body of knowledge and a specific domain, the method of self-study must be transparent with a detailed and clear data trail. Self-study must be systematic, "trustworthy," and validated over time. "Only in that way can the ideas be employed, applied, and retested by the teacher education community in ways that will help us embrace, discard, or transform those assertions; that is the essence of the validation process for the field" (LaBoskey, 2006, p. 258).

Self-study scholars have also addressed the critique about method by focusing on issues of validity and quality in self-study (Feldman, 2003). Two ways of doing this involve the use of critical friend validation groups and the encouragement of honesty and transparency in the research. Bullough and Pinnegar (2001) offered guidelines for quality in autobiographical forms of self-study research including issues of addressing the self within a contextualized and historical context of engaged practice and connections with others. There is caution about only addressing the self, being dishonest, and "the obligation to seek to improve the learning situation not only for the self but for the other" (Bullough & Pinnegar, 2001, p. 17). Samaras and Freese (2006) offer a structure for informal and formal self-study research, which includes work with critical friends and evidence of the impact of the research.

During the era of its formalization, self-study scholars broke with earlier paradigms and argued that self-study "is methodologically unique" (Pinnegar, 1998, p. 31). They asserted that "self-study is a methodology or a stance toward research, which employs many methods" (LaBoskey, 2004b, p. 1173). Hamilton et al. (1998) explain that "formal research does not provide teachers with the kinds of immediate answers they need for their classroom problems, nor teacher educators the tools to best support their students" (p. 238). They add that formal and quantitative methods have their place in research but are not useful for answering all types of questions and the ones self-study scholars pose. Explaining the impact of their research beyond their own personal and professional development has been at the forefront of the work of self-study scholars. As they provide detail about the impact of their work on students and programs, they are also responding to the personal/professional critique. Quality self-study is not narcissism.

And so we begin to see some of the major influences in the outgrowth of self-study and the influences and distinctions of their work from earlier paradigms. We also begin to understand how self-study research was refined as scholars addressed the critique and as they look toward the work ahead.

Looking Forward

S-STEP program chairs, Castle proceeding editors, and members developed and continue to discuss self-study as a school of thought. Zeichner (2007) surmises that much of the early work in self-study was about explaining its methodological aspects. Although this early work helped establish its legitimacy and bring it to a place of stature in the field, Zeichner argues that what is needed next is "how a study builds on the work of others" (p. 39). Questioning power, social justice, and discrimination issues, Bodone, Guðjónsdóttir, and Dalmau (2004) call the need for a continued discourse, asking such questions as "How have researchers used collaborative research relationships? . . . How do educators constructively transform these challenges into possibilities for growth and communal knowledge?" (p. 775).

When an organization documents, interprets, and assesses its development over time, it enables members to make sense of their past and discuss areas for improvement—to dialogue where they have been, what they have accomplished, and what they have learned. It also allows the self-study community to hold a conversation about its future of self-study research. Self-study members collaborated in a self-study of S-STEP; that is, they participated in an AERA symposium and electronic survey distributed through the S-STEP electronic mailing list, sharing comments about what attracted them to the field of self-study, how the community welcomed them in, how they practice self-study, and what sustains its scholarship and community (Samaras, Guðjónsdóttir, & Dalmau, 2009). S-STEP members have discussed Zeichner's (2009) call to speak out and disrupt the rhetoric of educational reform, not only as individuals but as a group, addressing the role of universities and teacher preparation in social justice issues (Samaras et al., 2009). Each of these efforts helped shape the quality and quantity of self-study writings within an intellectually safe and highly supportive cultural inquiry community, much like what we encourage teachers to develop in their classrooms.

KEY IDEAS

- The culture of a research community helps shape what it values in its practice.
- The culture of self-study research is diverse in multiple ways such as in geographic location, years of teaching experience, theoretical orientation, discipline, and topics studied.
- Self-study scholars are unified by their use of the self-study methodology rather than by a discipline, topic, or context.
- Self-study includes practitioners besides teachers, and that is called self-studyship.
- According to Kuhn (1996), paradigms emerge when researchers are attracted away from competing paradigms due to their dissatisfaction with the current methods available and the new method is open-ended enough to leave all sorts of problems for the redefined group of practitioners to resolve.
- The self-study movement was influenced by earlier paradigms such as teacher inquiry, reflective practice, and action research and is distinguished from them by its unique methodological components.
- Self-study teacher research began when researchers began to ask questions about the issues they found in their role as teacher educators much like they asked of their students.
- The Self-Study of Teacher Education Practices [S-STEP] Special Interest Group began in 1993 and grew into a community of scholars committed to developing a new paradigm for teacher education research.
- The Self-Study School was formalized through conferences, S-STEP, an international handbook, a journal committed to self-study research, and a plethora of book and journal publications.
- There has been critique of practitioner research and self-study research, and scholars have responded by offering clearer guidelines and suggested directions for its sustainability and future.

4

The Self-Study Methodology

Why and How

The greatest discovery from learning this methodology is related to data sources. Using art and visual representations allowed me to take a step back from the traditional text-based data sources in a safe environment. I didn't think I could do memory work at all, and even told classmates that I had a hard time remembering events. However, as soon as I started staring at old photographs from twenty years ago, I was able to recall some specific details. How exciting and freeing to learn that I am no longer bound by text. I never anticipated or appreciated the substance to visuals until completing this proposal.

—Tamie L. Pratt-Fartro (2007), *Reading Specialist, Stafford County Public Schools, Virginia*

CHAPTER DESCRIPTION

This chapter describes the self-study research methodology framed within a discussion of the culture of self-study. In this chapter, the Five Foci, or the methodological components of self-study, are first introduced: personal situated inquiry, critical collaborative inquiry, improved learning, transparent research process, and knowledge generation and presentation. Each of these methodological components is revisited in later chapters.

◆ Reading this chapter will provide an opportunity for you to become familiarized with the methodological components of self-study research, which are essential to understand in enacting a quality self-study research project.

While teaching a course in the self-study methodology, I observed that students learned the process best through their actual experiences in using it. The self-study research project enabled students to have a deeper understanding of the intersection of their personal histories and professional practices and their construction of new knowledge. Their situated inquiry gave self-study immediate applicability and illuminated the opaque, or as one student stated, "It helped show a hidden side of data, because it is gathered, in a sense, from 'the dark side of the moon.'"

Figure 4.1   Self-Study Methodology and Self-Study Methods

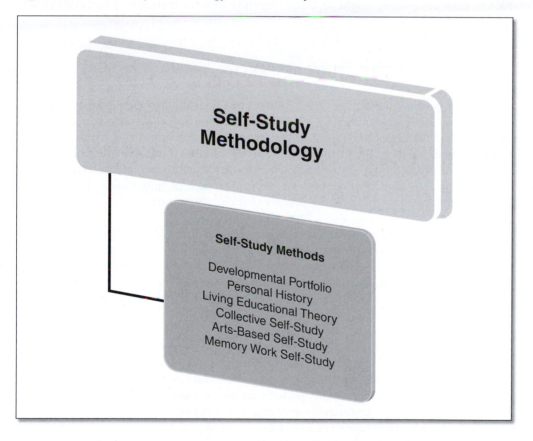

Self-study is a methodology or "a stance that a researcher takes towards understanding or explaining the physical or social world" rather than a way of knowing or doing research (LaBoskey, 2004b, p. 1173). You might find the notion of method

and methodology used interchangeably, but they are not the same. Wolcott (2001) asserts that method refers to "specific techniques" and methodology "refers to underlying principles of inquiry" (p. 93). The self-study methodology is "a body of practices, procedures, and guidelines used by those who work in a discipline or engage in an inquiry" and includes a choice of multiple **self-study methods** (Samaras & Freese, 2006, p. 56; see Figure 4.1, p. 67). Those practices, procedures, and guidelines are discussed in this text as methodological components of self-study or the Five Foci and are located in whatever self-study method you choose. Self-study employs a variety of methods, which you will be introduced to in the next chapter, that help the researcher capture the essence of the question being studied and think deeply about practice, its development, and its impact. As Loughran (2004) emphasizes, "There is no one way, or correct way, of doing self-study. Rather, how a self-study might be 'done' depends on what is sought to be better understood" (p. 15).

CHARACTERISTICS OF SELF-STUDY RESEARCH

One way of grasping the culture of self-study is by understanding characteristics and the nature of self-study as identified by some of its members. In that manner, you will be able to understand the underpinnings of self-study to better frame and enact your self-study teacher research project. For example, Barnes (1998) shared his observations on the characteristics of the self-study community, which he identified from his observations of the 1996 Herstmonceux (Castle) conference. A primary note of importance is that Barnes brought attention to the need for the *process* of self-study "to be made plain":

> The papers that did this began by explaining the institutional context, quoted next (rather than summarized) some of the evidence used, illustrated the processes of interpretation, including alternative views, outlined any changes made in the course being studied, and discussed general conclusions. Papers which had done this drew their audience into the process by which the conclusions had been reached. (p. xi)

Drawing from Schön's (1983) terms *framing* and *reframing*, Barnes (1998) views the central task of teaching as "making changes in how the various aspects of the task of teaching are perceived" (p. xii). Self-study requires collaboration and a disposition to openness so that the researcher can present a frame, perhaps an unconscious one; dialogue with critical friends about that frame; and reframe or change his or her way of looking at what is occurring in the classroom and take steps to enact new pedagogies. Barnes identifies three major characteristics he found in the conference papers:

1. Reframing

2. Collaboration

3. Openness (pp. xii–xiii)

Self-study leaders in the Self-Study School and its methodology, Loughran and Northfield (1998) offered 10 statements about the nature of self-study that align with and extend Barnes's (1998) viewpoints:

1. Self-study defines the focus of the study (i.e., context and nature of a person's activity), not the way the study is carried out.

2. Even though the term "self-study" suggests an individual approach, we believe that effective self-study requires a commitment to checking data and interpretations with others.

3. It is very difficult for individuals to change their interpretations (frames of reference) when their own experience is being examined.

4. Colleagues are likely to frame an experience in ways not thought of by the person carrying out the study.

5. Valuable learning occurs when self-study is a shared task.

6. Self-confidence is important.

7. Self-study outcomes demand immediate action, and thus the focus of study is constantly changing.

8. There are differences between self-study and reflection on practice.

9. Dilemmas, tensions and disappointments tend to dominate data gathering in self-study.

10. The audience is critical in shaping self-study reports. (pp. 11–15)

LaBoskey's (2004a) seminal work in naming the predominant characteristics of the self-study methodology describes the research design of self-study:

1. Self-initiated and focused

2. Improvement-aimed

3. Interactive

4. Multiple, primarily qualitative methods

5. Exemplar-based validation (pp. 842–853)

Describing self-study as self-initiated and focused, LaBoskey (2004a) explains that self-study researchers are conducting the research and studying themselves in that research. Their work is to improve their practice at the individual and institutional levels. Another characteristic of self-study methodology is its interactive nature, which according to

LaBoskey (2004a) is different from collaboration and can take various forms with the critical friend interactions as the data set. According to LaBoskey (2004a), mainly qualitative approaches and various self-study methods (e.g., action research, narrative, dialogue, and arts-based) have been employed by self-study researchers. Finally, the self-study field "is advanced by the construction, testing, and re-testing of exemplars of teaching practice" (LaBoskey, 2004a, p. 851).

Samaras and Freese (2006) identify the central characteristics of self-study:

1. Situated inquiry

2. Process

3. Knowledge

4. Multiple in theoretical stance, method, and purpose

5. Paradoxical: individual and collective, personal and interpersonal, and private and public (pp. 40–53)

Samaras and Freese's (2006) work on the central characteristics of self-study emerges from their practice and research in sociocultural theory. For example, the importance of situated theory, based on the Vygotskian (1981) tenet that learning occurs during situated and joint activity, was central to Samaras's (2002) self-study of teaching preservice teachers. In terms of process, Samaras and Freese (2006) state that "self-study is a systematic and sustained process where inquiry is longitudinal in nature" (p. 43). Self-study generates knowledge on the personal, professional, and program and institutional levels and "yields insights for program development involving school-university partnerships" (Samaras & Freese, 2006, p. 45). The multiple nature of self-study is presented by Samaras and Freese (2006) as multiple from theoretical stance, from research method, and from purpose. Its paradoxical nature again draws from the work of Vygotsky (1978) that cognition is always socially mediated, especially through language. Those paradoxes are presented through the view that self-study is individual and collective, personal and interpersonal, and private and public.

FIVE FOCI METHODOLOGICAL COMPONENTS OF SELF-STUDY RESEARCH

Drawing from this rich literature as well as other works (e.g., Bullough & Pinnegar, 2001; Feldman, 2003), a Five Foci framework was designed and includes the following components: (a) personal situated inquiry, (b) critical collaborative inquiry, (c) improved learning, (d) transparent research process, and (e) knowledge generation and presentation. It is important to reiterate that the framework has been gleaned, refined, and extended from almost two decades of work by self-study scholars and particularly from the work of Barnes (1998), LaBoskey (2004a), Loughran and Northfield (1998), and Samaras and Freese (2006) to provide a manageable format for you to *apply* it in a high-quality self-study project.

The Recursive Nature of Self-Study Research

Please note this important word of caution. Although the self-study methodological components are presented in a sequence and enumerated, there is a fluidity and recursive inquiry in self-study research (see Figure 4.2). That is, self-study research has a **hermeneutic** quality. Hermeneutic is "a research process whereby the researcher shifts forward and backward through the data with no predetermined assumptions to allow for the emergence of seemingly unrelated ideas and part-whole relationships" (Samaras & Freese, 2006, p. 12). The process is not linear in nature. You may pose your personal situated inquiry and then, after reading research in your literature review, find that your research question has shifted because of your change in focus. Likewise, you may propose a plan, but what you notice and/or read about during your literature review may cause you to change your original plan and the pedagogies you planned. Additionally, when you analyze your data, you might be able to discover seemingly unrelated ideas and part-whole relationships unless you hold predetermined assumptions and propositions. Critical collaborative inquiry is embedded in each step and is essential throughout the self-study process. Of course, ultimately the goal is to improve learning and contribute to the knowledge base of teaching, yet even those goals are evident during the process with discoveries along the way.

As you read through the methodological components, it is important to keep in mind that being systematic in the research process does not mean following a lockstep procedure (Mason, 2002). Quality research involves a continuous looking back and revisiting of your understandings. It requires that you acknowledge and embrace the fluidity of qualitative research. I understand how much a recipe is helpful, but ultimately, you are working to understand, uncover, and reframe your understandings of practice. That requires an openness to discovery and change during the research process.

Figure 4.2   The Recursive Nature of Self-Study Research

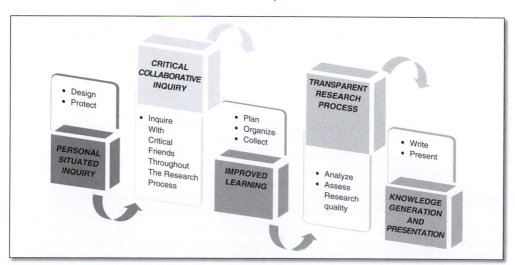

Now let's examine each methodological component. First, to gain an overview of each methodological component in the self-study teacher research process, read carefully through Table 4.1.

⚑ Self-Study Research Guidepost

FIVE FOCI FRAMEWORK

Table 4.1   Five Foci Methodological Components of Self-Study Research

#	Focus	Methodological Component
1	**Personal Situated Inquiry**	*Self-study teachers initiate and study their own inquiry in their classroom and utilize a self-study method aligned with that inquiry.* Self-study is a self-initiated inquiry of practice and draws from a practitioner's experience. Self-study teachers can choose from various self-study methods to inquire into their practice, explore who they are as a teacher, and self-assess their teaching. They consider the role culture plays in their theories and practices to assess its impact of their teaching.
2	**Critical Collaborative Inquiry**	*Self-study teachers work in an intellectually safe and supportive community to improve their practice by making it explicit to themselves and to others through critical collaborative inquiries.* Critical collaborative inquiry contributes to a validation of findings because the analysis extends beyond one's personal views, thus addressing potential biases. Paradoxically, self-study is both personal and interpersonal. It is the community that helps extend an individual's understanding. Critical friends encourage and solicit respectful questioning and divergent views to gain alternative perspectives. Critical friend teams serve as a validation group to provide feedback on the quality and legitimacy of each other's claims.
3	**Improved Learning**	*Self-study teachers question the status quo of their teaching and the politics of schooling in order to improve and impact learning for themselves, their students, and the education field.* Self-study is for improving and impacting learning. It is the "so what" of what we do as teachers. As self-study teachers work to improve their professional development, they impact students' learning, inform programs, influence policy decisions, and reform education.
4	**Transparent and Systematic Research Process**	*Self-study requires a transparent research process that clearly and accurately documents the research process through dialogue and critique.* Self-study includes a hermeneutic spiral of questioning, discovering, framing, reframing, and revisiting. The method you choose for self-study depends a good deal on your questions and the impact you seek to make in your professional practice and education writ large.

#	Focus	Methodological Component
		Self-study necessitates a disposition of openness to outside views, questions, and critique. Self-study teachers strive to make their practice explicit to themselves and to others. The transparency of the research process is enhanced through the review of critical friends who ask probing questions and offer alternative perspectives and interpretations.
5	Knowledge Generation and Presentation	*Self-study research generates knowledge that is made public through presentation and publication.* Self-study research contributes broadly to the knowledge base of personal, professional, program, and school development. Making the study public allows it to be available for review and critique. It contributes to the accumulation of pedagogical, content, and issue-based knowledge and serves to build validation across related work.

SELF-STUDY METHODOLOGICAL COMPONENTS

1. Personal Situated Inquiry

Self-study teachers initiate and study their own inquiry in their classroom and utilize a self-study method aligned with that inquiry.

This first methodological component indicates that self-study teachers value choosing their inquiries. You choose your question, context of study, and method of study. That means your project begins with your self-initiated inquiry and is driven from your questions situated in your particular context. You are the author of your research. It also means that you can consider employing various self-study methods and choose a self-study method that best aligns to your inquiry. What does the **personal situated inquiry** mean in self-study research?

Personal

In self-study research, personal experience is a valued source of knowledge (Loughran, 2004). Self-study draws from the authority of a practitioner's experience (Munby & Russell, 1994), which means that your voice matters in research. Research is grounded in the living issues of practice, and it incorporates the persons in their context or setting. The self-study method you choose depends a good deal on the question you choose and the approach that best assists you in answering your question.

Situated

As a teacher, you have the unique opportunity of a built-in or situated research setting—your classroom! *Situated inquiry* means that self-study "begins with your inquiry and is driven from your questions situated in your particular context" (Samaras & Freese, 2006, p. 40). It is that context in which you describe your inquiry and the context of that inquiry.

Grossman (2005), in addressing the question of context in studies on teacher education programs, notes that "the effort to make claims about the effects of particular pedagogical approaches is also hampered by lack of information on instructional context" (p. 448). Similarly, a detailed description of your classroom context will add to the study's value when others consider the strategies you enacted that contributed to your findings and outcomes. Loughran and Northfield (1998), in their discussion of the nature of self-study, made an essential point that "understanding the context is important so that the issues raised and conclusions drawn might be viewed in ways that help readers to relate the learning to their own situations" (p. 11). They further add that "defining the context becomes crucial, for the portrayal of the context shapes the focus of the study, but not the study itself" (p. 12).

The challenge for teachers is that they must not only be reflective but also manage the classroom that they are studying while they work to change it. LaBoskey (2004a) writes that "the practice setting must also be framed and reframed in sequences of reflective instances that are responded to with action" (p. 825) and with the input of colleagues in order to impact student learning.

There is a built-in motivation and investment in the research because you are the direct recipient of the results, which are immediate and relevant to your teaching and your students' learning (Samaras & Freese, 2006). Self-study provides relevance and utility to practitioners particularly because the inquiry is a personal and contextually bound study.

Inquiry

In general, teacher *inquiry* is "questioning and conducting research about one's teaching" (Samaras & Freese, 2006, p. 26). But self-study "demands a deep moral commitment to inquiry that connects the past in the present to imagine a new future in the concrete reality . . . as well as new possibilities" (Bullough & Pinnegar, 2004, p. 325). Inquiring into one's own practice leads to a clearer understanding of the complexities, dilemmas, and contradictions of teaching and learning for students and teachers alike (Loughran, 2004; Whitehead, 2004). Knowledge generated by practitioners' inquiries, as opposed to those of outside researchers, has immediate utility to the practitioner's context and toward efforts in educational reform (Cochran-Smith & Lytle, 1993, 2004). Your inquiry can be an issue or a problem that you believe needs your attention as a teacher. Your inquiry can be a **dilemma**, or a situation that does not have a "right" or "wrong" answer but requires you to make a decision informed by your research. Berlak and Berlak (1981) bring our attention to the many and integrated dilemmas inherent in teaching related to social, control, and curriculum issues. Your inquiry can also be something that is working well, and you want to explore the underpinnings of why it seems to be working.

2. Critical Collaborative Inquiry

Self-study teachers work in an intellectually safe and supportive community to improve their practice by making it explicit to themselves and to others through critical collaborative inquiries.

The second methodological component of self-study indicates that self-study teachers value a culture of **critical collaborative inquiry**. Self-study requires that personal insights be documented, shared, and critiqued to validate the researcher's interpretations (Loughran & Northfield, 1998). Critical friends work to mutually contribute to and enhance each other's research. They provide optimal feedback, enhance self-reflection, help articulate and make explicit one's thinking, and ease anxiety as they are continuously accessible and available (Breslin et al., 2008). Critical does not mean being judgmental or evaluative. Here, critical means receiving and offering honest, yet constructive, feedback that moves beyond technical advice and pushes you and your critical friend as researchers to question how your research efforts might be interpreted by your students and their families. Most important on a critical level, consider how your research addresses issues of social justice and equity and as van Manen (1977) prompts "from what 'is' to 'ought'" (p. 205).

While self-study entails a personal inquiry, it is also interpersonal, interactive, and collaborative. The nature of self-study research is paradoxical (Samaras & Freese, 2006). My personal frame for practicing self-study is through a sociocultural perspective based in the Vygotskian (1978, 1986) theoretical tenet that cognition is always socially mediated or influenced by others in social interaction particularly through dialogue. Individual learning and the social context are not separate. Learning does not occur in isolation and is dependent upon interactions with critical friends. Like self-study, the term *critical friend* may seem paradoxical, but you will read about the necessity of critique by trusted colleagues. Costa and Kallick (1993) describe the essential work of a critical friend:

> A critical friend, as the name suggests, is a trusted person who asks provocative questions, provides data to be examined through another lens, and offers critique of a person's work as a friend. A critical friend takes the time to fully understand the context of the work presented and the outcomes that the person or group is working toward. The friend is an advocate for the success of that work. (p. 50)

Critical friend work is mutually beneficial to participants and generates a participatory consciousness with others' perspectives informing one's own (Breslin et al., 2008). Working with critical friends allows you to have a support system that goes beyond weekly class sessions. It gives you a space in which you can name and articulate what you are coming to understand about your research. Conversations with critical friends allow you to dig beneath the surface of your teaching inquiry. Bodone, Guðjónsdóttir, and Dalmau (2004) call for a continued discourse in self-study where "collaborative dialogue contribute[s] to the iterative and ongoing process by which uneasiness, and even dissonance, becomes a catalyst for new perspectives, new findings and teachings, new action, and new questions" (p. 773). However, do not be mistaken that critical friends are just buddies. The role of the critical friend is to provoke new ideas and interpretations, question the researcher's assumptions, and participate in open, honest, and constructive feedback.

Advice From a Self-Study Scholar
Critical Colleagues

Knowing how to differ professionally, passionately, and constructively is critical if self-study researchers are to question the status quo and reach new understandings of teacher education. Knowledge communities are defined and strengthened as much by dilemmas as by their agreements, and as Common (1994) observed, "Differences are essential to knowledge of complex topics within a community diverse in experiences, interests and aspirations" (p. 266). However, conflict has also fractured communities, silenced voices, and outlawed sensitive topics. Understanding the resilient and strong forms of collaborative conversation that will persevere in the face of complex, conflictual viewpoints and harsh realities will be equally important to self-study researchers who wish to take a critical and transformative stance in their research (adapted from Bodone, Guðjónsdóttir, and Dalmau, 2004).

Hafdís Guðjónsdóttir
University of Iceland

Teaching is a challenging position that requires continuous attentiveness to students, schedules, lessons, and the daily tasks of a classroom and a school. What often gets missed in all the managing is not the tactics but the overall strategy and purpose of what we are trying to actually accomplish. Making our teaching and learning goals, behaviors, and changes explicit to ourselves and to others is one of the cornerstones of self-study teacher research. Mason (2002) in discussing the value of researching your own practice captures the value of this explicitness:

> By being explicit about *what* you are noticing, and by offering accounts to others, you can become aware of automatic behaviours which may not be entirely helpful, and of hidden assumptions and theories which may be driving these. By digging in your past experiences you may become aware of sources of those behaviours, as well as alternative ways of action. Only when you become aware of those behaviours, assumptions and theories can you examine them critically to see if they are helping you to achieve what you want to achieve. (p. 250)

Through collaborative inquiries, the researcher appreciates, and is receptive to, outside views and questions. Self-study involves risk taking and a level of vulnerability (Loughran, 2004). Self-study scholars incorporate the viewpoints and perspectives of colleagues to gain alternative perspectives and ongoing support for their research (see Photo 4.1). These new insights and questions can trigger new understandings of old ideas thus leading to further questions.

On a theoretical level, the notion of critical collaborative inquiry builds on the necessity and relationship between individual and collective cognition in professional development and within a learning community of engaged scholarship (Lave & Wenger, 1991; Samaras, Freese, Kosnik, & Beck, 2008). The dialogue is mutually beneficial and according to

Photo 4.1 Critical Friend Team

Vygotsky (1978) encourages new understandings. **Learning zones (LZ)** (Samaras & Freese, 2006), adapted from Vygotsky's notion of the zone of proximal development (ZPD), are "organic and diverse communities of diverse communities of expertise where learners co-mediate, negotiate, and socially construct an understanding of a shared task" (Samaras & Freese, 2006, p. 51). A **zone of possibility (ZOP)** (Kravtsova, 2006) occurs where instructor and students are learners open to new understandings generated through dialogue. Critical friends extend each other's zone of possibility in understanding their practice. Self-study, paradoxically, is individual and collective, personal and interpersonal, and private and public (Samaras & Freese, 2006).

Gadamer (2004) beautifully captures what I mean by **collaborative** from my Vygotskian (1978) lens—that is, "the communion" that occurs through the dialogue of critical friend inquiry and states, "To reach an understanding with one's partner in a dialogue is not merely a matter of total self-expression and the successful assertion of one's point of view, but a transformation into a communion, in which we do not remain what we were" (p. 371). Teachers who inquire into their practice with others receive "benefits from the support of colleagues engaged in similar enterprises and the scrutiny of the wider educational community" (Clarke & Erickson, 2003, p. 5). When you make your work available to the critique of others, it improves the quality of your research so that it is not limited to your viewpoint, judgment, or opinion.

McNiff and Whitehead (2006) explain that critical friends can serve as a validation group that meets regularly to share and review their data and thinking about their research. They essentially conduct **member checks,** examining and validating the researcher's interpretation of pieces of data to check interpretations. Collaboration with critical friends contributes to a validation of the findings because the analysis extends beyond one's personal views, thus addressing potential biases. Barnes (1998), in his observations of papers presented at the first self-study conference held in 1996, surmised that in supportive groups and dyads, "trusted colleagues help by validating one's experiences, ensuring that they make sense by asking for clarification, by offering alternatives and by reminding one of one's own values" (p. xii). LaBoskey (2004a) adds, "Self-study achieves validation through the construction, testing, sharing, and re-testing of exemplars of teaching practice" (p. 860). Kuhn (1996) explains exemplars as "concrete problem-solutions" (p. 187).

I was born in Annapolis, Maryland, and have lived there all my life. For as long as I can remember, each year I have watched and listened to the roar of the Blue Angels who perform an air show at the United States Naval Academy annually during Commissioning Week. Their work as a team of pilots with precision comes from their commitment to each other and to their mission. They cannot be Blue Angels alone. They communicate with each other and depend on each other. They are amazing to watch. I often wonder what it would take for teachers to work as a Blue Angels team. Granted, our work is different in mission, but our stakes are also high as we care for young minds and their developing talents. There is so much at stake for our world in our critical friend inquiries as teachers.

3. Improved Learning

Self-study teachers question the status quo of their teaching and the politics of schooling in order to improve and impact learning for themselves, their students, and the education field.

The third methodological component indicates that self-study teachers value a culture of improved learning for themselves and for their students. Self-study teachers question the status quo of their teaching, schools, the academy, and traditional research methodologies (Hamilton, 2002). The focus of the study is on "the self" but for improvement-aimed purposes (LaBoskey, 2004a). Ask yourself, "What is the value of this research to others? What is the 'so what' of this research?" This deliberate questioning is for the goal of improving your own teaching in order to impact your students' learning. **Improved learning** involves your understanding of what works and what does not work in your teaching. But remember, self-study is not just about you. Your goal is to positively impact students' learning. It is about how your research helps you know and teach your students better to improve their learning and plan for future instruction.

In *Studying Teacher Education: The Report of the AERA Panel on Research and Teacher Education,* a large-scale meta-analysis on studies conducted about teacher education programs, Zeichner (2005) writes that "one critical outcome that has been largely neglected in the teacher education research literature is *student learning* [italics in original]" (p. 743). In an effort to improve learning, self-study researchers enact pedagogical strategies, which LaBoskey (2004a) identifies as "an integral part of the methodology of self-study . . . and the interventions in our research design. These are the activities that embody our theoretical perspectives and pedagogical goals, our moral, ethical, and political values and agendas" to improve our practice and be authentic to our values (p. 834). As Ham and Kane (2004) explain about the self-study of teaching, "Teaching is by definition a socio-ethical act—it is to try to do good for another—and the actions or practices being researched are thus inevitably interactions with others and practices involving others" (p. 127). Self-study teacher educators value "walking the talk" (Hamilton & Pinnegar, 1998, p. 239; Samaras, Hicks, & Garvey Berger, 2004, p. 929)—that is, not just professing but practicing what they value.

Learning involves not only the cognitive domain. As an early childhood and human development and learning specialist, I appreciate and understand that as humans, we are quite complex. Our learning is influenced and affected by the ecology of our environment—a network of social, cognitive, psychological, emotional, and physical factors (Cole & Cole, 1996). We know that families play a key role in helping improve students' learning, and teacher educators and education students can play a role as facilitators in that process (Samaras & Wilson, 1999).

Self-study scholars have documented that the inquiries of self-study teachers impact the field of teaching in three unique yet highly integrated domains: (a) the personal, (b) the professional, and (c) the classroom, school, program, and/or institution (Kosnik, Beck, Freese, & Samaras, 2006). In terms of personal growth, self-study teachers question the taken-for-granted assumptions about their practice. They examine the alignment of their beliefs with their practice and contemplate the influence of their backgrounds, experiences, and culture on their teaching.

On a personal level, self-study scholars continuously work on examining the role they play in their research while they consider the stories they bring to their teaching. Their stories help remind them that their students also have stories of learning and stories about not learning (Samaras, 2002). For some self-study scholars, the focus has been on employing the personal history self-study method for "self-knowing, forming, and reforming a professional identity," for "modeling and testing effective reflection," and for "pushing the boundaries of teaching" (Samaras et al., 2004, pp. 913, 920, 924).

On a professional level, although complex, self-study supports the development of knowledge of the individual and the professional. There is a blending of the personal and professional with personal theory making as a gateway and "recognition that knowing and understanding the self is an essential aspect for generating change and developing new knowledge" (Hamilton & Pinnegar, 1998, p. 241). As Berry (2004), indicates, "At the same time, it [self-study] becomes a powerful and significant approach to researching teacher education" (p. 1304). Self-study teachers work to improve one element or aspect of their teaching. It has immediate utility and can lead to a greater sense of confidence, thus encouraging a teacher's continued and further work in self-study research (Samaras, Beck, Freese, & Kosnik, 2005).

On a program or school level, self-study scholars have worked in research communities conducting projects for improving their practice and programs with school colleagues. For example, self-study researchers have worked as grade-level or discipline-based teams, on school-wide curriculum projects, on district-wide restructuring efforts, and in partnerships between schools and universities (Beck, Kosnik, & Cleovoulou, 2008; Bell-Angus, Davis, Donoahue, Kowal, & McGlynn-Stewart, 2008; Hoban, 2008; Kessler & Wong, 2008; Mitchell & Mitchell, 2008).

Zeichner (2007) offers an interesting insight about a needed direction for self-study research in order to impact policymakers and the broader educational community. He calls for a "logical next step for this [self-study] movement" to focus on "the content of what has been learned from the research and how it builds on what others have learned" (p. 40). In that manner, the needed next steps are less about defending self-study as a methodology and more about its impact and contributions to the field. One way to move toward a focus of the impact of your study is to be transparent and systematic about your research process.

4. Transparent and Systematic Research Process

Self-study requires a transparent research process that clearly and accurately documents the research process through dialogue and critique.

The fourth methodological component of self-study research indicates that self-study teachers value a culture of **transparent and systematic research process**. Self-study research involves a transparency of your procedures and analysis, which you share with your critical friends and validation team.

Transparency

Transparent here means you are open, honest, and reflective about your work. Discussing the necessity of transparency, Wolcott (2001) offers valuable advice:

> Don't try to convince your audience of the validity of your observations based on the power of a fieldwork approach. Satisfy readers with sufficient detail about how you obtained the data you actually used. . . . The potential of your contribution will be greatly extended if you provide adequate detail about how you proceeded with your analysis. The unique combination of your field setting and you in it will never be replicated, but discussing how you analyzed your data can be a great help to other researchers with comparable field notes, experiences, and data sets of their own. (p. 93)

Hamilton and Pinnegar (1998) state, "The value of self-study depends on the researcher/teacher providing convincing evidence that they know what they claim to know" (p. 243). Self-study scholars must have a deep commitment to checking data and interpretations with colleagues to broaden possibilities and challenge perspectives to increase the credibility and validity of their work (Bullough & Pinnegar, 2001; Feldman, 2003; Loughran, 2007a; Whitehead, 2004). One way to check for transparency of your study is to conduct a self-assessment and critical friend assessment of the methodological components of self-study (see Critical Friend Inquiry 11.3) (Samaras, 2008), which are presented in Chapter 11.

Systematic Research

Being *systematic* along with the transparency commits you to having a plan and schedule to show your work to others, keeping an audit trail of your data collection, and sharing your data analysis with evidence of your claims. In order to contribute to a broader knowledge base, Grossman (2005), reporting on teacher educators' research, states that "closer attention must be paid to the circumstances under which data are collected, the relationship between research and students, and the manner in which data are analyzed" (p. 449). Bullough and Pinnegar (2004) corroborate with Grossman's position, stating, "Like any good research self-study must represent rigorous data gathering and analysis. . . . Methods must be transparent" (p. 340). The same criteria for being systematic in the reporting of your teacher research apply to you as a teacher researcher in your classroom.

Process

In terms of *process*, self-study is not a step-like or linear research methodology. Self-study is a change journey in a hermeneutic spiral of questioning, discovery, challenge, framing, reframing, and revisiting. It entails an open-ended research process that gives teachers permission to change their philosophy without incurring guilt over past practices and beliefs. Self-study is not a blaming game but a game changer for improving teaching (Samaras & Freese, 2006). Researchers and teachers do not have final answers to the issues they face, but they should be able to follow new developments and articulate and pose their own questions (Austin & Senese, 2004). Explaining why you chose a particular self-study method to help you answer your particular inquiry helps others understand your research goals and question.

Self-study also requires a disposition to openness and deep reflection as a tool to systematically inquire into one's teaching practice (Barnes, 1998; Samaras & Freese, 2006). As Bullough and Pinnegar (2004) explain, "When we commit to doing a self-study, part of that commitment is moving from critical reflection to creating and sharing an account of that reflection" (p. 321). Self-study incorporates reflection as self-study scholars dig deep to explore who they are as teachers, what puzzles them about their teaching, what role culture plays in their theories and practices, and what difference their teaching makes for their students. Whatever the query, their reflection is shared continuously with critical friends during the research process from its beginning to final report, in the question posing, research design, data collection, data analysis, and interpretations of findings. Reflection moves beyond the individual mind and is enriched through its transparency and the subsequent multiple perspectives and knowledge gained from the collaborative inquiry community.

5. Knowledge Generation and Presentation

Self-study research generates knowledge that is made public through presentation and publication.

The fifth methodological component of self-study research indicates that self-study teachers value a culture of **knowledge generation and presentation**. As Samaras and Freese (2006) argue, knowledge in self-study includes self-knowledge and acknowledging that as a teacher you are a "knower." Kincheloe (1991) reminds us that there is no knowledge without the knower. Knowledge also includes professional knowledge and "extends scholarship, ownership, and creativity into the hands of teachers as professionals" (Samaras & Freese, 2006, pp. 44–45). Self-study teachers generate knowledge for investigating and developing new knowledge about teaching with evidence that is immediate and personal and with significance to others. Knowledge also includes improving programs and schools. It can support and inform program reform and policy decisions thereby contributing broadly to the knowledge base of teaching. Self-study scholars create new knowledge as they reframe their practice through their questioning of the assumptions of their practices within the context and politics of schooling. This critical examination of teacher practices contributes to the knowledge and understanding of teacher education and the education reform movement (Zeichner, 1999).

There is a commitment in self-study to make one's work public because the audience is critical in both shaping and refining one's work and making it useful to others (Bullough & Pinnegar, 2004; LaBoskey, 2004a; Loughran & Northfield, 1998). Although the research may address a personal concern, a paradox of self-study is that it requires "going public" with one's work (Samaras & Freese, 2006). In that manner, the very act of recognizing any dissonance that comes forth through its sharing allows teachers to work toward real change with and through others (Russell, 2002). Self-study often involves an activist stance. Sharing the research with others moves the study beyond the self to raise issues of moral, ethical, and/or political reform (LaBoskey, 2004a). The knowledge generated and made public is useful to others because "accounts of it and therefore knowledge about it is added to the knowledge base of the teaching and research community" (Hamilton & Pinnegar, 1998, p. 243).

CRITICAL FRIEND INQUIRY 4.1

Critical Friend Research Memo 1

(*Sources:* Smith, A. (2008). Class assignment; Mercer, J. (2008). Class assignment.)

Take a moment to jot down your research question and write a **critical friend research memo**, or a letter to your critical friend as a way to more naturally talk about your research while also deeply thinking about it. Consider what you would be interested in studying/researching further and why. Construct a research question that relates to your interest. Be patient with yourself and the research process and know that your question will shift and be refined. This reconstructing of questions is natural and part of the research process. Write an opening research memo to your critical friend(s). You may choose to work in dyads or triads of critical friends. Post, read, and then respond to each other's memos in writing.

Consider:

Statement of your research question. Remember that a research question is an issue, a dilemma, or a tension that emerges from your situated context. The question should be one you care about and that ultimately matters to your students' learning. Plan for a focused question with a manageable inquiry and a feasible plan.

Significance of the problem to you. Reflect and write about the behaviors or issues you observed. What did you notice that you propose to change? How do you propose to make the change? Why are you so interested in this issue? What is your main message to others about this issue? Why is this question important to you and your students? Consider if this research question emerges from your learning experiences. What education-related life experiences help you make sense of the problem? What possible taken-for-granted assumptions do you have about the issue that merit study?

The broader educational significance. In what way might your research contribute to the field of teaching and schooling? What are the broader implications of your research for educational reform? This key component aligns with Focus #3: *Self-study teachers question the status quo of their teaching and the politics of schooling in order to improve and impact learning for themselves, their students, and the education field.*

Discuss:

- What components of my teaching would I like to better understand and/or improve?
- What am I noticing in my classroom?
- Why did I choose to explore this research project?
- Why am I so interested in this research topic? From where does this interest generate?
- Consider the role of personal history, culture, and identity in your research.
- What do I propose to change and how? What are some possible resources?
- What role do I play in the research that I am conducting?
- How would others benefit from my study of this topic?
- What do I hope for in my critical friend work?

✎ Student Examples:
Critical Friend Research Memo and Response

Dear Jim,

I have been pondering this research question now for 3 weeks. I am trying to narrow down on my area and subjects of focus. I believe I have found my topic of interest. I am interested in how I can keep seventh graders of all learning levels engaged. I am also interested in the personal self-study in how my transition from teaching ninth graders to teaching seventh graders had affected me mentally and emotionally and, most important, how I go about planning instruction. This topic is of great interest to me due to the culture shock I endured going from the high school level to the middle school level. Seventh graders are in another world apart from ninth graders. I am not used to the maturity level,

(Continued)

(Continued)

the level of babying that still exists, the "I can't open my locker" excuse, and the "I really have to use the bathroom" during class. Culturally, this was a shock for me. I was used to the ninth-grader mentality, and I thought I was ready to handle the seventh grader. As of right now, I have proved myself wrong. I have had to adjust to them just as much as they have had to adjust to me and the middle school that they will be spending the next 2 years of their life in.

I have chosen my fifth-period class in order to conduct my action research. So far, my fifth period is the most diverse, in terms of learners. This is a team-taught class with 29 students in it. Ten of them have individualized instruction programs and are on the team-taught teacher's roster. It is difficult to engage the entire class when doing an assignment. I want to focus on engaging all of the learners in this class at the same time. My team teacher and I just shake our heads in amazement as to how zoo-like the class has become. We set disciplinary boundaries and expectations for the students, but so far we have had no luck in the area of really getting through to them. I am interested in this class because it is a challenge for me personally. I love challenges and usually face them head on. I would have to say that this is my most difficult challenge yet, and I am afraid to face it, but that doesn't mean that I am going to go down without a fight.

The personal self-study aspect of my research is focusing on my past identity and experiences as a teacher. I still have the mind-set of high schoolers. Every day I have to force myself to remember that my students are only 12 and 13 years old, not 15. I have incorporated the interactive notebook in my classes this year because it worked really well in my classes last year. So far, it seems to be good for keeping all of my students' papers in one central location, but they forget to bring it to class. I am slightly frustrated with this process, but I am trying to overlook it and push forward.

I want to improve the engagement of my students. I have labs that are already made up for me, and they are boring. I can tell the students are bored, and I am beyond bored. I am trying to do the labs because the county dictates it and to come up with enrichment labs that do the same thing but in a more fun manner. This is especially difficult with the compounding of different levels of learners. Most of the activities are set up for gifted seventh-grade science students and just do not work. I have to go through and pick out the important pieces in order to get through the labs. I am hoping to find extra labs to reinforce the material but make it tailored so that every learner in fifth period can successfully complete the activity and hopefully learn from it.

I am the researcher in this role, as well as the one being studied. I want to study my students in order to help me better understand them as seventh graders and as individual learners. I have already learned so much about them as seventh graders, and I know there is much more to learn. I need to do some research about how 12- and 13-year-olds think. Maybe by gaining insight into their developmental minds I can better tailor the extra labs. I also know that this is a critical point in their lives where things begin changing. Puberty begins to hit, more responsibility ensues, and peer pressure needs to be confronted. I am the one being studied as well due to the fact that I need to learn how to work with the seventh graders. Certain things such as types of materials and the content need to be "watered down." I always want to spew out the most amount of information to my students because I love biology. I could expand the material with ninth graders, but I need to focus solely on understanding at the level of seventh grade because these students have never seen this material before.

I can hope for a friend and mentor in my critical friend work. I need support and guidance just like the students. I want to make sure that I am on the correct track in terms of questioning, gathering research, and compiling the data. I hope that my critical friend is there for me every step of the way. I have found that when people stick together when encountering new experiences they usually find the other side together.

Sincerely,
Amy

Dear Amy,

To address your concluding concern, I agree with you 100%. It is imperative that educators and researchers have conduits to share and discuss their concerns and findings. In that capacity, I will do my best to support you in your efforts. I feel as critical friends we have begun well. I immediately recognized intelligence in your words and that desire to reclaim the passion for teaching, which you were concerned was waning. I feel that this year will benefit you greatly, even if this is the only year you teach seventh grade. I have read that when people face daunting challenges, more often than not, they find ways to cope, and usually to succeed. I promise to help you in any way I can, even after our class has concluded.

As for your research project, I think you have picked the right class to study (both the class and your role). That class will be a challenge, and you must get the students in order first, prior to any teaching. I find that a reward system can have merit. I give 1 point per class to each student who comes prepared (paper, pencil, planner). I find that this small gift usually impacts most of the class, for if students make a mistake on a quiz, a project, and or homework, those cumulative points help keep their grade manageable. There are other techniques as well. Other seventh-grade teachers have explained that seventh graders want to be directed and should not be given a liberal reign. You may have to be even sterner than you have been so they know you mean business. Also, keeping them busy will help keep them organized. Make sure there is very little downtime between lessons. With two teachers, this can be done more easily, for one of you can direct, and the other reinforce.

With regards to the curriculum, I think that you have already realized that you will have to teach differently, for you said that the students do not have the prior knowledge or vocabulary. It is possible that many of your past ninth graders were very similar when they were in seventh grade. So the question is: Can you cover the curriculum you need to and get the students up to speed as well? In this challenge, I believe you will succeed; we only need to find the right way.

Your self-study has already begun. You seem very introspective, having already realized several of your concerns. As your research of your class progresses, I feel that many of your questions will be answered, for your passion for them to succeed will fuel your own desire to persevere and/or adapt to your new surroundings. I look forward to helping you on this journey, for I feel that your pathway will help me find my own.

Sincerely,
Jim

⧖ Take a pause here and look at Amy's exemplar brief in Appendix A to gain an overview of what these self-study methodological components look like in self-study teacher research. Again, please keep in mind that all student examples are presented to give you an idea of what self-study can look like. They are not presented as "the" model or something you should try to match. I encourage you to let your own ideas propel you forward and use the examples to see self-study research with a broad lens.

🖹 KEY IDEAS

- **Self-study methodology** is a stance that a researcher takes toward understanding or explaining the physical or social world.
- Self-study scholars have written about the nature and dispositions of self-study and the five methodological components of self-study (i.e., the Five Foci).
- Five Foci, or the methodological components of self-study research presented in this chapter, represent a synthesis of ideas developed by self-study scholars who have worked to refine the methodological components of self-study. The Five Foci provide guideposts for those interested in applying self-study teacher research.
- Each of the components highlights that self-study teachers are important participants in educational reform and can make a difference in students' learning.

  1. *Personal Situated Inquiry:* Self-study teachers initiate and study their own inquiry in their classroom and utilize a self-study method aligned with that inquiry.

  2. *Critical Collaborative Inquiry:* Self-study teachers work in an intellectually safe and supportive community to improve their practice by making it explicit to themselves and to others through critical collaborative inquiries.

  3. *Improved Learning:* Self-study teachers question the status quo of their teaching and the politics of schooling in order to improve and impact learning for themselves, their students, and the education field.

  4. *Transparent and Systematic Research Process:* Self-study requires a transparent research process that clearly and accurately documents the research process through dialogue and critique.

  5. *Knowledge Generation and Presentation:* Self-study research generates knowledge that is made public through presentation and publication.

Self-Study Methods

Why and How

Putting the coursework into a portfolio linked to the replicable to share with peers and was quite useful. The portfolio is easy to share with others and would be helpful to persons that are new to self-study to get a grasp of what it is all about.

—Deanna Breslin (2006), *Research Analyst*

CHAPTER DESCRIPTION

This chapter introduces various self-study methods that have been developed by self-study scholars, although it is not limited to these. You will find examples from students who found the methods useful. You will be introduced to the Critical Friends Portfolio, a developmental portfolio self-study method that is recommended as a manageable starting place for teachers new to self-study research. In this chapter, you will also be introduced to other self-study methods: personal history self-study method, living educational theory, collective self-study method, arts-based self-study method, and memory work self-study method. The examples are provided to assist you in seeing the applicability of each method as well as the diversity of methods. You will also find a chart of self-study research conducted by scholars who have employed various self-study methods to better understand their practice.

✦ Reading this chapter will familiarize you with some of the methods self-study scholars have designed and used to study their practice.

What is so fascinating about the self-study research methodology to me is that it entails multiple and diverse self-study methods. I had a front seat in observing my self-study colleagues create and enact various self-study methods over the years. What excitement watching Claudia Mitchell and Sandra Weber enact their memory work self-study in their academic literacy performance on a stage at the

Castle Conference in 2002. I too had found ways to include drama in my work with teachers, but their work brought first-person self-study into a clearer focus for me.

CHOOSING A SELF-STUDY METHOD

Self-study is multiple in method, theoretical stance, and purpose (LaBoskey, 2004a; Samaras & Freese, 2006). There are a variety of techniques and methods to choose from, but as in all qualitative research, "not only must choices be made among strategies, but commitments must be met in making them" (Wolcott, 2001, p. 91), and you "need to be assured that you are secure in the position from which you do your viewing and that your selection of a position is a reasonable and reasoned one, well suited to your purposes and your talents" (Wolcott, 2001, p. 92).

Self-study methods are multiple in nature and have been developed largely by and for self-study teacher educators (LaBoskey, 2004a; Lassonde, Galman, & Kosnik, 2009; Samaras & Freese, 2006). The method you choose depends on what you are trying to understand and how a particular method helps you achieve that understanding. There is not a single method or a "right" method (Loughran, 2004).

Although similar data can be collected for various self-study methods, consider these questions when deciding what self-study method you want to choose:

1. **Which self-study method would help me best explore my question?**

   a. Will I be working with a critical friend over time in creating a self-study developmental portfolio?

   b. Would examining my personal history in related educational experiences help me learn more about this question? Is my question related to a query about my personal and education-related life history?

   c. Am I interested in examining the alignment and authenticity of a particular pedagogical belief to my actual practice?

   d. Who are the participants in my study besides me? Will I invite school colleagues to join me? Would a collective self-study be a useful method to choose for that purpose?

   e. Would creating a collage, drawing a picture, or using some other art form assist me in getting at the underpinnings of this question?

   f. Would using memory work by searching through artifacts of my past enlighten my understanding of why I ask this question and seek answers about it?

2. **How can my research be best represented to share with others (e.g., through text, visual art, performance, or a combination of those)?**

3. **What can I learn from others who have used this self-study method or explored this question?**

Self-study methods may be explored informally as a way to gain practice in self-study research and also can be used to gather data, a component of a more formal project (Samaras

& Freese, 2006). Samaras and Freese (2006) coined the term **informal self-study approach** to "include activities that provide practice in exploring one's teaching and learning using reflection as a critical dimension; it does not necessarily involve formal data gathering" (p. 62). They describe a **formal self-study approach** as "a systematic research approach to explore one's practice" (p. 61).

Advice From a Self-Study Scholar

Informal Self-Study
Methods Demystify Research

I use informal self-study methods as a way of demystifying research. In my qualitative research course, students engage in and practice different methods of self-study research through "hands-on" activities. The informal activities raise students' awareness about how we, as teachers and practitioners, are often reflecting on our work. The activities also help students see how their day-to-day wonderings and dilemmas of practice are excellent starting points for thinking about potential research questions. In the class we discuss how self-study involves systematically exploring the tensions of practice and the dilemmas we encounter. The activities are designed to scaffold student learning by providing guided assistance, which starts with the informal activities and moves on to examples of formal self-study research (Samaras & Freese, 2006). Instead of implementing theory to practice, we actually use practice as a way of making sense of theory.

Anne R. Freese
University of Hawai'i

In the next chapter, you will be prompted to consider the alignment of your research question with your self-study method. In the meantime, let's take a look at six of the self-study methods that my students have found useful:

1. Developmental Portfolio

2. Personal History

3. Living Educational Theory

4. Collective Self-Study

5. Arts-Based Self-Study

6. Memory Work Self-Study

DEVELOPMENTAL PORTFOLIO SELF-STUDY METHOD

If you want a structure to sort and scaffold your inquiry and make it public and open to the feedback and critique of your peers, then a **developmental portfolio self-study method** will serve that purpose well (Samaras & Freese, 2006). The developmental portfolio self-study method "presents an opportunity to store, catalogue, and study your professional growth over a selected period of time" (Samaras & Freese, 2006, p. 68). A **Critical Friends Portfolio** (CFP), one way to utilize the developmental portfolio self-study method, is recommended especially if this is your first self-study research project. Your CFP systematically catalogues the process of your research process with critical friend inquiries in a manageable manner and "enables you to uncover new and not always apparent dimensions of our teaching" (Samaras & Freese, 2006, p. 69). It is a great fit for a semester-long self-study teacher research project. Please note that the CFP is much more than a storehouse of your work. My students report the portfolio helps them think through and advance their self-study teacher research project in a systematic and documented fashion.

You are invited to collaborate with your colleagues and catalogue your critical friend inquiries throughout this textbook. From my experience, students who take time to draft, share, and respond to each other's work throughout the development of their project do better on the final product because of the feedback and ideas generated from each other's work. You may choose to work with one peer or more than one peer in your critical friend team. You may decide to work in school teams or in other professional collaborations, within discipline and grade level or across them. The critical friend inquiries included in the portfolio involve a series of carefully constructed dialogic assignments designed from Vygotskian (1978) theory to scaffold your particular self-study research interest and your project development.

In your CFP you have an opportunity to formulate and state your own goals and visions, choose your inquiry, and document your development as a self-study researcher. It is a place to reflect upon your research focus over time, and with the support of your peers it can assist you in considering and sorting out the dilemmas you notice in your teaching. It is also a data house of your continuous thinking and your critical friend's feedback about your thinking throughout the research process. You will find the CFP particularly useful in your memos about validation of your analysis with colleagues. The CFP is a place to which you can return during and after your research to examine the process of your self-study.

You may also decide to include how you correlate your project with national standards from your specialized professional association and state standards in your CFP. When you create a portfolio, you are practicing the scholarship of teaching—that is, researching and documenting teachers' practice. According to Shulman (1998), "For an activity to be designated as scholarship, it should manifest at least three key characteristics: It should be public, susceptible to critical review and evaluation, and accessible for exchange and use by other members of one's scholarly community" (p. 5). Lyons and Freidus (2004) assert that the portfolio inquiry "provides a structured yet highly accessible process that simultaneously can be both a mode of inquiry and a means of documenting and representing knowledge" (p. 1074).

Although there are many types of portfolios, the CFP is uniquely designed for you to align the study of your practice with self-study methodological components. Another key component in a self-study portfolio is that you have an opportunity to dialogue about those with your critical friend. Critical friend inquiry is not limited to the developmental portfolio method, but it does provide a structure while you begin to experience the value of critical friends and learn from each other's work. Lyons (1998) empathetically captures the importance of personal professional accountability in the portfolio process and states, "For many teachers, their most prized ways of doing things have never been shared with others, and certainly have rarely been subjected to the insights or probing of critical friends" (p. 251).

The CFP is designed to provide you with opportunities to practice self-study methods informally as you learn about self-study and to scaffold your formal and final project with the support of critical friends. This combination of your beginning informal explorations toward your final polished self-study teacher research project honors your work as a developing self-study teacher scholar. Nonetheless, you are also encouraged and prompted to consider employing other self-study methods throughout the text, informally and formally, such as Critical Friend Inquiry 5.1 entailing a personal history self-study method.

The CFP encompasses a series of critical friend inquiries that give you practice in the self-study methodological component of critical collaborative inquiry. The critical friend inquiries are in essence a metaconversation you have with yourself about your research along with collegial conversations of your teaching and professional development. As you work with your critical friend(s) in the activities throughout this textbook, you can include each of them in your portfolio. You might place your first "I wonder because" critical friend inquiry as discussed in Chapter 1 in your Critical Friends Portfolio. As you complete each critical friend activity, be sure to date each activity. That's right. You are generating the very data that will help you write your final project.

Below is a preview menu of suggested critical friend inquiries that compose your Critical Friends Portfolio and align with the sections of your research report. It will give you an overview of activities that are purposely designed to guide you through the process of developing your portfolio and introduce you to other self-study methods informally. All activities are to be shared and discussed with your critical friend. You will find critical friend inquiries in the chapters ahead.

Table 5.1 is a chart of critical friend inquiries so that you have an accessible and easy frame to locate, organize, and reflect often on your portfolio data. Again, depending on your needs and time, choose the inquiries that call you to explore deeply.

5.1 Self-Study Research Guidepost
YOUR CRITICAL FRIENDS PORTFOLIO

Table 5.1 Your Critical Friends Portfolio

#	Critical Friend Inquiries	Description of Activity	Purpose of Activity Aligned With Research Components	Chapter Location
1.1	*I wonder about*	An introductory research activity prompts you to consider what you wonder about in your teaching, why you are curious about the topic, and who would benefit from your inquiry	**Research Purpose.** Serves to spark your thinking about what you want to study and helps break writer's block	1

(Continued)

Table 5.1 (Continued)

#	Critical Friend Inquiries	Description of Activity	Purpose of Activity Aligned With Research Components	Chapter Location
4.1	*Critical Friend Research Memo 1*	A research memo to your critical friend to share your thinking aloud about your research focus, rationale, and proposal	**Research Question, Rationale, and Proposal.** Designed for peer support and a feedback loop from another perspective as you work through your research question and proposal	4
5.1	*Education-Related Life History*	A narrative about a critical incident or nodal moment in your learning experiences and the role that culture played in the incident. Your narrative highlights how your background, culture, and learning experiences influenced your beliefs about teaching and student learning. *A personal history self-study method*	**Significance of Problem/Rationale.** Helps you explore how personal learning experiences and culture shape your practice, your students' learning, and your inquiry	5
5.2	*Self-Portrait of a Researcher*	An alternative format for presentation through self-portrait making; abstract or nonabstract using an art medium of your choice that depicts how you see your role as a self-study researcher. Include a curator caption describing key reflections. Can also be used as a data technique during your research. *An arts-based self-study method*	**Professional Role/Data.** Useful for constructing an understanding about who you are as a researcher and your professional development	5
5.3	*Research Artifact*	An artifact that you choose to represent the main idea of your research interest; includes a title using a metaphor that signifies the core meaning of this chosen object. *A memory work self-study method*	**Research Question.** Prompts your thinking about your research focus and is a useful tool for you to consider your research interest in a symbolic and representative manner	5

#	Critical Friend Inquiries	Description of Activity	Purpose of Activity Aligned With Research Components	Chapter Location
6.1	*Class Portrait*	A visual representation of your current classroom situation and your practice capturing the academic, social, and culture theater of your context, your role, your students, and the interactions of learning	**Observation: Participants, Situation, and Pedagogical Plans.** Provokes critical reflection about what is taking place in your classroom to help you capture the focus of the change you propose and the pedagogies you plan	6
6.2	*Haiku*	A haiku poem of three lines with 5–7–5 syllables in each respective line that captures your research topic and why the topic matters to you	**Articulate Rationale.** Encourages you to articulate a topic and why you chose it in a concise manner to yourself and to others	6
6.3	*Research Proposal: Narrative and/or Alternative Visual*	A narrative that articulates what you propose to study, why you are interested in the topic, and how you propose to go about exploring the research. The proposal may be in a narrative format and/or with a visual representation. The visual also includes a narrative of your ideas and plans. *An arts-based self-study method*	**Research Proposal.** Designed for peer support and a feedback loop from another perspective as you work through your research proposal	6
6.4	*Mapping a Literature Review*	An integrated mapping and representation of the key areas and ideas of your topic and your developing theories of related research and how that literature helps inform and focus your research problem	**Literature Review and Conceptual Framework.** Develops and extends your understanding of prior research; helps to inform and justify your research approach and pedagogical plans	6
7.1	*The Ethical Self-Study Teacher Researcher*	A memo to your critical friend outlining how you planned for the research ethics of your project to be framed according to the self-study methodological components	**Peer Review of Ethics.** Provides opportunities for dialogue and deliberation about the research ethics of your planned research project	7

(Continued)

Table 5.1 (Continued)

#	Critical Friend Inquiries	Description of Activity	Purpose of Activity Aligned With Research Components	Chapter Location
8.1	*Critical Friend Research Memo 2*	A research memo to your critical friend about your data collection	**Data Collection.** Provides support and a feedback loop from another perspective as you work through your data collection	8
9.1	*Interviewer and Interviewee*	A participant-observer experience of interviewing and being interviewed	**Data Collection.** Provokes reflection about interviewing from the perspective of the interviewer and the interviewee	9
11.1	*Critical Friend Research Memo 3*	A research memo to your critical friend about your data analysis	**Data Analysis.** Provides support and a feedback loop from another perspective as you work through your data analysis	11
11.2	*Dialogical Validity*	Peer critique and validation of your data analysis	**Critique/Validation.** Generates a reflective and critical dialogue for critique of your data analysis with critical friends	11
11.3	*Self-Assessment and Critical Friend Assessment of Five Foci*	A personal and critical friend assessment and analysis of how you addressed the self-study methodological components	**Self-Assessment.** Critique/Validation. Provides an opportunity for self-assessment driven from one's own efforts and situation; promotes personal professional accountability as a researcher	11
12.1	*Author's Chair*	A format for your presentation of your draft report including interpretations of data for public critique	**Writing/Presenting.** Facilitates dialogue, peer feedback, alternative perspectives of analysis, and refinement of final report	12
12.2	*Exit Paper*	An essay about your professional growth and your thinking about the process and product of your research project. Includes a self-assessment of how well you addressed the Five Foci, how you reframed your thinking, and possible next directions	**Discussion/Continued Professional Development.** Encourages researcher's self-assessment and reflection about research, knowledge, and future needed directions	12

PERSONAL HISTORY SELF-STUDY METHOD

In 2009, when President Barack Obama nominated Sonia Sotomayor as a judge to the Supreme Court, Ms. Sotomayor shared that one of the assets she brings to the professional position of Supreme Court judge is her life history particularly from an empathetic stance. Although the value of the nexus of the personal and professional is not appreciated or acknowledged by all, teachers as professionals also bring their life histories into their teaching (Goodson & Lin Choi, 2008). If you want to explore how your personal experience, culture, history, and learning experiences can inform your teaching, then you can employ a **personal history self-study method** (Samaras, Hicks, & Garvey Berger, 2004). This approach has also been called personal experiences methods (Russell, 2009) and education-related life history (Bullough, 1994; Bullough, Knowles, & Crow, 1991).

The personal history self-study method allows you to begin to reflect on your own learning that may have connections to your research interests and question. It is particularly useful to examine who you are as a teacher, your teacher identity, the motivations behind your teacher goals, and the constraints and supports you have experienced in reaching those goals. The personal history self-study method is one way to begin to develop an awareness of your development as a teacher and what current beliefs and values you bring into your practice. Impressed with how the personal history self-study method facilitates and drives classroom inquiry, I have adapted it in an education-related history activity. I found it to be one of the most effective ways for me to come to know my students and for them to get at the undergirding of their teaching passions. Julia's example below demonstrates the value of the personal history approach in understanding her research interest in students' second-chance assessment.

5.1 Student Example: Personal History Method—An Education-Related Life History

Julia B. Hiles, *Mathematics Teacher*

Not too many people left the small town in which I grew up. Most people graduated from high school, found a job locally, got married, and raised a family. While my parents were not college graduates, they knew there was a world beyond our small town and wanted my sister and me to be part of that world. They told us stories about London, where they met while in the Air Force, and showed us pictures of the places they visited in Europe. My mother, being a second-generation Polish/Greek American, shared stories of her mother's efforts to preserve this heritage. My father subscribed to *National Geographic* magazine, which I pored over while allowing my imagination to soar. I wanted one day to see all these places and have wonderful adventures. My goal of attending college was the first step in that direction.

During my freshman year, my high school decided to offer calculus to students in their senior year. To enroll in this class, students were required to take geometry and algebra 2 simultaneously sophomore year. I signed up for both classes, and I was psyched! Geometry was boring, but manageable. Algebra 2 was a different story. I was a member of a small subset of sophomores in a class of juniors—juniors who deplored our presence in *their* class. Our first quiz covered slope of a line and finding equations of

(Continued)

(Continued)

a line. I thought I understood the material, but the 40% I received on the first quiz implied otherwise. How discouraging! What went wrong?

I don't remember exactly how I finally triumphed over finding the slopes and the equations of lines. I think it was mostly brute force and strength and determination. In all honesty, I think I just learned it by memorizing a few problems to do well enough on the unit test. I am fairly certain I didn't truly understand the slope of a line until I learned it again in precalculus. What I do remember is the sting of failure, especially among a group of people who thought I was too young to be in their class. I remember questioning my abilities and wondering if I had made the right choice to take two math classes in one year. Did I overestimate my abilities? Did I sincerely understand the instruction?

As I observe my current precalculus students, I see my (young) self in them—highly motivated, over-achieving, and ready to take on the world. When they fail or do poorly, I wonder if they are questioning their abilities. I also wonder if they are just memorizing formulas or problems to pass a test without truly understanding the concept. Questioning ourselves and learning how to learn are part of our rite of passage in life. Are there ways to ease this rite of passage or guide it to constructive outcomes? While second-chance assessments can be helpful to these students on their academic journey, I question if they are the best strategy. A second chance may have forced me to relearn slope of a line and prevented me from memorizing the problems, but perhaps I *needed* this defeat to learn how to deal with adversity. I cannot predict the outcome of my research, but I hope it will at least give me some good insights as to the best approach to help my students be mature learners in a challenging environment.

Source: From Hiles, J. B. (2008). Class activity.

CRITICAL FRIEND INQUIRY 5.1

An Education-Related Life History

"As I look back, I can see the seeds of my values as an educator, a feminist, a caretaker, a humanist, and a bicultural Greek American in my childhood and adulthood. Each of these identities is so important in my work as an educator, and each of them is an integral part of me because of my life experiences. I did not try them on for size as an experiment; they passed through my body and became part of my being" (Samaras, 2002, p. 8).

The education-related life history activity may prompt you to consider the stories your students bring to your classroom. According to Vygotsky (1978) cultural and historical influences shape our development and knowledge about education. Self-study asks teachers to examine their own educational beliefs and cultural beliefs and values and how these inform and/or misinform their teaching. When teachers begin to look at their own education-related life history experiences, it helps them gain insights into their thinking about learning. As one of my former students, Dawn Renee Wilcox (2006), stated,

I really feel the self-study component is important for practicing teachers. I
believe that it is only when the teacher understands, reflects, and looks at events
that shaped his/her own educational experiences and beliefs that REAL growth or
change can occur in their teaching practices. I continue to use self-study and
teacher research in the professional development sessions which I coordinate.

Discipline and/or Grade-Level-Focused Option

You might also choose to focus your education-related life history narrative on an experience that is specific to the subject and/or grade level you teach. For example, a mathematics teacher found it useful to revisit and write about his experiences in learning mathematics.
An English teacher wrote of her literacy experience, and a kindergarten teacher wrote about
an experience he had in a "Show and Tell" activity.

Steps

1. Take time to think deeply and honestly about a personal learning experience that
   stands out for you and that was difficult for you or caused you to be concerned
   about something that mattered to you. Take time to be alone with your thinking. In
   quiet, we allow ourselves to ask deep questions about key moments in our learning.
   In this education-related life history, you may have been learning something new,
   something that you couldn't understand, or something that you did understand, but
   other factors may have been problematic in your learning the task.

2. Place yourself backward in this learning experience that you identified. *Visualize
   the full experience* and describe yourself as a learner fully and honestly. What are
   the images you see?

3. Next, write a narrative about a key education-related experience. Below are some
   suggested prompts to consider in your writing:
   - Include the role that your family background, culture, or way of being in the
     world impacted the situation.
   - Describe the context. Is it a classroom or outside of a classroom? Is there
     anything happening historically, socially, politically, or culturally that impacts
     this issue for you?
   - Identify key people who are involved in this experience with you (e.g.,
     teachers, a parent, other students). What role do they play positively and/or
     negatively in this scene? What is happening around you?
   - Offer details that allow us to see where you are and what is at hand. Why is
     this experience difficult or tense for you? What emotions are involved? Are you
     disconnected? Do you feel valued? What is the main issue or problem that you
     see going on here? Is the situation resolved?
   - Return to the question(s) you posed in Critical Friend Inquiry 1.1. Are there any
     connections between your wonderments and this experience? Do you carry
     any of your education-related life experience into your thinking about
     teaching? Explain.

4. Ask your critical friend to listen for any repeated statements and themes that he or she hears while you read your narrative out loud without interruption. Afterward, ask your critical friend what he or she noticed. Keep it simple and clear. Don't read into it or try to force an interpretation. Just pay attention to the actual statements and data. Be a good listener and one without judgment.

5. Exchange places with your critical friend and repeat the activity.

6. Take some time to work alone again, jotting down what you learned, the meaning you derived from this activity, and your discussion with your critical friend.

LIVING EDUCATIONAL THEORY

If you are interested in examining the alignment and authenticity of your beliefs and practices and generating theories of your lived practice, then the living educational theory (Whitehead, 1989, 1993) is a self-study method you might consider. Annemarie, a general education teacher who believes in student equity, asks herself if she is actually promoting that—that is, "How can I design a unit of instruction that would meet the needs of all learners in my inclusive classroom?" (Ratke, 2007, p. 3). Andrea, an elementary teacher who believes she applies new ideas she learns in professional development opportunities, such as effective questioning techniques, asks, "Has what I've learned in my professional development actually changed the way I teach for the better? Are my students becoming better learners of mathematics as a result of the changes I attempt to make? . . . Are my questions effective?" (Aiona, 2006, pp. 2–3). Andrea allows herself to be vulnerable in order to learn and openly question if her instructional practices are representative of her belief in inquiry-based learning.

5.2 Student Example: Living Educational Theory

Andrea M. Aiona (2006), *Elementary School Teacher*

I believe that one of the things that make my classroom a special place is that the climate is welcoming and open with regard to sharing ideas. I do wonder, though, to what extent I impose my own ideas on the students. Do I ask leading questions so that I can get the predetermined answers and conclusions that I have decided are valuable? Do I truly teach in an inquiry-based style wherein students are free to form their own conclusions? And, by achieving the latter, will the students really understand the mathematics that I am required to teach them?

Subsequent to my study on questioning, I wanted to look more closely at my motivations for decision making during my mathematics instruction and assessment by conducting a second pilot study in the spring of 2004. Because I merely looked at my questioning in the previous study, the data were limiting. I discovered that I needed to know the context in which the questions were being asked, the purpose and goals of my lessons, the subsequent questions posed as follow-ups, and how students responded.

The guiding questions were:

1. Why do I say the things that I say when I teach and talk with my students?

2. What does this say about the kind of teacher I am?

3. What can I do better?

I decided to examine the discourse that happened in my mathematics instruction and between students while they are engaged in tasks during classroom episodes. I sought to analyze the discourse that occurred in my class by observing my interaction with the class and individual students, and the interaction of my students with each other.

COLLECTIVE SELF-STUDY METHOD

Self-study can also be conducted by an individual or a school team using a **collective self-study method** (Samaras & Freese, 2006). You may choose to interactively examine an issue and implement a team or group project while you examine your role within that project. Davey and Ham (2009) call this a team-based approach to self-study. They talk about their "collective wisdom":

> Methodological collaboration in the self-study of teacher education practices comes in many forms and guises, ranging along various continuums of participation, purpose, and process from assistive support from another individual colleague at one end, to full blown cultural-collective studies undertaken by entire organizational and even national communities at the other. (p. 188)

Collective self-study has also been described as a self-study community as in a faculty teaching team that examined the components of its work (Samaras, Kayler, Rigsby, Weller, & Wilcox, 2006), a faculty and student research team exploring the development of a new course on self-study (Samaras et al., 2007), or a group of new professors who sought to learn together through conversations about their teacher education practices and scholarship (Kitchen & Ciuffetelli Parker, 2009). Kitchen, Ciuffetelli Parker, and Gallaher (2008, p. 158) "identified collaborative self-study as a means to 'building a culture of inquiry' that is 'reconfigured around team-teaching and facilitation of practitioner inquiry' (Grimmett, 1998, p. 264)."

ARTS-BASED SELF-STUDY METHOD

If you want to experiment with using an arts-based medium as a way to symbolize, represent, construct, or deconstruct your thinking about teaching, then you might choose to employ an arts-based self-study method (Weber & Mitchell, 2004). The **arts-based self-study method** "promotes and provokes self-reflection, critical analysis, and dialogue about improving one's teaching through the arts" (Samaras & Freese, 2006, p. 73). Researchers use a wide range of art forms to represent and reinterpret, construct and deconstruct meaning, and communicate their study of researching as they make it public: portraits, performance, photography, video documentary, art installations, multimedia representations, films, drawings, cartoons, collages, graffiti, signs, cyber graphics, videotape and digital recordings, computer-assisted technologies, diagrams, and found poetry (Griffiths, Malcolm, & Williamson, 2009; Hopper & Sanford, 2008; Mitchell, Weber, & Pithouse, 2009; Mittapalli and Samaras, 2008; Samaras & Freese, 2006; Tidwell & Manke, 2009; Weber & Mitchell, 2004). If you are attracted to this self-study method and want to explore it more formally, it would be worth reading the work of Griffiths et al. (2009), Hamilton and Pinnegar (2009), Mitchell and Weber (1999), Mitchell et al. (2009), and Weber and Mitchell (2004) on using art-based self-study to study your context. They offer excellent suggestions for using collage, photography, videotaping, and visual metaphors. You will find examples of students' arts-based self-study work throughout this text.

Critical Friend Inquiry 5.2 will be useful in extending your thinking and your discussion about the impact of your study on yourself as a self-study teacher researcher.

CRITICAL FRIEND INQUIRY 5.2

Self-Portrait of a Teacher Researcher
Arts-Based Self-Study Method

(Adapted from the work of Samaras & Freese, 2006, and Weber & Mitchell, 1996, 2004. Also see Richards, 1998.)

Purpose

Self-portraits are a form of text useful for reading, broadening, and communicating an understanding of one's self-study research practice and learning. Self-portraits generate data useful for researchers' professional knowing and can serve various research purposes:

- Understanding your interest in a particular research topic
- Developing or refining your research rationale
- Creating a visual representation of your research problem
- Understanding your role inside the research
- Reflecting on your development as an emerging self-study scholar (see prompts below)

Thus, the self-portrait becomes a source of data that informs the research and the researcher. Dialogue with peers about portraits is a means to construct and reconstruct your thinking.

Wonderings and Questions

- How do I see myself as a self-study scholar?
- How might I capture or depict my role in my research through a self-portrait?
- How does my self-portrait demonstrate my hoped-for change?

Process and Data Collection

1. Draw or make a self-portrait of how you see yourself as a developing self-study scholar. Choose your medium and materials (e.g., sketch paper, pencils, poster paper, markers, clay, crepe paper, felt, colored pencils, oil paint, watercolor sets, crayons, cardboard, wood). This activity does not require any artistic training in portrait making.

2. After you complete your self-portrait, step back and examine it carefully.

3. Then, reflect and write a reflection, narrative, poem, or short story about your portrait. Include your thoughts and reactions to what you have drawn. Below are some *suggested* prompts to consider as you critically examine your portrait:

   - How does this self-portrait relate to my research project?
   - Is this portrait related to a particular revelation in my research journey?
   - What does the self-portrait reveal about my perception of my identity and gender as a researcher? (Notice your clothes, props, physical features, expression, and so on.)
   - What is the context of my self-portrait? (Pay attention to the historical, social, and cultural context of your self-portrait.)
   - Is anyone else included in my self-portrait? Are there peers or professors or family and friends in the drawing? If so, what does it suggest about my relationship to those persons?
   - Are there objects in my self-portrait? Do they carry any special meaning to me and/or to others?
   - What would I title this self-portrait?
   - What might a curator write about this self-portrait?

Critical Friend Inquiry

After you complete your self-portrait, ask a colleague to react to your portrait without judgment. Your critical friend might also decide to share his or her self-portrait. Talk about what you are learning about each other. Share your hopes for yourself as a self-study researcher. Below are some *suggested* prompts:

- What do you wish was different in your teaching?
- What are your projected professional goals?
- What resources will you need?
- How will you go about achieving this goal?
- You may choose to extend this activity with a group of colleagues. If so, find somewhere where you can comfortably gather and spread out your self-portraits.
- What is your reaction to these images? How do others react to them?
- Hold a conversation about what you see in the group of self-portraits.
- Observe and comment on any commonalities, differences, and connections that emerge when comparing the set of portraits.
- What are the challenges and hopes of the researchers as portrayed through these portraits?

Evidence of Impact

- What awareness has this activity raised for you about who you think you are as a self-study researcher?
- Reflect on and document any differences you experience in your researching and any changes in your learning after you conduct this activity.

CHALLENGES IN CHOOSING A METHOD

There can be some overlap in self-study methods such as in arts-based self-study and personal history, but the main method employed is how you identify your method. Accept and utilize the overlap and what each method offers. For example, although Kavita integrated her personal history in her class project (Mittapalli & Samaras, 2008), she employed an arts-based self-study method as her research design (see Photos 5.1a, 5.1b, and 5.1c):

Photos 5.1a, 5.1b, and 5.1c   Self-Portrait of a Researcher

Source: From Johri, A. K. & Mittapalli, K. (2008, April).

I painted a self-portrait and shared it with peers in the self-study class. I learned about Madhubani art many years ago in India as an undergraduate student from a friend majoring in fine arts but I did not foresee its power in opening a pathway to my research process. The art form is deeply rooted in my history, culture, and experiences. . . . This art form provided me the required means to not only represent my self-development process in an artistic form but also gave me a way to express my inner self as an Asian-Indian woman examining her ways of knowing as she grows as an education researcher. (pp. 246, 254)

MEMORY WORK SELF-STUDY METHOD

The **memory work self-study method** (Mitchell & Weber, 1999) serves to "uncover the ways in which individuals build their identities . . . what we remember and how we remember the events in our lives to form the basis of whom [sic] and what we are today" (O'Reilly-Scanlon, 2002, p. 74). It is used to represent autobiographical inquiry with critical and reflective revisiting. Weber and Mitchell (2002) have worked with their students on memory work projects to help them make the past usable and inform their future goals. Memory work, like arts-based self-study, can also involve using the arts, artifacts, and other data.

5.3 Student Example: Memory Work Self-Study Method

Bernadine Pearson, *Accountability Analyst*

Memory work along with a personal history self-study was useful to this student in her exploration of her role in program evaluation targeting increasing college enrollment and her later conceptualization of her dissertation research. She presented her memory work self-study to a cohort of students and offered her advice (Pearson, 2009a):

- I examined my artifacts (i.e., memory book, pictures, and newspaper highlight the role of multicultural navigators in my life).
- My personal history with memory work paints the self-portrait of a model multicultural navigator.
- Find and identify your critical friends (multicultural navigators).
- Critical friends are multicultural navigators who help redirect your route to keep you toward the ultimate destination of a completed manuscript.
- They perform the role of a GPS (global positioning system) navigator for your writing.
- Find comfort in knowing your interest will appear to shift; in the end everything is connected to your personal conceptual framework.
- Asking the question "Why study that?" of my research challenged me to find something meaningful to pursue for my dissertation.

(Continued)

(Continued)

Sharing her dissertation research (Pearson, 2009b), Bernadine wrote,

We live in multiple social worlds, such as home, school, and our local community. Each of these social worlds requires its own navigation. We develop skills on how to navigate from information we are taught (explicitly or implicitly) from models or multicultural navigators. Bandura's (1997) Social Cognitive Theory states that student learning is a result of reciprocal interactions among personal factors (i.e., thoughts, goals, beliefs, and values), behaviors (i.e., research topics), and environmental factors (i.e., multicultural navigators/social models) (see Figure 5.1). Simply stated, Bandura's theory suggests that our thoughts, goals, beliefs, and values relative to specific social worlds (e.g., instructional techniques for teaching reading to second graders) are shaped by observing our models/multicultural navigators.

Figure 5.1   Reciprocal Causation

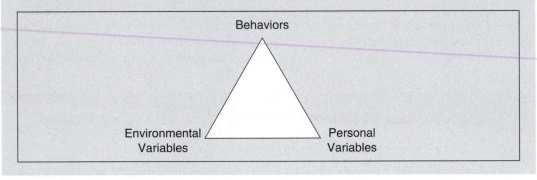

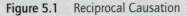

CRITICAL FRIEND INQUIRY 5.3

Memory Work Self-Study Method

I learn so much from my self-study colleagues. Critical Friend Inquiry 5.3 is adapted from the memory work self-study developed by Mitchell and Weber (1999). The purpose of this assignment is to allow students to cast a wide net on the scope and domain of the topic that they will later refine. I find that artifacts are a useful way to prompt my students to think about their research interest. The artifact, like a metaphor, stands for, represents, and expresses research interests in a nonlinguistic manner. I also bring a research artifact, not so much to model the activity as to be part of a growing class community. Below is an e-mail I sent my students, inviting them to practice an informal memory work self-study inquiry.

From	▶ asamaras@gmu.edu
Sent	Saturday, September 8, 2007 10:13 am
To	asamaras@gmu.edu

Cc	
Bcc	
Subject	Welcome to EDUC 675 and Bring Artifact

Hi all,

For our next class, please bring an artifact (object) to help us learn a little about your research interests. Then write a personal essay about your artifact. For example, in the past a student who was interested in improving children's reading brought in an old favorite book of hers. Another brought a bucket filled with treasures she collected at the beach that highlighted her interest in hands-on science inquiry as a teacher professional development science coordinator. Yet another threw a crumpled piece of paper across the room depicting his frustration for how his students view his homework assignments. It's a way for us to get to know each other's areas of study and research interests. Again, the artifact is a tool to prompt your thinking about your research.

See you for our next class,
Anastasia

Research Artifact

Steps

1. Choose an artifact that captures the main idea of your research interest.

2. Include a title using a metaphor that signifies the core meaning of this chosen object.

3. Write a personal essay on your artifact. Below are some *suggested* writing prompts:
   - Explain why you chose this object.
   - Share what the artifact represents in your research.
   - What is the time period of this artifact?
   - What role does your culture play in this artifact?
   - Are there others involved in this artifact memory? What role do they play? What is their influence on your thinking? Do they see things the way you do?
   - What metaphor would you choose to represent, symbolize, and reinforce the significance of this object to you?
   - Express an emotion that this artifact brings forth for you. Describe where that emotion generates from and might extend to in your teaching. Be descriptive.

With your critical friend, showcase and examine each other's artifact. Share your personal essays and what seems to be central to your research interest.

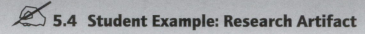

5.4 Student Example: Research Artifact

Dawn Renee Wilcox, *School Science Coordinator*

A science teacher, influenced by the time she spent learning about science with her grandmother through their walks on the beach, brought in a bucket for her research artifact (see Photo 5.2). The bucket was filled with symbolic "treasures" she had gathered from her teaching and learning experiences. She shares the symbolism of her bucket:

> Using the bucket metaphor has allowed me to create a visual that shows how everyone can have different items or experiences in their buckets. Teachers come with preconceived notions and ideas and it is important to know where they are when creating staff development that will encourage growth. Peers listened, showed support and offered feedback and brought out connections that I had missed myself. [This student is interested in supporting other science teachers' knowledge and practice of teaching about the natural world and science concepts through inquiry-based learning.] (Wilcox, 2006)

Photo 5.2   Research Artifact

What have self-study teachers asked using various self-study methods?

What kinds of questions have educators asked about their practice? What type of self-study methods did they choose? What was their context? Who were their participants? What types of data did they collect? What are the implications of their work? Table 5.2 provides a guide of the research components with an example included. You will find this chart provides a useful format for beginning to organize your own study.

5.2 Self-Study Research Guidepost

SELF-STUDY RESEARCH PROJECT FRAMEWORKS

Table 5.2 Self-Study Research Project Frameworks

Research Question	Self-Study Method	Context	Participants	Data Sources	Implications: So What?
How do I balance my multiple roles as an English department chair and teacher? (Adams-Legge, 2006)	*Developmental Portfolio Self-Study Method*	Secondary School	Self and professional colleagues	Surveys to teachers and other English department chairs in the district; author's ongoing reflective journals; department journal notes; visual concept map	Effective leadership practices in school settings
What contributed to my usage of inquiry-based science teaching? (Wilcox, 2006)	*Personal History Self-Study*	Elementary School	Self and critical friend	Narratives; self-portraits; artifacts; critical friend memos	Inspiring science teachers to utilize inquiry-based teaching as aligned with national science standards
What do I do and say to facilitate mathematical discourse? Has what I've learned in my professional development actually changed the way I teach mathematics? Are my students becoming better learners of	*Living Educational Theory*	Elementary School	Self and professional colleagues	Audiotaped recordings of lessons, Likert-based student surveys, student work samples, personal reflections	Insights for other teaching professionals for studying and facilitating mathematical discourse (e.g., increasing student participation, horizontal discourse, student sharing of solutions, improved teacher listening)

(Continued)

Table 5.2 (Continued)

Research Question	Self-Study Method	Context	Participants	Data Sources	Implications: So What?
mathematics as a result of the changes? (Aiona, 2006)					
Does my involvement in an electronic forum influence community building for our class? What constitutes effective practice in virtual teacher education? (Ham & Davey, 2006)	*Collective Self-Study*	University English Methods Course and IT course	Faculty, preservice English secondary teachers working with high school students and inservice teachers in IT courses	Postproject student and teacher interviews, written questionnaires. Ongoing tutor journal; regular iterative content analysis of discussions on Blackboard; teacher interviews; questionnaire. Professors' journals and meeting notes and critical friend inquiries	Implications for interpersonal student/faculty interactions in online learning environments. Students' self-regulation in online teaching environments deepened their need for professor feedback
How do I make sense of the "in-between-ness" of my roles as teacher and administrator? (Johri, 2007)	*Arts-Based Self-Study Method*	Elementary School	Self, critical friends, students, and school colleagues	Journals; self-portrait; critical friend memos; teacher and administrator interviews	Useful to teachers who are also administrators examining their dual roles, complexities, and impact
How can my early teaching diaries inform my current teaching? (Mitchell, 2006)	*Memory Work Self-Study*	University	Self as teacher and in relation to current students	Diaries of teaching as a beginning teacher; writing as textual evidence	Contributes to our understanding of the challenges beginning teachers often face. Looking at the future through the past

We are not at a loss for questions to ask about our practice. Keep thinking about your questions.

- Does my teaching philosophy align with my teaching? How do I live my values more fully in my teaching? (Gipe, 1998; Whitehead, 1989)
- What is the effect of my Asian American culture on my teaching of multicultural issues? (Oda, 1998)
- How does my collaboration in a professor network outside my university support my professional development? (Kosnik, 2008; LaBoskey, Davies-Samway, & Garcia, 1998)
- In what ways does my work with performing artists impact preservice students' perspective taking? (Samaras, 2000)
- How can I use a visual way of knowing to understand my teaching? (Mitchell & Weber, 1999)
- How have my education-related experiences shaped my teaching theory? (Bullough & Gitlin, 1995; Samaras, 2002)
- Can I use the World Wide Web for researching teaching-learning relationships? (Hoban, 2003)

Six self-study methods are introduced in this book. Nonetheless, self-study methods are not limited to these. Self-study researchers continue to write about and develop a large array of self-study methods such as interviews (Kosnik, Cleovoulou, & Fletcher, 2009); participatory research (Paugh & Robinson, 2009); self-study communities (Kitchen & Ciuffetelli Parker, 2009); literary and artistic methods (Galman, 2009); self-studies in teacher education accreditation review (Pinnegar & Erickson, 2009); co-autoethnography (Taylor & Coia, 2009); team-based approach (Davey & Ham, 2009); narrative inquiry (Chiu-Ching & Yim-mei Chan, 2009; Kitchen, 2009); dialogue (East, Fitzgerald, & Heston, 2009); social justice (LaBoskey, 2009); electronic technologies (Berry & Crowe, 2009); visual representation (Griffiths et al., 2009); photography for social action (Mitchell et al., 2009); visual metaphor (Tidwell & Manke, 2009); and collage (Hamilton & Pinnegar, 2009). Hamilton and Pinnegar (1998) argue, "Self-study is a methodology in which researchers and practitioners use whatever methods will provide the needed evidence and context for understanding their practice" (p. 240).

KEY IDEAS

- Self-study methods are multiple in nature and have been developed largely by and for self-study teacher educators.
- Self-study methods entail various approaches such as developmental portfolio self-study method, personal history self-study method, living educational theory, collective self-study method, arts-based self-study method, and memory work self-study method.
- When choosing a self-study method, you may find some overlap in self-study methods, but the main method employed is how you identify your self-study method.
- A Critical Friends Portfolio, designed using the developmental portfolio self-study method, is a purposeful and manageable self-study method to employ with critical friends throughout your project.

Your Self-Study Project

PART II

Curriculum belongs to teachers after all. . . . This creative ownership of the curriculum will be an invaluable asset in coping with the current approach to education reform, which relies all too heavily on high-stakes testing.

—*Anastasia P. Samaras (2002, p. xv)*

Part II is all about conducting your research project. In this section, you will find the information and practice activities to help you design, enact, and assess your self-study research project. Also included in this section are invitations to continue the critical friend inquiries, which you may also decide to include in your Critical Friends Portfolio. Chapter 6, "Design," describes seven key research design components of self-study including student examples. Chapter 7, "Protect," asks you to consider what it means to be an ethical researcher. You will be introduced to standards of research ethics and the role that your critical friend can play in that process. Chapter 8, "Organize Data," offers ways to effectively manage your large data set. Chapter 9, "Collect Data," includes techniques and guidelines for collecting your data. You will find examples of the types of data that self-study researchers collect and how they are aligned with their self-study method. Chapter 10, "Analyze Data," walks you through suggested steps in analyzing qualitative data. Chapter 11, "Assess Research Quality," offers a discussion and framework of the role that a validation group can play in helping you examine the quality of your research. Chapter 12, "Write," provides some friendly advice for writing. Chapter 13, "Present and Publish," offers guidelines for making your research public through presentation and publication and circles you back to reflect on what you learned about becoming a self-study teacher researcher.

Let your research process begin!

Design

6

Self-study could be seen as a way of "keeping it real." The "it" is the relationship between theory and practice. It keeps this relationship real by recognizing and formalizing the way we influence our practice. Doing so enables us to change because knowing our intents and beliefs opens us to others' perspectives and actions.

—Mary Jane McIlwain (2007),
Reading Specialist, Fairfax County Public Schools, Virginia

In this chapter, you will find a space for building a strong research design for your research project. A discussion is provided on the importance of having a design before you begin conducting your research while also appreciating the hermeneutic quality of self-study research. There are opportunities for thinking about your research question, guidelines for creating a critical friend team, ideas for observing your classroom, suggestions for articulating your rationale, advice for developing a literature review, and strategies for conceptually mapping the research you locate. This chapter has a great deal of information that is presented in sections. It is suggested that you read it in chunks as you begin to develop and enact your research project.

✦ Reading this chapter will provide an opportunity for you to acquire the tools you need for designing your self-study teacher research project.

As a Vygotskian researcher, I purposely designed collaborative learning experiences to guide preservice teachers as they construct their personal understandings about their teaching. I wanted to create a classroom aura that prompts students to work at the rough edges of their competence and understanding. I envisioned an environment of cognitive dissonance in which students' notions of teaching are challenged by moral and intellectual discussions with peers, cooperating teachers, and professors, and where students are permitted to make and share their mistakes.

DESIGN MATTERS

When I designed and first taught a course on self-study research, I encouraged my students to ask themselves the following questions:

- How can I author an inquiry driven from my questions situated in my particular context?
- What do I need to consider in being and having a critical friend?
- What is going on in my context that causes me to question my practice?
- How can I design a rationale that allows me to examine my role in the change I seek?
- What does a literature review entail?
- What self-study method should I use?

The design components in this chapter were developed from my understanding of what my students were telling me they needed to know as they developed their projects. These components warrant your serious attention before you enact your study.

SEVEN KEY DESIGN COMPONENTS

1. Author your research question.

2. Establish your critical friend team.

3. Observe your classroom.

4. Articulate rationale and proposal.

5. Frame your question within literature.

6. Align your question with self-study method.

7. Plan purposeful pedagogies.

To help you plan your research project, let's look at the seven key design components of self-study research for you to consider *before* you conduct your study (see Figure 6.1).

1. Author your research question.

A key component in designing your self-study research project is to be sure you are the author of your own research question that is situated within your own practice. This first key component aligns with the methodological component—that is, Focus #1: *Self-study teachers initiate their own inquiries and study them in their teaching context utilizing a self-study method aligned with that inquiry.* You will develop your research question from the authority and contextualization of your own experience and not someone else's (Munby & Russell, 1994). Like I tell my students, you have the privilege of asking your own questions

Figure 6.1   Seven Key Design Components

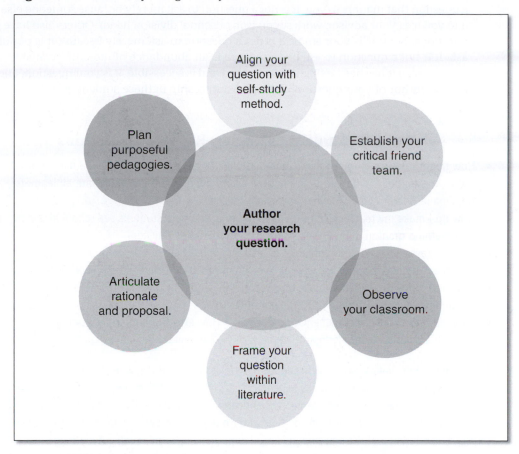

in the context of your own classroom. The one thing you can change in education is your own practice.

We live busy lives. The multiple demands of teaching sometimes force us to approach our work or project as another thing to get done. I have observed students grappling for ideas—any ideas—just to finish their project. When they settle on choosing any topic, they lose the opportunity to study a topic that matters to them and to their students. Unlike some research projects that might entail an administrator identifying a "felt need" that teachers would benefit from and gaining their buy-in (Tomal, 2003), self-study teachers identify their own problems *and* study the role they play in the intended reform. Some professional development coordinators have recognized the value of encouraging teachers to use self-study for professional development with questions generated from teachers themselves and supported through critical friend inquiries (Wilcox, 2008).

You know, my dear mother sent me a lovely birthday card reminding me that I was the author of my own life and work. The card said it was up to me to envision my work, sketch it out, develop an action plan, and make it happen. Similarly, self-study research is about a question that matters to you. It is not a question to ask merely because someone else gave it to you (i.e., your advisor, work supervisor, or school division head). Others also have good questions, but this is your study. It is not a question to ask merely because it is popular to ask. It is not a question to ask because there is an abundance of literature available about it or because it has been exhaustively studied and is accessible. It is your question, and you are the author of your question. Notice the authorship in these student questions:

✍ 6.1 Student Examples: Research Questions

- How might I design a unit of instruction that would meet the needs of all learners in my inclusive classroom? What strategies might I use to engage and accommodate all learners? Annemarie Ratke (2007), Elementary School Teacher
- How do I make my teaching of civics more rigorous and help students see school as a pathway to something greater? James Mercer (2008), Social Studies Teacher
- In what ways can I adapt my strategies of ninth-grade teaching of science to seventh graders and keep them engaged so they will want to learn? Amy Smith (2008), Middle School Science Teacher
- How do I motivate students to use new vocabulary, and how do I incorporate it throughout my classroom? Jennifer Soehnlin (2008), English Teacher
- What do I do to facilitate mathematical discourse? How effective am I in facilitating mathematical discourse? Andrea M. Aiona (2006), Elementary School Teacher

You might think back to your teacher education courses for a moment when you were asked to write your philosophy of education. Can you remember that? Now, consider asking yourself if your teaching philosophy and theoretical orientation authenticates your practice (Samaras, 2002; Whitehead, 1993). One of my students wrote in her final anonymous course evaluation in my teacher research course, "I have found that it is only through articulating challenges and trying out teaching philosophies that we find our own voices as teachers." So take some time here to articulate your teaching challenges, recall your teaching philosophies, and find your voice—as a self-study teacher researcher.

Be patient with the process of finalizing your research question. Your question will become clearer and sharper as you move through the research process. An arts-based self-study method may be a way that stimulates your thinking about your research question and helps you discover what you are really asking.

The arts-based self-study method allowed me to vacillate between concrete and abstract thinking in order to fully understand what research question I wanted to ask. Creating the art piece helped me visualize my thought processes and apply them in a concrete manner. Stepping back from the concrete artistic display then stimulated my mind to think more abstractly—drawing connections and developing metaphors for the objects used within the art piece. The cyclical process of concrete and abstract ideas finally propelled me to understand what questions I wanted to ask in my self-study research: *(a) How do we as teachers know it is time to move on to another job?* And *(b) What variables influence a teacher's decision to move onward to another position?* (Sell [Elementary School Teacher], 2009b)

2. Establish your critical friend team.

Establishing a critical friend team is an essential step in the teacher research process. Think back to your first critical friend inquiry in Chapter 1. Consider the role that your critical friend played in that work. Your critical friend is a trusted colleague who asks for clarification of your research and offers an alternative point of view in a constructive manner. You will recall that self-study research is not conducted alone and aligns with the methodological component, Focus #2: *Self-study teachers work in an intellectually safe and supportive community to improve their practice by making it explicit to themselves and to others through critical collaborative inquiries.*

Pamela Richards gives a very honest account about the importance of critical friends in writing. In her chapter in Becker's (2007) classic book, *Writing for Social Scientists,* she offers a most sobering reminder that those we trust help us trust ourselves and our writing: "Their responses convince me to trust myself" (p. 117). Richards finds a mutual trust and need with her peers who "already know how stupid I can be" (p. 116) and who hold a common history and related experiences. Critical friend inquiries are mutually beneficial and generate a participatory consciousness with other perspectives informing one's own. "You have to trust these people not just to treat you right (not to be competitive with you, not to tell tales when you mess up), but also to tell you the truth" (pp. 117–118).

Wade, Fauske, and Thompson (2008) note that critical friends are people tools:

In a self-study, where you're studying your own teaching, you really have to be concerned about this issue: I may not see something because of the very questions I've asked. So what tools can I use? One tool would be a colleague acting as a critical friend who takes observational notes, looks at the issues to criticize as well as commend, and then debriefs with me after class. Another would be analyzing the data together at the end of a course, in a more formal, qualitative way. So people would be the tools, especially teachers and researchers from different paradigms who would be willing to challenge my assumptions and ask the hard questions. You can't do a self-study by yourself. (p. 414)

A climate of trust with critical friends is essential to encourage a free flow of ideas among all participants of the community. Nonetheless, it takes practice being a supportive collaborator. It requires someone who provides encouragement and is also willing to ask probing questions to critically analyze the issues at hand. Over time, critical friends can become more comfortable with giving and asking for critique without lots of qualifiers. However, it is crucial that a climate of constructivist transparency and professionalism be established and reviewed often so that trust can build slowly over time.

Now consider if you want to expand the number of critical friends for your critical friend team, or perhaps you prefer working only with one partner. Some students like to account for any attrition that might occur along the way if a critical friend suddenly becomes inaccessible. Your critical friend(s) could be from a grade-level- or discipline-based school team or a group of teachers from diverse disciplines in your own school or even across schools.

3. Observe your classroom.

Your research question is your quest to understand your teaching and improve your students' learning. That notion aligns with the methodological component, Focus #3: *Self-study teachers question the status quo of their teaching and the politics of schooling in order to improve and impact learning for themselves, their students, and the education field.* Your question is generated from your noticing something worthy of study for your students, a dilemma or issue that emerges from your practice. It does not have to be a problem per se, but it must be something you want to explore, understand, and improve. Remember, your research should be focused on a problem that you care about and that will help you discover ways that teaching and learning might change.

I spoke with an anthropologist who had rushed to meet me on campus for his first visit. After hurrying to get to the meeting, he explained that his research training allowed him to quickly "read the land." Arriving out of breath, he exclaimed, "I could quickly see and appreciate the diversity, friendliness, and openness of your university through my noticing." Like anthropologists, teachers become attuned to reading and noticing classrooms. So go notice!

6.2 Student Example: Observational Notes

Amy Smith (2008), *Middle School Science Teacher*

I am teaching seventh graders, and my team-taught class especially seems to be off task at varying points of a lesson. It is every teacher's dream to be able to keep all students active and motivated throughout an entire lesson. My issue is with varying levels of learners and being able to create an active learning environment while not everyone is on the same pace. All of the students are involved because they all participate daily in the activities of the class. My team-taught class in particular takes longer to do assignments due to the fact that I am hesitant to move on while some will be left behind in the dust. I am noticing some students appearing bored after a particular activity. I want the entire class to be in an active environment from the moment they walk in until the moment they leave. I wrote in my journal log, "I feel as though the students are beginning to push my buttons in any way they can." My voice was diminishing, and my throat had begun to hurt from raising my voice to call attention to everyone. The "good" kids of the class just roll their eyes at me. This eye rolling is probably due to their disappointment in their peers' actions and their disappointment in me that I can't control the class. At the beginning of the year, this phenomenon was occurring daily. My team teacher and I worked diligently to combat the issue together. We devised a plan to always keep them on task in hopes that this would keep everyone engaged.

Below, you will find Critical Friend Inquiry 6.1, which you may elect to try. Get ready to snap a class portrait. It is an informal arts-based self-study method to help you see and read your classroom. Then share your noticing with your critical friend.

CRITICAL FRIEND INQUIRY 6.1

Class Portrait

When you think of a class portrait, you might picture one with students standing neatly and the teacher standing off to the side. The caption indicates the name of the school, the grade, and the school year.

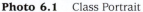

Photo 6.1   Class Portrait

Now make your class portrait come alive (see Photo 6.1). Design a visual and/or narrative representation of your current classroom situation and your practice capturing the academic, social, and cultural theater of your classroom, as well as your role within that context. Capture the action of your students interacting with each other and with you. You may decide to capture your class portrait through various art forms such as videotaping, photographs, a collage, sketching, or a combination of these. You might set up a camera or ask a peer to videotape your teaching so you can examine your role from a distance. Keep moving, widening, and narrowing your camera lens to see the situation from multiple perspectives.

You may decide to include **narratives** (e.g., reflections and interpretations of your research process) with visuals (e.g., journals, photo captions, or your analysis as a class portrait curator). A class portrait can provoke critical reflection about what is taking place in your classroom. It will provide a way for you to think deeply about your research question, to capture the focus of the change you propose, and to plan for solution strategies. Reflect on and observe what your medium teaches you about your classroom and construct a class portrait. Deconstruct your class portrait, describing what you are noticing in your classroom to your critical friend. This activity will bring you closer to your research question, rationale, and research proposal.

Take for example Sara, a practicing teacher who was "burnt out," exhausted, and disappointed after 2 years of teaching and struggled with classroom management. As she went to work noticing her classroom, she noted, "I really like to take charge of the classroom. . . . It is sometimes hard for me to let them [her students] get into groups and run discussions and guide their own learning" (Samaras, Beck, Freese, & Kosnik, 2005, p. 4). Trying to deal with 27 fourth graders who were constantly calling out and disrupting the flow of her lessons, she asked, "How can I harness classroom talking in a way that will allow for the open flow of ideas while showing concern for the common good and rights of all individuals?" (Samaras et al., 2005, p. 4).

Consider the following:

- What do you see happening in your classroom that you would like to change? Give specific examples of the situations and behaviors you have observed.
- What is going on that brings your attention to this issue?
- How would you describe what you see? Give specific examples.
- Who is involved?
- What is taking place?
- When and where does the issue or behavior occur?
- What do you think are the reasons for what you observe?
- What part do you play in this issue?
- What are your behaviors and challenges related to this issue?
- Are there any particular patterns or sequences to the behaviors you describe?
- How do your responses affect the situation?
- How might a peer see the same situation?
- If you asked your students to describe the situation, what do you think they might tell you?
- If you were a parent of one of your students, what might you want to change and why?

Next, step back and describe your hunches based on your observations—for example, what is going on, what causes it, and what are your plans? Present a summary of the observations, the hunches you identified through creating a class portrait, and begin to think about some possible causes and plans for change. Brainstorm potential pedagogical strategies for each of the causes you noted. Present a summary of your thinking and theory about the strategies as well as the possible positive and negative consequences of your actions. You may find it helpful to organize your classroom observations and pedagogical strategies in chart form.

Classroom Observation and Strategy Log

Observation Notes	Hunches	Possible Causes	Possible Pedagogical Strategies	Personal Beliefs, Values, and Theories Related to Strategies	Reflection on Strategies (Possible Positive and Negative Consequences of Enacting)

School Ethos and School Portrait

If you are working on a school-wide self-study project and/or working with a school-based team in a collective self-study, you might consider the "School Ethos Project" where teachers "examine their practicum school as if they were anthropologists" capturing a picture of the school and "the variability of school missions and their authenticity in practice" (Samaras, 2002, p. 65). You might also be interested in creating a "School Portrait." Modeled from the work of Lawrence-Lightfoot (1983), the school portrait assignment "provides the preservice teachers with an opportunity to apply research methods to questions and issues they encounter in their partnership school" (Freese, 2005, p. 124).

4. Articulate rationale and proposal.

Articulating a strong rationale is important to writing your research proposal. Have you ever found yourself talking on and on about something to someone that you haven't quite figured out for yourself? The same is true about explaining an undeveloped research proposal. Your goal next is to articulate a clear, crisp research rationale and proposal. Note how Martin, a mathematics teacher, uses the haiku assignment to help him develop his rationale.

In Chapter 1, you sketched out some of your wonderments. Now let's play with writing a haiku, writing a research memo to your critical friend, and then formalizing that work in a research proposal (see Critical Friend Inquiry 6.2). How have you planned to examine what role you play in the change you seek?

CRITICAL FRIEND INQUIRY 6.2

A Haiku Poem for Your Rationale

As a way to begin writing a research proposal, my students really enjoy first writing a haiku, which is a 17-syllable Japanese poetry form. I use it to help break their writing block about their research focus. I developed the idea after reading Janesick's (2004) work, *"Stretching" Exercises for Qualitative Researchers,* where she suggests that students write a haiku to capture their role as qualitative researchers. It's also an amazing way to articulate your research proposal. A haiku poem actually forces you to be concise, parsimonious, and articulate in a very short space. I ask students to write about their research topic and why they chose it in haiku form—that is, 17 total syllables:

Five syllables on the first line of the poem

Seven syllables on the second line

Five syllables on the third line

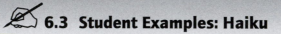 **6.3 Student Examples: Haiku**

Below are examples of haiku poems used to prompt thinking and articulating a rationale.

Mathematics teacher Martin Shaw (2008) asked himself, "How can I encourage students to really do homework and not just complete the assignment?" and wrote the following haiku:

Homework is no good!

But we must, to do better

Let's get it done, now.

In the next example, English teacher Sarah Craig (2008) was interested in studying her role in allowing students to choose their own vocabulary words in her goal of improving students' reading comprehension. She spoke from the perspective of her students:

I want to decide

Why can't I make a choice too?

It is my learning.

Try your hand at writing a haiku and share it with your critical friend. See if your critical friend can understand what you are studying and why you are studying it based on your haiku.

Now, let's continue the work of crafting your research proposal in a way that will help you build the narrative section of your proposal in your final research project (see Critical Friend Inquiry 6.3).

CRITICAL FRIEND INQUIRY 6.3

Research Proposal

This is the assignment I give my students in writing a research proposal.

This is a formative assessment with professor and peer feedback, so there is no grade, although it will be the basis and foundation of your final research project. You may also elect to add a visual representation to your research proposal. The idea is for the visual to help you figure out your "thesis" or main idea and not to enter an art show. If you decide to create a visual research proposal, after you do, ask your critical friend(s) to tell you what they "see" in this proposal.

Approach this assignment from where you are and honor its incompleteness as part of the research process. Ask yourself whether the written and/or visual proposal includes or demonstrates the following:

- An expansive list of your questions and wonderings
- A clearly defined focus and purpose
- Why you chose to explore this research project
- How you propose to go about exploring your inquiry and possible sources

What Are Your Questions and Wonderings?

Write your questions and look for how they relate to each other. Then write a clearly defined focus and purpose question.

A Clearly Defined Focus and Purpose

What is the problem/issue to be addressed?

Why You Chose to Explore This Research Topic

What is going on in your classroom that brings your attention to this problem or issue? What are your hunches about the reasons for this problem or issue? Why are you interested in this topic, and why does it matter to you, your students, and the field?

What Are Some Possible Sources for Exploring Your Inquiry?

What are some possible pedagogies you intend to enact? What do you intend to try? What are some possible data resources?

✎ 6.4 Student Example: Narrative Research Proposal

Kelli Frattini (2008), *Geosystems Teacher*

Questions and Wonderings

1. Does becoming a "peer helper" benefit both the lower-achieving students and the higher-achieving students?

2. Do enrichment activities help low- and high-achieving students better understand the material?

3. Should all students who complete assignments early be allowed to be part of the "100+ Club"?

4. Does it appear students are rushing to complete their work or that they really understand the material that much faster than other students?

5. Does the "100+ Club" give students incentive to push themselves beyond the level they typically work at?

6. What issues are present for differentiation of instruction?

Focus Question

How do I differentiate learning among all students in my geosystems classroom?

Why I Chose to Explore This Research Topic

The nature of a geosystems classroom encompasses a wide variety of learners. For this reason it makes reaching all students a very big challenge for me, especially as a new teacher. Originally I wanted to focus on the students who were not grasping the material as well as the majority of the class. However, I find that not only are the students who do not learn as quickly being left out; the largest population of students who are being left out actually includes the students who learn at a very high level, or more quickly than the average student. These students are often not challenged and have a lot of downtime in class. Finding a way to accommodate high-achieving learners has become increasingly more difficult for me. They are typically left out because they understand the material required, and more of my attention is needed on the students who do not grasp the content as quickly. This reasoning has left me wanting to find a way to include all students, not just the ones who understand the material or who do not, but the ones who are not challenged enough by this course and those who are not working in their zone of proximal development. Differentiating instruction for different-level learners in the same classroom has become the biggest challenge I have faced as a new teacher.

Possible Sources for Exploration

I have come up with a variety of activities that students who are high-achieving learners can participate in. These students typically work at a faster pace and can grasp the material at a very high level. For this reason I am exploring a number of ways for these students to enhance their learning and give them a more enriched learning environment. Students who finish assignments early and accurately can become part of the "100+ Club." Members of the club can choose from one of four activities to help them further learn the material.

- "Peer-Helpers"—Students will help their classmates with concepts that they do not understand. Teaching difficult concepts to their classmates will benefit both the "helper" and the other students. To be able to teach a concept the "helper" must understand the concept at a higher level.
- Enrichment Activities—Students will have additional activities or labs to help them further understand the content. These activities can be used in place of a missing assignment or can be added on to their unit test for extra credit.
- Review Games—There are a variety of Web sites posted on Blackboard that can help the student review for an exam, for a quiz, or even for Standards of Learning exams. No credit will be given, but the games will help the student further learn the material required.
- After-School Help—The teacher provides one-on-one instruction or students are tutored by a peer after school.

Alternative Visual Research Proposal

My students have found it beneficial not only to write but also to create a visual representation of their research proposal. Engaging in arts-based projects like this one allows you, as one student wrote, "to show a hidden side of data, because it is gathered, in a sense, from the 'dark side of the moon'" (Adams-Legge, 2006). This is similar to what Weber and Mitchell (2004) assert about the "ineffable" nature of arts-based self-study: "Arts-based methods of inquiry can help us access those elusive hard-to-put-into-words aspects of our practitioner knowledge that might otherwise remain hidden, even from ourselves" (p. 984).

Maxwell (2005) asserts that research proposals are in essence an argument that should cohere to its various components and be coherent to others. If we consider that a clear and coherent research proposal is a foundation for executing a quality research project or that, as Maxwell states, it should "hang together as an integrated whole" (p. 119), then art projects are tools to support that, literally and figuratively. I have found that students often struggle with where and how to begin writing about their ideas. Many have writer's block. The art-based self-study projects offer students an opportunity to visualize, conceptualize, and express their ideas in a nontraditional format. I have observed that the projects energize and propel students' work forward, allowing them to capture their thoughts in a format that the written word might miss. Creating a visual research proposal gives them agency as the composers and designers of their research and a concrete object that they can share with critical friends for feedback.

6.5 Student Example: Visual Research Proposal With Narrative

Deanna Breslin (2006), *Research Analyst*

I made an oil painting of a kaleidoscope (see Photo 6.2). It was a depiction of my collaborative experiences at work and school. This assignment helped me start conceptualizing my project on a deeper level, which helped ground the topic as well as give me a place to grow from as I continued to learn about self-study. I thought about my self-study project, my beliefs about collaboration, and my past experience with coworkers and classmates to make connections. The strongest connection I found was the blending that occurs between the two parts of my life—hence the colorful, well-blended painting. [This student's research project was later titled "Exploring Collaboration Through Self-Study in a Research Firm" (2006).]

Photo 6.2 Visual Research Proposal With Narrative

A Hallway Passing Statement

Now, after reflecting on and discussing your rationale and proposal with your critical friend, see if you can write a concise and articulate statement of your research project. Your compelling statement is a crisp, clear, and brief account of what you want to study, why you want to study it, and how you propose to go about studying it. And here's a tip to throwing out all the extra words you do not need: Imagine you are sharing your rationale with a colleague in the time you would have in passing and chatting with a teacher colleague in between classes—about half a minute! So next time you pass a colleague at school, share your hallway passing statement. Keep trying until you don't run out of time and your colleague tells you he or she understands what you are researching.

✍ **6.6 Student Example: Hallway Passing Statement**

Jennifer A. M. O'Looney (2006), *School Counselor*

My self-study is an attempt to examine my perspectives about the use of an assessment method called Response to-Intervention (RTI) as information for special education eligibility for students with learning disabilities and the shift in practice it might create.

5. Frame your question within literature.

Keep Digging!

Like those young children I mentioned in the beginning of this textbook who loved to play and dig in to learn, your literature review is a place to keep digging to better understand your research. A literature review entails a comprehensive review of the literature related to your topic with relevance to your research design, theoretical support, and questions, populations, or ideas that need further exploration and study. Looking through the literature enables you to situate your research in a broad field of the literature while also helping you refine your question and explore possible strategies already researched within that field. Once you have an idea of your research question, you can begin your review of the literature. Be sure to create some type of indexing method early on so you can keep track and make sense of the mass of literature available.

What Does a Literature Review Offer You?

1. A literature review allows you to understand your question placed in a broad field of knowledge examining journal articles, books, computer databases, documents, groups, organizations, and other sources related to your research topic. You may also include personal communications with those you interview about the topic.

2. A literature review offers you an opportunity to examine and evaluate what others have discovered about your topic, what strategies they have tried, and what findings resulted from their work. The literature review is "not a summary of various studies, but rather an integration of reviewed sources around particular trends and themes" (Glesne, 2006, p. 26).

3. A literature review gives you ideas about strategies you might employ. Make note of any research support you find through your review of the literature that supports your ideas for strategies. Stay organized. Chart or outline what studies have "relevancy, credibility, and similarity" to your research topic (Hendricks, 2006, p. 49).

4. A literature review is an ongoing process that you can use to continuously inform your topic and research (Glesne, 1999). Bogdan and Biklen (2007) propose that "after you have been in the field for a while, going through the substantive

literature in the area you are studying will enhance analysis" (p. 169). Keep reading and developing your literature review.

5. A literature review enables you to locate and build theories that connect to your research and thinking about your goals and strategies. Take notes and organize information gained on the theoretical tenets that inform your topic and enactment. Look for ways in which theory connects to the practices you have planned.

6. A literature review provides a wide range of information from different sources. For example, there is a difference between an article that is scholarly and one that is popular. You will want to be sure to include scholarly articles in your literature and popular ones if they are also useful. Scholarly journals report on original research or experimentation. They are substantial in content and sophistication of study and resources and are peer reviewed, whereas articles from popular journals are generally written to inform the general public, are shorter in length, and are not evaluated by experts in the field (see http://library.gmu.edu/mudge/Dox/scholarlypop.html for more information on scholarly articles).

> Interestingly enough, my professor from last semester is an expert in male adolescent reading. I sent an e-mail to him this evening asking for resources, tips, and so on. I'm very interested to hear back from him! I have found a ton of literature, and I'm almost overwhelmed by it. I have also found a social networking Web site to store and annotate links I find on my topic. It is starting to help me keep track of the things I am finding, and my notes help me when I go back and attempt to remember why they were important! I'm also planning on setting up an RSS (Rich Site Summary) feed, to see if there are other educators out there struggling with male adolescent readers. I have recently discovered an entire online community battling the same daily obstacles in their own classrooms. It is refreshing.
>
> —Patricia Demitry (2009), *English Teacher*

Using and Organizing Your Internet-Based Searches

If you are unfamiliar with the latest search engines, databases, and tips for searching library research databases and how to use them, I suggest that you contact a librarian to learn about them. Trust me. It will be worth your time. I have learned a great deal about the constantly changing world of library resources from marvelous librarians. You may decide to use a bibliographic management program such as Endnote (http://www.endnote.com/), RefWorks (http://www.refworks.com), or Zotero (http://www.zotero.org/) to help you organize and store your searches along the way and to help you manage, sort, and have easy access to citations that you will include in your reference section.

You may be tempted to conduct Internet-based searches through sites such as these:

Google (www.google.com)

Yahoo! (www.yahoo.com)

HotBot (www.hotbot.com)

KartOO (www.KARTOO.com)

Clusty (http://clusty.com)

However, computer databases such as ERIC, Education Full Text (by Wilson), ProQuest Research Library, and PsycINFO; search platforms such as ProQuest or EBSCO; and e-journal collections such as JSTOR are much more useful and sophisticated because they take you directly to journals and articles and the articles are indexed by subject, author, article type, and so on. A comprehensive computerized database platform, such as EBSCO, has features that allow you to search across multiple databases and store your searches in an online folder.

Most often, databases are accessible from a university library or school professional development library Webpage that requires that you log in with a password. You can check if computer databases can be accessed from off campus and which journals have been subscribed to and are available online. Many libraries add additional features to the databases that allow you to link to the full text of a journal article if it is available in this format through another source. Libraries give this feature different names, so check with your librarian to see if this is available. You can also look up journal subscriptions in the library catalogue or through a separate e-journal directory.

A teacher working in an after-school mathematics program presented the findings he had carefully organized and sorted during his literature review. Design an indexing method that works for you. Darwin used EBSCO's feature of storing articles he found and then created a summary sheet.

6.7 Student Example: Organizing Internet Searches

Darwin Kiel (2009), *Mathematics Teacher*

Effective Interventions for Low-Achieving Students

Griffin (2007) contends that effective interventions will (a) support students' full mathematical development, and not just a limited set of skills; (b) employ a developmentally sensitive curriculum; and (c) leverage inquiry-based approaches to learning. The literature presents numerous strategies that are effective for teaching students with difficulties in mathematics. Each of these practices accommodates the student characteristics described above:

☐ Start at students' level of understanding and teach concepts in the order naturally acquired (Griffin, 2007).

(Continued)

(Continued)

❏ Feature real quantities in authentic contexts that are meaningful to students (Allsopp, Lovin, Green, & Savage-Davis, 2003; Baker, Gersten, & Lee, 2002; Griffin, 2007; Woodward & Brown, 2006).

❏ Ensure that the sequence of instruction moves from the concrete, to the representational, to the abstract; make extensive use of manipulatives and visual models (Allsopp et al., 2003; Baker et al., 2002; Gersten & Clarke, 2007a, 2007b; Griffin, 2007; Woodward & Brown, 2006).

❏ Give students opportunities to use oral language to describe their mathematical understandings; use think-aloud strategies to encourage students to verbalize their thinking (Allsopp et al., 2003; Gersten & Clarke, 2007a, 2007b; Griffin, 2007).

❏ Employ systematic and explicit instruction to demonstrate procedures and to show connections between topical areas (Baker et al., 2002; Gersten & Clarke, 2007a; Woodward & Brown, 2006).

❏ Allow students to use natural strategies, but expose them to other problem-solving approaches; directly model both general problem-solving strategies and specific learning strategies using multisensory techniques (Allsopp et al., 2003; Baker et al., 2002; Griffin, 2007).

❏ Provide multiple and distributed practice opportunities to use mathematical knowledge and build proficiency (Allsopp et al., 2003; Baker et al., 2002; Gersten & Clarke, 2007b; Woodward & Brown, 2006).

❏ Utilize structured, peer-assisted learning activities to provide feedback and support (Baker et al., 2002; Gersten & Clarke, 2007a).

❏ Continually monitor students' performance and offer meaningful feedback (Allsopp et al., 2003; Baker et al., 2002; Gersten & Clarke, 2007a).

❏ Offer feedback to parents of low achievers; be specific, objective, and honest; report successes or progressions rather than failures or difficulties (Baker et al., 2002).

Bookmarking links to your discipline's professional organization and the resources it offers is another useful tool. Also search the Web sites of teacher professional organizations that publish journals and have online resources. For example:

Association for Childhood Education International (http://www.acei.org/)

National Association for the Education of Young Children (http://www.naeyc.org/)

National Council for the Social Studies (http://www.ncss.org/)

National Council of Teachers of English (http://www.ncte.org/)

National Council of Teachers of Mathematics (http://www.nctm.org/)

National Science Teachers Association (http://www.nsta.org/)

What Am I Looking for When I Conduct a Literature Review?

You may locate studies that are directly or indirectly related to your topic. It is useful to first skim resources to see if they are relevant to your study, to search using different keywords, and then to read sources that inform your work while making a list of topics and sources (Hendricks, 2006).

6.1   Advice From a Self-Study Scholar
Create a Concept Map

I recommend to peers that if you insert your research question in your header notes of your literature review, it will remind you to stay focused and not get too far off track in the wonderful field of literature treasures you may discover. Also helpful is to explore the references in articles that connect to your research. Creating a concept map of the big ideas and topics allows you to reflect on the bodies of literature that inform your work and how you employ those bodies of literature to conceptually map your research.

Jennifer R. McMurrer
Doctoral Candidate, George Mason University

Figure 6.2 (p. 132) shows Jennifer's concept map used for one of her self-study research projects. Notice how her literature review is connected to her research question: How can I improve my practice as a member of the team and contribute more effective and innovative methods to evaluate state student achievement data to better analyze the achievement gap?

These suggested prompts will be helpful to you as you read through the literature:

- What are the big ideas or concepts that jump out at you while you read through the literature?
- What have others found about this topic?
- What suggestions for future research do others offer that may be useful to your study?
- What key concerns have been studied?
- In what ways do others' findings have any bearing on your setting?
- How are the studies similar and/or dissimilar to yours?
- What has not been studied and seems to be missing in the literature?
- What theoretical lenses have others applied to the problem?
- What theories are useful to your question and ideas for pedagogical strategies?
- Do others cite specific theorists who help inform their work?
- What particular theories help inform your work?
- How do the insights of others help you reframe and refine your question?
- What common themes do you find across the research?
- If you created a concept map, what topics would be in your bubbles or bins?

Figure 6.2   Research Concept Map

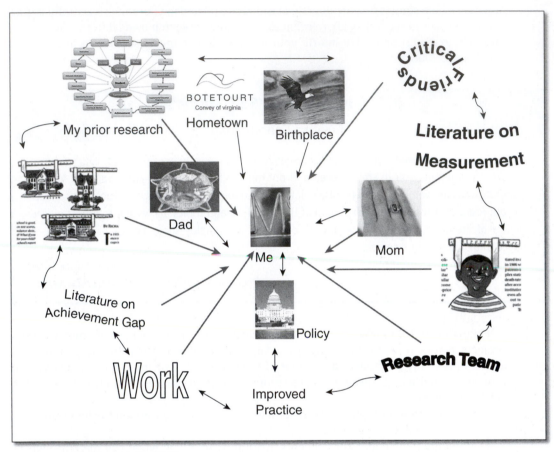

Source: From McMurrer, J. M. (2009).

Literature reviews inform your topic and pedagogical strategies. One of my students was interested in studying using blogs to enhance students' motivation in her science teaching. She was concerned that students were not critically reading what they found online about science. In her literature review, Katie found articles that made her rethink the problem. She wrote, "One theme I continually saw during my literature review was that literacy across different media was important to the development of student understanding and critical for our students in order to function in the world today" (Brown, 2008). She pondered, "Maybe students were not able to decipher valid research through the Internet because they lacked adequate literacy skills" (Brown, 2008). Further reading made her question if her students thought science was relevant to their lives. What is important to notice is how she integrates what she finds and how it informs her study. She does not just list the research she found in a list or book report form.

✎ 6.8 Student Examples: Literature Review Excerpts

Kathleen M. Brown, *Science Teacher*

Using a class blog of relevant science current events, I sought to meet "the challenge [of] making schools and classrooms, as much as possible, into 'worldly,' socially meaningful and relevant places" (Durrant & Green, 2000, p. 89). It seems clear to me now, having concluded my research project, that the conclusion of Turney (1996) is truer than I would have liked to admit. According to his study of how people interact with scientific information and integrate it into their lives, he discovered that "most people see the bulk of scientific knowledge as simply irrelevant to their needs and interests, and they are probably right" (Turney, 1996, p. 1087). I found Turney's conclusions about how the public uses scientific information to be very useful in self-reflection of my teaching practice. I am a bio mathematician by training, and my natural approach to and comfort level dealing with science concepts is not going to be similar to the approach most students or their parents naturally take. This supports my understanding of literature that science concepts must be made relevant to students if we are to expect to have any future scientists produced from our educational system.

Jennifer Soehnlin (2008), *English Teacher*

Fisher and Frey (2004) note that young children learn word meanings by having conversations with people, especially adults. During the conversations, they hear new words repeated several times. These oral language experiences help them learn how words are used and their meanings. It was this that made me want to see if modeling our vocabulary words would help the students use the words themselves. It seemed like Fisher and Fry (2004) and Allen (1999) focused on using new words in their vocabularies to teach students, but I hoped that by repeatedly using our vocabulary words in different contexts it would help the students incorporate them into their own vocabularies. I worked to teach fewer words well, teaching five words a week and adding our new words to the previous words we had already studied. I believed what the research was saying was true, that by modeling our vocabulary words over and over my students would begin to include them in their own vocabularies. I shared these researchers' enthusiasm with my students.

Over time, you will find the big ideas in the literature and how they connect and relate to each other and to your study. Unpack and keep condensing what the literature tells you as if you are unpeeling it to get at its core and then sorting it in bins. Begin to sketch out a conceptual mapping of the big ideas and domains you read about (see Critical Friend Inquiry 6.4). You will be able to gradually create your **conceptual framework**, which is an integrated mapping of the theories and phenomena that frame and shape your study and are informed by the literature reviewed.

Literature reviews are invaluable for generating ideas for your own pedagogies. Watch how Jennifer grabs ideas and adapts them into her practice. She also personalizes them as she weaves her thinking aloud with the literature. That is one style that worked well for her.

CRITICAL FRIEND INQUIRY 6.4

Mapping a Literature Review

With your critical friend discuss the following:

- What kinds of articles are you finding most useful?
- Where have you located your information?
- How are you organizing and keeping track of what you find (e.g., color-coded files, charts, matrixes, tables)?
- Have you explored storing them electronically?
- Have you backed up your files? Please no excuses that "the dog ate my homework" in this technological age.
- Are you typing your reference sheet as you go along? It is very important that you create a file on your computer or investigate if you have access to a computer program that stores and easily retrieves references (e.g., Endnote, Zotero).
- Have you been able to find commonalities across the articles and chapters you read?
- How do the findings from the articles and chapters inform your pedagogies and strategies?
- What theories do you find useful to your study?
- What are your big ideas (the bins and bubbles) in your conceptual framework/map? You might design a visual display using a computer tool insert function to create shapes, lines, and text boxes. You might also check if you have access to a computer program that allows you to visually organize and sort your thinking about the literature you find and how it fits into your research (e.g., http://www.inspiration.com/Inspiration).

6. Align your question with a self-study method.

Aligning your inquiry with a self-study method will give you an opportunity to maximize your exploration through a useful research lens or method. You might recall that in Chapter 5, you were introduced to various self-study methods. You might also remember that it was recommended that a developmental portfolio self-study method would align with a semester-long research project. You may, however, decide to explore using another self-study method that appeals to your learning style and that would help you explore your question.

The method you choose depends on what you are trying to understand and how a particular method helps you achieve that understanding. There is not a single method or a "right" method (Loughran, 2004). Recall that it is important to consider the self-study method that best aligns with your research purposes and how that method allows you to present your work to others. It might help you to look at Amy's research design planner to get an understanding of how her research question aligns with the developmental portfolio self-study research method.

6.9 Student Example: Aligning Research Question With Method

Amy Smith, *Middle School Science Teacher*

Research Question	Self-Study Method	Context	Participants	Data Sources	Implications: So What?
How can I create an active student learning environment in a team-taught science classroom? (Smith, 2008)	*Development Portfolio Self-Study Method*	Seventh-grade science classroom	Teacher, students, and coteacher	Presurvey; daily researcher log; student response to strategies; surveys; feedback from coteacher; videotapes of teaching; lesson plans; postsurveys	Improved teaching for students' interactive science learning; working with school colleagues to better integrate technology with real-life applications; effectively moving away from "cookbook" labs

You might create a table to help you see the components of your research design and check if the self-study method you chose works to answer your questions. Be ready to explain how the data you collect will help you answer your questions and why the self-study method you chose aligns with your research questions. Share your chart with your critical friend.

Your Research Design Planner

Research Question	Self-Study Method	Context	Participants	Data Sources	Implications: So What?

Note: It is highly recommended that you look ahead to the questions listed in Critical Friend Inquiry 11.2, *Dialogic Validity*, now as you are designing your study. Likewise, reviewing the questions posed in Critical Friend Inquiry 11.3, *Self-Assessment and Critical Friend Assessment of Five Foci*, will be very useful so you know what quality self-study research entails. Having a strong design will give you the foundation for enacting and later assessing the quality of your research project.

7. Plan purposeful pedagogies.

Make Your Inquiry Manageable

It is important to choose a manageable and purposeful inquiry given the time you have to work on it (e.g., a semester or yearlong project). Do not be tempted to just choose something to get it done. Choose an inquiry that matters to you and your students. Teaching is a time-demanding and time-consuming profession. Therefore, it is recommended that you focus on improving just one aspect of your teaching. Yes! Teachers do have a life outside of school and research. This will make your research project more manageable. You will feel a greater sense of accomplishment and be encouraged to go on to further needed changes (Samaras et al., 2006).

Kathleen shifted her original research question to make her project more manageable. Initially, she posed a very broad research question and didn't know where to go with it. She asked, "How can I ignite an inquisitiveness and appreciation of scientific inquiry in students?" Realizing she only had a semester and wanted to make an impact, she decided to narrow her focus by asking instead, "How can I ignite an inquisitiveness and appreciation of scientific inquiry in students by using a blog in my high school biology class?"

While planning for a manageable inquiry, this is a good time to brainstorm what activities and pedagogical strategies you might enact and what data those activities might yield. What student data do you have readily available that would be useful for your inquiry? We'll discuss data collecting in Chapter 9. Your activities and data collection have to be manageable. The initial strategies may change as you learn more about your question, and that's fine. Students also seem relieved when I explain to them that they do not have to have a final answer when their projects are completed. Nor do they have to look good. Talking about things that did not go as expected always gains them extra credit. After all, teaching and learning are lifelong and a continuous and intertwined process. Learning what may not work is also progress.

6.2 Advice From a Self-Study Scholar

Be Practical

The friction between personal involvement in the research theme, on the one hand, and the need to study this theme objectively, on the other hand, can be a complex one. Finding a balance between a perfect solution of this friction on the one hand and your possibilities (such as time, knowledge, and experience) on the other hand asks for a practical approach. Start your self-study by thinking about using data that are already available or easy to collect. Student portfolios and student evaluations are interesting data sources. Lessons can be videotaped. Do you use concept mapping or instruments like "The Wall" or "Pedagogical Analysis Schemes" in your lessons to structure students' thinking and experiences? These pedagogical instruments can also function as rich data sources.

Mieke L. Lunenberg, Fred A. J. Korthagen, and Rosanne Cathelijne Zwart
Vrije Universiteit, Amsterdam, The Netherlands

Use the Literature to Inform Pedagogies

Brainstorm potential pedagogical strategies generated from your noticing. Describe what teaching and learning strategies you plan to enact at this point in your classroom in order to address your research problem and question. Give a rationale for why you believe these strategies will be helpful for the issue you are studying and for teaching and learning in general. Again, these initial strategies are not "set in stone" and may change as you learn more about your problem.

You may find it helpful to organize your proposed strategies in chart form with data from your noticing. Incorporate any theoretical research evidence that supports the solution strategies you are proposing. Teacher educators at Victoria University in Melbourne, Australia, designed a semistructured protocol where students are asked to describe the situation, explain or interpret the situation, generate a personal theory about the practice, and propose strategies to change practice and improve the well-being of students and the community (Cherednichenko, Gay, Hooley, Kruger, & Mulraney, 1998). Regardless of how you decide to chart your plan, it is critical to reflect on the impact of your planned pedagogies before enacting them.

Notice how Amy charted and explained her plan and used the literature she found to support her strategies.

6.10 Student Example: Using Literature to Inform Pedagogies

Amy Smith (2008), *Middle School Science Teacher*

Plan of Action

Solution Strategy	Outcome	Research Supported	Considering Implementation
Computer-assisted technology	Students live in the technology age, and I want to see if they grasp science better by manipulating their learning with computers.	Yes (Bilgisayarh & Egitim ve Erisi, 2007; Tosun, Sucsuz, & Yigit, 2006)	Definitely. I haven't done any computer simulations or games, and I think it would be beneficial.
Interactive notebook	I want to bring a creative side to science and have the students learn the material while making it their own.	Yes (Associated Content, 2008; Stencel, 1998)	Already implementing on a daily basis; however, I don't think they understand the purpose or quality driven behind it.
Group work	Lab groups of four and partner work.	Yes (Pell, Galton, Steward, Page, & Hargreaves, 2007)	I already do, but I want the students to work cooperatively and efficiently.

(Continued)

(Continued)

Solution Strategy	Outcome	Research Supported	Considering Implementation
Hands-on activities	Using lab experiments to learn important science concepts.	Yes (Ginn, 2008; Haury & Rillero, 1994)	I already incorporate hands-on learning in my classroom, but I want to incorporate more.
Using food activities to reinforce	I find the students like food and that in turn causes them to like learning about the science concept.	No	I am trying to be creative and include enrichment labs to reinforce science concepts.

Reflect

What personal beliefs, values, and theories do you hold that shape your thinking about the issue and pedagogies you have planned? Consider your rationale for each strategy and the possible positive and negative consequences of enacting the strategies you are planning. Reflect on the implications of your pedagogical strategies for your students, your school, and the community. Incorporate any theoretical research evidence that supports the solution strategies you are proposing. These initial strategies are not "set in stone" and may change as you learn more about your question. Revisit your chart when you enact your study.

Deliberate the effects of your choices on students from an ethic of caring about them (Noddings, 1984). Reflect on the implications of your pedagogical strategies for students, teachers, your school, and the community (Ciriello, Valli, & Taylor, 1992). Consider not only how you will enact a change on a technical level (i.e., what you plan to do). Also consider the impact of your pedagogies on an interpretative level, or what that change might mean for your students. Equally valuable, consider your pedagogies on a critical level, or what ought to be in terms of what ethically and equitably should be occurring in your teaching and your students' learning experiences (van Manen, 1977). Ask yourself in what ways your action contributes to your commitment to social justice. Assess your plans in terms of the short-term and long-term consequences. Reflect on how your actions improve students' learning and well-being. Afterward, share your thinking aloud with your critical friend or critical friend team.

Be Ethical

It is essential that you plan for protecting your students by assessing the ethics of your pedagogical strategies, data collecting, and data reporting. Before proceeding with enacting your proposal, it is imperative that you read Chapter 7 on protecting your students. Walk through the critical friend inquiry at the end of that chapter. Although you might feel that your study will not harm your students in any way, the guiding questions presented will help ensure that.

KEY IDEAS

- A strong design and research proposal will serve you well in enacting and analyzing your study.
- Quality research involves a continuous looking back and revisiting of your assumptions and understandings. Ultimately, you are working to understand, uncover, and reframe your practice.
- *Before you enact your study,* plan for seven key design components:

  1. Author your research question.

  2. Establish your critical friend team.

  3. Observe your classroom.

  4. Articulate rationale and proposal.

  5. Frame your question within literature.

  6. Align your question with self-study method.

  7. Plan your pedagogies.

7

Protect

I began to wonder what makes someone a "good teacher." So I asked my sixth-grade students. "Assuming that I am a good teacher," I paused, "what is it that makes me a good teacher?" One boy spoke up and said, "Mrs. Wilcox, let me tell you the one thing that you do that makes you a great teacher." He paused for a moment and then pointed his finger at me and said, "You listen. I mean you really listen to what we have to say; lots of other teachers don't."

—Dawn Renee Wilcox (2006), *Science Coordinator,*
Spotsylvania County Public Schools, Virginia

CHAPTER DESCRIPTION

In this chapter, you are asked to consider what it means to be an ethical teacher researcher. A discussion about a code of research ethics and the role of professional educational organizations in developing ethical standards is presented. You will find key ethical issues essential to review in your research design: informed consent, deception, privacy and confidentiality, and accuracy. Since each research project is unique, you have the responsibility and obligation to check your research with your school division human subjects review committee and/or a university institutional review board to determine if you are acting according to ethical standards and federal requirements in protecting your participants. Included in this chapter is a critical friend inquiry to guide you toward assessing the ethics of your research. These guidelines and discussion are raised for you to carefully consider your research design and each of your research decisions.

◆ Reading this chapter will provide an opportunity for you to acquire a set of ethical research standards to carefully review with your critical friend before you launch your research project.

I recall hearing about a teacher who, studying her role in teaching about social justice, planned a strategy to impact students' understanding of the deplorable conditions of slave trade and travel. The teacher's idea was to ask students to imagine themselves as slaves and then direct them to crowd themselves into a small classroom supply closet where they would remain for a significant period of time until allowed to be released. Fortunately, the strategy was first shared with a professor and a critical friend and not enacted. It is important to think about human subjects' protection in a broad sense, psychologically, physically, and emotionally. The best laid plans and the best intentions do not always turn out as expected. As teachers we all want to meet our objectives, but never at the cost of harming others.

QUESTIONING THE ETHICS OF YOUR STUDY

Teachers and researchers can impact their students' lives both positively and negatively through their daily actions; really listening and caring about students as stated in the opening quote reminds us of the daily influence we have as teachers. That is all the more reason for standards for research ethics. It is easy to understand how standards for research ethics and proposal review came about when you think about what has gone horrifically astray in the name of research.

We have only to consider the Nuremberg war crimes, the atomic bomb, the Tuskegee syphilis study, and the Milgram shock experiments to appreciate the necessity for a code of ethics in research (Glesne, 2006). Sometimes, it is difficult to know the ramifications of your research. The one thing you can do is inform and discuss your research plan with your school administration.

Pause here and consider the ethics of your research project. Before you enact your study, ask yourself the general questions listed below as you think about possible dilemmas inherent in your research design. Since each research project is unique, the answers are not always clear cut. The key point is to deliberate about the ethical concerns your study may pose; to discuss them with and present them to critical friends, professors, school administrators, and review committees; and then to rework your research design as necessary.

Do I tell my students that I am conducting classroom research?	Yes, because No, because Not sure
Do I tell my students exactly what I am researching?	Yes, because No, because Not sure

(Continued)

(Continued)

Can I protect all of the participants' anonymity?	Yes, because No, because Not sure
Would colleagues question the ethics of my research?	Yes, because No, because Not sure
Do any of my pedagogical strategies cause harm to others?	Yes, because No, because Not sure
Can I enact my study in a manner that is equitable to all students and doesn't privilege some students over others?	Yes, because No, because Not sure
Have I considered how I will respect my students and their privacy?	Yes, because No, because Not sure
Will I need to receive permissions to access certain data?	Yes, because No, because Not sure
Should I be accessing the data I plan to collect?	Yes, because No, because Not sure
Can the reporting of my results release any sensitive information about students, families, teachers, the school, or the community?	Yes, because No, because Not sure
Will this study benefit my students and school and, if so, at what cost?	Yes, because No, because Not sure

There are many questions that begin to flood your thinking when you stop to question the complexities of research ethics related to your work. Yet your careful planning is crucial to protecting and respecting your students before you enact any pedagogical strategies, collect data, and/or report data. At the end of this chapter you will find Critical Friend Inquiry 7.1, *The Ethical Self-Study Teacher Researcher*, designed to guide your review about ethics in your research.

7.1 Advice From a Self-Study Scholar
Recognize Your Biases

As a counselor, I have been taught to know myself first; if I do not know my own biases, beliefs, stereotypes, hopes, and values, I will never be able to recognize when they are influencing my actions in life, especially my actions with a client. Using self-study, then, to become aware of your beliefs, values, and biases hopefully will give you a clearer picture, a stronger foundation, and a more open mind to begin to ask your questions.

Jeanmarie Infranco (2007)
Doctoral Candidate, George Mason University

SCHOOL DIVISION REVIEW

As a practicing teacher, your review will likely originate at your school division level. Before conducting any research, you must acquire the necessary permission from your school and district leadership. Any teacher research project, including one using self-study, requires a full transparency of your project with your school administration. If you are also affiliated with a university, then you will need to contact it as well (see the section on institutional review boards below).

As a teacher, any time you are using data generated by students other than for instruction such as for completing course studies, you need to gain permission from your school. The reporting of data about a school population or district, even when anonymous, becomes an issue of privacy. School divisions and research offices of school divisions may have a written agreement and a protocol that universities and colleges must complete and comply with for any research conducted in their schools (e.g., a written description of any research projects that are conducted in their schools as a part of course work and copies of projects and findings). A review measure some school divisions use is to hold all universities and teacher education programs to the same set of consistent standards with proposals reviewed by their office of researchers. School divisions also have the opportunity to benefit from the research conducted especially for projects that are mutually of interest.

In the student example below, notice (a) the transparency of the student's discussing her project and rationale with the principal, (b) her documentation of the process of having her project approved, and (c) the communication and consent letter she sent to families for their permission.

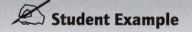 **Student Example**

Annemarie Ratke (2007), *Elementary School Teacher*

Process

In order to begin this self-study I needed to obtain permission from my principal. I informed him that my project would entail the implementation of a specialized unit of instruction based on Hawai'i

(Continued)

(Continued)

content standards but centered on the philosophy of inclusion. I conveyed to him my struggles with being able to reach all my students and suggested that this would aid me in engaging all learners through the general education curriculum. I reported to him that I would acquire parent and guardian permission to videotape my students prior to the start of the unit. Once I gained his approval I then approached the parents and guardians of my students.

In September 2006, I spoke to the guardians of my students during parent-teacher conferences. I explained to them the philosophy of inclusion and how I had hoped to implement it into our classroom with support of specific strategies in order to meet all learners' needs. The feedback I received from the parents and guardians was overwhelmingly positive. Each was supportive and enthusiastic about the project. Once I gathered parents' consent signatures to videotape their student for educational purposes, I was able to move forward.

Below is the consent letter that Annemarie sent to families and that she included in her project appendix.

September 14, 2006

Aloha Parents and Guardians!

It was so nice to see many of you at parent teacher conferences this past week. I enjoyed meeting with you and celebrating your child's success thus far this school year.

As was mentioned in our meeting, I would like to formally ask for your permission to videotape your child in our classroom for educational purposes only. I am currently enrolled in a cohort of classes focused on the philosophy of inclusive education at the University of Hawai'i. Inclusion is a way of teaching all children, general education and special education students, together. Inclusive education embraces all learners and their specific academic needs in the general education curriculum. Throughout my studies, I have learned research-based practices that, once implemented, will aid in the academic successes of our children. With the permission of our principal, I have designed a literacy unit of instruction that I hope to apply to our classroom this fall and winter. I would like to videotape the unit in order to reflect on the application of inclusive practices within our classroom. The video will only be used to inform others of the promise inclusive education holds for our students.

If you are not comfortable with having your child videotaped please feel free to let me know. Your student will still take part in all lessons and activities; we will just make sure not to film his or her face.

Again, let me say that it is a pleasure to be working with you and your child this year. Thank you for taking time to fill this form out.

Mahalo!
Mrs. Annie Ratke

STANDARDS OF RESEARCH ETHICS

Ethical Responsibility to Know

As a teacher researcher, you will need to develop an awareness of your ethical responsibility about how to gain information with regard to human dignity, individuals' lives, and their psychological and physical well-being. When I was completing my master's degree in human growth and development, I learned a powerful statement that still centers my thinking about the core of research ethics: "Every person is unique and worthy of respect." That seemingly simple sentence reminds us of our responsibilities and obligations to others as teacher researchers. This principle of respect for the worth and dignity of the lives and cultures of all people is a very serious matter. As professionals and in our continuous efforts to improve our practice, it is our obligation and responsibility to ensure that, in the process of researching, we do not bring harm to others—to students, families, colleagues, or the school community.

Furthermore, it is our responsibility to pay attention to the legal aspects of our misinformed or misguided behavior when conducting research (Manos, 2006). School divisions and universities expect their students to know and honor professional ethical standards. For example, at George Mason University, students are expected to practice the professional ethical standards that encompass their work as researchers and according to principles of fairness, honesty, integrity, trustworthiness, confidentiality, and respect for colleagues and students both within the university classroom and in their teaching classroom (see http://cehd.gmu.edu/teacher/professional-disposition/).

Ethical Responsibility to Protect and Respect

As we focus our lens on self-study teacher research proposals, one of the key concepts of research ethics is protection. Some would even argue that in teacher research the "researchers are obligated to respect 'research subjects,' and not just protect them" (Lee & van den Berg, 2003, p. 99). In teacher research, one is both the researcher and the practitioner making decisions that can impact others. Mitchell (2004) presents the argument that teaching naturally involves making efforts to improve students' learning through modifications in the teachers' instruction; "they are merely doing a study of what is/is not occurring in their classroom" (p. 1439). That is, as a part of teachers' daily lives, they intervene, collect data, and make needed changes, and "the great majority of teacher research projects involve little or no risk to students" (p. 1438). Nonetheless, Mitchell also insists that "researchers need to be able to demonstrate that they are aware of these obligations, of the sorts of unpredictable outcomes that they may face, the possible ethical implications of these and how they will deal with them" (pp. 1438–1439).

Careful consideration of ethics related to pedagogical strategies, data collection, and data reporting phases of practitioner research should be conducted. Yet, "in most cases, the ethical problems and dilemmas are associated with the last of these" (Mitchell, 2004, p. 1393).

Addressing the ethics of accountability in qualitative research, van den Berg (2001) notes the difficulty in protecting participants especially through data reporting when one makes the research public. The reporting can become problematic when the information gained is controversial and yet unethical for the researcher not to include (e.g., reporting that a principal paddled students 218 times in 2 years) (Lee & van den Berg, 2003). In my own self-study of teaching research, I included participants in the research process of data interpretation (Samaras et al., 2007). In that manner, participants became "coresearchers" with a voice in the findings and with their perspectives serving to hold me as a researcher more accountable to the reported findings.

7.2 Advice From a Self-Study Scholar

Question Power, Social Justice, and Discrimination in Research Relationships

How will *critical friendships,* or variously named collegial partnerships, assist researchers to question power, social justice, and discrimination? Misuse of power, social injustice, and discrimination is culturally and systemically generated and therefore potentially embedded in the habits of educational communities and environments, including research relationships and processes. These *invisible* scripts may be either reinforced or challenged by collaborative research relationships (e.g., mutually reiterated assumptions about power and agency between students and faculty). How have researchers used collaboration with colleagues, students, and significant others to raise consciousness about hidden oppression and misuse of power? How do educators constructively transform these challenges into possibilities for growth and communal knowledge? (Adapted from Bodone, Guðjónsdóttir, & Dalmau, 2004)

Mary C. Dalmau
Victoria University, Australia

Role of Professional Organizations

Research ethics have gained a great deal of attention by professional educational organizations. The organizations have developed codes, standards, dispositions, and principles of research ethics. Manos (2006) defines a code of ethics as "a series of statements that crafts an image of a professional role. . . . It's a shared framework for professional responsibility that affirms educators' commitment to the core values of our field" (pp. 2–3). For example, professional organizations such as the National Education Association (NEA) have established a code of ethics about the necessity for a commitment to students and the profession. The preamble (see http://www.nea.org/home/30442.htm) states,

> The educator, believing in the worth and dignity of each human being, recognizes the supreme importance of the pursuit of truth, devotion to excellence, and the nurture of the democratic principles. Essential to these goals is the protection of freedom to learn and to teach and the guarantee of equal educational opportunity for all. The educator accepts the responsibility to adhere to the highest ethical standards.

Educational professional organizations at the national level (e.g., the National Council for Accreditation of Teacher Education; see NCATE, 2007) have created professional standards and dispositions to ensure that teachers are well prepared to help all children learn and that they have the knowledge and skills to do so.

The American Educational Research Association (AERA, 2004) states, "It is of paramount importance that educational researchers respect the rights, privacy, dignity, and sensitivities of their research populations and also the integrity of the institutions within which the research occurs. Educational researchers should be especially careful in working with children and other vulnerable populations."

In similar reference, the American Psychological Association (APA, 2003), outlining ethical principles for educational researchers, states, "Psychologists respect the dignity and worth of all people, and the rights of individuals to privacy, confidentiality, and self-determination." Professional ethics entail many components, and for the purposes of your research let's look at key concepts that have been addressed in standards in research ethics. One useful framework for ethical standards, which applies to teacher educators and teachers alike, was developed by the American Educational Research Association in 1992 and revised in 1996 and in 2000. Topics related to research ethics include the following:

1. Informed and voluntary

2. Confidentiality

3. Deception

4. Sensitivity to established policies and activities

5. Participant withdrawal

6. No exploitation for personal gain

7. Mindful of cultural, religious, gender, and other significant differences

8. Responsibility: mindful considerations in reporting

9. Protection: mindful of negative consequences

10. Communicate

11. Anonymity

AERA Ethical Standards

AERA (2004) lists the following guiding standards on its Web site:

II. Guiding Standards: Research Populations, Educational Institutions, and the Public

(Italics were added on key components.)

(Continued)

(Continued)

A.
Preamble.

Educational researchers conduct research within a broad array of settings and institutions, including schools, colleges, universities, hospitals, and prisons. It is of paramount importance that educational researchers respect the rights, privacy, dignity, and sensitivies of their research populations and also the integrity of the institutions within which the research occurs. Educational researchers should be especially careful in working with children and other vulnerable populations. These standards are intended to reinforce and strengthen already existing standards enforced by Institutional Review Boards and other professional associations. Standards intended to protect the rights of human subjects should not be interpreted to prohibit teacher research, action research, and/or other forms of practitioner inquiry so long as: the data are those that could be derived from normal teaching/ learning processes; confidentiality is maintained; the safety and welfare of participants are protected; informed consent is obtained when appropriate; and the use of the information obtained is primarily intended for the benefit of those receiving instruction in that setting.

B.
Standards.

1. Participants, or their guardians, in a research study have the *right to be informed* about the likely risks involved in the research and of potential consequences for participants, and to give their informed consent before participating in research. Educational researchers should communicate the aims of the investigation as well as possible to informants and participants (and their guardians), and appropriate representatives of institutions, and keep them updated about any significant changes in the research program.

2. Informants and participants normally have a *right to confidentiality*, which ensures that the source of information will not be disclosed without the express permission of the informant. This right should be respected when no clear understanding to the contrary has been reached. Researchers are responsible for taking appropriate cautions to protect the confidentiality of both participants and data to the full extent provided by law. Participants in research should be made aware of the limits on the protections that can be provided, and of the efforts toward protection that will be made even in situations where absolute confidentiality cannot be assured. It should be made clear to informants and participants that despite every effort made to preserve it, confidentiality may be compromised. Secondary researchers should respect and maintain the confidentiality established by primary researchers. In some cases, e.g., survey research, it may be appropriate for researchers to ensure participants of anonymity, i.e., that their identify is not known even to the researcher. Anonymity should not be promised to participants when only confidentiality is intended.

3. Honesty should characterize the relationship between researchers and participants and appropriate institutional representatives. *Deception* is discouraged; it should be used only when clearly necessary for scientific studies, and should then be minimized. After the study, the researcher should explain to the participants and institutional representatives the reasons for the deception.

4. Educational researchers should be *sensitive to any locally established institutional policies or guidelines for conducting research.*

5. Participants have the *right to withdraw* from the study at any time, unless otherwise constrained by their official capacities or roles.

6. Educational researchers should exercise caution to ensure that there is *no exploitation for personal gain* of research populations or of institutional settings of research. Educational researchers should not use their influence over subordinates, students, or others to compel them to participate in research.

7. Researchers have a *responsibility to be mindful of cultural, religious, gender, and other significant differences* within the research population in the planning, conduct, and reporting of their research.

8. Researchers should carefully consider and minimize the use of research techniques that might have *negative social consequences*, for example, experimental interventions that might deprive students of important parts of the standard curriculum.

9. Educational researchers should be *sensitive to the integrity of ongoing institutional activities* and alert appropriate institutional representatives of possible disturbances in such activities which may result from the conduct of the research.

10. Educational researchers should *communicate* their findings and the practical significance of their research in clear, straightforward, and appropriate language to relevant research populations, institutional representatives, and other stakeholders.

11. Informants and participants have a right to remain *anonymous*. This right should be respected when no clear understanding to the contrary has been reached. Researchers are responsible for taking appropriate precautions to protect the confidentiality of both participants and data. Those being studied should be made aware of the capacities of the various data-gathering technologies to be used in the investigation so that they can make an informed decision about their participation. It should also be made clear to informants and participants that despite every effort made to preserve it, anonymity may be compromised. Secondary researchers should respect and maintain the anonymity established by primary researchers.

According to Christians (2000), "By the 1980s, each of the major scholarly associations had adopted its own code, with an overlapping emphasis on four guidelines" (p. 138). Those four key research ethics guidelines include issues of the following:

1. Informed consent

2. Deception

3. Privacy and confidentiality

4. Accuracy

Informed Consent

One of the most important steps to take in your research is to let your students, their families, and your school administration know that you are conducting classroom research in order to improve your teaching practice and students' learning. When you explain your research purpose to students and families, it is your responsibility to let them know (a) the purpose of your research, (b) what their participation will involve, (c) that their involvement is confidential and voluntary, and (d) that you will not penalize them for not participating. They can also withdraw from the study at any time and without penalty. They each have the right to be informed about the research and any possible consequences. It is imperative that you keep in mind the well-being of your students above any research goal. Be sure to gain approval for your research from families and your school. You should also check with your university instructor or advisor who is familiar with university requirements and review boards.

You should receive a written **informed consent** form, or an agreement by the participants, parent, or legal guardian to allow you to use information collected for stated research purposes in a study before you begin conducting research. The requirement for consent in research must be from a legal guardian, and state laws differ on who can be a legal guardian. Be sure to use clear language that participants easily understand. If you plan to use any information from students' work or to quote students in your final report, you need to have that approved by participants and your school. You also need permission to access and use information in **student records**. The Family Educational Rights and Privacy Act of 1974 (FERPA or the Buckley Amendment) has regulation-specific requirements for the use of records that have to be met. Once you acquire permission, be sure to remove any identifying information on students' work if you include it in your report.

Deception

Informing your students and their families about their participation in your research is the first step in creating an honest relationship with them. Similarly, it is not ethical to deceive them and tell them the research is about something else to gain information from them. Your students have the right to know if you are recording or taping them and for what purpose. If you think that telling them the purpose of your research will sway or influence their behavior, then you might rethink your research question and reframe your research. For example, examining issues of poverty and learning would require a sophisticated level of thought and caution, and you would have a social responsibility to your students and society (Fine, Weis, Weseen, & Wong, 2000).

You are in a delicate position as both a researcher and a teacher working with students over a semester- or yearlong period of your study. This notion of **positionality** entails your position and influence within the institutional hierarchy of schooling, especially in your role as teacher of the students you are studying. The research you conduct should be carefully considered not for "issues of convenience" but for "why it has to take place in our sites or with our own students" (Anderson, Herr, & Nihlen, 2007, p. 132). You recall studying your personal inquiry in your situated practice to improve that practice. Your role inside of the inquiry is a methodological component of self-study research, that is, Focus #1: *Self-study teachers initiate their own inquiries and study them in their teaching context utilizing a self-study method aligned with that inquiry.*

Share your intentions as a lifelong learner with your students. Explain that, like students, teachers also learn by understanding what they don't know yet and want to know better. When your students see and understand that you are also a sincere and active teacher learner striving to improve your practice to help them learn better, you will likely gain their respect and involvement. Self-study teachers are vulnerable to any discoveries in their uncharted research journey. You might share that effective teachers always work to question and improve their practice. Self-study research is not something you do to others but is something you do with your students to the benefit of all. This is known as **utilitarian ethics** or that "the right course of action should be what satisfies all, or the largest number of people" (Taylor, 1982, p. 131).

Privacy and Confidentiality

As a teacher researcher you have the responsibility to protect your participants' identities and check that your data do not include any identifiable information. Also ask yourself, "Can I ensure privacy and confidentiality?" Once you decide what data you will need to answer your research question, ask yourself, "Whom do I contact for access?" (Maxwell, 2005, p. 100). Any access to students' files and other confidential information should not be given without permission from the appropriate authorities.

Be careful that you do not leave data, students' files, test scores, or other confidential records lying around on your desk and that you store confidential material in a safe and secure file. Participants' privacy and confidentiality are a part of your contract with them unless they agree otherwise. Be sure to use pseudonyms for your students, colleagues, schools, and school communities. In that way, you have taken steps to protect participants from harm through identification as much as possible. If you promise participants that their personal information will be anonymous—that is, that their identities will not be known to you—then that is exactly what needs to happen. Anonymity can be planned for in the research design by asking someone else to remove names in your data and use random numbers or codes for participants with all records carefully stored.

Accuracy

Your ethical role as a teacher researcher demands your accurate designing, noticing, collecting, reporting, analyzing, and reporting of data and results without fabrications, omissions, or alterations. Designing and fairly administering questionnaires, surveys, interviews, or any other instruments are your ethical responsibility as a researcher. Keeping accurate records that can, if necessary, be immediately available to your instructor and school is also your responsibility.

Evelyn Jacob (n.d.) encourages teacher education students to practice the cultural inquiry process as they consider the possible cultural influences of what they are noticing and their wonderments about their practice. Teachers are prompted to consider mismatches between school and class curriculum and students' experiences, meanings, and cultural negotiations. As in self-study research, teachers are encouraged to examine the beliefs, values, and interactional patterns they bring to the issue and to its resolve. Consider the questions Jacob designed located in the online Self-Study Resource Center, which will be useful to assess your interpretation of your classroom situation.

Teacher research is not a game that you play with people's lives. It is not conducted to make your study turn out in a way that makes you look successful. I explain to my students that they will not receive a lower grade if their pedagogical strategies do not lead them to their hoped-for results. They always smile when I tell them that they will receive extra credit if they share their mistakes and what they learned from them. Research is a process of discovery, and because there are discoveries, we cannot know their outcomes. Your data and findings, regardless of what they yield, tell an important story and should not be altered to fit what you want them to show.

You recall that another methodological component of self-study is that you dialogue about your research through collaborative inquiry—that is, Focus #2: *Self-study teachers work in an intellectually safe and supportive community to improve their practice by making it explicit to themselves and to others through critical collaborative inquiries.* It is essential that you report your data accurately and that you are honest about the accuracy of your data with your critical friends.

Critical friends are key in the process of ethical research review. Anderson et al. (2007) corroborate that critical friends can "pose challenging questions to each other or to help think through the various dilemmas" (p. 144). Robinson and Kuin Lai (2006) also suggest to "use learning conversations . . . to test your own and others' assumptions about the impact of your research on others" (p. 71).

Accuracy also includes properly crediting your colleagues and including their names only with their permission (MacLean & Mohr, 1999). Also essential is properly crediting resources you find useful in your research and literature review to avoid plagiarism. If you have any questions about copyright law, you should contact your librarian and legal departments for information to ensure that you have followed legal procedures in copying and using information.

INSTITUTIONAL REVIEW BOARDS

Most universities have procedures for conducting research through a review committee. According to Glesne (2006), by 1974 the federal government required that an **institutional**

review board (IRB) be established for any organization that receives federal funding for research involving human subjects for review of the proposed research. Aligned with many of the research standards established by professional organizations, the major principles of IRBs involve (a) participants' informed consent, (b) the right to withdraw, (c) protection from harm and risks, (d) that the benefits outweigh all potential risks, and (e) that the research is conducted by a qualified researcher who understands and abides by a research code of ethics (Glesne, 2006).

The institutional review process grew out of the work of experimental research in science and especially from the projects that brought our attention to the extent researchers would go in the name of advancing science without human regard. Zeni (2001) was inspired to write a book addressing the ethical issues of practitioners when personally encountering that the ethical issues developed for experimental research were not aligned to practitioner research. Zeni argued that practitioners faced ethical issues that "tended to be ambiguous, context-specific, and therefore resistant to generic regulations" (p. xi). Situated studies are not clear cut. Mitchell (2004) agrees: "Protocols that are well established and appropriate for bio-medical research, where the researcher is positioned as a neutral outsider, are often criticized by those involved in practitioner research as being inappropriate when applied to the insider research" (p. 1394). Asserting that the institutional review process "has an uneasy fit with qualitative research in education, especially research by insiders in schools," (p. xvi), Zeni (2001) nonetheless acknowledges that "any research involving people and social institutions must involve ethical decision making" (p. xv).

Every IRB is unique, so you must check with your review boards before you begin conducting your research. A good guiding principle, regardless of the research, is to always check with your university instructor if you are taking a course and the IRB of your school and/or university to be sure your research has met the required standards. Inquire if you need to submit your research to a human subjects review board or a committee and whether you have to complete a training module often offered online through the IRB Web site. Two important factors that indicate a review is needed include (a) that the study involves humans and (b) that you are intending to make your findings generalizable; in either case you will need to contact your IRB or the committee or school district department that monitors research in schools. The Office for Human Research Protections (OHRP) is the federal office that enforces the regulations for human subjects research. According to the OHRP, "Research means a systematic investigation, including research development, testing and evaluation, designed to develop or contribute to generalizable knowledge" (U.S. Department of Health and Human Services, 2007).

I have conducted self-study research of my own teaching practices. In self-study research, you are the main participant studying your practice, yet since it is "research" as described above, you still need to contact your IRB. In a faculty course self-study portfolio study (see the proposal abstract below), I received an expedited review process, or one that does not have to be reviewed by the full committee of the IRB. Nonetheless, the study had to be submitted for review with documented communication processes between investigators and reviewers and required informed consent from students.

Project Title: Self-Study Through a Faculty Course Portfolio of Teaching

Principal Investigator: Anastasia P. Samaras

College of Education and Human Development, Graduate School of Education, George Mason University

Abstract: This research uses existing data to report on a professor's course portfolio in a newly designed self-study qualitative methodology course for doctoral students. The professor openly conducted and evaluated a self-study of her design and teaching of the new course. Although it was not the intent to present or publish the work, the resulting data base is rich and worthy of professional sharing. This work extends from the work of Cerbin (1993) and Gipe (1998) whose work highlights the value and components of course portfolios toward improving teaching and students' learning. It also responds to Boyer's (1990) call for an expanded vision of scholarship, which includes identifying and making public new teaching discoveries, integrating a scholarship of teaching across disciplines, and applying and transforming our ways of thinking about teaching. Students come from various disciplines and professional fields inside and outside of teacher education and contribute to each other's understanding of the self-study process. The work incorporates students' informal class activities included in their critical friend portfolios developed in tandem during the semester-long course and their assessment of the professor's teaching. Students completed self-study research projects with the goal of learning and integrating the self-study methodology into their thesis, which resulted in five "developing self-study of scholarship" exemplars. This work extends self-study of practices to fields outside of teacher education to self-studyship (Samaras & Freese, 2006). The notion of learning zones (Samaras et al., 2006), adapted from Vygotsky's (1978) conception of zone of proximal development, was used to frame this research. Data were drawn from multiple sources in the professor's and students' informal self-study activities resulting in formative and summative assessment measures. Data were analyzed using a constant comparative method (Glaser & Strauss, 1967) resulting in the themes of mentorship, community building, and professional development. This paper includes a discussion of what is both useful and problematic in developing a course portfolio and the value of this research in advancing the quality of scholarship, particularly for doctoral study and education programs.

CRITICAL FRIEND INQUIRY 7.1

The Ethical Self-Study Teacher Researcher

Protecting students is so very important in teacher research. In order to find a space to think through the ethical questions about your research, you might take advantage of the opportunity to write a research memo to your critical friend of your assessment of the ethics of your study. You will find some prompts below that are aligned with the self-study methodological components you have come to know. Miles and Huberman (1994) recommend the value of

Photo 7.1   Critical Friends Review Research Ethics

this memo and state that "an occasional 'ethics issues' memo or study team meeting helps sur-face the sorts of mild worries that often prove to be a distant early warning" (p. 296).

Describe and discuss your research proposal with your critical friend. Talk specifically about your role, your participants, the planned pedagogical strategies, data collecting, and the data reporting you have planned. Collaborate with your critical friend(s) to openly discuss any-thing you are not quite sure about in terms of any possible negative impact or harm to others. Hold a thorough discussion about the ethics of your self-study proposal (see Photo 7.1).

Below are some suggested prompts for your consideration and discussion with your crit-ical friend. The prompts are framed according to the Five Foci, or the self-study method-ological components integrated throughout this text. Describe your research to your critical friend and ask yourself the following questions:

1. **Personal Situated Inquiry**
   a. Where does my research take place?
   b. What is my role in the research?

   c. Have I used my position as teacher or researcher to coalesce information and results from my students or participants?

   d. Do any ethical issues immediately present themselves to me and to my critical friend?

   e. What dilemmas does this research pose to others and myself?

   f. Am I competent and responsible in enacting this research?

2. **Critical Collaborative Inquiry**

   a. How do I plan to share the process and progress of my research with my critical friend(s)?

   b. Will the anonymity of my participants be protected during my critical friend inquiry?

   c. Have I encouraged my critical friends to offer me honest feedback about ethical issues such as my positionality in the study, the impact of my pedagogical strategies, the accuracy of my data and interpretations, and any anticipated negative effects and long-term consequences?

   d. How will I document my research process and make it available for public review and critique by my critical friends?

3. **Improved Learning**

   a. Who are my participants?

   b. What is the value of my research to my participants and others?

   c. What is the "planned for" positive impact of my study?

   d. What are the risks of my research to others?

   e. Are there any trade-offs to participants in conducting this research?

   f. Do some participants benefit more than others?

   g. Are some participants more at risk because of my research?

   h. Could my research be embarrassing to anyone?

   i. Do the planned pedagogical strategies include responsible and effective teaching and learning components that will not harm anyone?

4. **Transparent and Systematic Research Process**

   a. Have I checked with my university, school, and review boards to find out if my study needs to be reviewed? Have I shared my research proposal with my school administration?

   b. How do I plan to inform my participants? Have I explained to my participants that I am collecting data in order to improve my practice?

   c. Have I secured all needed permissions and consent forms?

   d. Can I ensure that my participants (e.g., students, colleagues, and school administrators) will not be identifiable to others?

   e. What types of data do I plan to collect?

   f. How do I plan to collect data in an accurate manner?

g. Will data on students be kept confidential, or is it possible that some data cannot be kept confidential?

h. Do I foresee any problems with enacting my planned pedagogical strategies?

i. Will my interpretations of data be harmful to any of my participants?

j. How do I plan to check for the accuracy of my interpretations?

5. **Knowledge Generation and Presentation**

a. Does my study contribute to the education field?

b. In what way does this study challenge the status quo of teaching and schooling?

c. Could others misuse my results in any way?

d. Could I misuse the results in any way?

e. Can my research yield any sensitive information? Will my reporting or interpretations of data be harmful to any of my participants or to my school?

f. Do I anticipate any long-term ethical issues regarding my study?

g. Have I acknowledged the role of my colleagues, or would that acknowledgement pose problems?

h. Have I acknowledged any sponsorship of my research through grants, course credit, or consulting?

i. Has my research undergone a review by a human subjects review board?

KEY IDEAS

- Carefully reviewing and assessing the ethics of your research is essential to protecting others.
- School divisions and universities expect their students to know, protect, and respect research participants.
- Professional organizations have established a code of ethics and research standards about the professional commitment teachers have to students, their families, and the community.
- Protecting and respecting participants is a concern, especially through data reporting when one makes the research findings public.
- The American Educational Research Association has developed a useful framework for teacher educators that is also useful to teachers in assessing ethical research standards.
- Four important principles regarding research ethics include (a) informed consent, (b) deception, (c) privacy and confidentiality, and (d) accuracy.
- Research involving humans and with the intention of making findings generalizable requires review.
- Universities and schools have procedures for conducting research through a review committee. Every school and university is unique, so you must check with the review committee at your university and school.
- Reviewing your research proposal with critical friends allows for dialogue and critique about the ethics of your research framed in the self-study methodological components.

Organize Data

I collected data during two distinct stages of this study, the research phase and the enactment phase. Multiple methods ensured I collected the data needed to best answer my question. These methods included (a) constructing and deconstructing a personal narrative, (b) analyzing five years of teaching evaluations, (c) collecting and analyzing student essays, (d) collecting and analyzing professor essays, and (e) developing artwork representative of both my problem and the outcome of my study.

—LaKesha Anderson (2009)
Doctoral Candidate, George Mason University

CHAPTER DESCRIPTION

The chapter offers guidelines for organizing and managing your data, which is essential for later data analysis and transparency of your data collection: what you collect, how you collect it, and when you collect it. A template is provided to guide you through your data collection (i.e., the data you will collect before, during, and after your study). You are also asked to consider the alignment and significance of your data to your research question and the types of data your pedagogical strategies will yield.

✦ Reading this chapter will guide you in organizing your data to make your project manageable.

I remember when I was working on my dissertation. I had collected volumes of data. Feeling overwhelmed about how to organize them all and where to begin the data analysis process, I exclaimed to my husband, "I have all these data to analyze!" Ted responded with kind support, "Yes, you have data!" My dissertation advisor, Greta G. Fein, always rejoiced when she had data and exclaimed, "I love having data!" Now, I know just what she meant. I love my data too. Researchers tend to have a slobbering love affair with their data. Choose your attitude about your data and consider how privileged you are to have data to organize and analyze.

ALIGNMENT OF DATA WITH QUESTION

You might now be saying to yourself, "I have this big research project to do, and I feel over-whelmed with it all!" You may be wondering what data to collect. On the other hand, you may have so many data that you do not know where to begin. Or you may be looking ahead and worried about how you will analyze and write about the data. One thing I tell my students is not to think about their project all at once but to just chip away at it, little by little; just keep moving!

And yet, careful and thoughtful planning in designing your research makes a difference in how easily you move forward. Be sure you are collecting data that are aligned with your research question. Before you begin to think about what data to collect, take time to revisit and reflect on your research question. What are you really trying to do? What is the main purpose of conducting your research? Patton (2002) asserts that "purpose is the controlling force in research. Decisions about design, measurement, analysis, and reporting all flow from purpose" (p. 213).

In any type of research, the question is not really "What data should I collect?" as much as it is "How will the data I collect help me answer my research question?" Related to that big question, ask yourself, "Are my data aligned with my research question and the purpose of my research?" "Is there research that I found in my literature review to support my pedagogical strategies?" and "What data will a pedagogical strategy yield that might be useful?" (See Photo 8.1.) "Good" data, in any methodology, are data that help you answer your research question.

Photo 8.1 Pedagogies Yield Data

✍️ **8.1 Student Example: Research Planner**

Patricia Demitry (2009), *English Teacher*

Notice how this English teacher uses a researcher log and a student questionnaire as data to assess the impact of one of her pedagogical strategies.

Research Question	Pedagogical Strategy	Possible Outcomes	Research Supported	Data Sources
How can I change my pedagogy to help struggling male adolescents in reading?	Increase in experimental and kinesthetic learning through drama enactment. I want to see my students up and out of their seats, engaging in the text, and actively participating.	Lessons will attempt to adjust classroom to specific male-oriented learning style. Refrain from constant lecturing, note-taking, etc. Introduce movement and energy.	Do male students comprehend reading material with greater understanding when utilizing movement and action? YES (King & Gurian, 2006)	Researcher log; student questionnaire about the activity.

Self-Study Teacher Researcher Log

The lesson I created linked the curriculum being studied, *The Catcher in the Rye*, and positive reinforcement of masculine-prone behaviors. Using video cameras, students were separated into groups and asked to perform scenes from the novel. Creating their own videos, students were responsible for turning the narrative into a script, assigning roles, staging their videos, shooting the film, and splicing the scenes. At the conclusion of the lesson, we made popcorn and viewed each group's movie. Observing my students, paying special attention to my adolescent male students, I viewed their engagement with the technology as well as the novel. Particularly interesting, the struggling male readers were flipping through the text, furiously rewriting the narrative, and laughing with their peers. This activity simultaneously created a community of learners engaged in a common goal, while leading to mastery of the content. I was anxious to survey my students at the conclusion of this activity, because my observations were extremely positive. Using the same two questions, carefully surveying the lesson and not my students' ability to answer a questionnaire, I diagrammed their interest and engagement with the activity.

Student Questionnaire

"I liked this activity."

1-Strongly Disagree	2-Disagree	3-Undecided	4-Agree	5-Strongly Agree
0	3	0	10	12

"I have a better understanding of the class reading/discussion after this activity."

1-Strongly Disagree	2-Disagree	3-Undecided	4-Agree	5-Strongly Agree
0	0	6	15	4

The following comment by Miller and Crabtree (2000) is particularly useful in thinking about what data you should collect:

> A *methodologically convincing story* answers the question, How was the research designed and done? It is important that the researcher make explicit how and why the research design, sampling strategies, and data collection and analysis techniques fit the question and research context. (p. 623)

Be patient and purposeful about the process of learning to collect data while you also try it out in the same time frame. What data do you plan to collect to help you understand the underlying problem? When you designed your study, you charted possible pedagogical strategies you would employ and what data each of those strategies would yield. Once you refine your research question, you will see that your data genuinely emerge from the pedagogical strategies you choose. Those strategies were designed from your continuous observations and data collection. That's why it's called a research process.

In self-study teacher research, you want to be sure you are collecting data that provide information about your efforts to improve your practice and your students' learning. You want to also capture your metaconversation and thinking about the process. Your data should be focused on examining your practice (i.e., the impact of your practice on your students and the impact of your practice beyond your classroom toward educational reform). Those data can be generated from you, from your students, from other participants, and from your colleagues as external observers (McNiff & Whitehead, 2005).

Plan Carefully

Here are a few examples of why you need to plan carefully:

> Let's say that you are planning to interview students to gain their perspectives of your pedagogical strategies. Then you will need to carefully plan whom you want to interview and why; how you will obtain permission to interview; how you will protect confidentiality; where you will conduct the interviews; and the types of questions you will ask.

If you plan to collect observational data, you will need to explain whom and what specifically you are observing and how these observations will be conducted. Will your observations be formal or informal? Will you take field notes? When? How often will you observe?

You plan to collect artifacts of students' work. Which artifacts will you choose? Whose artifacts will you choose? How do you explain your selection of data? Why is it important to have these artifacts? Have you asked for permission to use them? Where will you store the artifacts securely?

All of these questions are much easier to answer if you let the inquiry and question drive the study instead of just collecting data without a purpose in mind. Just having lots of data is useless if they are not connected to what you are studying. The bottom line is that careful planning of data collection is a very important step. Collecting baseline data will help you see what is taking place before you enact your study. You may elect to conduct a survey or questionnaire before you begin enacting your pedagogical strategies that would be followed up with a postsurvey or -questionnaire if that information might serve your inquiry. Results from a piece of data may suggest to you that you need to collect additional data. Think ahead and plan. Plan how you can collect data to examine your current pedagogical strategies. Consider what data might be informative to the pedagogical strategies you might enact. For example, a science teacher, interested in improving students' science literacy, found through a presurvey that her students were gaining much of their information about science from the Internet.

✍ 8.2 Student Example:
Surveys on Students' Science Reading Sources

Kathleen M. Brown (2008), *Science Teacher*

This prestudy survey was completed by 97 students enrolled in Biology I. These students have a C (2.3) or lower GPA (grade point average) and have not been particularly successful in science previously. I have a hunch that a lack of interest in science and poor reading comprehension combine to make important and relevant science concepts difficult for these students to master.

Presurvey

	No News	Newspaper	Online News	Pop Culture	Science News
Out of 97 Biology I students	26	11	60	91	6

This chart reflects five major themes in the free-response answers that I collected from the presurvey questions. I should note that I emphasized that any news such as Yahoo! e-mail headline news counted as online news. If headline news feeds were not counted as online news, I suspect from my observations that many more students would be in the "No News" category. Consequently, I decided to develop a science current events blog to link disconnected science concepts to real life. Then a postsurvey was administered in a class required to use the blog to examine the impact of using the blog.

Postsurvey

	Prefer blog format for reading	Prefer paper for reading	Prefer blog as strategy	No preference or nonpreferring
First Period Bio I	31	2	26	7

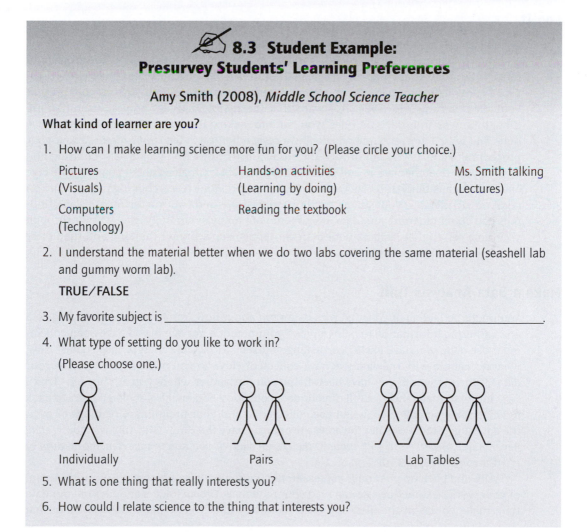

✎ 8.3 Student Example: Presurvey Students' Learning Preferences

Amy Smith (2008), *Middle School Science Teacher*

What kind of learner are you?

1. How can I make learning science more fun for you? (Please circle your choice.)

    Pictures
    (Visuals)

    Hands-on activities
    (Learning by doing)

    Ms. Smith talking
    (Lectures)

    Computers
    (Technology)

    Reading the textbook

2. I understand the material better when we do two labs covering the same material (seashell lab and gummy worm lab).

    TRUE/FALSE

3. My favorite subject is _____.

4. What type of setting do you like to work in?

    (Please choose one.)

    Individually   Pairs   Lab Tables

5. What is one thing that really interests you?

6. How could I relate science to the thing that interests you?

Recall that self-study is purpose-driven research. Self-study scholars have insisted on the need for transparency in data collection and data analysis, which includes describing your multiple data sources and strategies they enacted.

As you proceed to enact your project and collect your data, keep in mind the self-study methodological component of a transparent and systematic research process—that is, Focus #4: *Self-study requires a transparent research process that clearly and accurately documents the research process through dialogue and critique.* Keep an accurate and detailed documentation of all the data you collect.

DOCUMENT

Log It

Writing about the unexpected and confusing events along with your frequent descriptions and interpretations of those events is a documentation of your insights, questions, and reflections about your research (MacLean & Mohr, 1999). Miles and Huberman (1994) provide a convincing argument for employing matrixes as a way to both organize and present your data analysis. However, they warn that the matrix data are only as useful as the thoughtfulness and "decision rules" you put into making them and logging what you have done and why. They recommend keeping a researcher log to feed your matrix about your procedural steps as you go through the study. Clearly, describing data sets, charting and sharing your documentation, and your conceptual decision making about your data are crucial to the plausibility and believability of your report. Your researcher log helps create an audit trail to increase your study's validity and to assess and confirm the theories and findings you conclude from your data. Document your analysis carefully as you move through your data set. In that fashion, your critical friend(s) can see your thinking and then offer their input and perspective.

Make a Data Analysis Trail

You might be feeling overloaded with data right about now. You have been collecting data and gathering information to help improve your practice. Yet, while you have been collecting those data, you have likely been asking yourself, "How will I analyze these data?" Now, what do you do with the data you have collected? How do you make meaning of all your data? Knowing where you have been helps you remember where you are headed. That's why it is essential to keep a trail of your data collection and analysis so you can trace back to what data you collected, when you collected it, and your preliminary readings of what the data suggested. Consider the advice the Queen gave the King: *"The King went on, 'I shall never, never forget!' 'You will, though,' the Queen said, 'if you don't make a memorandum of it'"* (Carroll, 1998, p. 130).

Write and back up your ongoing researcher log so you have a global positioning system of your work so someone else can read your road map. Create folders and files of your data trail, make copies of the files, and send them to yourself via e-mail. Make notes of first glances of your data as you move through your study. For example, if you administered pre-strategy questionnaires or kept checklists during your study, it is important to keep track of those and your readings of those along your data journey trail. Don't hesitate to capture your ongoing ideas during your research. Bogdan and Biklen (2007) explain, "You do not have to prove ideas in order to state them; they must be plausible given what you have observed. Do not put off 'thinking' because all of the evidence is not in. Think with what data you have" (p. 172).

Miles and Huberman (1994) argue that your first audience in the documentation process is "the self," then the readers, and then other researchers (p. 280). They state that "documentation is not a separate, onerous task carried out for 'someone else.' It's a method of improving the immediate analysis task being carried out, advancing the sophistication of later analyses, and deepening the confidence you present in your conclusions. The value of friend, colleague, reader, replicator, meta-evaluator, or auditor responses comes later as an add-on" (p. 286). And as you know, critical friend responses are not considered an "add on" in self-study research. The collaborative inquiry of critical friends is a distinguishing methodological component of self-study research.

Show Your Work

I remember my mathematics teachers always insisting that we show our work on how we arrived at our answers. Students may think that just having the "right" answer is enough. Yet, showing your work allows others to see your thinking and interpretations as well as your misinterpretations. Wolcott (2001), in speaking about qualitative research, writes that "the potential of your contribution will be greatly extended if you provide adequate detail about how you proceeded with your analysis" (p. 93).

In their discussion of drawing and verifying conclusions in qualitative research, Miles and Huberman (1994) contend, "When procedures are left so opaque, we have only vague criteria for judging the goodness of conclusions: the 'plausibility,' the 'coherence,' or the 'compellingness' of the study" (p. 281). They also remark on the essentialness of audience and the need for an exchange of information for public critique: "Qualitative studies cannot be verified because researchers don't report clearly on their methodology, and they don't report clearly on their methodology because there are no shared conventions for doing so. . . . We need better descriptive information" (p. 281).

Write down as specifically as you can how you went about analyzing your data and interpreting the findings. Walk us through the steps you undertook. Explain how you sorted through, organized, and analyzed your data. Explain how you managed a large amount of data as you attempted to make sense of it. The description of your data analysis tells others what you learned and how that led to your reframed understandings of your research. Explain the procedures you employed for finding patterns in your data. Did you identify codes and then categories? Did you make notes of repeated behaviors? Did you create visual displays? Did you quantify some data? What concerns did you raise about your analysis along the way? Providing a detailed and transparent analysis will allow others to see the steps you took increasing your credibility as a researcher. If there are limitations, then state those. Include the role that critical friends played in your analysis and interpretations.

The analysis section of your final report is the documentation and reporting of the data you analyzed. You may decide to also include key analyses summarized in such a manner that helps make your data understandable to your reader (e.g., in a table, chart, or pie graph). You can include the "homework" and detail of your analysis in your appendix so your readers don't get overwhelmed with your data. What you decide to include in your analysis section of your report is based on the question(s) you posed and the quality and quantity of the data that are responsive to those questions. Where you might include a few sentences that help support a claim or bring attention to a finding, a more complete example of a data piece could be placed in your appendix.

Your Critical Friend Research Memos

Since you have been writing memos to your critical friend all along, you have data for your data analysis. Your critical friend research memos can be part of your data set. The memos are your cataloguing and documenting of your questioning, collecting, and analyzing of your data.

Perhaps you utilized visual memos incorporating the arts in thinking about your data analysis by including a drawing and/or concept map with your critical friend research memos. Hubbard and Power (1999) note that **visual memos** "can help a researcher work out relationships in a different way than narratives can and can be especially helpful when there is too much information or too many categories to present as text" (p. 114).

Research memos, both visual and narrative, "are primarily conceptual in intent [and] don't just report data; they tie together different pieces of data into a recognizable cluster, often to show that those data are instances of a general concept" (Miles & Huberman, 1994, p. 72). Nonetheless, as we try to make sense of a shifting set of theories, Miles and Huberman caution that it is important to see recurring regularities and "remain open to disconfirming evidence when it appears" (p. 246). Theory making takes place while you continuously organize any incoming data and analyze your data.

CATEGORIZE

Matrix It

One technique my students find useful in organizing their data is to insert it into matrixes, now made easier with computer word processing. Check your computer word processing program for easy and ready-made and custom-designed matrixes, graphs, concept maps, charts, and tables that allow you to insert your data for making sense of them through graphic displays.

Quantify It

You may also have data that can be quantified and thus can be counted using spreadsheets or a program such as Excel. For example, you may decide to graph the data you quantified for analysis from questionnaires incorporating data from Likert scale scores or from surveys where you tabulated students' attitudes and/or test scores. If you are making the claim about the quantity of a particular item, then presenting those items by the quantities and the mean may allow others to see the convincing evidence.

Color It

Computers allow you to highlight text, fill in boxes, and change the font color. When analyzing data, a teacher researcher may apply different colors in the text to identify possible codes and eventual categories.

OVERLAPPING RESEARCH PHASES

Understand that data collection is a time-consuming process. It involves a great deal of effort and time in observing, interviewing, and assessing (Tomal, 2003). The process requires very careful planning and monitoring with a tentative timeline. Just like in good teaching, you don't just grab an activity to do, but you first look at your objective and what you want to accomplish. Extensive planning allows you to be flexible with unexpected demands and changes.

And yet, data collection is not a linear process. That is, you are always assessing students' current needs and adjusting your strategies. You are progressing from your hunches, collecting data about the changes you are attempting, and assessing the impact of those changes. One way to help you organize your data collection and strategies is to think about them in three overlapping research phases:

Phase I: Data collecting *before* enacting your study

Phase II: Data collecting *during* the enactment of your study

Phase III: Data collecting *after* enacting your study

Of course, there's overlap in the research process or what you might consider as three phases of your research, but it will mark the process and progress of your research. This is just one way to plan for what data you will collect, for what purpose, and when. Your analysis will be ongoing, regardless of the research phase, and we'll talk about that more in Chapter 10.

When you think about it, you have been informally gathering data all along your research journey. That's how you knew you had an issue you wanted to address. Your hunch likely came from your observations of events in your classroom, comments made by students and peers related to the issue, and your personal reflection. As teachers, we collect baseline data on the current situation and then check students' progress in order to look back and see if the changes we made had an impact. Collecting data before enacting your study is useful to plan for the strategies conducted during your study. Your pedagogical strategies will generate much data. Then, collecting data after enacting your study is also important so you can take a retrospective look reflecting on your role in the research and examining the impact of your work.

So what are your decisions for data collection, and what purposes do they serve during each phase of your study?

Phase I: Data Collecting Before Enacting Your Study

This is a good time to look back at your classroom portrait critical friend inquiry presented in Chapter 6 where you were prompted to notice your classroom for student improvement in your research design planning. What did you write about? How did you gain that information? How can those data be useful to examine later in your study? What data did you collect before enacting your study? Include your descriptions and statements made by students.

Phase II: Data Collecting During the Enactment of Your Study

Describe what data you will collect and the purpose of each piece of data that is generated from your strategies. You need to determine a feasible schedule for collecting and analyzing your data with plenty of time to write. Also factor in the time for giving and receiving critical friend feedback on drafts and your rewriting and polishing.

Include data that involve your cataloguing, examining, observing, and interviewing. Include your personal notes, journaling, and research memos to your critical friend as data. These notes and reflections and early readings of data are also data. Incorporate any theoretical research you gleaned from your literature review that offers research support for the solution strategies you are proposing.

Describe what teaching and learning strategies you plan to enact at this point in your classroom in order to address your research question. You may find it helpful to organize the dilemma or issue, possible causes, and possible benefits and consequences of strategies in a chart format (Ciriello, Valli, & Taylor, 1992). Give a rationale for why you believe these strategies will be helpful for the issue you are studying and for teaching and learning in general.

These initial strategies are not "set in stone" and may change as you learn more about your problem or question. Reflect on what information you will gain from each strategy you plan to enact. Reflect on the implications of your pedagogical strategies for students, teachers, the school, and the community.

Revisit your design plan sketched at the beginning of your study. You planned various strategies based on your professional assessment of what might work. Joe Maxwell (personal communication, August 15, 2009) asserts that as a researcher you should "include how you attempt to understand HOW and WHY a particular intervention works, what factors affect its success, how it is experienced by participants, and what unintended outcomes it may have. . . . You want to understand the WAY in which something happens, the importance of the context in which it occurs, and its multiple effects, not just *whether* it has a particular result."

Phase III: Data Collecting After the Enactment of Your Study

After you enact your pedagogical strategies, look back at your research memos. Describe the effects and impact of your efforts. Explain what you enacted, why you enacted it, how you enacted it, and when you enacted it.

 Take some time to sketch your data collection ideas during each phase. You will find some ideas in the chart below.

My research question is . . .

Research Phase	Data Techniques	Purpose	Timeline
Phase I *Before* enactment of study	Classroom portrait: your observations of noticing	Collecting observations of students' behaviors during reading time provide information about . . .	Week 1
	Presurvey of students' attitudes about . . .	Giving a presurvey before I . . . will help me . . .	Week 2
	Student records	Student records will allow me to assess students' standardized test scores over time and . . .	Week 2
	Critical Friend Memo 1	Peer support and feedback	Week 3
Overlapping of Phases I and II			
Phase II *During* enactment of study	Semistructured interviews	The reason I want to conduct interviews is to . . .	Week 3
	Focus group	A focus group will add to the interview data in terms of . . .	Week 4
	Questionnaire	A questionnaire will allow me to read students' written narratives about . . .	Week 4
	Critical Friend Memo 2	Peer review of data	Weeks 3–4
Phase III *After* enactment of study			
	Researcher log	Looking back at my researcher log, I will . . .	From the beginning of research study
	Critical friend research memos	Critical friend research memos capture the development of my research over time and will be useful for . . .	From the beginning of research study
	Self-portrait	The self-portrait depicts my . . .	Week 9

Below is an example of a professor who asked, "How can I improve my teaching and better understand how to be both an effective researcher and an engaged and helpful professor? How has my culture impacted my teaching and my views of being a professor?" She used the chart to catalogue, organize, and understand her data. Notice that because of the recursive nature of self-study research, there is overlap during Phase I and Phase II.

✍ 8.4 Student Example: Research Planner

LaKesha Anderson (2009), *Doctoral Candidate and Instructor, Department of Communication, George Mason University*

These data provided for a rich, meaningful representation of my culture and its impact on my desire to teach, my ways of teaching, and my current struggle with finding joy in and time for my teaching. It will also provide me with a set of "guidelines" or "best practices" for how I might proceed as I advance further as both a professor and a scholar. The chart below captures the data techniques I completed, the purpose for completing those steps, and the research phase in which they were completed. A timeline indicating when each step occurred is also included.

Research Phase	Data Techniques	Purpose	Timeline
Phase I: Before enactment of study	Analyze prior semesters' teaching evaluations	To gain a better understanding of how students perceive my course and my teaching, particularly course rigor and fairness	Already collected; analysis completed March 1–5
	Narrative	To frame my research focus in my culture and describe my struggle to balance being a young professor who wants tenure but also wishes to remain a strong educator; enables me to attend to my physical and emotional experiences over the years	Completed through critical friend memos; revision completed April 30
Phases I and II	Critical friend memos	To better develop my research question and gather feedback on data analysis procedures as well as validation for findings and suggestions for improvement	Ongoing throughout Phases I and II
Phase II: During enactment of study	Collect and analyze student journals	To understand how past students metaphorically view me (as a "farmer or cobbler") and why they view me in this way; this will help me better understand if students perceive me as the farmer I hope and think I am.	Request students to journal: Feb. 23–March 1. Analysis completed March 21–23

Research Phase	Data Techniques	Purpose	Timeline
	Collect and analyze professor journals	To understand how those who have been straddling the line between teacher and researcher are doing so; do they feel they are metaphorically more farmers or cobblers, and do they feel they are straddling the line successfully?	Request professors to journal: Feb. 28–March 1. Analysis completed April 6
	Artwork: self-portrait	To create a visual representation of my problem and "solution."	Artwork completed April 2
Phase III: After enactment of study	Self-assessment	Implementing this study will open up knowledge about how I came to this problem and how my culture impacts my teaching. After completing the study, I can reassess my goals and ideas and see how I can grow from this experience, as well as assess how my students might be better served in the future.	Self-assessment to begin May 20 and remain ongoing as a reflective process
	Teaching evaluations	Future teaching evaluations can help me determine if there is a change in how students perceived my class before and after the study; also, I will add qualitative questions on the evaluation in hopes of more specifically evaluating my effectiveness as an instructor.	End of each semester (fall and spring) and summer session
	Research memo to critical friends(s)	In a research memo to my critical friend, I will ask how my friend thinks I have grown from this project, as well as ask for suggestions on how I might continue to improve my practice.	Memo to critical friend produced and e-mailed by May 10

CRITICAL FRIEND INQUIRY 8.1

Critical Friend Research Memo 2

Data Collection and Pedagogical Strategies

- What is the context of your study? Describe the community, the school, and your classroom.
- Who are your participants?

- Share your planned data collection and planned pedagogies, the data generated from the pedagogies, other data, and your timeline in a research memo to your critical friend.
- What kinds of data do you plan to collect in each data collection phase?
- Why did you decide to collect these data?
- Can you offer a rationale for each piece of data you will collect?
- Collect and date all data that you collect.
- Describe each planned strategy and the data each yields to help you answer your research question.
- You might write about an experience and/or an interaction that led you to a new way of seeing your classroom and thinking about what data would be useful (e.g., concept mapping, photography, and videotaping).
- Discuss how you plan to organize your work.
- Respond to each other's memos.

KEY IDEAS

- Foremost in data collection is the need to align your data with your research question. It must be meaningful and responsive to addressing the purpose of your research.
- The chapter presents guidelines for data analysis to (a) document, (b) categorize, and (c) chart your data.

  Charting your data collection and strategies can include three overlapping research phases:

  Phase I: Data collecting *before* enacting your study
  Phase II: Data collecting *during* the enactment of your study
  Phase III: Data collecting *after* enacting your study

  Organizing your data assists your in examining and presenting them to your critical friends for their review.

Collect Data

My first exposure to any form of qualitative research was in my senior year of college when I went to a village with a group of students to conduct interviews with some farmers to understand their ways of using rice production methods in their farms. It was an assignment on research to practice. The whole experience turned into a methodological shock and a revelation! Shock because I had no idea that "the other side" of the fence existed and revelation because it was a research data technique!

—Kavita Mittapalli (2006), *Research Analyst*

CHAPTER DESCRIPTION

The chapter includes techniques for collecting data through cataloguing, examination, observation, and interviewing. Included in this chapter are descriptions of data and examples of the alternative forms of data collection that self-study researchers have used. Guidelines are included for collecting different forms of data. This chapter also highlights the importance of a transparent and systematic research process in terms of documenting the data collected.

✦ Reading this chapter will provide an opportunity for you to learn multiple ways of collecting data and guides specific to each technique.

We had collected gargantuan volumes of data to study our work in the first self-study research methods course taught at our university (Samaras et al., 2007). To make the large data set manageable, Dawn Renee created a table to help us sort out and see our primary and secondary data sources with a column for each class assignment. The rows of the table included the following headings: (a) each class assignment and description, (b) the context, (c) the impact of each class project in learning about and meeting the self-study methodological components, (d) how the student approached each project, (e) the role of peers in the learning process, (f) what the project added to their current field of study, and (g) notes and reflections. The columns included each coresearcher's name so we could each insert our comments. After that, as coresearchers, we were easily on our way to analyzing.

DATA GATHERING TECHNIQUES

There are many types of and numerous ways to collect **data**, or what Bogdan and Biklen (2007) call "the rough materials researchers collect from the world they are studying . . . [which] include materials the people doing the study actively record . . . [and] what others have created and the researcher finds" (p. 117). In self-study, *you* are "the people doing the study" and actively recording. Cataloguing is a self-study method of recording and sharing your thinking about your research and your role in it throughout the research process. Self-study "primarily utilizes the characteristic qualitative research tools of observation, interview, and artifact collection, although clearly with different kinds of emphases" (Cole & Knowles, 1998, p. 48) (see Table 9.1).

*Keep in mind the purpose of collecting data is to help you explore your research question. There is not a recipe for how much data to collect or what data to collect. Do not worry about what types of data your peers are collecting. Make your data collection purposeful and meaningful to your research project.

⚑ 9.1 Self-Study Research Guidepost

SELF-STUDY RESEARCH DATA COLLECTION

Table 9.1   Self-Study Research Data Collection Tools

Data Technique	Description and Usefulness
Arts-Based Data	Artifacts from classroom and/or school (e.g., books, bulletin boards, school mission, school newsletters); also can include arts projects completed by researcher (e.g., self-portraits, haiku poems, classroom portraits), which provide an alternative format to uncover something that more traditional formats of data collection may not afford
Concept Maps	Visual displays that highlight connections and links of "big ideas"; document your understanding of a phenomenon by visualizing the relationships and complex ideas among concepts and the dynamics and connections between them
Critical Friend Research Memos	Letters you write to your critical friend as a way to more naturally discuss and present your research while also deeply thinking about it. Spark new ideas and promote dialogue to gain another's interpretations of and perspectives on your research.
Interviews	Notes and/or transcripts from meetings with students, peers, families, or school administrators through various formats: *in person*—formal or informal interviews with structured or semistructured prompts, audiotaped interviews, videotaped interviews; *written formats*—questionnaires, surveys, checklists; useful for gaining perspectives of participants and obtaining information on questions related to research; journalist's prompts—*who, where, when, what, why,* and *how* are useful

Data Technique	Description and Usefulness
Narratives	Stories, journaling of your ongoing record, essays, other reflections about your study; can include education-related life history; interpretations of visual data and story of your research process; can include narratives by participants
Observations	An ongoing record of classroom events, student behavior, school events; useful for noting any repeated behaviors, common occurrences, and patterns and also anomalies or things that break away from a usual pattern, outliers, unique events; researcher can be a participant while he or she conducts the observation and/or be a nonintrusive nonparticipant in the observations
Self-Study Teacher Researcher Log	Notebook that documents the self-study teacher researcher's meta-conversation to himself or herself and to critical friends of an unfolding of questions, reflections, meaning making, and shared insights of his or her self-study research project; can include notes, reflections, and preliminary ideas on the unfolding, enactment, and assessment of pedagogical strategies
Student Records	Examination of student records (e.g., academic progress, transcripts, attendance, promotion and retention records, and discipline referrals); enables you to learn about students' school performance
Visual Memos	Visual display of data (e.g., sketches, painting, objects); incorporate the arts to assist the researcher in thinking about the research and sorting out relationships and concepts in data

Wolcott (2001) categorized data-gathering techniques in three major headings and depicted them on a tree with three branches to represent the techniques of (a) examination, (b) observation, and (c) interviewing, respectively. Similarly, Hendricks (2006) presents three main data collection techniques: (a) examination of artifacts, including student-generated and teacher-generated work; (b) observational data, such as research logs, videotapes, and checklists; and (c) inquiry data, such as individual interviews, focus group interviews, surveys, and questionnaires.

Referring to the tree diagram representing qualitative research strategies, Wolcott (2001) wrote of expectations that others might add to the tree and "develop sections of the tree in greater detail" (p. 92). Responsive to that call, I add **cataloguing** or a data-gathering technique to memo and document the self-study teacher researcher's metaconversation to him- or herself and to critical friends of the unfolding of understandings and shared insights of his or her self-study research project. That places the researcher inside the research to be at the vantage point of seeing the research from the inside out. The cataloguing documents the welcomed subjective stance of the self-study researcher and the objective stance of critical friends in the data collection and data analyzing process.

Offering advice to social scientist researchers, Mills (1959) claims that expert researchers take notice, organize, and record their experience because "experience is so important as a source of original intellectual work" (p. 197). Our plans and thinking are not single-shot events in our research, and "by keeping an adequate file and thus developing self-reflective habits, you learn how to keep your inner world awake . . . the file helps you build up the habit of writing" (p. 197).

The Critical Friends Portfolio was designed as your file or what Mills (1959) calls "intellectual production" (p. 199), which catalogues the raw ideas about your research that you openly share with critical friends. It is in essence a metaconversation about the development and process of your research. A Critical Friends Portfolio allows you to create a teacher researcher log of your sorting, meaning making, and documenting of your research. It is more than your interesting thoughts. The critical friend inquiries support and provide evidence of the transparency of your data collection and analysis. The inquiries validate that your thinking about your research has extended beyond yourself. These data will be useful to writing your final reflections and discussion section. You will find the critical friend inquiries under the heading of "Cataloguing" in Table 9.2. As you know, critical friend inquiry is essential in self-study research.

Please note that the critical work is not limited to the critical friend inquiries presented in this text. Furthermore, the inquiries are suggested and not required. You may pick and choose which ones to complete although you are encouraged to read through each of them and utilize them to support your research as time permits.

Table 9.2   Data Collection Techniques

Cataloguing	Examination	Observation	Interviewing
A self-study teacher researcher log of your sorting, meaning making, and documenting of your research. It includes your notes, reflections, and preliminary ideas on the unfolding, enactment, and assessment of pedagogical strategies. It can also include your notes and hunches on any connections of your practice to theories. This is the metaconversation you have with yourself and critical friends about your research and the process of your research. Cataloguing is useful to writing your discussion on reframing your practice (i.e., what you learned and its impact on your students). Suggested cataloguing of critical friend inquiries is offered throughout the text and includes those listed below:	Student records including records of students' academic progress, transcripts, attendance, promotion and retention records, and discipline referrals	Participant and nonparticipant observations	Interviews: notes and transcripts from formal and/or informal interviews; structured, semistructured, audiotaped, and/or videotaped interviews with students, peers, families, school administrators

Cataloguing	Examination	Observation	Interviewing
Education-related life history	Student portfolios	Peer observations of your teaching	Surveys
Self-portrait of a researcher	School handbooks, curriculum guidelines, textbooks, documents, school and community demographics	Drawings of observed student activities	Group interviews
Research artifact	Student daily work	Videotapes of students	Questionnaires
Classroom portrait; includes notes on your noticing of students, interactions, and pedagogical strategies; artifacts of the classroom; photographs, drawings, and videotaping of classroom including your role as teacher	Students' projects, presentations, performances	Observations of student talk	Checklists
Critical friend research memos	Student journals, diaries, quick writes	Anecdotal notes	Focus groups
Haiku of research	Student self-assessments	Case studies of students	Rating scales (e.g., self-efficacy); self-concept, attitude; confidence; learning preferences
Chart, graphic organizer, or concept map of literature review	Student and group standardized test scores	Field notes	Stories obtained through interviewing
Research proposal; narrative and/or visual	Student and group scores on state and district tests	Observations of how classroom space is used; interactions within that cultural theater	Oral histories

(Continued)

Table 9.2 (Continued)

Cataloguing	Examination	Observation	Interviewing
Ethical review assessment with critical friend	Student scores on discipline and/or grade-level competencies	Observations of school space and activities	Inventories
Dialogic validity	E-mails and correspondence	Visual recordings of events and spaces	Record sheets
Self- and peer assessment of self-study methodological components	Classroom Web 2.0 space; Blackboard, blogs, wikis	Vignettes of observed activities	Student portfolio interviews

Advice From a Self-Study Scholar

Exploring Ontology

Self-study of practice research exists in a space between. It exists between biography and history. It is conducted in the midst of practice, and it exists in the space between self and other. As a result, when we design these studies, we need to make sure that we collect data that will allow us to explore that space between self and other where practice grows. We need to record our thoughts and our actions as well as our students' experience in that space. In this way we are able to uncover what is the ontology of the setting and construct rigorous, coherent, trustworthy accounts of our practice.

Stefinee Pinnegar
Brigham Young University

9.2 Self-Study Research Guidepost

SELF-STUDY TEACHER RESEARCHER GUIDES FOR CATALOGUING

- **Log it, draw it, and/or perform it.**

  Cataloguing is an invaluable tool to you as a self-study teacher researcher in collecting data about your self-study and your role inside that research. Cataloging is an ongoing record of your understandings, questions, and experiences during the research process. The Critical Friends Portfolio offers you a chance to write, draw, or perform your data along with multiple opportunities to share your question posing, questions, and insights with your critical friend as your research unfolds. You are generating theories and meaning of your practice to improve it and trying to make sense of what is taking place. Cataloguing is essential to that meaning making.

The cataloguing data document and make transparent your analysis and serve as an audit trail that will be useful to insert into your final project. As teachers, we take mental snapshots of our actions and reflect on what is working and what is not working all the time. Making that thinking concrete through written and/or visual formats provides a file that you can access again and again and share with others. You will likely see your data "tell" you something while you are collecting them and in your early readings of your data. Those hunches may change, but they are valuable to notice and record. Keep a **self-study teacher researcher log** and memos of your thinking as you move through your research. Memos are your "think pieces" about the research over time (Bogdan & Biklen, 2007, p. 122). It is very important to document your contemplations about what you are noticing in your early readings of the data or what Glaser (1978) calls "theorizing" (p. 110). Do not hesitate to capture your raw ideas during the research. "You do not have to prove ideas in order to state them; they must be plausible given what you have observed. Do not put off 'thinking' because all of the evidence is not in. Think with what data you have" (Bogdan & Biklen, 2007, p. 172). Memos are in essence your field notes and can be used as data to journey, understand, self-critique, and analyze your data (Maxwell, 2005), albeit in self-study research, the memos are shared with critical friends. Students find their engagement in planned critical friend conversations quite useful in their understanding of self-study and their research project.

• Embrace critical friend research memos as data.

You are encouraged to write and receive critical friend research memos, or letters that you write to your critical friend as a way to more naturally talk about your research while also deeply thinking about it. Critical friend research memos can spark new ideas and promote dialogue to gain another's interpretations and perspectives on your research. The critical friend research memos are data and are useful from the beginning of the research until the completion of your project. Date all memos. You may decide to title your memos and also include artwork to represent your thinking and progress over time. You will also benefit from sharing the critical friend inquiries with your classmates who can further contribute to your thinking about framing and reframing your practice. Critical friend(s) can prove useful in your data collection and analysis as they provide alternative perspectives on interpretation to increase the validity of your research.

The memos provide an open and inviting forum for your questioning, thinking, strategies, and data collected that can be made public to your critical friends and others. Critical friend research memos will serve you well if you take time to be thoughtful and detailed while you are writing and responding to them. *Then tell the story of your research or the process of your coming to understand and interpret your research.* My students have reported that it is quite beneficial to maintain informal communication and memo writing with critical friends as they continue their studies. Many have sustained their work as critical friends and continued to work together on other research projects after our course ended.

- ## Purposely organize, index, and store.

    Create a personal system for organizing your data (e.g., computer folders and files, a wiki space shared with your critical friend, an accordion folder or portfolio for student work, a binder that allows you to insert and remove materials). Organize according to your focus. Add pockets for nonwritten sources such CDs, videos, visual representations, and projects. You are encouraged to store materials electronically and with copies of folders in other locations. As I tell my students, with technology, scanning, digital photography, and free space for storing files on the Internet, we can no longer use the excuse, "My dog ate my homework."

    Design a system for easy retrieval with data purposely sorted, indexed, and organized to align with the components of your query. Be sure you have a master file of what you collected and how you decided to sort each data set. Use color-coding, numbers, or whatever makes sense to you and the way you make sense of things. Place each catalogued item in your critical friends portfolio. These catalogued items are data for your self-assessment of addressing the self-study methodological components after you complete your study.

- ## Use technology.

    Use technology to support your data collection management and analysis with computer-based matrices, metamatrices of master charts (Miles & Huberman, 1994). Consider the use of computer software programs for sorting and storing, spreadsheets, tables, charts, PowerPoint, concept mapping, and data analysis software.

- ## Read for purpose, continuously.

    Read your catalogued items during your study to direct and inform your ongoing work.

- ## Share.

    Share and review your catalogued items, and especially your critical friend research memos, often with your critical friend to gain alternative perspectives. Look back to inform your looking forward. Examine and discuss what you are thinking about the data during the research process.

✍ 9.1 Student Example: Data Chart

Corey Sell, *Elementary School Teacher*

On the following page is an example of a teacher using the cataloguing technique in his self-study research with notes added about the purpose and a timeline. He also charts data techniques he used for examining, observing, and interviewing.

*Notice that although Corey had identified an area of research focus, his research question is not clear in the beginning of his research. Most typically, research questions are refined during the self-study research process.

Key: Four Categories of Data-Gathering Techniques

1. Cataloguing
2. Examining
3. Observing
4. Interviewing

Phase I. Cataloguing

Data Techniques	Purpose	Timeline
1. Digital Artifact of Research	Uncover a research topic of interest to me.	1/09
2. Journal on Artifact	Attempt to uncover deeper meaning within artifact and its relationship to a research topic of interest.	2/09
3. Critical Friend Research Memo 1	Discover my research interests within a narrative format.	2/09
4. Revised Critical Friend Research Memo 1	Reflect on my research topic incorporating comments made by critical friends.	2/08/09
5. Research Proposal	Abstract research proposal in the form of a sculpture that attempted to get at my research question.	2/09
6. Critical Friend Research Memo 2	Narrative format of my research proposal where I tried to capture in words my research question and rationale behind it; my cursory attempt to set up a data-collecting table.	3/09
7. Critical Friend Work on Critical Friend Research Memo 2	My reflections on the critical friend work on this memo brought me closer to my own research question.	3/09
8. Journal on Meeting With Anastasia	To unravel what I really want to know in my research and begin to develop more coherent methods of data collection.	3/09
9. Revised Critical Friend Research Memo 2	To document my new research question and my new data collection techniques during the study.	3/09
10. Self-Portrait (Revised Research Proposal)	To deconstruct my former arts-based research proposal in order to reconstruct from the pieces of it an arts-based, abstract representation of my new question.	3/09
11. Critical Friend Research Memo 3	To begin the conceptualizing of how I will document, organize, and analyze my data using my final research question. Also to gain feedback on these initial processes.	4/09

Source: From Sell, C. (2009). *Moving on: What lights our path towards emancipation?* Paper submitted in partial fulfillment of course requirements in Advanced Research Methods in Self-Study, George Mason University.

SELF-STUDY TEACHER RESEARCHER GUIDES FOR EXAMINING

- ## Examine with a focus.

    Examining archived data provides information about the school, the school community, and students' past performances and profiles. Examining also includes students' ongoing developments, progress, and understanding of learning. Again, focus on the documents and artifacts about your context and participants, which will help you tell the story of your research more fully. Give specific attention to examining data that allow you to paint the research scene with a broad brush while also detailing the specifics of your participants' perspectives with a fine brush. Notice if those specifics are reframed over time, repeatedly, and why.

- ## Collect, record, and organize.

    Collect, record, and organize school records and data early in your study. Take time to put the data into the method section where you are asked to describe your school and school community.

- ## Be careful of time.

    Don't take too much time or get bogged down in plowing through statistical data about your school or students. Instead, use the data to help you gather baseline data and with consideration for how they inform your context and purpose. Many schools and school divisions have demographic data available on their Web site.

- ## Examine carefully.

    Use the data to inform, but not bias, yourself against attempting particular pedagogical strategies. Gather information with an open mind, not to just affirm your hunches, but to give you an opportunity to consider rival explanations of your original thinking. Take notes as you move through your research process instead of waiting until all your research is completed.

- ## Be ethical.

    Remember to follow ethical procedures. Gain permission for accessing records and including any information you decide to include in your report. Maintain confidentiality of all participants, the school, and the school district. Safeguard and later destroy any copied material.

SELF-STUDY TEACHER RESEARCHER GUIDES FOR OBSERVING

- ## Formalize your daily observations.

    Observations allow you to collect firsthand data on individuals, groups, programs, processes, or focused behaviors and activities (Stevens, Lawrenz, Sharp, & Frechling 1997). You might be asking yourself, "How can I conduct observations while I am also teaching?" Now consider the reality. You observe your classroom every day you teach as a participant observer or as "both participant in and observer of the situation" (Punch, 1998, p. 188). You make mental notes of comments students make and click visual images of student interactions and behavior. Be mindful of keeping abbreviated notes or a checklist of those comments and visual images.

- ## Be planful.

    Observations are useful in helping you decide on a research focus. Observing allows you to step back and look, analyze, consider what needs your attention. Use pre-strategy observations to help you zero in on and refine a research question under development. Once you decide on your focus and purpose, be planful that the data you collect will actually be useful to you. Conducting observations is time consuming so you want to consider if the observations will serve the purposes of your study.

- ## Be aware of your cultural bias.

    When you are observing, consider if you are capturing the facts or your interpretations and judgment of a person or situation. Have you reflected on how your cultural lens may distort your perceptions and how you judge others? Record actual statements and details and be weary of liberal adjectives, adverbs, and modifiers in what you record. Include the positive that is occurring which is also valuable data. Kalmach Phillips and Carr (2006) advise teacher researchers to "realize that you may misjudge others' actions based on learning expectations" (p. 70). Personal opinion can also be recorded, but duly noted as your opinion to share with your critical friend.

- ## Be complete.

    Include a description of the context, the particular class, day, time, and situation. Provide detail to explain the scope of a scene, incident, or behavior. Include interactions of others involved in an episode.

- ## Be specific.

    It's easy to make a quick generalized note of your interpretations and evaluations of incidents or behavior. Consider what you are reading into an observation, embrace that perspective, and write about it. Share it with your critical friend. Next, work at capturing what students actually said without your judgment of the students. Write direct quotes when possible. Make notes of any clues that help frame the fuller picture such as body language, interactions and reactions of other people involved and the subsequent responses of students. Also, look for what is not happening (e.g., the lack of response, off-task behavior, uninvolvement in a group project, etc).

- ## Be ethical.

    Students are aware of much more than we might think. Consider if your observations hinder or hurt your participants in any way. Does your observing influence students' behavior and reactions to the strategies you are enacting? Will the data you collect be embarrassing to students or others? Share your observations and reflections with your critical friend to help establish a trustworthiness of your work.

SELF-STUDY TEACHER RESEARCHER GUIDES FOR INTERVIEWING

Interviews allow you to gather descriptive data on participants' points of view about the research in question and in their own words. They provide an opportunity for you to ask specific and/or general questions depending on your research question.

• Decide on type of interview.

Interviewing can take many forms. You might decide to conduct informal or formal interviews or use a variety of formats and questions in different interviews throughout your study. Structured individual interviews include the same set of specific pre-established questions that each participant answers (Fontana & Fey, 1994). You might want to conduct a semi-structured interview which has a set of questions that you will ask but that also includes probes, clarifications, or extensions prompted by your respondents' responses.

Perhaps, you will decide that you want to conduct a group interview or a focus group where you can interview several people at the same time (Punch, 2005). Asking a group a set of questions will also capture the group dynamics in response to the questions you ask the group (Patton, 1990). Questionnaires and surveys are essentially formal types of interviews. Whatever you decide, be purposeful with any interviews collected. Interviews are very time-consuming. If you are planning to transcribe the interviews, do that early in the project. There are new technologies available for recording and transcribing easily through voice recognition although it will require learning how to use the equipment. Careful planning and organization are required.

• Clarify purpose of interviews.

Consider why you are conducting the interview. Prepare your questions to carefully align with your research goal and purpose and to help you answer your research question. Carefully craft each research question that will help you answer your research question. Maxwell (2005) asserts, "Your research questions identify the things that you want to understand; your interview questions generate the data you need to understand these things" (p. 69). Can you explain why you are conducting the interview? Can you present a rationale for your decisions on whom to interview and why? How many people will you interview and why? What information are you trying to gain from interviewing them? Why is gaining information from them important to you?

- **Develop purposeful questions.**

    Before you begin interviewing, plan your interview interaction, develop your questions carefully, and revise and pilot your questions (Glesne, 2006). One way to think about the interview design is to put on the hat of a journalist and ask questions that get at the *who, what, where, when,* and *how* of your research focus. A good idea is to pretest your interview questions and share them with your critical friend for feedback and suggestions. The questions you ask might be context or problem specific, descriptive, clarifying, and/or contrasting in nature. Kosnik, Cleovoulou, and Fletcher (2009) state, "Interviewing has a strong appeal to self-study researchers because it allows them to gather in-depth data on very specific topics" (p. 55) and yet researchers "may need to make the familiar strange and 'detach' themselves from the topic being studied" (p. 60).

- **Plan ahead.**

    Plan the logistics of the interview from beginning to end. Allow for time to set up any equipment as well as time in between interviews to account for transition time and if the interview runs longer than you planned. Include some time to take notes and prepare for the next interview. Decide if you will take notes, audiotape, and/or videotape. If you decide to use audio, transcribe the interview as soon as possible after the interview so any confusing comments are more easily retrievable. Videotapes also document the body language but may inhibit participants' comfort level and willingness to express. Transcribing and videotaping require that you gain participants' permission before you conduct the interview.

- **Be a good listener.**

    It is important to establish some initial rapport with your interviewee before launching into the questions. Maintain good eye contact and show you are interested in your interviewee. Think of "the interview as a conversation" (Kvale, 1996, p. 19) and yourself as a "research instrument" (Kvale, 1996, p. 147) who can influence the information you obtain from your interviewee. Ask clear questions that you have first piloted on others not in your study. Be a good listener, sensitive, and nonjudgmental. Don't agree or disagree; merely acknowledge what you hear. If your interview is semistructured, use prompts such as "Tell me more about that." "Can you give me an example of that?" "Please explain that to me." Use wait time and don't try to answer the question for your respondents. Thank your respondents.

- **Be ethical and culturally responsive.**

    Review the chapter on ethics and consider the ethical issues embedded in your interview. Consider the consequences of the study and how you will obtain informed consent, maintain confidentiality of the interview subjects, and check for any oversimplification of your interviewees' words (Kvale, 1996). Gain permission to interview, audiotape, and/or videotape your interviews. Maintain confidentiality. Conduct the interviews in a private setting. Be aware of any sensitive matter that you might ask about and/or share in your final report.

During your analysis of the interview, be careful not to add an extra layer of meaning, bias, or interpretation when examining the language and culture of your respondents (Fontana & Frey, 2000).

ALTERNATIVE DATA COLLECTION TECHNIQUES

In an effort to study their particular research topics in their contexts, self-study researchers have boldly stepped outside the norm in using alternative formats not only to collect data but to see it in a new light through dialogue with critical friends. Self-study researchers have used a wide range of art forms to represent and reinterpret, construct, and deconstruct meaning and communicate their study of researching as they made it public. Self-study research has included less commonly used forms of data such as visual/image-based arts (e.g., portraits, performance, photography, video documentary, art installations, sculpture, multimedia representations, films, drawings, cartoons, graffiti, signs, cyber graphics, and diagrams). A look through the edited collections of self-study research highlights the variety of data found in self-study research (Kosnik, Beck, Freese, & Samaras, 2006; Lassonde, Galman, & Kosnik, 2009; Loughran, Hamilton, LaBoskey, & Russell, 2004; Tidwell & Fitzgerald, 2006; Tidwell, Heston, & Fitzgerald, 2009). Self-study research has included data such as photography (Mitchell & Weber, 1999); drawings (Weber & Mitchell, 1996); found poetry (Hopper & Sanford, 2008); self-portraits (Mittapalli & Samaras, 2008); diaries (Mitchell, 2006); videoenthographies (Chan & Harris, 2002); artifacts (Allender & Manke, 2004); performance (Weber & Mitchell, 2002); improvisations (Samaras, 2000); image theater observations (Placier et al., 2006); collage (Hamilton & Pinnegar, 2009); narratives (Kitchen, 2009); and e-mails and online discussion board interactions (Ham & Davey, 2006).

No Artistic Talent Required!

When I assign arts-based self-study work, I assure students that artistic talent is not a requirement. The art is a medium of expression and not to enter an art show. In order to work in self-study research, a learning community of trust, openness, and care is essential (Samaras, Freese, Kosnik, & Beck, 2008). I encourage them to give themselves permission to explore their research in a medium of their choice so that they might carefully consider what they want to research and why. Suggesting the use of abstract representations seems to lower students' anxiety (Samaras, 2009).

In conducting a self-study of a new course I designed, I wrote in my researcher log:

I used examples of self-portraits that artists have made but students told me they found the portraits intimidating. I think it's best to merely give verbal examples of the range of media one can use and let them know that all projects can be abstract. In reflecting back, I could have done a better job explaining the self-portrait. As young children, we draw ourselves all the time and then as we get older, we feel intimidated that others might judge our artwork. I need to remember that students might not have been asked to use art for some time and the novelty needs a better introduction.

It is not that self-study researchers just use these alternative formats, but they use them to "get at" something that more traditional formats of data collection have not afforded them. Students' personal narratives can prompt a professor to examine the significance of race in identity formation processes (Brown, 2002). A former teaching diary can serve to assist a professor to study her novice teachers' struggles with beginning teaching (Mitchell, 2006). A piece of art can spark a deep reflection with significant insights about one's practice (Hamilton, 2005).

Eisner (1991) talks of epistemic seeing in **arts-based data** as "the kind of knowledge secured through sight" (p. 68), which encompasses working to see what we know before we make claims.

Self-study researchers have found arts-based data useful in teaching about social justice (Placier et al., 2006); in promoting teacher education and students' reflection (Hoban & Brickell, 2006) and for rethinking teacher professional images (Mitchell & Weber, 1999; Mitchell, Weber, & O'Reilly-Scanlon, 2005).

Some would argue that artistic forms have allowed self-study researchers to abstract a deeper conceptualization and expression of what they seek to better understand (Weber & Mitchell, 2004). Using the arts as data encourages connections of the self to practice, individualizes meaning making, provokes critical analysis and interpretation, and encourages dialogue about improving one's practice through the arts (Galman, 2009; Samaras, 2009). While traditional research forms create an understanding of the research situation through the processes of experimentation, observation, and control, the arts allow students to sketch and create an understanding of a situation through a descriptive analysis and encourage outside interpretation (Barone, 1995; Barone & Eisner, 1997; Eisner, 1993, 1995). Chenail (2008) notes that some may question, "Is arts-based research practice really research?" and he comes to the conclusion that "all forms of research can inform, perform, reform, and transform what we think we know about the world around as well as ourselves as researchers and readers" (p. 10). Self-study research has demonstrated the value of using alternative data collection formats particularly for researchers' efforts to reform education and work toward social justice.

Below is an excerpt from the research of Arvinder Johri (2007). Her self-study research project was done with the objective of exploring her professional identity in her dual roles as teacher and administrator. Her inquiries included the following:

1. How am I perceived as an administrator and a teacher by my faculty and administration?

2. How are the perceptions connected to my gender, cultural, and religious identity?

3. How do I perceive myself as a teacher and an administrator?

4. What do I want to achieve in the role of a teacher or an administrator?

5. Am I willing to give up one for the other? If yes, why?

✎ 9.2 Student Example: Arts-Based Self-Study

Arvinder Kaur Johri (2007), *English Teacher and School Administrator*

My self-study arts-based project was an ambitious endeavor to symbolically represent my research questions. During the brainstorming phase of my project I created a conceptual collage of my dual professional roles, students' expectations, my expertise in the area of teaching and administration, my professional passions, my cultural identity, my childhood ambitions, my acknowledgment of the undercurrents of cultural misplacement, and my future action plan. As a child growing up in India I had multiple opportunities to watch and admire dancing peacocks from close proximity. My grandmother used to tell me a folktale about a peacock who would cry after scrutinizing its ugly legs. This realization of ugliness especially in its state of blissful dancing during rain would bring tears to the peacock's eyes. My self-portrait unravels this antithetical aspect of life. The legs, disconnected from the plumage, are placed on the top right corner as a stark revelation of friction and tensions that come with the acclaim and accomplishments (see Photo 9.1).

Photo 9.1   Self-Portrait of a Teacher and Administrator

My self-study art project of a peacock motif symbolizes my connections with students, and I feel compelled to make a pragmatic positive difference in their lives. As a researcher, the ugly feet of the peacock are symbolic of the friction, tensions, and ugly power equations related to my professional roles that need to be faced and resolved. The plumage represents my diverse professional roles seeking balance and harmony of form and mind. In my two roles I have been juggled between different calls, changing visions, and shifting agendas, and I have repeatedly felt the need to find balance and harmony among my conflicting priorities. The ritual of feather renewal is a reminder for me as a self-study researcher to reassess the effectiveness of change frequently.

Questioning the status quo, thinking of the "what ifs" and the "why not," and reflecting on how change can modify the organization and improve productivity are essential to a self-study practitioner. The eyes in the feathers belong to my students who have moved from the periphery to the center. This was the most surprising element in my self-portrait. Conceptually when I was trying to visualize my self-portrait, I had not identified the symbolic significance of the eyes. Only during the process of painting the plumage did the eyes gain their own meaning and identity. I realized that my self-study wondering related to my professional identity will define my role in my students' life and therefore should be carefully explored and analyzed.

9.3 Student Example: Data Artifact

Mary Adams-Legge, *English Teacher and Department Chair*

Mary, who is also an avid knitter, knit a hat as a representation or artifact of her experience as a teacher and department chair wearing many different hats (see Photo 9.2, p. 190). It became an informative piece of data in her final project.

Each layer of the hat had a different color with unique features and textures representing the components of her work: the knottiness and friction, the spheres of influence, and the complexity. She writes, "It [the knitted hat] forced me to conceptualize my role more minutely, looking at more of the subtleties of the position. I used color, texture, shape, combinations, and process to represent the different roles of my job." [This student's self-study research project was later titled "'Juggling Hats': A Self-Study of an English Department Chair"; see Adams-Legge, 2006.]

Because of the multiple methods of self-study, the methodology includes approaches adapted from other disciplines such as the life history work of sociologists, the portrait making of artists, and the artifact exploration of anthropologists. Self-study researchers seek out other disciplines not only for the data analysis of their findings but also for the conceptualization of their research question and the data collection of their research project. For example, a researcher studying student differentiation might find it useful to engage in an arts-based self-study method to reflect on and improvise the individual differences in learning, which then would be shared and performed with a group of critical friends who also participated in the activity (see "Differences Through Drama" in Samaras & Freese, 2006, pp. 169–171).

Photo 9.2   Self-Portrait of an English Teacher and Department Chair

Faculty and students have recognized the value of cross-disciplinary work and the importance of modeling it for their students. Student and faculty perspectives on drama and improvisation exercises were data in the collaborative research conducted by Placier et al. (2006) to teach the "ideals of democracy and social justice" and in the research by Samaras (2000) to teach preservice teachers perspective taking. Improvisation exercises were utilized and "allowed us to recognize that we can understand others on the inside even if on the outside they seem very different from us" (Samaras, 2002, p. 139).

Hubbard and Power (1999) also note the value of alternative ways of seeing data and findings and explain, "By trying to come up with a poem, or doing a quick role-play with peers based on a critical incident in your project, you will see new dimensions in the work. The findings will also shift and change before your eyes, even though your data will remain the same" (pp. 128–129). Data can also be represented through dramatic portrayals, short stories, and poems (Glesne, 2006). Using "poetic transcription" by creating poems from interviewees' words "the researcher creates a third voice that is neither the interviewee's nor the researcher's but is a combination of both. The third voice disintegrates any appearance of separation between observer and observed" (Glesne, 2006, p. 200).

Hopper and Sanford (2008) brilliantly utilized a poetic form in their data analysis to capture student teachers' perspectives of university and school-integrated courses: They interviewed students, analyzed the interviews into themes, and arranged extracts from actual words and themes of the interview analysis into a poem to represent the student voices, and then they asked the students to validate their composition. They write, "Using spaces, word emphasis, positioning on the page, line breaks, metaphor and imagery, the poetic form creates a structure that engages the reader in the text in a way that differs from more formal academic presentation of the findings" (p. 35). If you are drawn toward using the arts in your data collection and data analysis, you will find numerous examples in *Handbook of the Arts in Qualitative Research* (Knowles & Cole, 2008).

QUANTIFIABLE DATA

Students often ask if they can include numerical data in their projects. Many have developed a single conception of research from their science courses as experimentation with a hypothesis, a control group, and statistics. Some believe that their research requires higher-level mathematics and analytical procedures with large numbers of "subjects" with the researcher conducting an experiment and having a control group. My students have used computer programs (e.g., Microsoft Excel) to easily conduct basic statistical operations, such as calculating the auto sum, mean, medium, and mode of sets of data. Some have misconceptions that teacher research requires "proving" a way of doing something. Research is not limited to experimental designs. Furthermore, in any research, we are always building knowledge, and that knowledge shifts as we learn new things about old ideas in our work and from the work of others. As teacher researchers, you are part of generating that knowledge about your teaching and the content you teach.

For example, an elementary teacher interested in facilitating classroom discourse in her teaching of mathematics brilliantly integrates standards in her discussion and analysis of a transcribed audio recording, which she meticulously analyzed for the quantity of student discourse.

9.4 Student Example: Analyzing Quantitative Data

Andrea M. Aiona, *Elementary School Teacher*

The *Professional Standards for Teaching Mathematics* (NCTM, 1991) state that the discourse of a classroom—the ways of representing, thinking, talking, agreeing, and disagreeing—is central to what students learn about mathematics as a domain of human inquiry with characteristics of knowing. Discourse includes both the way ideas are exchanged and what the ideas entail: Who talks?

About what? In what ways? What do people write, what do they record, and why? What questions are important? How do ideas change? Whose ideas and ways of thinking are important? Who determines when to end a discussion? The discourse is shaped by the tasks in which students engage and the nature of the learning environment; it also influences them.

In order to answer the question "Who talks?" I counted the number of lines of transcripts to find that approximately 2,499 out of 6,808, or 36.7% of the transcribed lines, were those of students. Episodes 5 and 9 have the least amount of student lines of dialogue. On November 2 (Episode 5), I had lectured the students about being unprepared for class by not completing work and studying for announced assessments. My interactions with the students were more short and commanding. I had reached my wit's end on this day, possibly resulting in less student dialogue.

Table 9.3   Percentages of Student Lines of Dialogue in the Full Transcript

Episode	Number of Student Lines	Number of Total Lines	Percent of Lines Students Spoke
1: October 14	489	1219	40.0
2: October 18	252	676	37.3
3: October 19	452	1263	35.8
4: October 21	271	617	43.9
5: November 2	310	972	31.9
6: November 3	125	237	52.7
7: November 4	315	791	39.8
8: November 8	116	310	37.4
9: November 9	169	723	23.4
Total	2499	6808	36.7

Data in self-study research can include both qualitative data and information that can be quantified, tabulated, and analyzed using statistics. But do keep in mind that self-study is a form of qualitative research (Pinnegar & Hamilton, 2009). Quantifying your data does not mean you are conducting a quantitatively designed study (Mills, 2007). You can include quantifiable data within your study if they inform your research. Some data such as surveys, questionnaires, and checklists can be quantified, and the results can be presented in a quantifiable format (Mertler, 2009). Displaying numerical data can be an effective way to make an argument for an interpretation. You will find that it is easy to display your quantifiable data visually with easy-to-use tools accessible through your computer. For example, my students have used the "insert" tool on Microsoft Word to easily display their data in tables, concept maps, diagrams, line and bar charts, and pie graphs.

As a classroom teacher, you have access to a great deal of numeric data from your students' assignments, quizzes, exams, standardized tests, and other performance measures. If you deem that data will help you address your question, then you should also include them in your research.

✍ 9.5 Student Example: Analyzing Quantitative Data

Julia Hiles (2008), *Mathematics Teacher*

A secondary education mathematics teacher interested in the value of offering students second chance assessments (SCA), or review and retaking of quizzes, found that tabulating students' survey responses and then comparing them to her colleague's student responses was useful for obtaining students' perspectives. She also administered a survey to students who chose not to participate in second chance assessments.

Julia notes, "The responses for the survey are relatively similar for each group. Next to the noticeably different responses, I have placed a bullet mark (•). 'Noticeably different' is defined as possessing medians and modes varied enough to have a significant impact on the weighted average. The students agreed the SCA helped them learn the material by forcing them to go back and review their mistakes. They also agreed learning was more important than grades, but wanted their grades to reflect their learning. An interesting contrast between the students who took the SCA and those who did not, occurred for the question, 'I have trouble deciding what to study.' Participants agreed or strongly agreed with the question, while nonparticipants disagreed or strongly disagreed. This would suggest the students are capable of learning the concepts, but need to find the best method to 'make it their own'" (Hiles, 2008).

Table 9.4   Hiles Participant Survey/Colleague Participant Survey

	Julia's Class			Colleague's Class		
	Wt. AVE.	**Median**	**Mode**	**Wt. AVE**	**Median**	**Mode**
I have taken a Second Chance test to improve my grade.	4.92	5	5	4.68	5	5
I have taken a Second Chance test because I felt the first grade I received didn't reflect what I actually understood.	4.67	5	5	4.09	5	5
Learning is my priority, but I want my grade to reflect my learning.	4.64	5	5	4.23	5	5
I understood the material better when I took the Second Chance test.	4.25	4.5	5	4.07	5	5
I didn't prepare properly for the first test because I was overwhelmed with work for my other classes.	3.83	4	4	3.64	4	4,5

(Continued)

(Continued)

	Wt. AVE.	Median	Mode	Wt. AVE	Median	Mode
I have trouble deciding how or what to study for tests.	3.50	3	3 and 5	3.02	3	4
• Knowing I can take the Second Chance helps me relax when I take the test the first time.	3.91	4	4 and 5	2.66	2	2,3
I didn't prepare properly because I knew if I did poorly, I could just take the Second chance.	2.00	1	1	2.25	2	2
I'll be honest. I didn't study for the first test.	2.00	2	1	2.20	2	2
I learned from the mistakes I made on the first test.	4.42	4	4	4.55	5	5
I still didn't understand the material the second time.	2.33	2	1 and 2	2.21	2	2
I made careless errors on the first test.	4.42	4	4	4.52	5	5
My mistakes on the first test were because I choked.	3.00	3	2 and 3	2.70	2	3
I prepared less for the Second Chance than the first test.	2.83	3	2, 3, 4	2.58	2	2
I didn't understand the material the first time I took the test.	2.92	3	2	3.00	3	4
I was more confident taking the Second Chance than the first test.	3.75	3.5	3	3.96	4	5
I am sure I can do an excellent job in this class.	4.00	4	5	4.02	4	5
I prefer classes that are challenging so I can learn new things.	3.75	4	3.4	3.59	4	3

	Wt. AVE.	Median	Mode	Wt. AVE	Median	Mode
• I think what I am learning in this class is useful for me to know in other classes and in the future.	4.33	5	5	3.30	4	4
I think what we are learning in this class is interesting.	3.75	4	5	3.10	4	4
Understanding this subject is important to me.	4.17	4	4	3.66	4	4
I always try to learn from my mistakes.	4.67	5	5	4.25	4	4

Also keep in mind that whether you use qualitative data or quantifiable data, your data are only as good as the instrument you design to measure them. That's why the early explorers didn't know there were other planets. They did not have the powerful telescopes or other instruments to see them. You may also discover that some of your data are not sensitive enough to measure what you hoped they would measure. When you conduct your analysis, some data may end up in a discarded pile. Don't worry about that. Store these data in a "take out" file for later review. You can offer a discussion of why they were not effective pieces of data to collect and what they did not measure or how they ended up not being very useful for answering your inquiry.

Critical Friend Inquiry 9.1 is a participant observation experience designed to give you an opportunity to "see" others and to consider the importance of asking questions that inform your research.

CRITICAL FRIEND INQUIRY 9.1

Interviewer and Interviewee

- Ask your critical friend to describe a critical incident that occurred in his or her classroom and how it is related to his or her research question. A critical incident may be at the underbelly of a larger self-study inquiry although it is not the inquiry itself. First, prepare what you consider to be the "right" interview questions that will help you address the following research question: "How does my critical friend understand the relationship of a critical incident in his or her classroom that appears to be connected to his or her research question?" The critical incident could have been a segment of your critical friend's noticing his or her classroom.

- Interview that person for 15 minutes. Completely give yourself to that person as a listener. Ask that person to tell you about the dilemma.
- Notice the details of words, gestures, voice, vocal pattern, posture, appearance, and actions of your interviewee.
- Keep notes on verbal and nonverbal communication.
- Write a segment of a piece of your interview that tells us something about the dilemma and situation described.
- Exchange places with your critical friend and reflect on your role as the interviewer and the interviewee.
- Write a reflection on how you approached collecting data through the interview.
- What was most difficult for you?
- Would you change anything the next time you interview someone?
- What did you learn about the interviewing process?
- Share your reflection on interviewing with your critical friend.

KEY IDEAS

- Transparency in research includes a detailed documentation of the data you collected.
- Data-gathering techniques include (a) cataloguing, (b) examination, (c) observation, and (d) interviewing.
- Cataloguing is a self-study data-gathering technique.
- Self-study research can include a variety of data commonly collected in qualitative research.
- Self-study may also include alternative and creative forms of data collecting borrowing methods from other disciplines such as the humanities and the arts.
- Self-study research can also include data that are quantifiable.

Analyze Data

I reread my personal history on why I felt the need to incorporate technology into lessons. My narrative was much more helpful after analyzing the other pieces because it helped me see ideas that were common throughout my other data. For example, I mentioned in my narrative my desire to help students understand how science could be used in the real world. A common theme in the way I used technology in class revolved around that theme. In addition, each of the teachers I surveyed mentioned real-world application as a way I used technology.

—Amos O. Simms-Smith (2009),
School Administrator, Fairfax County Public Schools, Virginia

CHAPTER DESCRIPTION

In this chapter, you will find both general and specific discussion for analyzing your data and with student examples. This chapter offers a general overview about analyzing data but not with the intention that this is all you need to know about qualitative research, which is a very broad topic. For an in-depth discussion about how to analyze data in qualitative research, I suggest you visit some of the seminal works on qualitative research listed in the Self-Study Resource Center. The self-study methodological component of the need for a transparent and systematic research process is again emphasized in this chapter in terms of describing your data analysis.

◆ Reading this chapter will provide an opportunity for you to gain a broad overview of data analysis and detailed steps in how to proceed.

> Self-study research is a hermeneutic process: *a dance of data collection and data analysis.* Consequently, data collection and data analysis are not linear processes. Data analysis is not something that is done after you finish collecting all your data. To the contrary, it is recommended that you begin your early and preliminary analysis of data *as* you collect them so that you can begin to manage them systematically, store them for easy access later, and "see" and document what is happening as your research proceeds. You will return to the full data set in your data analysis, but beginning to reflect and take notes on what is happening *during* your research will serve you well in your final data analysis work.

RESEARCH AS A RECURSIVE ACT

Self-study research is not a linear process. As Bogdan and Biklen (2007) explain, "Data are the particulars that form the basis of analysis. . . . Data are both the evidence and the clues" (p. 117). So often we like to think of research in a linear format where we just move along to each component of a project in a step-like fashion. But research doesn't happen that way. Research is a recursive act that requires revisiting earlier steps, reexamining your data, and reassessing your preliminary interpretations based on incoming data. Keeping in mind that research is a recursive act, take notes of your readings. Addressing analysis of interview transcripts, Seidman (2006) offers this recommendation:

> During the process of reading and marking the transcripts, the researcher can begin to label the passages that he or she has marked as interesting. After having read and indicated interesting passages in two or three participants' interviews, the researcher can pause to consider whether they can be labeled. What is the subject of the marked passage? Are there words or a phrase that seems to describe them, at least tentatively? Is there a word within the passage itself that suggests a category into which the passage might fit? (p. 125)

Trust the process and accept the messiness of not knowing or having a final answer or theory. You sort and classify information all the time for your students to help them understand material instead of just presenting it as a series of facts. That's why reading and rereading your data and taking notes on issues or events that stand out and are repeated or patterned in some way are so useful to you. During the process of your reading and analyzing your data you are making meaning of your data.

The brain is an amazing organizer and meaning maker. Caine and Caine (1994), in their groundbreaking work on principles of brain-based learning, explain that researchers have discovered that we are wired to make and find meaning as "the brain is both artist and scientist, attempting to discern and understand patterns as they occur and giving expression to unique and creative patterns of its own" (p. 89). Your brain is constantly taking in data as you collect them and drawing hunches, seeing surprises, and noticing things you wouldn't expect to find. Having generated data, you have already started to draw meaning from the data. You might have noticed statements from students that were similar or were in contrast to each other; behaviors that seem to be reoccurring; and factors that were closely associated, linked, or sequenced. As you gained new information, you might have clustered or chunked similar information into mental bins. Those data were likely arranged and rearranged in your brain as more new information arrived. Your smaller files might have been placed into a larger file or category. Or maybe you had a general topic that came to you and then you found smaller parts that fit that category, like in the game of *Jeopardy*.

Whether your thinking was deductive or inductive, what is powerful is that you noticed what was happening while you were making mental, and hopefully written, memos about your noticing to share with your critical friend. Miles and Huberman (1994) offer techniques to draw meaning from qualitative data, which include this noticing and making sense of data in various ways (e.g., noting patterns, themes, and interrelationships; seeing plausibility; clustering; using metaphors; examining contrasts and comparisons; and making conceptual/theoretical coherence of what the data mean). They describe metaphors as "pattern-making devices," "decentering devices," and "ways of connecting findings to theory" (p. 252). Notwithstanding, as researchers we learn quickly that if we draw conclusions too early, or with little information, our premature conclusions are discarded.

Bogdan and Biklen (2007) also ask qualitative researchers to consider using metaphors, analogies, and concepts:

> We get involved collecting data in a particular place and become so captured by the particulars, the details, that we cannot make connections to other settings or to the wide experiential array we carry with us. Ask the question, "What does this remind me of?" about different aspects of the setting. (p. 169)

Again, although you may be able to notice patterns rather easily, keeping notes of that meaning making is necessary so you don't forget it. It's making sense of the whole of the parts that takes the researcher to another level to conceptually reveal a bigger picture. This is a research story worth sharing because it demonstrates the point of how data can reveal patterns that help you understand the context you are researching.

I began my coding life as a graduate student in a master's program in human growth and development where I observed adolescent behaviors in my civics classroom for a research project. I learned to notice and pay attention to what are called "repeated behaviors" when I conducted case studies of adolescents. During my doctoral program where I worked on a project examining the impact of microcomputers in young children's learning and play choices, I was invited to join *The Computer Discovery Project* (Church & Wright, 1986) research team as a logger of children's computer interactions.

In the process of writing anecdotes, I couldn't help but notice a fascinating pattern. I observed that the interactions of the 5-year-olds with their teachers, especially in their talk and length of "playing" at the computer, were dissimilar with different teachers. I saw both a pattern and a contrast and wrote memos about it along with lengthy and specific anecdotes. I tried to write as much of the actual statements made by the children and teachers. I noticed that when the teacher offered indirect and open-ended prompts, the children stayed longer at the computer. That data really jumped out when I looked at the variance in the length of time children stayed at the computer, which I had recorded in my log. Also, when teachers' language was more facilitative and they served to foster children's investigations, children's stories were language rich, creative, and filled with joint problem solving (see Wright & Samaras, 1986).

CODING

One process of sorting and beginning to make sense of your data is through coding. Read and reread your data. Pay particular attention to any repeated statements, behaviors, and actions across your data set. Reflect on your work and learning. Read back through the items you have collected and consider what you are learning about your students and your role as teacher. Give yourself time and permission to reflect honestly and to study your role as a researcher. The process of noting regularities and patterns, topics, chunks, or classifications assists in condensing your data and also helps guard against facing a data overload after you have collected all the data (Miles & Huberman, 1994). **Codes** are "tags or labels for assigning units of meaning to the descriptive or inferential information compiled during a study" (Miles & Huberman, 1994, p. 56). You may include descriptive codes with abbreviations (e.g., LC = learning community), interpretive codes (e.g., ES = emotional support), or pattern codes (e.g., TP-PS = teacher prompted–peer supported). You may decide to create a "start list" or a priori codes determined from the study's theoretical framework (Miles & Huberman, 1994). Be certain to create a master file of what your codes stand for and the meanings you assign them. It is absolutely essential to create a key of what your letters or colors represent. You won't remember the abbreviations when the data become fuller. Trust me. I've learned that the hard way. Also, you may find that your initial codes change or are discarded because there is not sufficient support for keeping them. Don't be discouraged. That discarding is bringing you closer to understanding your research.

Another technique for managing your data analysis is placing different-colored sticky notes on a large piece of poster paper. Although it is old-fashioned, the beauty of this technique is you can move the sticky notes around as you reread the data and create categories from the codes using different-sized and -colored sticky notes. The disadvantage of this technique is the sticky notes are not permanent as they lose their stickiness over time with your repeated shifts in deciding the best fit for a code into a category.

Additionally, when you create only hard copies of your data, the data are less portable, retrievable, and secure. Some students use index cards, which can also get lost. Nonetheless, if you are someone who likes to "touch the data" by handling each handwritten data piece, then it is a useful way for you to organize your data. You can always type or scan the hard copies into a computer file. Whatever technique you decide to use for your data analysis, be sure it is one that is reliable so you can share the process of your data trail with your critical friend. Keep your research question and the purpose of your study at the forefront while also being open to the unexpected and begin to code.

Advice From a Self-Study Scholar
The Importance of Self-Study Research

The life force of self-study is the personalization of learning, but not the self-indulgence of learning. Self-study researchers are not interested in producing feel-good educational research where everything turns out wonderful because the researcher says so. Instead, self-study researchers are deeply intent in looking deeply, closely, and clearly at the unvarnished truth. Questions are not so much answered as new questions are engendered as a result of a valid inquiry into one's own teaching practices and/or the study of an educational policy. This constant ambiguity, the inability to underline truth with certainty but to clarify it with estimated solutions and educated assumptions, is what makes self-study a dynamic and ever-evolving research tool and a valid and living thesis for this text. Without self-knowledge, there can be no self-doubt, and without self-doubt, there can be no real teaching.

Jeffrey Kaplan
University of Central Florida, Orlando

Below is an example of coding conducted by a teacher working as an English for Speakers of Other Languages (ESOL) teacher in a science classroom and exploring how ESOL students' success in the classroom might be improved using one-on-one instruction.

*Notice the recursive nature of his research (i.e., how the rationale is embedded within his education-related life history and social justice, which was presented as an example in the wondering critical friend activity in Chapter 1, and how his rationale drives the study and the interview questions he selects). He charts the data across three of his ESOL students (i.e., three cases) to help him make sense of the repeated codes.

✎ 10.1 Student Example: Rationale and Coding Cases

ESOL Teacher

Rationale

The rationale for this research was created to investigate the effects one-on-one instruction can generate on ESOL students. The idea of researching this topic occurred to me based on the personal connection that I have with the topic, since I was once labeled as an ESOL student. As a biology teacher whose schedule includes three team-taught ESOL/biology classes, I want to be able to provide my students with the adequate instruction. This instruction will hopefully allow each individual student to succeed in the classroom by allowing all of them to feel comfortable when participating in lectures, labs, and activities; by achieving higher grades; and by receiving a passing grade in the ESOL exam at the end of the year. I believe the current education, especially the teaching strategies, being provided to ESOL students can be improved and expanded. I frequently encounter situations in which my ESOL students seem confused and upset with themselves because they are not able to understand the material implemented.

Source: Student Work (2008). *Improving ESOL instruction based on my one-on-one instruction.* Paper submitted to the Secondary Education Program, Graduate School of Education, College of Education and Human Development, George Mason University in partial fulfillment of the requirements for the degree of Master of Education.

DATA ANALYSIS

This teacher highlighted statements expressed by more than one student with the same color (see Table 10.1). Work with your critical friend to try your hand at this data excerpt and share what codes you find across the three cases.

CODING CATEGORIES

Another inductive process used in data analysis is called coding categories to help you sort descriptive data by topic. Bogdan and Biklen (2007) describe **coding categories** as "terms and phrases developed to be used to sort and analyze qualitative data" (p. 271). Accordingly, Bogdan and Biklen note that coding categories could include codes about the setting, participants' definitions of the situation, participants' perspectives, participants' thinking about people and objects, processes or changes over time, activity or behavior codes, events, strategies, relationships, narratives, and reflection about your methods. Examining the elements and properties of codes will help you sort them conceptually using coding categories and with a focus on your research question.

Table 10.1 Coding Cases

Interview Questions	Studying Biology and English at Same Time	Teacher Behavior	One-on-One Instruction	Having Another Biology Teacher Who Did Not Speak Spanish	Teacher and Student Interaction	Team-Taught Classes	Study at Home	Attitude About Taking Biology
Miguel	"I feel good because I am able to learn both."	"You explain things over and over again until I know them."	"I feel better when you explain one-on-one because I feel like I do well. I can do more."	"I don't think for me it would have worked if I had another teacher. You are able to explain it in Spanish and another teacher would not have been able to do that. I can probably work faster and quicker with you."	"It makes me feel good that you approach me because you come up to me and someone is taking care of my grades and me. It is a helping hand."	"You teach us what you have to teach us, while the ESOL teacher walks around explaining while you talk. You use your hands and slow the way you talk."	"I study at home sometimes. One day before the test."	"I was excited."
Felix	"Most of the time it is biology words that I get confused about, not English."	"You explain clearly, and you have a lot of patience."	"You read out loud to me, and you correct me when I am wrong."	"Always helpful that you speak Spanish and you can explain in our language when we don't understand."	"It does help that you approach us because when we don't understand something we are able to understand it better."	"ESOL teacher translates to simpler terms."	"I look at my binder once a week."	"Good!"
Raul	"I get confused about bio words, not with English."	"You have a great deal of patience when explaining."	"You use a lot of expression, speak slowly, and use Spanish to explain when confused."	"Helpful when you speak in my language."	"It helps when I don't understand something."	"You use 'fancy' biology terms."	"I look at my binder once to twice a week."	"Excited!"

Your research question may draw you toward focusing on a particular type of code. I often use coding categories to provide a structure and organization to analyze with more focus. Let's say, for example, you want to examine what your students think about a new pedagogy you are employing as I did with my students (Samaras et al., 2007). Then Bogdan and Biklen's (2007) code of "perspectives help by subjects" (p. 175) would be useful. Or perhaps if you wanted to examine families' views of utilizing computers with their children in an after-school family literacy program (Samaras & Wilson, 1999), then "subjects' ways of thinking about people and objects" (Bogdan & Biklen, 2007, p. 175) would be a helpful way to code.

CATEGORIES AND CONNECTIONS

As you analyze your separate codes, you will begin to see the relationships and connections among and between them and create a category that will represent "a unit of information composed of events, happenings, and instances" (Creswell, 2007, p. 64). Temporarily title that unit of information as a **category**. Categories will likely be retitled when you have integrated and collapsed them into larger or better-titled categories. This happens when they are reorganized in their relation to each other and as any new data are analyzed. Similar to codes, there may be an overlap in the categories whereby they can be renamed, combined, and/or discarded if they do not demonstrate sufficient support or saturation. Move them to a file marked "discarded" for your personal documentation.

Researchers sometimes refer to categories as themes (Corbin & Strauss, 2008). They write that "the following **themes** emerged from the data," and what they are presenting is their interpretation and a thematic analysis presented in categories. Keep documentation of what you discarded and why to review with your critical friend when you examine the validity of your study. Be prepared to explain the final categories you selected based on the evidence you found. Creating codes and categories is a purposeful research activity and not one that should be done quickly or haphazardly. Miles and Huberman (1994) offer this advice on the importance of structure in coding:

> Whether codes are created and revised early or late is basically less important than whether they have some conceptual and structural order. Codes should relate to one another in coherent-study important ways; they should be part of a governing structure. Incrementally adding, removing, or reconfiguring codes produces a ragbag that usually induces a shapeless, purely opportunities analysis. (p. 62)

You might think of categories in a similar fashion to concept mapping where the separate topics or issues can be named under a category because they all seem to belong to that classification. Indeed, you may find drawing a map or sketch will help you sort and organize your data and help you see the links between the codes while you also condense your data. This is not to suggest that data analysis in qualitative research is merely a listing or chunking of data. Instead data analysis is a process of understanding and interpreting your data. You are trying to decipher what the data tell you about your question and your interpretation of the data within a particular context. Consider how your categories tell the story of your study and your restorying or framing and reframing (Schön, 1983). Data analysis takes time, but the time and effort help you understand what is happening in your classroom as demonstrated in the next example.

✍ 10.2 Student Example: Transparency of Data Collection

Annemarie Ratke (2007), *Elementary School Teacher*

Before I began the unit of instruction, I needed to assess my students' learning to develop a profile so that I could create lessons and activities that would be appropriate for all students. After compiling the students' profiles, I designed activities that supported the research related to community building, differentiated instruction, and cooperative learning based on third-grade reading and writing standards that were suitable for the story *Charlotte's Web*. After the lessons and activities were created, I chose specific days for the videographer to videotape our class.

I requested the videographer to visit our class when we were incorporating specific strategies such as community building, differentiated instruction, and cooperative learning into our literature unit. She visited our classroom 3 times throughout the unit for an approximate number of 6 hours. The activities she recorded were fundamental for an inclusive classroom. Hence, I deemed it an appropriate time for her to capture the implementation of such strategies. We used one fixed camera to portray the lessons and activities. I wore an attached microphone on my shirt during the filming. When the videographer interviewed students we changed the microphone so that their voices could be heard. I appointed specific things I wanted her to film, and then she filmed anything else that she thought our research could benefit from.

After each morning of filming I was prompted with questions regarding the strategies that we tried that day. Some of the questions included the following:

1. How did this activity create community? Was this what you anticipated?

2. Do your students know the difference in activities when you differentiate assignments?

3. How did you tap into the students' prior knowledge?

4. Would you try this strategy again?

Most of the conversations were a synopsis of what worked that morning or what didn't work. I also described how I felt throughout the lesson. Once the videographer had captured several lessons on video, I then had to go through all the raw video footage and decide what I wanted to include in the final product. While I was viewing the raw data I charted the time and wrote brief notes describing what was happening during that time. Following this, I coded themes that I thought would require me to reflect more deeply. Rossman and Rallis (1998) refer to coding as the process of organizing material into "chunks" before bringing more meaning to those "chunks." I used four different colors on the video notes to show the difference between the themes. After I coded the themes, I added another column to the charts titled "Findings." Under the findings column I added more details reflecting upon what I viewed while editing the video clips. For the themes that fell under strategies and implementation of activities, I added descriptions of those tasks.

Video Analysis

The purpose of this formal self-study was to design a unit of instruction and implement strategies that would meet the needs of all learners in my inclusive classroom. Afterward, I would reflect upon the results of such implementations. The information was gathered through a videotaped analysis of teaching. Several themes emerged from the videos, and this self-study focuses on the theme of implementation of strategies and activities that embrace all learners in an inclusive general education setting.

> Notice how she uses narratives to catalogue her thinking. Also interesting is how she took video notes to describe the situation and, along with cataloguing her reflections of the situation, she names repeated themes that emerge. A sampling of the analysis from six videotapes collected over a 3-day period is included.

Videotape Analysis #1

Day 1

Time Recorded	Video Notes	Themes	Reflection
11:30–12:30	Farm animal books Students' background knowledge	Activity Engagement	Teacher explained activity thoroughly. Students were all engaged and on task.
15:59–22:30	Directions of community building activity 1st time without talking	Strategy Engagement	Community building activity was introduced clearly. Students were engaged and worked cooperatively on task following instruction.
24:20–26:52	2nd time talking	Engagement	Students were frustrated more easily with one another.
27:33–29:43	Review of activity How did this activity create community?	Engagement Strategy	Teacher reviewed the purpose of community building strategy. Students articulated how they felt about it.
36:15–end of tape	Did you know cards Explanation of activity	Strategy Activity	Differentiated cards helped everyone become involved. Teacher directed students effectively.

Community Building Activity: Line-ups . . . students each had a card with a letter on it. They had to find others with the same color card and spell a character's name from *Charlotte's Web*. The first time the students could only communicate with visual cues. The second time the students could talk to one another.

(Continued)

(Continued)

Did You Know Cards: Students were given (differentiated) cards with facts about E. B. White, the author of *Charlotte's Web,* written on them. In cooperative learning groups, students had to share their facts aloud in a round robin share.

Videotape Analysis #2

Day 1

Time Recorded	Video Notes	Themes	Reflection
00:00–11:08	Students reading the cards Round robin share Groups reading cards and helping one another Answer questions about cards	Engagement Strategy Engagement Engagement	Students are implementing strategy effectively. They are engaged and helping one another. Teacher is observing while students work cooperatively.
15:22–24:30	Explanation of spider cards Mix & Freeze Student response	Activity Strategy Engagement	Teacher explanation is unclear. Mix & Freeze strategy is not implemented smoothly. Students do not seem engaged.
32:35–end of tape	Rohan reading aloud Lucia reading aloud Teo reading aloud	Engagement	Students are reading their facts aloud; however, partners don't seem to be focusing on them.

In Annemarie's reflections and recommendations from this work, you will notice how carefully she describes what she learned from the analysis of the strategies she enacted. She openly shares what she might have done differently and that she learned to generate knowledge not only for her own teaching but for other teachers who might also be interested in a similar inquiry.

Self-Study Reflections

The purpose of this formal self-study was to design a unit of instruction and implement strategies that would meet the needs of all learners in my classroom and then to reflect upon the results of such implementations. I have learned a great deal about myself as an educator and as a member of a classroom community through this experience. As excited as I was about all that I had been learning through my studies, I believe that applying my knowledge to my classroom has enabled me to see more clearly the importance of a well-planned lesson and thoughtful delivery of a lesson and the imperativeness of engaging all learners throughout a lesson or activity. When I first started viewing the videotapes I couldn't believe how boring I was while instructing the students. I felt that I didn't capture my students' attention before giving instructions for tasks. In addition, my instructions were unclear and confusing for many of the activities. I believe this is why some of the activities did not go smoothly. Had I taken time to check students for understanding, then I think there would have been less bewilderment by the students. However, as the unit progressed I believe I got better at introducing concepts, assignments, and activities. I felt more comfortable with the inclusion of students of all abilities and was able to get to know each and every student personally. As a result, the students became less confused and more engaged, and the content of what we were learning became more clear.

I am overwhelmed with so much joy after completing this project. I feel a renewed sense of passion for teaching. I don't feel intimidated by overwhelming standards or bleak data of students' performance. I don't hesitate when a new student transfers into our class or when a student's behavior is reckless. Instead, I now know I have knowledge on how to make a child's experience in school more appropriate for him or her. Additionally, I have a strong desire to deepen my understanding of practices related to inclusive practices and curriculum design. I am not hesitant on learning new ways of teaching all children. I hope to push forward professionally through professional development courses and perhaps more university credits.

Moreover as a result of this unit I have formed sincere, personal relationships with each of my students as a result of careful attention to their individual needs. I believe that I have reached all my students at a level that I wasn't able to before I tried these strategies. I have made it possible for them to demonstrate their learning in various forms. Therefore, my students have felt success and now have more desire to work toward their third-grade goals. I cannot say that they will all be reading third-grade text or that they will write a five-paragraph essay without flaw. However, I can say that their interests in school have sparked. Their relationships with their peers have strengthened. Our classroom is truly a community now. We rarely have conflicts or major behavior problems in our classroom. Also, my fully included special education students have a stronger motivation to stay in the general education setting. They are working much harder on homework and class work and are participating in class much more frequently. In fact, shortly after we ended our unit on *Charlotte's Web* a special education student who had been fully included in our class wrote me a note that said, "I love you Mrs. Ratke. I love school. I love our class. Thank you for letting me be with you." This little note and my overwhelmingly positive experience with this project has made me secure in my philosophies of inclusive education.

You might also consider how the data connect across the full data set by identifying key relationships that bind and connect the data together. Maxwell and Miller (2008) have contributed the *categorizing strategies* and *connecting strategies* method in qualitative research, which entails analyzing data according to two types of relationships: those based on similarity (categories) and those based on contiguity (connections). Accordingly, they note when you look for the similarities and differences you are creating a category, and codes is a categorizing strategy. When you look for connections between your categories you are looking not for the similarities and differences of your data but for the "juxtaposition in time and space, the influence of one thing on another, or relations among parts of a text" (Maxwell & Miller, 2008, p. 462). That is generally done by "identifying key relationships that tie the data together into a narrative or sequence and eliminating information that is not germane to these relationships" (Maxwell & Miller, 2008, p. 467). (See Mittapalli & Samaras, 2008, for a good example of categorizing and connecting strategies.)

Maxwell (2005) notes that codes should not be limited to only placing data in bins or in organizational categories. Making sense of what is going on requires "substantive and/or theoretical categories . . . that make some sort of claim about the topic" (p. 97). Qualitative researchers generate theory from their data by making and supporting their claims and using related literature to justify their claims (Freeman, deMarrais, Preissle, Roulston, & St. Pierre, 2007). Thus, you need concentrated time to process your data and as Bogdan and Biklen (2007) recommend "undisturbed time because if your concentration is continually broken by other tasks, you are not as likely to get a sense of the totality of your data" (p. 185). You are an interpreter, a meaning maker, and a theory maker, albeit for purposes of improving your practice through constructing meaning rather than for the purpose of making any final claims of knowing (see Charmaz, 2006; Pinnegar & Hamilton, 2009).

CONSTANT COMPARATIVE METHOD AND GROUNDED THEORY

Self-study researchers may employ an inductive approach in their data analysis—that is, the **constant comparative method** (Glaser & Strauss, 1967; Strauss & Corbin, 1990), which entails "taking information from data collection and comparing it to emerging categories" (Creswell, 2007, p. 64). That is, you are constantly comparing initial codes as new data come forth from your multiple data sources to develop and saturate the category. The constant comparative method involves a line-by-line reading of data and making note of codes. Glaser and Strauss (1967) explain that the decision to stop coding is based on the researcher's assessment of exhausting the dimensions of the categories to the "point of theoretical saturation" (p. 69). Look at your data until they saturate that category or when you "find information that continues to add until no more can be found" (Creswell, 2007, p. 64).

Using the constant comparative method in grounded theory may be challenging for those who like more structure. In a **grounded theory** study, researchers "set aside, as much as possible, theoretical ideas or notions so that the analytic, substantive theory can emerge" (Creswell, 2007, pp. 67–68). This means the researcher moves from the specific instances of participants' actions to generate general understandings about teaching practice and education. Nonetheless, Creswell (2007) argues that grounded theory is a systematic approach that involves examining initial categories in open coding, to reassembling data in axial coding and identifying propositions in selective coding, which "assembles a story that describes the interrelationship of categories in the model" (p. 65).

You are theorizing or making initial claims during the research, but this meaning making continues with an interchange of collecting and analyzing. This process continues until most of your data have been collected so you can check and assess the quality and validity of your initial coding against incoming data and until a theory of what is happening can be developed. In self-study research, you are in essence generating a working theory grounded in the data of your practice and attempting to make meaning of it. You also recognize that your understanding is always under construction as you continuously frame and reframe your practice with continued study.

CONCEPT MAPS

Concept maps can be a useful visual tool to help you make sense of your data. A **concept map** is a technique for visualizing the relationships and complex ideas among the big ideas or concepts and the dynamics and connections between them (Novak & Gowin, 1984). In my teaching of preservice teachers, I studied how my students found concept maps useful in generating an understanding between their conceptions of unit planning and their usage of content knowledge in an interdisciplinary unit they taught (Samaras, 2002). In turn, students found concept maps useful to understand their own students' concept attainment of the units they taught. Preservice teachers developed preplanning and postplanning concept maps of their understanding of unit planning and preplanning and postplanning concept maps of their background knowledge of their unit topic. The visuals captured the development of their ideas and the links they made. The concept maps were useful for me as a teacher to see how my students were understanding what I was trying to teach them and their own analysis of "seeing" their thinking about teaching.

In similar fashion, Hoban and Brickell (2006) in their work with preservice teachers used diagrams "as tools for reflection" (p. 239) on the dynamics of teacher-learner interactions before and then again after a 2-week practicum in schools. Concept maps are a useful strategy for generating, connecting, and communicating complex ideas. Linking phrases demonstrate that the concept "gives rise to," "results in," or "leads to" another concept (Novak, 1995).

Photo 10.1   Using Computer Programs

COMPUTER SOFTWARE TOOLS

While you are conducting your data analysis, allow yourself to see your categories collectively as you try to make sense of them by writing or typing them on a piece of paper and reflect about the relationships of the words you post. You might try a computer program such as Wordle (http://www.wordle.net/) to make a word wall of your categories. Post your word categories. Think about them. Examine them in space. Then reorganize them as you see the connections and links between them in your own word wall. What are your theories about what is taking place in your study?

Computer software, such as *Inspiration,* is another visual tool you could use to post and decipher the major concepts or factors that you are studying. You can also use the visual insert features on your word processing program. For example, Microsoft Word has a feature called "SmartArt" that provides numerous frameworks for building your own concept maps with inserted text. Again, the format you use will depend on what you are sorting, trying to better understand, and aligning with your research question and the ongoing questions that surface during your analysis (e.g., List, Process, Cycle, Hierarchy, Relationship, Matrix, or Pyramid). Don't get bogged down in the technical or the artistic aspects of computer tools and software. Using the tools is not to make your data look interesting. Rather, use the tools to make sense of your data. Use what tools work best for you to help you see your data. It may be that a pencil drawing or mapping is your way of making sense of your data. The tool is just that: a tool. It's people who do the interpreting.

There are also computer software tools that allow you to sort, organize, store, analyze, and access large amounts of data. Keep in mind as Bogdan and Biklen (2007) note that the computer program "does not do the analysis for the researcher" (p. 187). The programs have different features and require training. Some programs are designed for coding and retrieving (e.g., HyperQual, NVivo, The Ethnograph); others include coding and theory building (e.g., AQUAD, HyperRESEARCH, QCA); and others include conceptual network building (e.g., ATLAS.ti, MECA, SemNet) (Miles & Huberman, 1994). The programs are especially useful for extensive data collection and long-term studies such as these is and dissertations (e.g., NVivo). Keep in mind there is no magic bullet in data analysis. It takes a lot of work, time, and thoughtfulness. Computer programs are only as useful as the information you enter into the program (see Photo 10.1 on the previous page). Maxwell and Miller (2008) also note that some computer programs can limit your opportunity to see the connections in data as many are limited to creating and sorting categories, which "may lead to neglect of connecting strategies" (p. 473).

How might I analyze and interpret my data?

1. Read your data as you collect them.

2. Write notes, share research memos, and share interpretations of your ongoing data with your critical friend.

3. Reread your data often and with time to think about them.

4. Begin coding data as you gather them.

5. Organize the types of data you collect. Keep a file of your code labels and your color-coding scheme.

6. Decide on a way to organize your data to help you try to make sense of them (e.g., tables, matrices, concept maps, charts).

7. Make notations of **emic coding** (i.e., a participant's own words) and **etic coding** (i.e., your interpretation of others' words). Emic codes represent your first level of analysis.

8. Conduct pattern coding and clustering of common ideas: Search for regularities, recurring words, statements, patterns, topics, discrepant evidence, and negative cases.

9. Formulate and reformulate categories as you continue to read through your data and memos.

10. Determine if there are organizational categories or broad topics as well as more specific ones. Keep trying to get a sense of the big picture of what is happening. What is the narrative or your interpretation of what these data within your situated context tell us?

11. Examine for any connections among the data using "connecting strategies" (Maxwell & Miller, 2008, p. 467), or those that demonstrate relationships to each other. Make note of those along with your preliminary interpretations of the data.

12. Consider your findings in light of the research support you gleaned from your literature review.

13. Share the interpretations and the categories and themes you identified and verified by the data with your critical friend.

14. Practice dialogic validity with your critical friend (see Critical Friend Inquiry 11.1).

15. Receive peer feedback and revise conclusions.

KEY IDEAS

- Self-study research is not a liner process and instead is recursive in nature.
- Codes, categories, and coding categories are techniques for sorting and analyzing data. Exploring connections among categories allows the researcher to examine relationships among the categories.
- The constant comparative method entails "taking information from data collection and comparing it to emerging categories" (Creswell, 2007, p. 64).
- In grounded theory study, researchers "set aside, as much as possible, theoretical ideas or notions so that the analytic, substantive theory can emerge" (Creswell, 2007, pp. 67–68).
- A concept map is a technique for visualizing the relationships and complex ideas among the big ideas or concepts and the dynamics and connections between them (Novak & Gowin, 1984).
- Computer software tools allow you to sort, organize, store, analyze, and access large amounts of data and are only as useful as the information you enter into the program.

Assess Research Quality

Having to explain my collage to my classmates really started the questioning process of what did I ultimately hope to find from this project and how did I envision getting there. Critical questions about my possible methods were key in helping me examine what I was planning to do.

—Jennifer A. M. O'Looney (2006),
School Counselor, Prince William County Public Schools, Virginia

CHAPTER DESCRIPTION

This chapter offers a discussion about the need to collect multiple and different sources of data to improve the quality of research. Critical friends create a prism effect and serve to present alternative points of view and interpretations of your data. Issues of transparency, validation and trustworthiness, reliability, and generalizability are addressed in this chapter. A detailed outline and rubric is provided for your self-assessment and your critical friend assessment of how well you addressed the Five Foci or the self-study methodological components in your research.

✦ The chapter offers guidelines for assessing your study with a discussion of the role that a validation group can play in that process.

I sit at my computer, plug in my headphones, and sign on to Skype. I'm excited to see that Hafdís, Mary, and Jennifer are also signed on. Hafdís connects us on a four-way conference call, and the fun begins. I hear the phone ring and see the phone receiver icon flashing on my computer screen. I press the icon and say hello. Across three continents, we gather to talk about our research and celebrate our efforts as four women working to make a difference in teacher education.

We send files ahead of time through e-mail and also through Skype during our bimonthly meetings. During the development of an electronic survey, we send tracked edits to each other to assess

---

the quality of our questions. Jennifer and I refine a final version and send it to our research team and then to the Self-Study of Teacher Education Practices (S-STEP) electronic mailing list. We later send our preliminary codes of our individual analysis of our multiple data set. Hafdís and I write memos about the process and meaning making of this sharing. Mary prompts us to constantly consider the big questions and to dialogue about our diverse interpretations. As we hang up, we say good morning, good dinner, and good night across the time zones and continents.

MULTIPLE SOURCES OF DATA

Essential to the quality of your study is that your data are derived from multiple and varied sources and perspectives so that you can analyze your research questions from more than one data source or perspective. Understanding the multiplicity of data is especially valuable for considerations of your study's validity. Having multiple data sources increases your validity.

The notion of multiplicity in data gathering and analysis as central to research design is known as **triangulation** and can include examining or triangulating of information and/or perspectives from your data, investigators, theory, and methods (Denzin, 1978). Using multiple data sources and methods leads to the development of diverse perspectives on an issue or a problem. Practicing triangulation and not relying on a single source helps crosscheck your data and addresses the issue of confirmability (Mills, 2007). Bogdan and Biklen (2007) note that the term *triangulation* may be confusing and advise against using it because "it confuses more than it clarifies, intimidates more than it enlightens" (p. 116). Instead they recommend, "If you use different data-collecting techniques—interviewing, observation and official documents, for example—say that. If you collected data from many subjects, about the same topic, say that. If more than one researcher collected the data, say that" (p. 116).

A fascinating, albeit maybe equally misunderstood variation of triangulation is known as **quadrangulation** (McKernan, 1996), which includes multiple participants working to coanalyze data (e.g., external researchers, participants, and project teams each working with the teacher-researcher with the goal "to make a thorough appraisal of the problem, bringing all those with a role into the evaluation process" [p. 188]). Another interesting approach that also promotes multiple ways of knowing is **multiplism**, which "refers not only to multiple methods but also to multiple triangulation, multiple stakeholders, multiple studies, and multiple paradigms and perspectives" (Miller & Crabtree, 2000, p. 615). Self-study scholars can collaborate with researchers using other methodologies, both quantitative and qualitative, to study the same topic to find new connections and theories through a multimethod and cross-disciplinary approach.

Richardson (2000) offers a postmodern and creative analytic approach to extend data gathering and validity through **crystallization**. That is, she looks beyond "the triangle—a rigid, fixed, two-dimensional object"—and uses the metaphor of a crystal, "which combines symmetry and substance with an infinite variety of shapes, substances, transmutations, multidimensionalities, and angles of approach. . . . Crystals are prisms that reflect externalities and refract within themselves, creating different colors, patterns, and arrays, casting off in different directions. What we see depends upon our angle of repose" (934). Recognizing the limitations of triangulation, Kalmbach Phillips and Carr (2006) recommend that "overlaying the concept of triangulation with the metaphor of a crystal, as presented by Richardson (2000), enriches the concept and honors the complexities of teaching and learning" (p. 75).

Embracing the concept of crystallization, Janesick (2000) has masterfully harnessed the power of using the arts in qualitative research. Janesick (2004) writes, "I like to think that crystallization incorporates the use of other disciplines, such as art, sociology, history, dance, architecture, and anthropology, to inform our research process and broaden our understanding of method and substance" (p. 392). Ellingson (2009), in her book *Engaging Crystallization in Qualitative Research,* notes the unnecessary dichotomy of art and science in research and writes, "When scholars argue that we cannot include narratives alongside analysis or poems within grounded theory, they operate under the assumption that art and science negate one another" (p. 5). Intertwining methods may be a conduit for the researcher to see and make sense of something with new insights. Self-study researchers may intertwine several self-study methods, such as personal history and arts-based, using one perhaps more prominently than the other. The multiple angles of each method, like a crystal, may lead to a better understanding of the research. Having multiple and varied data sources and perspectives is important to the quality of your data.

Envision critical friends as prisms.

Use varied data sources *and* multiple perspectives. Although qualitative researchers are encouraged to use multiple data sources to triangulate their data, they often miss the opportunity to consider critical friends as a data source. Unique to self-study research, critical friend perspectives are data sources that allow you to dialogue about your research sources and process to gain multiple perspectives from colleagues. The critical friend inquiries in this textbook are designed using various learning modalities to prompt you to reflect upon and record an account of your insider point of view enhanced from the feedback of critical friends.

I assert that critical friends work as the **prism effect** to allow you to alter your view through a different medium (i.e., your critical friend helps illuminate new ideas and show you something that may be present all along but not obvious or visible to you alone). They present alternative sides to your research (see Photo 11.1). Critical friends, like the faces of a prism, are not parallel to each other, so the differing angle may unveil something that neither critical friend can see alone. In the same manner in which the surface of a prism will determine if a ray of pure light can be reflected and shown through, each critical friend must be receptive to listen to, although not always accept, the feedback and ideas presented.

Photo 11.1   The Prism Effect

CRITICAL FRIEND INQUIRY 11.1

Critical Friend Research Memo 3

Data Analysis and Interpretation

Read and reread your data. Pay particular attention to any repeated statements, behaviors, and actions across your data set. Reflect on your work and learning. Read back through the items you have collected and consider what you are learning about your students and your role as teacher. Give yourself time and permission to reflect honestly and to study yourself as a researcher. Take a moment to think back along your research journey when you made meaning from a series of seemingly separate observations. Consider the questions below and write a research memo to your critical friend about your data analysis and interpretations.

*Some of the questions might not be relevant yet and will need to be revisited when you are further along in your data analysis. Make notes on what you need to discover and what you need to refine. Keep thinking, "Process . . . process . . . process."

1. What types of data did you collect?

2. Did you collect enough data?

3. Were your data varied?

4. Is it easy for others to understand what data you collected related to your strategies?

5. Walk us through the steps of how you made sense of your data.

6. Did you provide a detailed, descriptive, and accurate description of your analysis?

7. Do your research notes reflect the way you began to group or categorize your hunches into mental bins?

8. What patterns and relationships among categories did you note in your data? Pull those notes out now and share them aloud with your critical friend. Discuss if the noted patterns remained throughout the study or if they shifted.

9. Select a segment of data that you coded from one of your data sets. Work with your critical friend to gain alternative perspectives and to member-check your analysis.

10. Are you being open to outcomes other than those you planned?

11. Have you been honest about any personal bias you brought to the study?

12. What are your preliminary interpretations?

13. How would others view your interpretations?

14. Share the themes you noted in your data.

15. Did your data help you answer your research questions?

TRANSPARENCY, VALIDATION, EXEMPLARS, AND TRUSTWORTHINESS

Let's look at further research considerations of assessing the quality of your study: transparency, validation, exemplars, and trustworthiness and also reliability and generalizability. The self-study methodological component(s) related to each of these topics are brought to your attention in the discussion. Reflect on how well these quality issues are addressed in your research. Then you will find a critical friend inquiry with a list of questions so you can self-assess the quality and validity of your self-study research with your critical friend.

Transparency

If you kept a detailed log on what you did during your data collection and data analysis, then you are able to share that with your critical friends—that is, Focus #4: *Self-study requires a transparent research process that clearly and accurately documents the research process through dialogue and critique.* Self-study necessitates a disposition of openness to outside views, questions, and critique. Self-study teachers strive to make one's practice explicit to oneself and to others. The transparency of the research process is enhanced through the review of critical friends who ask probing questions and offer alternative perspectives and interpretations.

As Bullough and Pinnegar (2004), who were at the vanguard of quality issues in self-study research, argue, "Like any good research self-study must represent rigorous data gathering and analysis" (p. 340). Although their work is specific to autobiographical self-study research, the guidelines they offer have been integrated into the methodological components for self-study research presented in this text. This recognized need for quality in conducting and reporting self-study research was a major impetus in writing this book or what Samaras and Freese (2009) call "the need for brighter guideposts" (p. 13).

The field of self-study research has developed and continues to develop as a school of thought. During its formalization period and afterward, self-study scholars worked to formalize self-study research by offering suggestions for improving the quality in the reporting of data analysis (Feldman, 2003; LaBoskey, 2006; Loughran, 2007a). I observed in the early self-study conference proceedings (Kosnik, Freese, & Samaras, 2002a) that while self-study scholars wrote in detail about their experiences and subsequent discoveries in their practice, on several accounts, there was less detail about how researchers arrived at those conclusions. Hamilton and Pinnegar (1998) make the case that "the value of self-study depends on the researcher/teachers providing convincing evidence that they know what they claim to know" (p. 243). Keep in mind, as McNiff and Whitehead (2005) state, that "data and evidence are not the same thing . . . you now have to decide which pieces are directly relevant to what you are claiming to have achieved" (p. 92). Samaras and Freese (2006) provide a detailed example of a teacher's data collected in a series of videotape and dialogue journal analyses including the teacher researcher's categories, descriptions, and findings (pp. 92–95). Whether you decide to chart your analysis, place it in a table or matrix, or color-code it as text, what is important is that, as Feldman (2003) purports, self-study researchers should "provide clear and detailed descriptions of how we collect data . . . provide detail of the research methods used . . . [and] provide clear and detailed descriptions of how we constructed the representation from our data" (pp. 27–28).

Validation, Exemplars, and Trustworthiness

You will recall the issue of validation and trustworthiness is addressed in the self-study methodological component, Focus #2: *Self-study teachers work in an intellectually safe and supportive community to improve their practice by making it explicit to themselves and to others through critical collaborative inquiries.* Critical friends play a key role in inquiring if the data collected accurately gauge what you sought to measure (i.e., validity). Critical friends are also key in validating your assumptions and interpretations of the impact of your research on student learning.

Assessing the quality of your work demands "tactics for drawing and verifying conclusions" (Miles & Huberman, 1994, p. 277) with others. Those tactics include validation, trustworthiness, reliability, and generalizability. Prominent self-study scholars Loughran and Northfield (1998) make the case that "colleagues are likely to frame an experience in ways not thought of by the person conducting the study. . . . The requirements for reliability and validity are addressed in the way the self-study is developed. They include the involvement of others, and the interplay of ideas, questions and challenges introduced through interaction with others" (p. 13). Critical friends push each other to explore areas that might be uncomfortable and circumvent "rationalizing or justifying one's action or frames of reference" (Loughran & Northfield, 1998, p. 7). In the early stages of the formalization of self-study, Cole and Knowles (1998) strongly encouraged self-study researchers to "explicate goals, intentions, and processes . . . so that appropriate appraisals can be made about the value of such work" and "work toward maintaining the integrity of self-study research through explicit adherence to methodological standards (broadly defined)" (p. 231).

Procedures for validation coming out of the "traditional positivist criteria of internal and external validity" and experimental model have been recast as trustworthiness and authenticity in the work of practitioners and constructivists (Lincoln & Guba, 2000, p. 158). Janesick (2000) recommends "replacing validity, generalizability, and reliability with qualitative referents" (p. 393). Mishler (1990) likened validation to the fabled Gordian Knot and stated, "The apparent increase in rigor and precision of successive advances in methods have brought us no closer to resolving the special problems faced by inquiry-guided researchers" (pp. 416–417). Instead, Mishler proposed a "new perspective" about validation as the "social construction of knowledge" or "whether the relevant community of scientists evaluates reported findings as sufficiently trustworthy to rely on them for their own work" (p. 417).

Mishler concurs with Kuhn (1996) on the role and importance of exemplars or "concrete models of research practice" (Mishler, 1990, p. 415) in research as helping shift and validate emerging research paradigms. If we consider that in practitioner research validation is "not a statistical property but rather a social, mutual, and cumulative process of formulating and implementing practice, collecting data on the results of implementing practice, sharing and discussing the results, refining the questions, and trying out recalibrated practices" (Pine, 2009, p. 83), then Mishler's work calls self-study teachers to present their work as exemplars and make them available for critique. Craig (2009) agrees with Lyons and LaBoskey

(2002) on the need for exemplars in narratives of self-study and elaborates on what those exemplars might look like:

> Because self-studies interrogate practice and often use narrative in a variety of ways, it makes sense to filter representative self-studies through the criteria Lyons and LaBoskey proposed. Such an approach would add to the body of knowledge concerning what is known about the trustworthiness of self-study of teaching and teacher education practices research in two important ways: one, rather than taking narrative in self-study for granted, as often is the case in both qualitative and quantitative types of research, narrative would be placed at the forefront of discussion; and two, the approach would offer a productive response to Zeichner's (2007) recent critique of self-study inquiries. (pp. 23–24)

Self-study is viewed as constructivist as "it includes elements of ongoing inquiry, respects personal experience, and emphasizes the role of knowledge construction" (Samaras & Freese, 2009, p. 8). If presented in rich detail and quality, the knowledge generated from self-study research can be useful to others. Self-study scholars such as Lyons and LaBoskey (2002) and Mittapalli and Samaras (2008) have worked to create exemplars so other inquiry-guided researchers can gauge the **trustworthiness** or "the degree to which we can rely on the concepts, methods, and inferences of a study, or tradition of inquiry, as the basis for our own theorizing and empirical research" (Mishler, 1990, p. 419).

Hamilton and Pinnegar (2000) in speaking about the work of teacher educators call for integrity and trustworthiness as necessary to make informed judgments about practice for the good of students and their students. By systematically collecting data, questioning and dialogue with colleagues, and articulating motivations and the process of a reframing of their practice, "we can evaluate individual practices, understand teaching better, change our practice to respond to the needs of our students and, most importantly, create practice that stands as an embodied testament to our belief" (p. 238). Establishing trustworthiness is strengthened by using multiple and varied data sources (i.e., triangulation), which increases the credibility and affirming of your interpretations (Glesne, 2006).

Pine (2009), conducting a literature review on validity, identifies a dozen ways to consider validity based on the existing literature, which he cites extensively:

1. *Catalytic validity* or "To what extent has the research energized participants to know and understand reality so they can transform it?" (p. 85)

2. *Consequential validity* or "What are the value implications of the research?" (p. 85)

3. *Democratic validity* or "To what degree has the research been done in collaboration with all stakeholders?" (p. 85)

4. *Dialogical validity* or "To what degree has the research encouraged and generated a reflective and critical dialogue among all participants in the research?" (p. 86)

5. *Ethical validity* or "Have the elements of human subjects protection such as permissions, confidentiality, privacy, and truth been present throughout the research process?" (p. 86)

6. *Interpersonal validity* or "Was the research characterized by interpersonal openness and trust?" (p. 87)

7. *Outcome validity* or "To what extent are the findings of the study worth paying attention to?" (p. 87)

8. *Process validity* or "To what degree has triangulation been used to guard against biased views of events?" (p. 87)

9. *Public validity* or "To what extent have the researchers made the results of their research public and engaged in a dialogue about it?" (p. 88)

10. *Recursive validity* or "Has research been systematically conducted but in a way that is responsive to evolving understandings and circumstances in the research?" (p. 88)

11. *Social justice validity* or "To what extent has the research addressed issues of social justice, diversity, equity, civic discourse, and caring?" (p. 88)

12. *Values validity* or "Have the researchers articulated and justified their own intentions and beliefs for the research?" (p. 89)

Summarizing the work of Anderson, Herr, and Nihlen (2007), Pine (2009) notes the importance of critical and open debate among the participants and peers about the outcomes of the research. Pine (2009) presents this notion of "validity as inquiry" and agrees with Lather (1986) that "rather than seeing validity criteria as a form of intellectually 'policing' research, we need to move toward 'validity as incitement to discourse'" (pp. 83–84). Note it was suggested in Chapter 7 that you conduct a cultural inquiry of your research as proposed by Jacob (n.d.) as well as review the ethical validity of your research.

One way to help you make sense of the extensive literature about the multiple issues of validity is to practice dialogical validity, adapted here to include critical friends, and public validity. In Critical Friend Inquiry 11.2 below, I have adapted the notion of dialogical validity and public validity to be practiced among critical friends by incorporating the guidelines for identifying and dealing with validity and credibility threats proposed by Maxwell (2005).

CRITICAL FRIEND INQUIRY 11.2

Dialogical Validity

Practice dialogical validity with your critical friend and as a validation group with another dyad of critical friends. For example, you can recognize and explain to your critical friends the limitation that intensive, long-term involvement was not possible within the limits of the course and project. You should also note any influences and biases that may have impacted your data in unexpected ways (e.g., students wanted to tell you what you wanted to hear; your different behavior or reactions to students resulted in the different behaviors).

Below is a series of questions or a checklist for validity adapted from the work of Maxwell (2005, pp. 109–114). Ask your critical friend to ask you the following questions to help you examine the validity of your study.

1. Over what period of time did your data collection and strategies take place? What are the implications for the length of your involvement and activity on the outcomes of your study? Will you include a discussion of time restraints in your limitations discussion?

2. Present the data you collected as specifically as you can. Include what you collected, when you collected it, why you collected it, and how you collected it. Was it "rich" and varied to provide a clear picture of your context and topic?

3. Did you systematically solicit feedback and critique about your study? Did others check your ongoing interpretations of data?

4. Have you considered if and how your role as teacher and your position as teacher in the study impacted the results you obtained? Do you think any of your strategies influenced how you saw your students and/or how they reacted to you?

5. Were there any instances or outliers that didn't seem to fit with the data? Did you examine the discrepant data carefully to assess plausible reasons?

6. Did you practice triangulation and/or crystallization, collecting data from various sources and using a variety of methods?

7. Did any of your data present an opportunity for you to quantify them? Did you present how and if the quantitative support added any new information to your interpretation?

8. If your study involved multiple cases, did you provide a discussion of a within-case and a cross-case analysis as well as "assertions or an interpretation of the meaning of the case" (Creswell, 2007, p. 75)?

9. Have you been honest with your reporting? Could you have been mistaken about any outcomes?

10. Have you provided sufficient evidence to support your claims?

11. Do you see any flaws in your research design for collecting, analyzing, and interpreting your data that posed threats to the validity and credibility of your study?

12. What do you see as the major strengths and areas for research design refinement in your study?

RELIABILITY

You will find the research consideration of reliability addressed in the self-study methodological component of Focus #2: *Self-study teachers work in an intellectually safe and supportive community to improve their practice by making it explicit to themselves and to others through critical collaborative inquiries.* Additionally connected to the issue of reliability is Focus #4: *Self-study requires a transparent research process that clearly and accurately documents the research process through dialogue and critique.*

You may decide to use **check coding** on a coding sample with your critical friend (i.e., "when two researchers code the same data set and discuss their initial difficulties," [which] "aids definitional clarity but also is a good reliability check" [Miles & Huberman, 1994, p. 64]). When two coders working independently arrive at similar conclusions it improves the reliability and consistency of a measure. LaBoskey (2006) concurs with Loughran (2004) noting,

[We need to] make our learning from self-study more accessible to others by stating the "assertions" that result from that research clearly and boldly. Only in that way can the ideas be employed, applied, and re-tested by the teacher education community in ways that will help us to embrace, discard, or transform those assertions; this is the essence of the validation process for the field. (p. 258)

GENERALIZABILITY

You will find the research consideration of generalization addressed in the following self-study methodological components: Focus #1: *Self-study teachers initiate their own inquiries and study them in their teaching context utilizing a self-study method aligned with that inquiry*; Focus #2: *Self-study teachers work in an intellectually safe and supportive community to improve their practice by making it explicit to themselves and to others through critical collaborative inquiries* (i.e., where the research has been reviewed with critical friends); and Focus #5: *Self-study research generates knowledge that is made public through presentation and publication* (i.e., where the implications of your study are considered by others in terms of applicability to their own contexts).

Even though your study is limited to your context and not generalizable beyond your classroom, you are attempting to demonstrate "the ability to design a coherent and feasible study, providing evidence that you are aware of the key issues in your proposed research and ways of dealing with these, rather than requiring a completely worked-out design" (Maxwell, 2005, p. 118). Providing a rich description of the context and the research process promotes its generalizability to others; "generalizability is not a claim that can be made by the self-study researcher without wider interaction with colleagues. Such interactions allow validation of experiences and ideas and, thus, self-study reports can be considered as an invitation to readers to link accounts with their own experiences" (Loughran & Northfield, 1998, p. 13).

Let's return to the self-study methodological research components presented throughout this text and add a self- and peer assessment component on the quality and validity of your self-study research. This is an essential critical friend inquiry for you (see Critical Friend Inquiry 11.3). It is designed to guide you in your self-assessment and your critical friend's assessment of the way you addressed the methodological components of self-study research. As teachers and learners, we also honor that our work is always under development, so look at this not as a summative but rather as a formative assessment.

Please note: The questions in Table 11.1 are *prompts*. You do not need to answer each one. Compose an essay on how well you addressed the Five Foci and on recognizing that the category of "developing critique" is appropriate for emerging self-study scholars. The activity is designed for you to be aware of issues of quality and validity and to work toward them as you continue your work as a self-study teacher researcher.

CRITICAL FRIEND INQUIRY 11.3

Self-Study Research Guidepost

SELF-ASSESSMENT AND CRITICAL
FRIEND ASSESSMENT OF FIVE FOCI

Table 11.1   Self-Assessment and Critical Friend Assessment of Five Foci

Focus	Methodological Component	Self-Assessment	Critical Friend(s) Assessment
Personal Situated Inquiry	*Self-study teachers initiate and study their own inquiry in their classroom and utilize a self-study method aligned with that inquiry.* Self-study is a self-initiated inquiry of practice and draws from a practitioner's experience. Self-study scholars can choose from various self-study methods to inquire into their practice, explore who they are as a researcher, and self-assess their practice. They consider the role culture plays in their theories and practices to assess its impact.	Did you clearly articulate your research question? Does your research question draw from your authority and experiences as a practitioner? Did you design a manageable inquiry with extended opportunities for change? Is the inquiry driven and generated from your questions situated in your particular context? Does the research have immediate utility to your setting and to others' work? Have you adequately described your context so readers might consider the generalizability and implications of your findings to their contexts? Did you thoroughly describe any historical information that is pertinent to this research?	__ Yes __ No __ Developing Critique:
Critical Collaborative Inquiry	*Self-study teachers work in an intellectually safe and supportive community to*	Have you involved critical friends in your inquiry?	__ Yes __ No

Focus	Methodological Component	Self-Assessment	Critical Friend(s) Assessment
	improve their practice by making it explicit to themselves and to others through critical collaborative inquiries. Collaboration contributes to a validation of findings because the analysis extends beyond one's personal views, thus addressing potential biases. Paradoxically, self-study is both personal and interpersonal. It is the community that helps extend an individual's understanding. Critical friends encourage and solicit respectful questioning and divergent views to gain alternative perspectives. Critical friend teams serve as a validation group to provide feedback on the quality and legitimacy of each other's claims.	Is the exchange among critical friends in the learning community respectful, constructive, and bidirectional? Did you describe the role critical friends played in supporting and validating your research? How did your critical friends help you test your analysis, thinking, and interpretations? Is there evidence that you reframed your thinking from the critical friend input? How did your critical friends' responses contribute to your analysis and reframed thinking? What was it like to have a critical friend and to be one?	__ Developing Critique:
Improved Learning	*Self-study teachers question the status quo of their teaching and the politics of schooling in order to improve and impact learning for themselves, their students, and the education field.* Self-study research can support and inform school and program reform and impact policy decisions.	Did you provide evidence of the value and impact of your work for those you work with, to yourself, and to others? Did you describe if the knowledge gained in this study improved personal, professional, program, and/or unit development? What is the "so what" of my research? Does your inquiry serve to inform policy and educational reform? Does your inquiry inform social justice issues?	__ Yes __ No __ Developing Critique:

(Continued)

Table 11.1 (Continued)

Focus	Methodological Component	Self-Assessment	Critical Friend(s) Assessment
Transparent and Systematic Research Process	*Self-study requires a transparent research process that clearly and accurately documents the research process through dialogue and critique.* Self-study includes a hermeneutic spiral of questioning, discovering, framing, reframing, and revisiting. The method you choose for self-study depends a good deal on your questions and the impact you seek to make in your professional practice and education writ large. Self-study necessitates a disposition of openness to outside views, questions, and critique. Self-study teachers strive to make their practice explicit to themselves and to others. The transparency of the research process is enhanced through the review of critical friends who ask probing questions and offer alternative perspectives and interpretations.	Did you clearly explain what data you collected; how you collected them; why you selected them; and when you collected them? Have you explained the theoretical stance to your work? Did you explain why you chose a particular self-study method and how the method allowed you to effectively explore and answer your research question? Did you collect sufficient data from multiple sources and techniques to support your claims? Did you provide detailed documentation of an audit trail of your data analysis? Did you include a discussion documenting the adequacy of data collection and analysis? Did you discuss the quality control procedures and the steps you took toward establishing trustworthiness of your self-study? Did you describe the role that critical friends played in the validation of your findings? Did you provide evidence of reflective reframing and transformative thinking? Did you return to answering your research questions in your findings?	__ Yes __ No __ Developing Critique:

Focus	Methodological Component	Self-Assessment	Critical Friend(s) Assessment
		Since self-study is a hermeneutic process with spiral questioning, did you explain how your research led to refined or new research questions?	
		Were you critical of yourself in your research role?	
		Were you willing to share your concerns?	
		Were you willing to receive constructive criticism?	
		Were you open to new ideas and different perspectives?	
		Did you reflect on your role as both researcher and researched?	
		Did you share this self-assessment with your critical friends?	
Knowledge Generation and Presentation	*Self-study research generates knowledge that is made public through presentation and publication.* Self-study research contributes broadly to the knowledge base of personal, professional, program, and school development. Making the study public allows it to be available for review and critique. It contributes to the accumulation of content- and issue-based knowledge and serves to build validation across related work.	Did you provide a discussion on what new knowledge was generated from your research? Did you note what your study contributes to the field at large? In what way(s) did you share your research, or how do you intend to make your research public for review and critique?	__ Yes __ No __ Developing Critique:

KEY IDEAS

- Essential to the quality of your study is that your data are derived from multiple and varied sources and perspectives.
- The notion of multiplicity in data gathering and analysis as central to research design is known as triangulation.
- The prism effect allows you to alter your view through a different medium (i.e., your critical friend helps illuminate new ideas and show you something that may be present all along but not obvious or visible to you alone).
- Research considerations of assessing the quality of your study include transparency, validation, exemplars, trustworthiness, reliability, and generalizability.
- Self-assessment and critical friend assessment of the Five Foci provide an opportunity for dialogical validity and public validity of your research.

Write

If you want to engage your reader, tell a story because stories are much more memorable than theoretical abstractions. Focus on a telling incident, rather than a long, chronological narrative. After sharing with your reader the essential, compelling details of the incident, you can then explain what the incident reveals about you at the time of its occurrence as well as what you have gleaned from it since.

—Janet Jakusz Favero (personal communication, July 6, 2009),
*Upper School Learning Specialist, Writing Lab Coordinator, and
Learning Department Cochair, The Key School, Annapolis, Maryland*

CHAPTER DESCRIPTION

In this chapter, you are encouraged to write the story you know better than anyone else since you have lived it as a teacher and researcher throughout the research process. Some friendly writing advice is offered about the writing process including making time to write with an established and regular routine, writing from Day 1, participating in a research and writing community, sharing your work with critical friends, and believing that you have an important story to tell. Guidelines are offered for crafting the findings and discussion sections of your final research report. The chapter focuses on the methodological component of self-study research of knowledge generated through writing.

♦ Reading this chapter will provide an opportunity for you to learn about habits for writing, techniques for structuring and formatting the writing of your research, and the importance of critical friend support and critique in that process.

As a doctoral student, I was part of a doctoral support group affectionately known as *The Greta Girls* and composed of a handful of women, all of whom worked with the same advisor. We worked to balance our family and academic lives and tried to keep each other on track with both. I recall telling these colleagues how I found myself cleaning my house instead of working on writing about my project. And I don't even like to clean my house! They totally understood my procrastination and offered their empathy.

SOME FRIENDLY WRITING ADVICE

You have worked to validate your data analysis and interpretations with your critical friends. You have presented how you collected data, your data analysis trail, and how you made sense of your data. Now you are ready to write up your final and formal research report. Why write about your research? As teachers, we recognize that our classroom is a unique learning environment filled with unique students. And yet, we also realize that, as teachers, we face similar challenges and can learn from each other. When you write up your research project and communicate your findings with others, you are advancing the field of teaching and information about your research topic. You are generating new understandings about teaching and learning. Making time to write about your project allows others to learn from you.

Writing is a process. I often hear students indicating they will write their paper when they have a big block of time. Now, let's be realistic. How many of us have a big block of time as teachers to just write and close out all other responsibilities? Even if you had time and a remote place to work, like a beach house or a lakeside cabin, how would you organize and manage time to write? What are some structures for effective writing?

Many scholars have written about the habits of effective writing, how to avoid writing blocks, how not to procrastinate, how to become confident and comfortable with your writing (Boice, 1990, 1994, 1996), and giving yourself permission to be a good writer without getting caught up in the "power of rules" or early negative writing experiences (Becker, 2007; Brodkey, 1996; Elbow, 2000). There are countless books on editing, writing style, and grammar (e.g., Becker, 2007; Strunk & White, 1979; Williams, 1994). Scholars highly recommend sharing your early writing with colleagues (Gray, 2005; Richards, 2007), which you have done through your critical friend work. Figure 12.1 offers some friendly advice gleaned from a large array of resources and also from a course I developed titled "Dissertation to Publication" to provide guidelines for emerging scholars to write and publish their work.

Get a routine and keep it.

Life moves forward quickly. Daily living swallows up our time. We often sigh and wonder, "Where did all the time go?" We get busy and busier with things that push us away from other things we planned to do. Routine matters, and keeping it matters more. If you have ever tried to start something new and wanted to sustain it, then you know that routine matters. Otherwise, the activity gets put on the back burner and may just stay there. It may be like that treadmill you bought and meant to get back to: Without a routine you never really hit your stride. Also, "Like golfers who play only occasionally, sporadic writers can expect to struggle and think of giving up the game" (Boice, 1994, p. 237). Explain to friends and family that this writing is important to you. We make excuses to others instead of promises to ourselves. How do you make writing a routine, like brushing your teeth or exercising?

Figure 12.1   Some Friendly Writing Advice

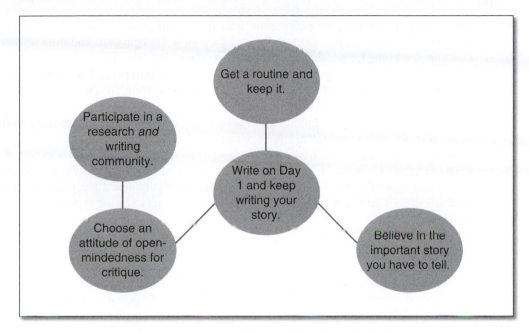

First of all, stop waiting for the right time and the right place, and set a routine to write. Make an appointment on your calendar to write. Post your calendar in front of your computer. Your routine can be that you write in the early morning. You might set a specific time, like 8 p.m. each evening. Gray (2005) states, "Writing daily, even for 15–30 minutes, greatly increases scholarship productivity compared to writing infrequently in big blocks of time ('binges')" (p. 13).

Use the recommended Self-Study Research Project Timeline presented in Table 2.2 and adapt it to your schedule. But have a schedule, plan ahead, and monitor your progress. Also schedule breaks and find small ways to reward yourself as you reach the goals you set for yourself. Writing does not have to be painful and can actually be quite enjoyable. Moxley (1997) recommends "a change in your writing environment . . . to help you see your work in new ways" (p. 13). The problem with not having some routine is that it becomes too easy to find things to purposely distract you. Just work to keep a momentum going and don't procrastinate (Boice, 1996).

Write on Day 1 and keep writing your story.

You wrote something on Day 1 of your research (i.e., your pondering about your research question). You have been writing all along as you moved through the research process. The critical friend inquiries served to scaffold your work and offered you a structure for ease of this next step (i.e., writing up your formal research project). You first wrote about your ideas, what you wondered about in your teaching, and why you cared about the topic. You took notes about your research rationale and wrote a research proposal. If you keep in mind that the research and writing are continuous throughout your project, that frame of mind will propel you to finish. As you learned earlier, it's essential to begin your literature review and continue searching for relevant research during your study. Take Gray's (2005) good advice, "Don't wait to start writing until you finish the literature review—and don't wait until you finish your research either" (p. 30). Write about what you are planning to do. Write about what is going on in your classroom during your study.

Each of the critical friend inquiries was designed to structure a space for writing, to break down, scaffold, and organize your large writing project. The critical friend work was in essence small drafts of a larger draft. It's interesting how "calling something a 'draft' can be a device to relieve tension, a way to suspend your overly critical reading of what you have written, a way of putting aside your feelings of inadequacy" (Bogdan & Biklen, 2007, p. 210). One of my critical friends, Clare Kosnik, always reminded our self-study writing group, "Nothing is in stone," and that gave us something to push up against, shape, and reshape. Perhaps you will want to share early thinking and/or quote yourself or an insight that marked a turning point in your thinking about your research question or problem with your critical friend. Drafts are meant to be changed, so honor the incompleteness of your work. Writing is not the same as editing. Just get things on paper. You can later polish and edit, which takes time.

Also take time to reward yourself. Take artistic leave by going to a performance or a museum; or take a walk in the park. I always discover new ideas when I move away from my computer for a while to think with fresh eyes and also to let others' creativity spark and ignite my own.

Advice From a Self-Study Scholar
Writing Backward From the Results

Self-study scholars using qualitative methods do not write in a straight line. They design a study, write a proposal, review studies on the topic, and plan a way to answer their focused research question. However, when they draft the results section, they begin to revise the methods section to reflect what they actually did and the changes they made to help them address their inquiry. Likewise they revise the literature review to delete any article that is no longer relevant to the direction the study actually took and to add any that are related to unexpected findings. As they go, they note on the side any implications, should-have-dones, should-do-nexts, and so-whats that rise to attention, thereby forming the conclusion. Repeating such forays from results to literature to conclusion and back as needed, they craft a compelling narrative. The very last step is to rewrite the introduction, drawing the reader onto a clear path through the argument to what now seems like a logical conclusion.

Linda May Fitzgerald
University of Northern Iowa

Participate in a research *and* writing community.

Writing does not have to be a lonely craft. Indeed, "Isolation not only hurts writers in terms of loneliness and understimulation. It makes writers work harder than they need to" (Boice, 1994, p. 243). Using the design for self-study research presented in this book, you have been receiving continuous feedback from your critical friends from the day you started. You talked about your early research ideas and interests. You thought about and developed a purpose statement and a rationale. You wrote memos about your data collection and data analysis. Now, write as if you are still talking to your critical friend. Each of the research memos to your critical friends is a valuable piece of writing with sections that can be cut and pasted into a report. You might have kept a researcher log or wrote journals about your research. Those writings have components that may be useful to include in your report.

The fascinating impact of collaborating with critical friends is that you learn from them and through them by sharing your drafts. They in turn learn about their research from offering you feedback. By offering them your critical eye, you may notice revisions also needed in your work. Wolcott (2001) speaks on the reciprocal benefits of review: "Editing the work of others also affords opportunity to recognize desirable practices in their writing that we are not always able to discern on our own" (p. 114). Wolcott further adds that providing editorial review not only affords you valuable experience but engages you in the collective responsibility for improving the quality of research. In speaking of this "transformative power of reviewing," Graue (2006) asserts that peer review "is a lot of work, but in the big scheme of things it is a pretty important investment. Surprisingly, the investment is not just in others or in the field. It might just be in you" (p. 41).

Photo 12.1   Writing Support Group

Sharing your drafts with writing groups and experts and discussing your work with each other allows you to gain ongoing feedback, encourages you to stay on schedule, and assists you in moving beyond a place where you feel stuck in your writing (see Photo 12.1, p. 231) (Bogdan & Biklen, 2007; Glesne, 2006; Gray, 2005). Don't underestimate the importance of the editing advice you gain from others and provide for them (Klein, Riordian, Schwartz, & Sothiros, 2008). Pay attention to the edits colleagues give you to save you time later (e.g., grammar, punctuation, or using American Psychological Association style). DeAngelis (2008) recommends keeping "a running list of errors you tend to make or that professors have commented on in your papers" (p. 41) so as not to repeat the same mistakes later.

Choose an attitude of open-mindedness for critique.

Boice (1994) offers extensive "rules for comfort and fluency" in writing and emphasizes that researchers must pay attention to how they react to and learn from mistakes: "The best way to handle criticism is to anticipate it, acknowledge it, and learn from it" (p. 244). I have observed how well some critical friends offered and received critique in faculty teaching groups (Samaras et al., 2006), in a class setting (Samaras et al., 2007), and with my colleagues (Kosnik, 2008). My former students reported, "We have learned that working with a critical friend requires accessibility and an open mind throughout the writing process. . . . The role of a critical friend is pivotal to the developmental process of self-study research. That is why optimal feedback provided by critical friends is invaluable to each student's formal self-study research project" (Breslin et al., 2008, p. 33).

Critical friend work isn't something done as a one-shot peer review or after the writing begins. It begins on Day 1 and continues throughout the project so researchers become more accustomed to soliciting, receiving, and giving each other feedback. Prolonged engagement matters. Critical friend work can be problematic (Schuck, Aubusson, & Buchanan, 2008; Schuck & Russell, 2005). Being open-minded is eased when you are working with colleagues you have worked with over time, but that is not enough. Trust builds gradually and allows you to "learn how to listen better" (Gray, 2005, p. 63). You may agree with Bogdan and Biklen (2007) who argue, "People who really care about your development will engage you and discuss the good and the bad" (p. 215). Indeed, self-study requires a stance of vulnerability and confidence and a disposition of openness to outside views, questions, and critique (Loughran, 2004).

Believe in the important story you have to tell.

Remember those young children I mentioned in the beginning of the book whom I observed getting their hands dirty in order to learn? I spent countless hours observing and working with children during my doctoral studies in early childhood education. Another amazing thing I have observed about young children is that their early writing can be prompted by the stories they tell and often enact during their dramatic play.

If you observe young children in a circle time, in a dramatic play center, outside on a playground, or even riding in a car, they anxiously tell their stories. They gain practice in putting their ideas together, sequencing them, and articulating them to others. There are a setting, characters, a plot of some sort, and not necessarily a grand conclusion to their stories. There may not be a clear introduction, a body, and any final thoughts. Nonetheless, the storytelling will serve their later writing development. With time their story structure improves. Yet, as adults we forget we have important stories to share and that we can tell our stories. Yes, you can tell your research story. Believe in its impact for others. You add knowledge to the field of teaching by telling and writing your story.

Below is Critical Friend Inquiry 12.1, which my students find quite useful.

CRITICAL FRIEND INQUIRY 12.1

Author's Chair of Draft

One way of sharing your writing drafts with critical friends is to use an Author's Chair format. It is a format that allows you to see if your story is coherent and clear to someone else. "The term Author's Chair comes from language arts and is an activity where writers present their own writing to peers who ask questions of the author" (Samaras, 2002, p. 89). You are, after all, the author of your research, which was the first recommended principle in designing your research presented in Chapter 6. The Author's Chair format capitalizes on the social dimensions of writing and facilitates perspective taking. It is recommended that this activity include both oral and written drafts of your work. That is, give your critical friend an electronic copy of your draft ahead of time and then share it orally. Your critical friend can track comments on your paper and then present questions for you to consider during your oral presentation of the draft.

As in all the critical friend work, reverse roles and repeat the activity again with your critical friend's research. Below are some *suggested* prompts:

1. Read the central question of your research. Your critical friend(s) will comment on its clarity.

2. Explain your rationale for this research. Your critical friend(s) will offer you feedback on its authenticity to your question.

3. Read a segment of your literature review that demonstrates your understanding of applying theories to your practice. Your critical friend(s) will discuss the clarity of your presentation of theory and practice.

4. Describe your data collection set. Your critical friend(s) will offer feedback related to how well the data align with your research question.

5. Offer the details of your data analysis. Your critical friend(s) will ask you to pause when something doesn't make sense and ask for clarification.

6. Present your major findings. Your critical friend(s) may ask for further explanation of your findings. Your critical friend(s) will offer comments on completeness and the evidence you provide for your interpretations.

7. Read the major points you make in your discussion about the impact of your study. Your critical friend(s) will prompt you to clarify and extend components that may need further thought.

After your draft sessions with your critical friend, the next step is to formalize your self-study teacher report. Below is an example of critical friend feedback after the reading of a first draft:

12.1 Student Example: Critical Friend Feedback on Writing

Darwin Kiel, *Mathematics Teacher*

Martin,

I do have some comments and suggestions. It looks like you have adequately addressed every item in the template/rubric. You have been thorough, and your analysis and interpretation of the data is good.

I know that you constructed this report from parts and pieces, so at this point, I would suggest that you work at "polishing" the overall document.

Print the entire document and find a comfortable chair. Read through the whole report. Pretend that you did not write it and that you have never seen it before. Just try to follow what the guy is saying and see the big picture.

Read it through again to look for potential edits. Do not make changes right away; just mark the candidates. Look for duplicated phrases and ideas. Look for statements that do not advance the story. Look for phrases that might be made clearer.

Now look over the candidates you marked and consider what changes you want to make. Rewrite anywhere you see an opportunity for improvement.

I hope this helps you. See you Monday night.

From,
Darwin

Sources: From Shaw, M. (2008); Kiel, D. (2008). Class activity.

WRITING YOUR RESEARCH REPORT

See "Suggested Research Project Headings Template" for accuracy of what exactly should be included in your report. Some general advice and examples are included below.

Writing Your Introduction

You can easily insert your earlier writing about your research question, rationale, and literature review. That is the beauty of writing your report as you move through the research

process. You have written critical friend memos and perhaps some other critical collaborative inquiries, which will also be useful in your introduction.

Writing Your Method Section

The method section includes (a) a detailed description of your context; (b) a detailed description of your participants; (c) a detailed description of what data you collected, your rationale for collecting each data set, how you collected your data, and when you collected them;
and (d) a detailed description of your pedagogical strategies.

Describe Your Context

You will know the context of your study and your participants early and can insert those
descriptions into the report. Write a detailed description of your research context
including the immediate and broader environment (e.g., your classroom, school, and
school community). Students often find demographic information on school and school
district Web sites although they never include the actual names of schools or school
divisions.

Below is an example of a social studies teacher describing the context of his research:
(a) community, (b) school, and (c) classroom.

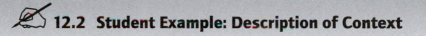 **12.2 Student Example: Description of Context**

James Mercer (2008), *Social Studies Teacher*

Community Demographics: Kingfield Township. The community of Kingfield Township is composed
of approximately 45,000 people. Kingfield Township is the main feeder of students for Kingfield Junior
High School. Kingfield Township lies within the planning district of Bloom Hill.[1] This district has a
6-to-1 ratio of Caucasians to African Americans (the next closest ethnic group).[2] Other minority groups
include Asian/Pacific Islanders and Hispanics. Of the population of 45,000 people in the township,
families comprise a little over 12,000 people.[3] According to a recent census, there are approximately
6,000 children who fall within the range (6–17) attending school in the township. Kingfield Township
is considered a middle-class community, with a majority of its 18,000 households earning over
$75,000 per year or better.

School Demographics: Kingfield Junior High. Kingfield Junior High is a very diverse community.
There is no one ethnicity that has a majority. Caucasians have a plurality at 35% of the population,
followed by African Americans at 27%, Hispanics at 18%, and Asians at 13%. We have a few

(Continued)

---

[1],[2],[3]Adapted from county statistics; Planning District Profile

(Continued)

families from Europe and the Middle East. In my classes, I have students from Russia, Lebanon, Egypt, and Tunisia. I believe the diversity of our school will benefit our students in the long run, for they will have a greater capacity of empathy for other cultures and ethnicities. We have had some great discussions this year generated from the students' cultural backgrounds. One student explained the differing cultural practices of Islam, comparing his family's view in Tunisia to Saudi Arabia's view (Wahhabism). Although the school has a large foreign base, of the 997 total students, 79% of those students are English proficient.[4] Scholastically, Kingfield Junior High has climbed steadily in the last few years. Last year, 85% of the students passed their Standards of Learning (SOL) exams, up 2.1% from the previous year, with 40% of those students reaching the advanced level (up 16% from the year before).[5]

Classroom Setting: Room 6022. When you enter my classroom, the first thing you might notice is that I have tried to create a welcoming setting. My desk is not in the front, like a traditional class setting. This was done for two reasons. First, I want my students and fellow teachers to know that my room is always open and that I am available to meet their needs. In my experience, when a teacher has his or her back to the door, he or she does not want to be disturbed. Second, when my students are working, I have a unique perspective from my desk, to be able to assess their level of work ethic, or aptitude for the assignments. The desks are set up in a "U," facing the front dry-erase boards. This format allows me to have equal access to most of the students in the room. It also allows for sections of the room to work as teams during certain lessons.

Describe Your Participants

Your research should include a detailed description of your research participants with demographic information. Below is an example involving a science teacher that highlights just how useful it can be for a researcher to gather information about the context and participants to inform a research question and possible pedagogical strategies. Notice how the data collected about the participants are useful to the researcher's understanding of the research problem. Research support from the literature review is integrated in the discussion as demonstrated in the example below.

[4,5] Middle school demographics

✎ 12.3 Student Example: Description of Participants

Stacy Dumaresq (2009), *Science Teacher*

"How can I as a science teacher best help my ESOL
[English for Speakers of Other Languages] students learn science content language?"

Participants

The participants of my study are the students in my eighth-period adapted biology class. The class consists of 14 students ranging in age from 14 years old to 18 years old. The students have been in this country anywhere from 1 to 5 years. Two girls and 12 boys participated in the study. The students come from 11 different countries. They are from Sierra Leone, Bangladesh, Pakistan, Ethiopia, Vietnam, Korea, Peru, El Salvador, Bolivia, Puerto Rico, and the Dominican Republic. There are seven different languages spoken by the students of my adapted biology class, including Bengali, Krio, Urdu, Amaric, Korean, Vietnamese, and Spanish. The students have varying levels of science background knowledge. Three of the students took a biology class in their native country. The rest of the students have been taught anywhere from a few months' to a year's worth of concepts.

The students in my adapted biology class are required to take the same Standards of Learning as all other students. This proves to be especially challenging because, though they may know the biology content, they may miss a question because they don't understand the vocabulary. I have often noticed that when my students encounter a word they do not know, they just give up and guess instead of trying to decipher the word's meaning. ESOL students have an especially difficult time with science because not only are they still working on learning basic English literacy, but they also need to locate, interpret, and apply an entire science vocabulary (Carrier, 2005). Though the students may be relatively fluent in conversational English, many are still lacking in science content language because it is used so much less frequently on a day-to-day basis. The content language can also be very confusing to ESOL students because there are many terms in the English language that sound very similar but have very different meanings (Carrier, 2005). For instance, in my class we use the term *concentration* to mean the amount of solute in a solvent. When I ask the students in my adapted biology class if they know the meaning of the word *concentration*, they usually say, "Yes, it means to think or focus really hard on something." Though that is a correct meaning of the word, it is not the meaning I am looking for in the science classroom.

Writing Your Findings Section

What a great feeling! You have now collected and analyzed your data. But you don't want to leave your work in that form. The next step is to write up and explain your interpretations based on your analysis. Restate your research question and the data you collected, and then list and enumerate the findings or the major themes that emerged from your data. Circle back to the research question you posed and what you discovered. Explain how your research helped you answer that question. This is where you get to tell your story about the study. You really have been writing your report from the beginning of this book. You should be able to incorporate into your paper and refine much of what you have already written.

I find students often get confused with the difference between the analysis section and the findings section. The analysis section of your final report is the documentation and reporting of the data you analyzed. Your interpretations of the data generated from your categories and the evidence you found to support them are generally reported in a section titled "Findings," which appears after your data analysis section. It is recommended that you use subheadings of your key findings or themes in your findings section to help your reader follow your claims supported by your data. Provide sufficient detail to justify and build a case for your findings and conclusions.

Providing one or two good examples may help illustrate a point you are trying to make. As the researcher, you really do know what happened in your own research. So don't be afraid to state it in your own words. Sometimes, researchers include too many quotes or lengthy quotes rather than offer the most significant comments. Use quotes to support your interpretations and "to provide a definitive enunciation of a key point" (Murray & Lawrence, 2000, p. 188), but don't overuse them. Your quotes should be selective and short and help you make a case or illuminate a finding (Glesne, 2006). Quotes should not be used to carry all the weight of your argument (i.e., don't expect someone to just read the quote and figure out the finding). Offer enough context so the quote makes sense to readers (Robinson & Kuin Lai, 2006).

There are different styles of including quotes (Booth, Colomb, & Williams, 2003; Creswell, 2007):

1. Embed the quotation within your own sentence (e.g., They felt pushed outside their comfort zones and "forced to clearly map out a plan and organize thoughts to communicate them").

2. Write the quotation to stand alone and introduce it with a colon or an explanation (e.g., In terms of curriculum design, course projects required peer feedback. A student stated: "The activities you have planned to build relationships and promote socialization and feelings of trust have created a positive and rich learning environment").

3. Set off long quotations of 40 words or more in a block quote.

Most of all, I realized that I had to trust dismantling the power relationship I held as "professor." I worried that students would take advantage of me, and I wrote about that to Anne, who served as my critical friend. Although I explained that I really wanted their feedback at the beginning of the course, they weren't sure if they should offer it. I also serve as a doctoral advisory committee member for two of the students. As they read the self-study literature, I believe they understood that self-study scholars genuinely ask for others' perspectives. Once I trusted the process and let go of the "I" and "thou" power position, wonderful learning took place. I observed empathy, care, and consideration for one another's research and efforts. When students also let go of their position as "student," they became a different kind of learner, and we became more than a class or a course to take (Samaras et al., 2007).

Writing Your Discussion Section

Discuss what you have learned after conducting your study. Present how your research links or does not link to what other researchers have found about this topic. In the discussion section of your report, "the focus shifts from a close examination of the data to the big picture, by linking the findings to the original research question and the literature (prior research) and discussing their implications" (Robinson & Kuin Lai, 2006, p. 186). Offer a narrative of the impact of this research on your students' learning and for improving your teaching. Provide a thoughtful discussion of the implications of your research to your school, families, community, and education on a broad level. Wolcott (2001) argues against a grand finale or conclusion and recommends, "Rather than striving for closure, see if you can leave both yourself and your readers pondering the essential issues that perplex you" (p. 123). While you learned a great deal from this research, discuss what questions presented themselves for further study. Since research and teaching are processes, we have the opportunity and responsibility to continue to learn.

Your discussion of the impact of your research can be presented in three sections, either separately or in an integrated fashion: (a) discussion about the impact of your research on your students, (b) discussion about the impact of your research on your teaching, and (c) discussion about the impact of your research on the education field. Let's look more specifically at ideas for discussing the impact of your research on your teaching and professional development.

Critical Friend Inquiry 12.2 will also be useful for developing your reflections and writing about the impact of your research on your teaching.

CRITICAL FRIEND INQUIRY 12.2

Exit Paper

Teachers sometimes assign students exit papers so they can reflect on what they learned at the end of a class, a unit, or a course. Now, here's an opportunity for you to have a space to think deeply about what you learned about self-study teacher research and your project. Analyze and write about your research journey. Write an exit paper assessing your development as a self-study teacher scholar and how well you addressed the Five Foci in your project. This section can be adapted for the section of your final research project titled "Impact on Teacher." You may decide to use the rubric provided, complete a self-assessment of your exit paper, and then share it with a critical friend for his or her assessment as well (see Table 12.1). Below are some *suggested prompts.* You do not have to answer all the questions.

You might ask yourself:

1. What did you learn about yourself as a teacher researcher?

2. How has your perception of your inquiry changed? What became important and apparent? Insights? Next steps?

3. What were critical events that influenced your thinking while conducting your study?

4. Are there paradoxes that capture the essence and process of this work? These might include disharmony/harmony; despair/hope; status quo/change; struggle/success; or consistency/possibilities.

5. What role did critical friends play for you? What kind of critical friend were you?

6. What was your greatest aha or discovery?

7. What would you do differently next time in your research? What do you want to continue doing?

8. How well did you address the Five Foci or the methodological components of self-study research?

9. What are the most significant contributions of your work to students, to other teachers, and to the field?

10. What new questions emerged from your study that warrant further study?

Self-Study Research Guidepost

SELF-ASSESSMENT AND PEER RUBRIC ASSESSMENT OF EXIT PAPER

Table 12.1   Self-Assessment and Peer Rubric Assessment of Exit Paper

Distinguished 10 pts.	Proficient 9 pts.	Basic 8 pts.	Unsatisfactory Below 8 pts.
Personal Situated Inquiry Evidence of deep reflection and analysis about research situated in professional practice	Evidence of reflection and analysis about research situated in professional practice	Evidence of some reflection and analysis about research situated in professional practice	Little or no evidence of reflection and analysis about research situated in professional practice
Critical Collaborative Inquiry Significant reflection of evidence and effort to share and contribute to peers' research; significant movement beyond your own perspective and with contributions to professional knowledge base	Evidence of reflection and effort to share and contribute to peers' research; significant movement beyond your own perspective and with contributions to professional knowledge base	Some reflection and evidence of effort to share and contribute to peers' research; significant movement beyond your own perspective and with contributions to professional knowledge base	Little reflection and evidence of effort to share and contribute to peers' research; significant movement beyond your own perspective and with contributions to professional knowledge base

Distinguished 10 pts.	Proficient 9 pts.	Basic 8 pts.	Unsatisfactory Below 8 pts.
Learning as a Self-Study Scholar Honest and thorough appraisal of impact and understanding of self-study and its application in improving your teaching and your students' learning	Honest and good appraisal of impact and understanding of self-study and its application in improving your teaching	Honest and average appraisal of impact and understanding of self-study and its application in improving your teaching	Weak appraisal of understanding of impact of self-study and its application in improving your teaching
Transparent Research Process Consistently asking and exploring difficult questions about the complexities of research and self-study methods; excellent articulation of research misconceptions and thorough discussion of reframed understanding	Asking difficult questions about the complexities of research and self-study methods; good articulation of research misconceptions and good discussion of reframed understanding	Asking some difficult questions about the complexities of research and self-study methods; satisfactory articulation of research misconceptions and discussion of reframed understanding	Minimal questioning about the complexities of research and self-study methods; undeveloped summary of research misconceptions and reframed understanding
Writing and Presenting Excellent and clear organization, writing, and language mechanics; evidence of full participation in sharing exit paper with critical friend and integration of critical friend feedback	Good organization, writing, and language and language mechanics; good participation in sharing exit paper with critical friend and integration of critical friend feedback	Average organization, writing, and language mechanics; average participation in sharing exit paper with critical friend and integration of critical friend feedback	Poor organization, writing, and language mechanics; poor participation in sharing exit paper with critical friend and integration of critical friend feedback

Impact of Your Research on Your Teaching

In the discussion section, include your reflections and assessment of conducting your self-study research project informed from your exit paper. Explain how this research may have changed you as a professional, how it may affect your future practice, and what you might like to further explore. It is important to leave your reader with the idea that you have said something important about this problem, that it matters, and the next steps needed.

✐ 12.4 Student Example: Impact on Teacher (Excerpt)

Amy Smith (2008), *Middle School Science Teacher*

This research project has opened my eyes to a whole new thinking process about planning and administering the knowledge to the students. I want to have my students actively learning. I have been using hands-on activities easily because I am a science teacher and the nature of science teaching involves lab work. I need to make the learning meaningful and engaging in order for the students to get anything out of the lesson. You cannot just simply say, "Oh, it's hands on," and let the students go. To learn by doing, they must be able to also retain the information. I am still on the hunt for activities and strategies that will make me feel like I am reaching the students. I want to bring more real-life scenarios into the classroom so the students realize that they aren't just learning biology because the school system mandates it. I want to make sure that I am constantly being critical of myself and being honest as well.

WRITING YOUR ABSTRACT

When you are almost finished writing your research paper, write a single, articulate, concise paragraph of 120–150 words, double-spaced, and on a new page after the title page. An abstract describes your purpose, context, method, key findings, and implications. The abstract is inserted at the beginning of your paper, but you can't write it until you have completed your study as you don't have the findings or implications until that point. Keep in mind the same hallway passing statement principle you learned while composing your research proposal. Brevity is beautiful and a good research craft to learn. Craft a clear, crisp outline of your research that invites readers to read your paper.

It is imperative that others can understand what your study entailed and what was found. The clarity and completeness of your abstract will influence peers' decisions to read your full report, accept your work in a conference program, or consider it for funding and awards (Robinson & Kuin Lai, 2006). If you are considering submitting your work for publication, remember that the abstract is the first thing a reviewer sees after your title offering the reader a synthesis and "a sense of 'knowing' the story to come" (Murray & Lawrence, 2000, p. 194). The abstract may be thought of as the "'critical signpost' to a research report" (Murray & Lawrence, 2000, p. 193) and as such should be written with great care.

Writing the "Good" Abstract

1. Read the abstracts below carefully.

2. What do they demonstrate to you about the purpose of an abstract?

3. Choose one abstract and decide how it demonstrates the purpose you noted.

4. Discuss with your critical friend if it is a "good" abstract and why.

Student Examples of Abstracts

Abstract

The purpose of this research project was to increase the science literacy of students through the use of a current events blog. A science current events blog was created to link disconnected science concepts to real life. Students were presurveyed to determine what news they choose to follow and how they get their news. Students had three opportunities to participate in a class blog, the third of which was required. A postsurvey showed that students preferred blogging over reading about science. It was not clear if students were more likely to make connections between science theory and real life after blogging, but it did prove to be a positive strategy for promoting science literacy. By all types of students, the current events blogging activity was preferred over pen and paper literacy initiatives. In conclusion, blogging to make content more relevant and significant to students' lives is a viable science literacy strategy. (Brown, 2008)

Abstract

This research project, originally undertaken to determine how to motivate students to learn civics at a more rigorous level, also became a study of investigating students' and professional colleagues' perceptions of a rigorous civics curriculum. I employed several qualitative methods including presurveys, surveys, interviews, and a Likert scale evaluation of current and former students, as well as teachers. The analysis revealed that a majority of the students have diverse notions of how rigor is defined. Teachers, on the contrary, as stated in their surveys, do hold a universal definition of how rigor should be defined and an understanding of its impact on students' learning their respective curriculums. Teachers also have the responsibility to help students understand that they should challenge themselves in their educational development. Furthermore, they should provide the scaffolding necessary to support their students' endeavors in a more rigorous curriculum. (Mercer, 2008)

1. Does the abstract state the *main purpose of the research?*

2. Does the abstract describe the *method of data collection employed?*

3. Does the abstract include the *key findings?*

4. Does the abstract state the *major conclusions and implications?*

5. Overall, does the abstract explain *what the researcher did* and *what was discovered?* Does the abstract provide an accurate synthesis of the research conducted?

SUGGESTED RESEARCH PROJECT HEADINGS TEMPLATE

Below is a suggested heading and subheading template for your formal research report:

On the title page, include a running head with an abbreviated title in uppercase letters flush left with the page number flush right, and the title of the paper, author's name, and author's professional affiliation centered on the page.

Abstract

An abstract is a single, articulate, concise paragraph of no more than 150 words that describes your purpose and the context, method, key findings, and significance of your research. Create a page break from the title page. The running head and page numbering continue throughout the report.

[Include the title of your paper centered on the page.]

As per American Psychological Association (APA) style, the introduction does not need a heading; the first paragraphs are assumed to be the introduction. Introduce the purpose of the study set within the background and context of your classroom. A good introduction allows your readers to gain an overview and outline of the purpose of your paper. Present a *rationale*. Discuss the personal significance of this work to you as a teacher and the broader educational significance. Include your experiences, perspectives, and goals that influenced and shaped your interest in this research.

Statement of Research Problem/Question

Research Problem

Describe your research problem/question that emerged from your observation of and reflection on an issue, a tension, or a dilemma in your classroom.

Research Question

State your personal and manageable research question situated in your context. The question is meaningful to you and purposeful for improving your practice to impact learning for yourself and your students.

Review of the Literature

[Include headings of relevant topics found in the literature.]

Conduct a comprehensive review of the literature related to your topic with relevance to your research design and usefulness to extending knowledge of the field. Include in your discussion an integrated conceptual mapping of theories and phenomena that framed and shaped your study and were informed by the literature reviewed.

Method

Context: Description of the Community, School, and Classroom Setting

Provide a detailed description of the research context including the immediate and broader environment (e.g., your classroom, school, and school community).

Participants

Provide a detailed description of the research participants with demographic information.

Data Collection

Provide a detailed description of the pedagogical strategies you enacted and the multiple data sources you collected to help you understand the underlying problem and assess the impact of your research.

Data Analysis

Provide a detailed and transparent data trail describing your data analysis. Include the procedures used to make meaning of your data and formulate preliminary and concluding interpretations including dialogue, critique, and validation with your critical friends.

Findings

Provide a discussion and an explanation of your interpretations of your data analysis with evidence for your claims. Include the themes identified through your analysis as subheadings. If you conducted case analyses, present those using subheadings of themes identified within and across the cases you studied.

Discussion and Implications

Impact on Participants

Provide a discussion about the impact of your study on your students' learning. Learning involves more than cognition and can include other impacts (e.g., motivation, emotions, and attitudes).

Impact on Teacher

Provide a discussion of the impact of your research on your understanding and reframing of teaching. Include a self-assessment of how you addressed the self-study methodological components. Include new questions that emerged from your study and warrant further and continued study.

Impact on Education Field

Provide a discussion and an explanation of what the findings of your study mean for the broader field and possible areas for further study. A good conclusion should make clear what you believe the paper has contributed to your understanding of teaching, its impact on your students' learning, and why it is important to the field.

Limitations

Include the limitations that you and your critical friends identified in your dialogic validity activity.

References

This is your bibliography. You should only include references you have actually cited in your report. Nothing should be listed in the bibliography if it has not been cited in the report. Use APA style for references. In addition to referencing the *Publication Manual of the American Psychological Association* (2009), it's relatively easy to find examples online of APA style for writing your report and references (e.g., http://owl.english.purdue.edu/owl/resource/560/01/).

Appendix

The appendix can include data that will help the reader better understand your research but perhaps are not needed within the body of your report (e.g., questionnaires you administered, interviews, samples of student work, additional displays of data, examples of your researcher log). Label your appendix items within the report and also title them in the appendix (e.g., within the report, "Students completed a Likert-type scale on their interests in working with peers [see Appendix A]").

WELCOMING PEER CRITIQUE

Why wait for a professor to assess your project? Why not conduct your own assessment of your research report and then ask a peer for his or her feedback? Welcoming self- and peer critique has worked for you all along in this project. Below is a suggested rubric to guide you and your critical friends' assessment of your project. Include your comments beyond a yes or no response.

Self- and Peer Assessment of Self-Study Teacher Research Project

Criteria for Assessing the Research Report

Abstract

- Have you provided a single, articulate, concise paragraph of no more than 150 words?
- Does your abstract concisely describe your purpose and the context, method, key findings, and significance of your research?

Comments:

Introduction/Rationale

- Have you stated the purpose of your study in the broader context of your work?
- Have you clearly and concisely explained why this research is important? Have you addressed the broader educational and social significance of this research?
- Have you offered perspectives that shaped this question for you?

Comments:

Statement of the Research Problem/Question

- Have you clearly and concisely stated the research problem?
- Have you clearly and concisely stated your main research question and any subquestions?

Comments:

Review of Literature and Conceptual Framework

- Did you conduct an ongoing literature review that informed your research?
- Is the review relevant and connected to your study?
- Is the review adequate, coherent, and analytical?
- Does the review include references from a variety of sources?
- Is the review integrated into a conceptual framework with a mapping of the theories, literature, and phenomena that help inform your study?

Comments:

Method

- Have you described your research context and the community, school, and classroom context?
- Have you included demographic information of participants?
- Did you include your reflection of the problem (e.g., behaviors observed, possible causes)?
- Have you explained the reasons for your planned pedagogies based on your noticing of your classroom and the literature reviewed?
- Have you described in detail what data you collected, how you collected them, and when you collected them, including data generated from your pedagogical strategies?
- Are your data from multiple sources?
- Did you include a description of the pedagogical strategies you enacted?
- Did you explain how you analyzed your data and include a data audit trail?
- Have you included and explained the role of your critical friends in your data interpretations and validation?
- Did you explore using visuals and technologies for analyzing and displaying your findings in a coherent manner?

Comments:

Findings

- Did you restate your research question and what was found through the research?
- Are the findings thoroughly and adequately presented?
- Is there convincing evidence to support your themes?
- Is there connection and coherence among the separate themes?
- Did you explain your findings to your critical friend to gain his or her perspective on your interpretations?

Comments:

Discussion

- Have you adequately explained the possible implications of your study to your students' learning?

- Have you adequately explained the possible implications of your study to your teaching and reframing of your practice? Revisit your original research question. Take a retrospective journey and reflect back on the "self" or your role and the conscious (and perhaps at the time unconscious) consequences of your actions in the process of studying your teaching practice.
- Have you adequately explained the possible implications of your study to the education field?
- Have you adequately explained the relevance of your study to national and state education standards?
- Have you discussed any limitations?
- Have you identified areas for future research possibilities?

Comments:

References and Appendix

- Did you follow the APA style for your report for a running head, page numbering, references, citations, and the appendix? Does the report include a title page with project title, author's name, and author's professional affiliation?
- Are references current and from different sources?
- Are all references cited in the research report included in the references? Have you provided a complete reference list of all print and nonprint (Internet) references?

Comments:

Organization, Grammar, and Mechanics

- Is the report coherent, concise, and well structured with a clear purpose?
- Is the report grammatically correct with proper usage of language?
- Does the report have your distinctive focus and voice? Have you used professional language (i.e., no jargon)? Have you written in an accessible style and presentation?

Comments:

Overall Comments:

Exemplary: Substantially meets the project and report requirements. All criteria addressed fully.

Accomplished: Meets the project and report requirements. Criteria adequately addressed.

Developing: Meets some, but not all, of the project and report requirements. Weaknesses in addressing some of the criteria. Consider revision.

Undeveloped: Does not meet the project and report requirements. Weaknesses in addressing the majority of the criteria. Needs significant revision.

KEY IDEAS

- You have an important research story to share and formalize in a written formal report.
- There are many habits for effective writing.
  - ✓ Get a routine and keep it.
  - ✓ Write on Day 1 and keep writing.
  - ✓ Participate in a research *and* writing community.
  - ✓ Choose an attitude of open-mindedness for critique.
  - ✓ Believe in the important story you have to tell.

- The findings section involves explaining your interpretations based on your strategies and the data those strategies generated.
- The discussion section includes a narrative of the impact of this research on your students' learning, on your teaching, and on the education field.
- The abstract briefly and clearly describes your purpose and the context, method, key findings, and implications of your research.
- Welcome peer critique as an opportunity to refine and polish your final paper.

Present and Publish

From	▶ Deborah Tidwell
Sent	Tuesday, January 1, 2008 6:28 p.m.
To	Deanna Breslin, Kavita Mittapalli, Anastasia P. Samaras, Mary Adams-Legge, Jeanmarie Infranco, Jennifer A. M. O'Looney, Arvinder K. Johri, Mary Jane McIlwain, Bernadine Person, Tamie L. Pratt-Fartro, and Dawn Renee Wilcox

Congratulations on the acceptance of your proposal for The Seventh International Conference on Self-Study of Teacher Education Practices. I will be the primary editor for your full paper throughout the proceedings preparation process. Please feel free to contact me directly with any questions you may have.

—Deborah Tidwell (personal communication, August 15, 2009)

CHAPTER DESCRIPTION

This chapter discusses the importance of making your research public through presenting it broadly. You will find an invitation to create an interactive presentation along with pointers for presenting your research. An example of a self-study proposal and proposal criteria are included to help you gain an idea of a proposal process. Also included is advice about presenting your research as well as advice on getting published. The chapter focuses on the methodological component of knowledge generation and presentation along with an invitation to celebrate your efforts as a self-study teacher researcher.

✦ Reading this chapter provides guidelines for presenting and publishing your research.

> I literally ran to the conference session. I couldn't wait to hear this researcher speak. I had read so much of her work, and it was so connected to my own research. I arrived at the session early because I figured it would be packed. I found a seat and anxiously waited for the talk. Instead, and to my great disappointment, the presenter first passed out a paper of her research and then proceeded to read the whole thing for 20 minutes, running out of time to address audience questions. We know that good teaching and presenting are more than just telling.

A **poster presentation** is "a visual display—including printed text, maps, diagrams, photos, and artifacts—that summarizes the problem addressed, how it was researched, and the outcomes of the investigation" (Wolcott, 2001, p. 153). After your presentation, you might consider asking for permission to display your poster in your faculty lounge, school division office, or board of education office. That is an easy way to showcase your work with high visibility to multiple audiences.

THE IMPORTANCE OF PRESENTING YOUR RESEARCH

You have written your research report and are ready to share it with colleagues in your class, school, and/or community. It is crucial that you share the research you have enacted so others can learn from you. Remember, you have an important story to tell that contributes to the body of knowledge about your research topic. Remember, when you make your work public, you allow your work to be available for review and critique. Communicating your work to others allows you to gain new perspectives, network and learn from others' work, and hear concerns and acknowledge the work yet to be refined (McNiff, Lomax, & Whitehead, 2003). Furthermore, sharing your work contributes to the accumulation of content- and issue-based knowledge and serves to build validation across related work. This aligns to the methodological component, Focus #5: *Self-study research generates knowledge that is made public through presentation and publication.*

It is important to share your work with others as it demonstrates your efforts to improve your teaching and to impact student learning. That information is useful to your students, colleagues, school, school district, and profession (MacLean & Mohr, 1999; McNiff et al., 2003). You have generated new knowledge that may be beneficial to your colleagues who are facing similar dilemmas. Your work may spark a school-wide reform because you are able to bring an important issue to colleagues' attention. It can make a difference in other schools facing and struggling for solutions to related problems and projects. By sharing your work, you model the essence of continuous professional learning and teachers as lifelong learners.

Finding outlets to present your work locally can be as simple as sharing your work at a department or faculty meeting. You may decide to submit your work to a school district conference, at national professional conferences, electronically on teacher Web sites, and to a journal for publication. It is useful for others to learn about self-study research, so presenting your research to audiences who are not familiar with it broadens the general knowledge base about teacher research.

*Be sure to check the journals and professional conferences of your discipline's professional organization, which are excellent outlets for your presentations and publications. For example, in the United States:

American Alliance for Health, Physical Education, Recreation and Dance

American Association for Health Education

American Council on the Teaching of Foreign Languages

American Library Association/American Association of School Librarians

Association for Childhood Education International

Council for Exceptional Children

Educational Leadership Constituent Council

International Reading Association

International Society for Technology in Education

National Art Education Association

National Association for the Education of Young Children

National Association for Gifted Children

National Association for Music Education

National Association of School Psychologists

National Association for Sport and Physical Education

National Council for the Social Studies

National Council of Teachers of English

National Council of Teachers of Mathematics

National Science Teachers Association

Teachers of English to Speakers of Other Languages

More programs are listed at http://www.ncate.org/public/programStandards.asp?ch = 4.

*Be sure to also visit the Writing and Publishing Resources and the Presentation and Publication Outlets in the Self-Study Resource Center on the accompanying text Web site.

CHALLENGE THE STATUS QUO OF PRESENTATIONS

Self-Study Presentations

Like effective teaching, conducting an effective presentation is a craft. If you want others to know about your research, it's paramount that you say it in a way that they will want to pay attention to what you have to share. We live in an exciting and interactive world, learning from each other through our conversations, questions, and ideas. Never just read your paper. Engage your audience. Self-study presentations tend to be highly interactive with creative introductions and participant activities (e.g., a reader's theater, a dramatic piece, a poetry reading, the use of photographs or other media, a song using sign language). Self-study scholars aim to promote dialogue between the presenters as a way to gain feedback and alternative perspectives of their work and extend the discourse of self-study in the educational community. Bodone, Guðjónsdóttir, and Dalmau (2004) argue that the "intercommunal collaboration" of self-study scholars has advanced self-study scholarship:

Since its inception the Self-Study of Teacher Education Practices Special Interest Group (AERA) has brought the self-study community together to share and review members' work and clarify methodological, ethical, and practice issues. While the history and analysis of this process is yet to be written, we introduce the idea here that this international and intercommunal collaboration has been a major influence in the development of the discourse and practice of the self-study of teacher education. (p. 750)

At conference sessions sponsored by S-STEP, there are a variety of formats used including round tables, paper presentations, and interactive symposia. There is an introduction of papers by a chair, the presentation of researchers' work, and a conclusion with comments and critique by one or more discussants.

Dalmau and Guðjónsdóttir (personal communication, September 24, 2009) serving as S-STEP program chairs for a number of years summarized some of the formats used in the past for presentation and dialogue in an interactive symposium format:

Presentation and Dialogue

Presenting teams have used a number of strategies to ensure that each of the papers forms the basis for a dialogue with participants about the paper topic and key self-study-related issues. Teams have used a number of strategies to support this dialogue. For example:

Breaking into paper-focused groups. Participants are asked to form smaller groups with presenters of one of the papers for more intense discussion. Usually the presenter uses 20–25 minutes of the time to present her or his paper followed by a discussion. These groups report back to the whole group at the end of the session. Sometimes the symposium is organized around a key question, which all groups address in their discussion.

Variations. Sometimes groups are constructed differently (based on available space in the room, number of participants, or congruent topics covered by pairs of presenters). In one session some years ago presenters worked in pairs with slightly larger groups.

Round-robin. Participants are divided into smaller groups, and presenters move around the room spending some time with each group.

Activity. Some presenters have also included within one of the structures described above the opportunity for participants to engage in some form of activity related to their topic.

If you have been working with critical friends in dyads and/or larger validation groups, you already know much about each other's research. In a teacher research course with 15 students and only 160 minutes of class, I asked each student to share his or her research project in an 8-minute presentation that included a one-page handout of a special research resource that others might find useful and applicable (e.g., a research tool, a survey that can be adapted to peers' classrooms, a technology tool discovered, a student exemplar that highlights the impact of the research, or a personal reflection to share). We sat around a large conference table, learned about the research conducted informally, and each walked away with 15 useful resources.

✎ 13.1 Student Example:
Presentation With Application Handout

Below is an example of a study tool that Stacy and her school colleagues use. She presents it as an example of her research efforts to improve her ESOL [English for Students of Other Languages] students' learning. Her classmates particularly appreciated this handout since they are all working to help their students pass the Standards of Learning test and it is a ready tool they can easily use in their teaching.

Standards of Learning (SOL) Review Project

Stacy Dumaresq (2009)

Purpose:

To create a study tool covering all material from biology that could be included on the SOL biology test in May. The tool may be also used on the final exam *if completed*. The project will count as 33 % of the overall final exam grade.

Materials:

- 7 sheets—8.5" x 11" letter size unlined paper (will be provided)
- colored pencils, markers, crayons, etc.
- 1 piece colored construction paper (will be provided)

Procedure:

1. Fold 8.5" x 11" paper width-wise (hamburger style).

2. Number your pages, beginning with the very first page. You should have 28 pages.

3. Staple your pages together like a book.

4. Page 1 will serve as your table of contents. You can handwrite it or create one on the computer—your choice. Use the calendar in the table below to make your table of contents.

5. Each unit will be given 2 pages for information. The first page will always be on the left side of the book with an even number. The unit pages should open to each other!

6. Each unit is worth 5 points and must follow all guidelines in order to receive full credit.

7. On the unit pages, draw diagrams/illustrations that relate to concepts within the unit topics—you are *not* to use words unless they are labels!

8. Be sure to include the topics listed.

9. Fill in both pages entirely! There should not be any white space in your book.

10. *It is important that you draw your understanding. By using too many words, you will not be allowed to use your book on the final exam!* Even if only 1 page is wrong, your entire book is wrong. The entire book must be done properly in order for you to be allowed to use it on the final exam.

11. Glue the grade sheet onto the last page (p. 28).

Calendar:

Table 13.1   Example of Research Tool Handout

Weeks	Topics	Due Dates
1	Nature of Science	February 26
2	Biochemistry	March 6
3	The Cell	March 12
4	Energy	March 20
5	Cell Cycle	March 26
6	Central Dogma	April 17
7	Inheritance	April 17
8	Genetic Technology	April 23
9	Natural History	May 1
10	Taxonomy	May 7
11	Ecology	May 15
12	Human Body Systems	May 22

Additionally, presenting your research formally is excellent practice for presenting professionally. However, consider how you might challenge the status quo of presentations that rely only on lecturing. As a teacher, you already have a repertoire of ideas for presenting information. We know there are so many ways you can think about presenting your work. There are a variety of conference session format ideas listed and described on the American Educational Research Association (AERA) Web site (http://www.aera.net/meetings/Default.aspx?menu_id = 22&id = 578&terms = explanation + of + session + formats&searchtype = 1&fragment = False).

Just like your students, adults don't like to be talked to, lectured, or bored to death with a reading of your report. Conducting an effective presentation is conducive to getting your story heard.

I have been attending professional conferences for decades and have observed a wide variance in the quality of presentations of research. AERA has made available several articles with tips for presenting effectively on its Web site (http://www.aera.net/Default.aspx?id = 299). Also see "Effective Presentations" by Erin B. Lindsay (http://www.research.ucla.edu/era/present/index.htm).

Below is my advice about presenting your research gleaned from the work above and my own experiences.

ADVICE FOR PRESENTING

1. **Announce who you are**. You would be surprised how many people begin speaking and assume people know who they are and their professional affiliation.

2. **Stay cool, calm, and collected** and enjoy what you have worked hard to learn and now have the opportunity to share. Use a friendly and inviting tone. Be appreciative, and not defensive, about feedback.

3. **Speak slowly** and slower than you think. You know your research well, but it's new to your listeners. Additionally, we tend to talk too quickly if we are nervous or if we are trying to tell everything we know.

4. **Don't read your paper**. You may decide to read a quote or segment that helps you make your point. Establish eye contact.

5. **Engage/involve your audience** in some way. Prompt and inspire audience members to think about questions and be curious about your work. Be clear if you are inviting audience participation during and/or after your presentation. Be aware that some audience participants can talk for a very long time.

6. **Offer an inclusive presentation**. Adapt your presentation for individuals with disabilities. For example, if you decide to use a video clip or DVD, check if it has closed-captioning. Consider the many English as a Second Language learners sitting in audiences. If translators are available, leave pauses for them to catch up and continue to talk to your audience and not the translators.

7. **Incorporate visuals** that are readable and easily understood and appreciated by audiences as another form of communication. If you use PowerPoint, remember, the point of using PowerPoint is to highlight the points. Include simple points posted in large print. Do not include paragraphs that are too detailed for your audience to absorb and in a font too small to be read.

8. **Offer a brief, usable handout** that includes your name and contact information. You have accrued lots of information. Now simplify it for others and offer points that are useful for their work.

9. **Watch your time**. Everyone runs out of time. And please don't waste your time telling your audience you don't have much time. Respect your timekeepers. Nobody likes someone who abuses the time allotment, which ultimately causes problems for speakers who follow you.

10. **Close your presentation** with a synthesis of your main points and/or take-away points.

WRITING YOUR SELF-STUDY PROPOSAL

Self-study scholars have presented their research to gain feedback about the quality of their work. The interactive conference sessions allow for them to reflect on how their work represents self-study research. Program chairs Mary Dalmau and Hafdís Guðjónsdóttir created a handout designed from their work in reviewing S-STEP conference proposals, noting areas most commonly needing further development in the proposals they received and reviewed. The guidelines are offered as questions we have raised as a community that need our continued attention. Notice the self-study methodological components embedded in these abbreviated suggestions.

Reflections on Writing a Self-Study

The full report can be found on the S-STEP electronic mailing list at
http://sstep.soe.ku.edu/aera/.

Hafdís Guðjónsdóttir and Mary C. Dalmau
(personal communication, September 24, 2009)

The Self-Study of Teacher Education Practices AERA 2002 papers were reviewed by a great team of 13 experienced members of the SIG. What follows are my reflections on issues raised by reviewers and proposal authors.

Contribution to self-study of teacher education discourse

One of the reasons the special-interest group exists and sponsors programs at conferences is to promote and support the improvement of teacher education practice though self-study. Papers and presentations are not simply about telling the world what we have done—they are about facilitating dialogue, creativity, and scholarship among us. Thus, at the end of our writing and presentation, authors, readers, and participants will have learned something new, reframed issues in their own practice, and developed new questions.

Self-study methodology

Was it simply claimed? Could I picture the study?

Questions: Did the authors do the self-study to confirm something they already knew? What were the new questions that emerged? How was the methodology organized so that questions were generated?

Data: Was there more than a list of data collection tools (e.g., interviews with students, journals, surveys)—was there evidence of the type of data collected and the way the data were used in the study? What evidence was there that authors did more than think about what others need to do (e.g., "We found that students did not . . ." or "We found that students needed to . . .")?

Reframing: What evidence was there of authors responding to data by questioning their assumptions and their practice? How did they reframe their way of looking at their work? In what ways did the authors attempt to look again and newly at their work?

Transformative nature of self-study: Could I see and understand the nature of the transformation that was in process in the authors' practice?

Meaning and knowledge: What was the evidence of how the researchers came to new understandings and how they tested that knowledge?

Collaboration, going beyond the self: Was collaboration simply claimed? Was there any evidence that the researchers had gone beyond their immediate circle and questioned their work with folks of different or divergent perspectives and experience?

Community and knowledge generation

What does this mean when we come to building knowledge from our research and practice? Is there any evidence in our papers to illustrate the nature of our learning community?

13.2 Example of AERA Self-Study Proposal

The criteria used by reviewers are presented in the highlighted boxes so you might gain a better understanding of how criteria are integrated into an actual proposal. Also see "The Proposal Review Process."

A Self-Reflective Journey of a Researcher and a Teacher-Administrator Seeking Answers Through Arts-Based Self-Study

Arvinder K. Johri and Kavita Mittapalli (2008)

Submitted to S-STEP, 2008

Preferred Session Format: Paper Discussion

Purpose/Objectives

We examined our ways of knowing and learning through arts-based self-study methodological processes as outlined by LaBoskey (2004) and Samaras and Freese (2006). The purpose of self-study is to bridge the gap between theory and practice, to fully understand the situated knowledge of practice, and to explore and extend these new understandings in public ways (Loughran, 2007). Although we come from different streams of education research and professional lives, our paths converged when we applied self-study to our respective practices. One of us learned how doctoral students conducted qualitative research (Study 1) while the other explored her professional identity in the dual roles of teacher and administrator (Study 2). Our self-portraits sealed our efforts to apply self-study to our practice. We present our different journeys in our paper.

Choice of Problem/Topic

Notice how the purpose of the study is stated clearly and at the beginning of the proposal (i.e., "The purpose of self-study is to bridge the gap between theory and practice, to fully understand the situated knowledge of practice, and to explore and extend these new understandings in public ways [Loughran, 2007]. . . . One of us learned how doctoral students conducted qualitative research [Study 1] while the other explored her professional identity in the dual roles of teacher and administrator [Study 2]"). Specific research questions and the rationale for the study are also included in the next paragraphs.

Our research questions included the following: How do I learn qualitative research? What are the stages of my evolution as a researcher? How do I find meaning from my participants' perspectives of the research process they are trying to understand? How am I perceived as an administrator and a teacher by my faculty and administration? How are the perceptions connected to my gender, cultural, and religious identity? How do I perceive myself as a teacher and an administrator?

As self-study researchers, we offer a discussion of utilizing arts-based self-study methods as a research tool. This tool promotes and provokes self-reflection, critical analysis, and dialogue about improving one's research through the arts (Samaras & Freese, 2006). As arts-based self-study researchers, we use a wide range of art forms to represent and reinterpret, construct and deconstruct meaning, and communicate our study of researching as we make it public. It can take many forms including visual-/image-based arts (e.g., portraits, performance, photography, video documentary, art installations, multimedia representations, films, drawings, cartoons, graffiti, signs, cyber graphics, diagrams). As in teaching practices, reflection on one's research practice and self-study are important components of the push for closer examination of an individual's pedagogy and are linked to ideas about the development of knowledge through better understanding of personal experience (Loughran & Northfield, 1998).

Although there is a large body of research related to the self-study of teacher educators and teachers, (e.g., Hamilton, Pinnegar, Russell, Loughran, & LaBoskey, 1998; Loughran & Russell, 1997, 2002; Russell & Korthagen, 1995; Samaras, 2002), there are limited examples of its usefulness to practitioners outside of the teaching profession. By way of using arts-based self-study methodology, we intend to add to this small but growing pool of knowledge in the field of self-study and inform both students and educators alike.

Theoretical Framework

The lens used to frame our investigation about self-study is through symbolic interaction-ism theory (Blumer, 1986; Mead, 1934). Symbolic interactionism, or interactionism, is one of the major theoretical perspectives in sociology. Blumer (1986) and Mead (1934) empha-sized the subjective meaning of human behavior, the social process, and pragmatism. Interactionists focus on the subjective aspects of social life, rather than on objective, macrostructural aspects of social systems. One reason for this focus is that interactionists base their theoretical perspective on their image of humans, rather than on their image of society (as the functionalists do). For interactionists, humans are pragmatic actors who con-tinually must adjust their behavior to the actions of other actors. We can adjust to these actions only because we are able to interpret them (i.e., to denote them symbolically and treat the actions and those who perform them as symbolic objects). The process is aided by our ability to think about and to react to our own actions and even ourselves as symbolic objects. Thus, the interactionist theorist sees humans as active, creative participants who construct their social world, not as passive, conforming objects of socialization.

Theoretical Framework

The study was clearly informed by theory, and a rationale is offered in how the researchers make the claim of how theory informed their study.

Methods

Data were collected during a semester-long course. For Study 1, the primary data sources included (a) semistructured interviews with three advanced-level doctoral students and (b) memos written during and after the interviewing process. Secondary data included (a) self-study course peer feedback and classroom presentations and discussions, (b) self-portrait and narrative (i.e., arts-based self-study method), (c) professor's feedback, and (d) correspondence with critical friend. For Study 2, the primary data sources included (a) semistructured interviews with 11 teachers and an administrative assistant and (b) eval-uations from principals. Secondary data included (a) self-study course peer feedback and classroom presentations and discussions, (b) correspondence from critical friend, (c) self-portrait and narrative, (d) professor's feedback, and (e) student-teacher portfolio.

In Study 2, all participants were asked basic demographic questions at the start of the inter-view followed by questions pertaining to how they perceived the researcher as a teacher and an administrator; to their views about her attire, culture, and religious affiliation; and to her relationships with the principal, students, and faculty and her power equations with them.

Based on critical friends' letters exchange and peer feedback and correspondence with the professor and course readings, we painted two self-portraits. Study 1's self-portrait reflected the journey and an objective and factual representation of a previously held notion about research, which was positivist, to a naturalist mode of inquiry and now to the current status of looking at a "mixed" view of conducting research. The art form, Madhubani, not only provided the required means to represent a self-development process in an artistic form but also gave the researcher a way to express her inner self as an Asian Indian woman examining her ways of knowing as she grows as an education researcher.

Study 2's self-portrait was that of a peacock motif that symbolized the researcher's connections with students. Growing up in India, she had admired peacocks for their majestic beauty and their intricately designed feathers. She often wondered why this immortal beauty was tarnished by such long, ugly feet. She had been exposed to the myth of a dancing peacock that cries out in agony when it sights its own ugly feet. The myth affirmed that perfection needs an antithesis to hold its potential for being translated to narcissism in check.

Self-Study Methodology

Since this proposal includes two studies, each researcher explains how she used the arts-based self-study method in creating her self-portrait along with multiple other data sources.

Participants

For Study 1, three graduate students, one male and two females, were interviewed. They were all advanced-level doctoral students who were working on their dissertations at the time of the interviews. All of them had some qualitative research experience though they had come from strictly quantitative professional backgrounds. One of them was an engineer. The second participant was an accountant, and the third was an educator with an interest in brain research and teaching. They had all taken at least one of the two qualitative methods courses being offered in the doctoral program. For Study 2, 11 teachers and one administrative assistant were interviewed. Nine of the participants were Caucasian, two were African American, and one was African. Eleven of the participants were females, and one was a male. Their teaching experience ranged from 35 years to 10 months. Seven of the 11 teachers had exposure to teaching only in a Catholic school setting, and 4 of them had teaching experience in public, parochial, and international schools.

We were also participants in our respective studies: in Study 1 as a researcher who constructed her ways of knowing and thinking about conducting research, and in Study 2 in her dualist role as a teacher and an administrator in an unusual school environment.

Data Analysis

For data analysis, we used the categorizing and connecting method (Maxwell & Miller, 2008). The categorizing method was done to develop codes in each of the transcripts based on similarity of emerging codes and to compare them across the data set. The connecting method was used to connect the various codes within each transcript. In order to form categories across the interviews, a separate category profile for each individual participant was developed and then grouped according to the categories formed. This semester-long study culminated in a self-portrait and an accompanying narrative, which were in tandem to education research and the self-study methodology.

> ## Evidence/Data
>
> The independent and multiple data sources are discussed in the method section with specific detail about participants and how the data were analyzed. Someone should be able to read your analysis and understand exactly what you did. This is tricky because proposals are limited in word length.

Findings, Conclusions, Interpretations

In Study 1, the data analysis revealed the various techniques the three participants learned in the advanced qualitative research methods course, which included making connections within their research work/profession, having a context in which to base their findings, understanding their participants' perspectives, conducting research that is valid and reliable, understanding their role as a researcher, issues of reactivity or bias in research, being flexible with the research and interview questions, peer feedback, and reflecting on their work. Some of the statements made by the participants were "Qualitative research is a 'focused,' 'technical' way of knowing and conducting research. I have learned the various paradigms. I have used concept maps and narratives in my research, and have found the interactive design approach useful for my research." "Qualitative research is an open process." "You need to have a deep passion for what you want to do in qualitative research. If you don't, maybe it's not for you." "Qualitative research is flexible; you design as you go!" "You as the researcher and the instrument 'color' the research and the background you are in; you have to take that into account when you conduct qualitative research and try to be unbiased." The interviews sparked the researcher's thinking about her way of knowing and thinking about conducting research.

She then created a self-portrait that depicted the self-representation in the stages of her self-development as a researcher—an agriculture science student trained in a positivist view of the world, the stage of being exposed to the naturalist mode of inquiry, and the current stage being that of a self-examining researcher who wants to take a middle ground of using both the methods in research with an equal leverage. The self-study provided a platform for the researcher to continue to question, examine, and reexamine her thought processes as an individual who is evolving as a researcher from a more positivist to a mixed-method researcher.

In Study 2, the interviews with teachers and the administrative assistant helped in understanding how all of them perceived the researcher as an administrator and as a teacher. It also helped her find the nuances of connections to her cultural and religious identity defining or clarifying her professional identity. Some of the statements made by the participants were "It never entered my mind that you are an Indian, non-Catholic female." "Your ethnic attire was a refreshing change, and I think it is important for the students to experience diverse cultural attires." "You guided the principal with great expertise, and sometimes the roles were reversed between the two of you." "You did not make your being an Indian non-Catholic a point, so the point was never taken." All the teachers were of the opinion that the researcher's professional joy resides in teaching and not in administration. The interviews revealed that being successful in her profession was not an issue in her search for professional identity as she was respected and regarded as an administrator and a teacher who was dedicated to her students. She realized that holding on to the position of an administrator should not be with the objective of gaining power or an elevated status or as an act of proving herself to others.

The self-portrait of a peacock motif symbolized this researcher's connections with students, and she felt compelled to make a pragmatic positive difference in their lives. For her, the ugly feet of the peacock are symbolic of the frictions, tensions, paradoxes, and ugly power equations related to her professional roles that need to be faced in the open and resolved. The plumage represents her diverse professional roles seeking balance and harmony of form and mind. The ritual of feather renewal is a reminder for her as a self-study researcher to reassess the effectiveness of change frequently. The eyes in the feathers belong to her students who are constantly keeping a check on her next move.

Conclusions/Interpretations

The researchers present their findings and support them with data and quotes used sparingly and integrated into their discussion.

Contribution and Educational Implications

The two studies can serve to inform students and researchers in their process of learning to do qualitative research and to encourage teachers and administrators to self-reflect in their current practices to improve their professions using the self-study arts-based genre. The study will help bridge the gap of extending arts based self-study from teachers and educators to practitioners.

Contribution to Self-Study Discourse and Teacher Education

In this section, the researchers state concisely how their work adds to the knowledge base of qualitative research and teacher education.

Membership Appeal

As noted, it is important to assess where to submit your proposal for the best fit of your work and membership appeal.

Quality of Writing/Organization

Proof your work so you do not get marked down for that category. The total amount of points can make a difference in acceptance.

References

Blumer, H. (1986). *Symbolic interactionism: Perspective and method.* New Jersey: Prentice Hall.

LaBoskey, V. K. (2004). The methodology of self-study and its theoretical underpinnings. In J. J. Loughran, M. L. Hamilton, V. K. LaBoskey, & T. Russell (Eds.), *International handbook of self-study of teaching and teacher education practices* (Vol. 1, pp. 817–869). Dordrecht, The Netherlands: Kluwer Academic Publishers.

Loughran, J. J. (2007). Researching teacher education practices: Responding to the challenges, demands, and expectations of self-study. *Journal of Teacher Education, 58*(1), 12–20.

Loughran, J. J., & Northfield, J. (1998). A framework for the development of self-study practice. In M. L. Hamilton, with S. Pinnegar, T. Russell, J. Loughran, & V. K. LaBoskey (Eds.), *Reconceptualizing teaching practice: Self-study in teacher education* (pp. 7–18). London: Falmer.

Loughran, J. J., & Russell, T. (1997). *Teaching about teaching: Purpose, passion, and pedagogy in teacher education.* London: Falmer Press.

Loughran, J. J., & Russell, T. (2002). *Improving teacher education practices through self-study.* London: RoutledgeFalmer.

Maxwell, J. A., & Miller, B. (2008). *Categorizing and connecting as components in qualitative data analysis.* In P. Leavy & S. Hesse-Biber (Eds.), *Handbook of emerging methods.* (pp. 461–475). New York: Guilford.

Mead, G. H. (1934). *Mind, self and society.* Chicago: University of Chicago Press.

Russell, T., & Korthagen, F. (1995). *Teachers who teach teachers: Reflections on teacher education.* London: Falmer Press.

Samaras, A. P. (2002). *Self-study for teacher educators: Crafting a pedagogy for educational change.* New York: Peter Lang.

Samaras, A. P., & Freese, A. R. (2006). *Self-study of teaching practices primer.* New York: Peter Lang.

THE PROPOSAL REVIEW PROCESS

First, finding a good fit for which conference, section, division, or special-interest group to submit your proposal to is key to its acceptance. Also, knowing how your proposal will be assessed is always helpful in writing it. Although the criteria may vary over time, "good" proposals address objectives or purposes, theoretical framework, methods, data sources, results, and scholarly significance. For self-study proposals, reviewers look for the self-study methodological components to be embedded in the proposal. Seeing examples of accepted proposals is useful. Asking peers and experts to review your proposal is also valuable. Below is an example of proposal review criteria and an example of a review for the Johri and Mittapalli (2008) proposal noted above.

In S-STEP, reviewers are encouraged to offer narrative feedback in addition to the numerical ratings. Also, notice how although the proposal was accepted, the critique provides an opportunity for authors to refine their paper before their presentation.

> I very much appreciate the authors' foci on how their culture and narratives emerge through an art-based genre in research design. . . . At the same time, it is not made explicit enough for what reason the authors undertake their study—that is, why is it important to researchers, administrators, and teachers to become aware of their multiple roles and how their background impacts their professions? Furthermore, as the theoretical framework sounds interesting and appropriate for the study put forward, I would recommend that the authors make more explicit how it does inform their studies in particular. Overall I think the authors have an interesting and very important topic to work from, but they need to make a stronger argument for why it is important for practitioners to engage in this kind of work.

Ratings on the same proposal will differ, and this can be disheartening for the author if there is variance in the scores. As a proposal length is limited, it is often problematic for the author to include all the required criteria. It becomes a real test of brevity and conciseness and improves with paying attention to the reviewer comments and working to improve future submissions. Program chairs use the multiple reviews to make a final decision on the proposal's merit while also working within the constraints of how many session slots have been allocated to the special-interest group. Below is a review worksheet of someone who was very impressed with the Johri and Mittapalli (2008) proposal. It is presented to show you the criteria used at the time of this review, which may vary slightly from year to year but with the same basic criteria.

Sub Unit:	SIG-Self-Study of Teacher Education Practices	
Review Worksheet	Individual Submission	(3/3)
Review #xxx:		
Criteria		*Rate*
Choice of Problem/Topic		5/5
Theoretical Framework		5/5
Self-Study Methodology		5/5
Evidence/Data		5/5
Conclusions/Interpretations		5/5
Quality of Writing/Organization		5/5
Contribution to Self-Study Discourse		5/5

Contribution to Teacher Education	5/5
Membership Appeal	5/5
Would You Attend This?	5/5
Overall Recommendation	5/5
Comments to the Author: I have read six proposals, and this was the best by far in terms of research, interest of topic, and theoretical framework. I can't wait to attend this session.	

In addition to presenting your work, another important way to make your work public is by publishing it. Below is my advice about getting your work published gleaned from various sources and from my own experiences.

ADVICE FOR GETTING PUBLISHED

1. **Believe in the important story about teaching you have to tell**. The story you tell is to generate knowledge about the topic you chose. It is a story that others can learn from, regardless of the results. It is your story and yet one others can relate to and extend in their contexts.

2. **Share your manuscript** with critical friends and get their continuous input on your writing. Participate in a writing and publishing support group. Also ask others who are well published for their feedback on your manuscript. Ask advanced scholars about the "dirty little secrets" to getting published.

3. **Decide on the audience** who will most benefit from your research.

4. **Choose a journal** that best fits your research focus and audience. This important step is often overlooked. Get a sample journal copy. Don't hesitate to contact and speak with the editors to sort out if your manuscript is a good fit for the journal's mission. Talk to others who have submitted to the journal. Look at the types of articles and topics already published in the journal over the last couple of years. Who is the editor? What is her or his stance? Who is on the editorial board? Who are the reviewers? *Carefully* read the journal's criteria. Write specifically to its specs.

5. **Keep researching and writing**. Researching and writing take time. If you are interested in publishing more than once and becoming a more prolific writer and contributor, then this advice is for you. That is, if you want to develop a habit of researching and writing, then have a short-term and a long-term plan. I tell my doctoral students, "Keep cooking!" with one project in the pot almost done (a manuscript ready to submit), one pot in the making (research in progress), and

one pot ready to cook (your ideas for your next research project). Having both a short-term and a long-term plan is important since the turnaround time from submitting to hearing back from journals can take up to 6 months for some journals.

6. **Accept the long process of revision**. A polished manuscript takes time and multiple revisions. The best writers revise many times. Don't send your manuscript out until it's in good shape. Journals are not your editors but can give you great insights. That will take longer than if you solicit advice from scholars and peers.

7. **Embrace critique and be persistent**. You will receive a note that your manuscript has been received. If you don't hear back about the acceptance, revision, or rejection from your journal within a reasonable time, then e-mail or call the editor. It's very seldom that no edits are needed. Write specifically to each concern and address how you have responded and corrected any concerns. Once you receive the reviews, listen to the reviewers' concerns. Send out your revisions after you have stepped back from your manuscript and then looked at it again. Carefully read what the reviewers' concerns are really about. Smile often and consider how fortunate you are to receive feedback on your work. Reviewers offer invaluable information to improve your writing and research. Writing is a process and requires that you are persistent and committed to writing and rewriting. You have the opportunity to present a high-quality manuscript, and that just takes work and time. Never give up.

8. **Celebrate your efforts!** Your effort counts. If your manuscript is rejected, see that as an opportunity to learn from the reviewer comments and make revisions. Rewrite. Send to your second choice of journal. Be persistent, be diligent, and have faith in your own abilities and hard efforts. It will happen. Writing is a habit of mind and heart. Enjoy the discoveries along the way.

KEY IDEAS

- Self-study teacher researchers make their work public through presentation and publication to allow it to be available for review and critique.
- Conducting an effective presentation is conducive to getting your story heard.
- Self-study scholars aim to challenge the status quo of traditional presentations.
- Consider the challenge and opportunity to design and enact a creative research presentation.
- Be informed about getting published.
- Celebrate your research and writing efforts.

CLOSING REMARKS

One of the biggest challenges we face as teachers is the continuous demand to implement new programs, curricula, and standards. Instead of getting frustrated and diverted with these new directions that can cause division within your school community, embrace these changes together as a community and as a process instead of as an end result. It is important to remember that your colleague's teaching journey may be different from yours but it is the mutual respect and listening to each other that ultimately improves students' learning.

—Irene Pantelides Meehan (personal communication, July 14, 2009), *Special Education Resource Specialist*

COMING FULL CIRCLE

In the beginning of the textbook, you were invited to get your hands dirty and to dig into the messiness and uncertainties of studying your practice. You were presented with three reasons why you should do so.

1. Personal Professional Accountability

2. Applicability

3. Reforming in the First Person With Critical Friends

You have now explored and experienced conducting a self-study teacher research project. Reflect back on each of these components and the experiences you engaged in throughout the text as you developed an understanding of self-study by doing it. You developed a repertoire of self-study teacher research. Through your Critical Friends Portfolio you explored getting your hands dirty with colleagues so you could learn with and from each other. I hope you had an educative research journey as you designed, developed, and enacted a self-study teacher research project.

1. You had an opportunity to question your practice, hold yourself *personally and professionally accountable* to your students, and reframe your understanding of teaching.

2. I also hope you accepted the many invitations to explore and *apply self-study in your teaching practice* and that you will return to the critical friend work again and again. Look back at your Critical Friends Portfolio as it documents the process of your research project.

3. Finally, I hope you felt success as you *initiated and crafted a research project with the support of colleagues* and with the ultimate goal of *improving and reforming education* for a more just system of schooling for all learners and teachers.

Celebrate and Continue Your Research Journey—*A Wondrous Field*

Taking a retrospective journey of your role allows you to see where you have been and where you want to go, dirty hands and all! You likely wished you had more time to collect data, try out additional pedagogies, collaborate more with a school team, and create a more finished final product. The time period for this study might not have allowed you to research for as long as you would have liked because it was within a one-semester course. Your time will come for that. Now that you understand the self-study process as a whole, you can apply it in research that requires more time. The good news is that teacher research is a journey and one that you can continue. Your study likely presented additional questions and ideas for your teacher research. Follow those ideas. A course introduces you to why you should conduct teacher research and how you can go about that. A professional teaching career offers you a lifetime of chances to explore your teaching.

Perhaps the dilemmas we face in teaching are the essential inquiries that lie in "the swampy lowland" (Schön, 1987, p. 3). I agree the problems we face as teachers are most often ambiguous and messy because of the nontechnical solutions they require. Professionals expect and embrace that challenge. I also see that our self-study and our messy inquiries take us to *a wondrous field* with many interesting diversions and paths that afford us the opportunity to engage in a research journey with critical friends (see Photo 13.1). It is not an easy road, but it is one worth taking nonetheless.

Photo 13.1   A Wondrous Journey

Take time now to appreciate and celebrate the process of all your hard work and its impact on your students, on you, and on schooling and the education field. Seize the promise of your personal and collaborative inquiries yet to be fulfilled. Imagine what your research has taught you about the next steps in studying your practice. As self-study teacher researchers, we continue to develop and explore our practice with the hope that *the best is yet to come.*

Self-Study Teacher Research Exemplar Brief Highlighting Five Foci

This is an abbreviated project frame presented to highlight the Five Foci. You will find components of Amy's research throughout the textbook.

CREATING AN ACTIVE STUDENT LEARNING ENVIRONMENT

> *"We are the toughest critics for ourselves, but our students are the ones that we must reach."*
>
> —Amy Smith (2008), *Middle School Science Teacher*

My background is in biology. I only have one year of teaching experience, and that was gained teaching ninth-grade biology. This year has been a huge transition for me in my teaching. I am faced with two difficult challenges this year. I have been assigned to teach a new subject, life science, and to a new group of students, seventh graders. This is the first year that I am teaching seventh-grade life science. It is also the first year that I have ever had a team-taught class. Within the first week of teaching, I realized that I was going to have to change my methods of instruction in order to capture all of the students in my fifth-period team-taught class. It was evident to me that there were varying levels of learners, as well as different types of learners. I want to capture the attention of every student and find out the best way to incorporate the curriculum around the method that works best. I easily became frustrated with myself due to lack of preparedness for teaching seventh graders in a team-taught class. I want to refine my teaching practices to fit seventh graders and hopefully improve learning and student engagement in the process.

Significance of Problem to Me

There are county limitations as to what I can and cannot do in terms of lab experiments in the classroom. I hope to be able to supplement the labs already in place in order to help fifth period be in a more active learning environment. Relating the science in the classroom to things of interest to the students seems to be one way to really capture their attention. I want to look at my teaching styles and teaching practice in order to refine my methods that are currently in place. I have never taught in a team environment before, and I want to get as much out of the experience as possible for myself, my students, and my teaching colleague as a team teacher. I think that the students will get more out of my life science class if I make it meaningful for them. I want to reach every student and open their eyes to the world of science around them.

Broader Educational and Social Significance of the Problem

Any success that I have in making a more active learning environment will help the students throughout their academic career. They will hopefully find a value in the work that they are doing and see that it is important to learn about different topics and subjects. If the students can become active learners in science, then they can do it in any subject. If I am successful in finding methods to create an active learning environment, more team-taught classes could implement the strategies in order to reach their students as well. If I find data supporting my theories, I might be able to share my research with my department chair and the special education department chair in order to update practices and certain aspects of the curriculum and instruction portion of seventh-grade science.

> **Improved Learning:** Notice Amy is committed to improving her students' learning by studying her teaching practice. She questions the status quo of her teaching and the politics of schooling in order to improve and impact learning for herself, her students, and the education field.

Research Question

How can I create an active student learning environment in a team-taught science classroom?

> **Personal Situated Inquiry:** Amy clearly initiates her own inquiry and studies it in her teaching context and asks, "How can I create an active student learning environment in a team-taught science classroom?"

Review of the Literature

This research set out to discover the best methods to use to create an active learning environment in a team-taught classroom. Active learning happens when students are given the opportunity to take a more interactive relationship with the subject matter of the course. "Research has shown that an active learning environment can be an exceptionally effective teaching technique. Regardless of the subject matter, when active learning is compared to traditional teaching methods (such as lecture), students learn more material, retain the information longer, and enjoy the class more" (TA Consultants, 2008). These methods will also be applicable to regular and honors classes, but my sole focus for this research is in a team-taught environment. I found literature that pertained to elementary school students through college students. It seems as though most teachers are searching for the secret to maintaining or creating an active learning environment in every subject and grade level. My literature review yielded a variety of different methods to encourage students to become active in their learning. After giving the students a presurvey about how they learn, I discovered that most of them enjoy using technology and working in groups.

[Amy continues to explain how she searched the literature for ideas and research to support her students' learning.]

Method

Context and Participants

"Greenville Secondary School" is 37% White, 29% Black, 18% Asian, and 16% Latino. The numbers of males and females almost equal each other: 51% of the students are males, and 49% of the students are females. Around 29% of the students are on free or reduced lunch, and 21% of the student population has limited English proficiency. Greenville Secondary School instructs students from 7th through 12th grade. The entire school has approximately 2,500 students. The participants come from my one team-taught science class. There are 28 students in the classroom and two teachers: myself and my team teacher.

Data Collection

I used several different methods for data collection to ensure that I had enough and varied data to conduct my research. The following data were collected: (a) a presurvey, (b) teacher daily journal, (c) Likert scale survey post each student activity, (d) my team teacher's thoughts on teaching and classroom environment as well as the thoughts of my critical friend, (e) microscope activity, (f) computer-based activity, (g) edible cell activity, (h) interactive notebook, (i) postsurveys, and (j) feedback from my critical friend.

Data Analysis

Student Analysis

After each activity, the students were given a survey with a Likert scale and the same two questions each time. The Likert scale was based on a scale of 1–5, where 1 = *hated it*, 2 = *didn't like it*, 3 = *undecided*, 4 = *cool*, and 5 = *awesome*. The two questions asked each time were: "Did this activity make learning fun?" and "Do you want to do more hands-on labs when possible?" I charted, graphed, and tabulated all the results of students' perspectives of each activity.

Team Teacher's Thoughts

I asked my team teacher what I could do differently to actively engage every student in the class. I also asked her to fill out the same Likert scale that the students did in the postsurvey.

Personal Journal Log

I wanted to look at my own personal thoughts in order to gain some insight into my own self-study practices and to critically look at my activities. Each day I recorded my thoughts about my frustrations with the class and the activities and what I thought went well throughout the period.

Transparent and Systematic Research Process: Amy's full report includes extensive explanation and detail about this step of the research process: her planned pedagogies and rationale, the data collected, her analysis, and critical friend memos used to validate her interpretations.

Findings

I was able to compile the categories from each activity into overarching themes resulting in (a) engaged and learning, (b) fascinating, (c) keeping interest, and (d) an amusing class-room environment.

Engaged and Learning

Looking at my three sources of data from my students, my team teacher, and myself, I was able to triangulate my data, which resulted in the theme of *engaged and learning* for the microscope and computer activities. The students were more interested in the activity being fun and exciting, while the team teacher and I saw evidence of learning while having fun. The students made comments such as "I liked being able to move the words." They rated the activity as *cool* or *awesome* on the Likert scale, and 85% of the students said that the microscope activity made learning about microscopes fun.

Fascinating

Another theme resulting from my analysis was that students found the pedagogies fascinating. For example, the students were extremely interested in the edible cell, but it may have been for the reward in the end of eating the cell. The students made comments such as "This is awe-some" and "Very fun," and 92% of the students gave the activity an *awesome*. Some students even asked me if they could create a higher scale on the survey because it wasn't a good mea-sure of how exciting the activity was. It was a reinforcement activity to review the parts of the cell with the students. . . . My team teacher said: "I think they were more interested in eating the cell, although it was a good idea." I think we agree that it has the potential to be a fascinating activity with a hands-on–based approach and group collaboration, but there needs to be some tweaking of the activity to make sure students are actually learning in the process.

Keeping Interest

The theme of *keeping interest* may have emerged because none of the students were too par-ticularly fond of using an interactive notebook. I wanted to keep the students interested in the notebook because it can be a very resourceful tool for them to use in the classroom and in the future. The students responded: "It should be optional, not graded," and "I hate tak-ing notes." They think that the notebook is just a tedious way to get them to cut and paste things into a spiral notebook. This is not the case, and I don't think I did a very good job introducing the interactive notebook and why it is important. . . . In order for the interac-tive notebook to fit into an active learning environment I might need to rethink a couple of things. Last year my students loved the interactive notebooks. I was sort of biased going into my active learning environment question thinking that seventh graders would love it too. Maybe I presented it properly, and they are not mature enough to understand its importance. It really struck me that this wasn't more of a favorite with my students.

Exciting Classroom Environment

This theme was supported largely from reading my own journal log. When I was reading my thoughts I could sense the fun in the activities and in my writing voice when recording my thoughts. I wanted to incorporate fun in the classroom, so I came up with the word *exciting* to capture how I felt the classroom involved the students. This entire unit where I was trying to make a more active learning environment opened my eyes to many things. I am striving to incorporate these ideas back into my old curriculum. I want to incorporate cooperative learning activities with the hands-on while using computers. I think this combination will lend itself to an active learning environment, which will set all students up to be successful.

Discussion and Implications

The implications for this study would be that focusing on creating an active learning environment should be a priority in every classroom, especially in science. The findings that I uncovered are supported through the literature and from my discussions with colleagues. . . . Group work facilitates leaders and encourages collaboration among peers. Incorporating computers in the classroom not only brings in the everyday technology but also gives the students a chance to relate to the outside world and apply their knowledge to real-world scenarios. There is not a definite answer as to how to create an active learning environment. I found that by incorporating some of these methods together, the students were more active in their learning and seemed to have fun while doing so. My research was limited by time and by participants. I will continue this research to try to find the best solution for every student.

Perception of the Problem

I don't think that creating an active student learning environment has totally eliminated the excess chatter and students being off task at times. I do think that by creating the active learning environment the students were more actively engaged in their activities. By employing the strategies of hands-on, computers, and group work, the students seem to be more interested in what they are doing and are learning the material as a result of the interest. It has become more evident to me that I need to employ more varied and creative approaches to getting students to want to learn the material. It is important to have a backup plan in case it doesn't work out the way you planned. That is the beauty of teaching; it never occurs the same way twice. Your instruction is always different, and the students' thoughts and outcomes from the assignment are always different. . . . My future goal is to make the interactive notebook fun and engaging.

Self-Study

When I read back on my researcher journal from the beginning of October, it took me back to my lessons. I was able to see what worked with my classroom management technique, my lesson plans, the interaction between students, and the engagement level of the activity and classroom environment. . . . My revelations really occurred when I saw my fifth-period class excited about learning science. My curriculum is not only mandated, but the labs are already set in place. A lot of these labs in my opinion are "cookbook" labs where all of the steps are laid out for the students. Every educator is told to push for inquiry, but that is very difficult with the types of labs that I must teach. In the beginning of the year I added some enrichment labs where the students had to think about the problem and were not given all of the parts of the experiment. The students really seemed to enjoy being the investigators and acting like real scientists. This is where I got the idea for my research project and wanting to create an active learning environment. From this point on, my research will not cease. For each unit, I am going to push my boundaries to try to find ways to make the students interactive and allow them to be the scientists. Not only do you learn more by doing, but you learn more by being active and engaged in what you are learning about.

Usefulness

I can say that I was a resource for the research. I looked at what I was offering the students and reflected on my role in my personal journal log. I can say that my experience with ninth graders last year drove a lot of my thinking processes. I know what the students are going to need to know for ninth-grade biology, so I know what to reinforce and what isn't going to be as important. I was used to the ninth-grade mentality where the maturity level, organizational skills, and flexibility with class demands are totally different. The strategies and ideas that I used last year seemed to work. All of my students passed their Standards of Learning exams and were able to retain the information. I wanted to be able to adapt my lessons to the seventh-grade mentality. I had to scaffold my instruction in order to come up with a solution that would work for the students.

> **Knowledge Generation and Presentation:** Amy has reflected on what her study adds to the knowledge base of creating an active student learning environment in her science classroom. In her discussion section, she presents the value of this study to her students, to her teaching, and to the field in general. Her study was made public through class presentation sharing with school colleagues.

Role of Critical Friend

My critical friend was a great support network for me. He was always there to lend an ear, and to give helpful suggestions as to where to go. My critical friend was especially helpful due to the fact that we are employed at the same school. I think that if this project was carried out on a larger scale and for a longer period of time, it would definitely impact the standards for teaching in any environment. Science should not be the only discipline that uses a hands-on approach on a regular basis. All subjects should try these methods and see if they help create a more active learning environment. We have to reach students one at a time, but why not do it with things that they enjoy?

> **Critical Collaborative Inquiry:** Amy worked with her critical friend James Mercer in an intellectually safe and supportive community to improve her practice by making it explicit to herself and to him through critical collaborative inquiries. In turn, she was an equally valuable resource and critical friend to James. Her team teacher also served as a critical friend as they collaboratively worked to improve students' learning.

Self-Study Is Not Just for Classroom Teachers

Below are some examples of practitioners, other than teachers, who have found the self-study research methodology useful to the practice. The abstracts and links are provided so you can access them easily.

A Research Methodologist's Self-Study

Mittapalli, K., & Samaras, A. P. (2008). Madhubani art: A journey of an education researcher seeking self-development answers through art and self-study. *The Qualitative Report, 13*(2), 244–261. Retrieved December 3, 2009, from http://www.nova.edu/ssss/QR/QR13-2/mittapalli.pdf

Abstract

This study is situated within a self-study research methods course to scaffold doctoral students' explorations of the intersections of their culture and research interests using arts as a tool. Embracing the arts as a research method, the first author painted a self-portrait using the vibrant colors of Madhubani art, which holds cultural significance to her. She utilized Blumer's (1986) and Mead's (1934) theory of symbolic interactionism to explain the process of her self-development as a researcher. Combining her self-portrait with an earlier research study proved valuable as a conduit for understanding and interpreting her work as a research methodologist. This study is valuable to others interested in studying their practice and research identity through an arts-based research method.

Teacher Educators' Self-Study

Samaras, A. P., Kayler, M. A., Rigsby, L. C., Weller, K. L., & Wilcox, D. R. (2006). Self-study of the craft of faculty team teaching in a non-traditional teacher education program. *Studying Teacher Education, 2*(1), 43–57. Retrieved November 30, 2009, from http://www.informaworld.com/smpp/content~db=all?content=10.1080/17425960600557462

(Continued)

(Continued)

Abstract

We share our self-study research of faculty building a successful collaborative culture and team teaching experience in a unique master's program for experienced teachers. As part of self-study and reflective practice, this faculty team shared its collaborative experiences with teachers. This transparency had positive effects on the teachers' perceptions of faculty and on their own teaming experiences. To frame our work, we use the perspective of learning zones adapted from Vygotsky's conception of zone of proximal development. A multivocal perspective on the processes of faculty professional development and program development is presented.

A Science Coordinator Exploring
Self-Study in Teachers' Professional Development

Wilcox, D. (2008). *Project science inquiry: An exploration of elementary teachers' beliefs and perceptions about science teaching and learning.* Submitted in partial fulfillment of the requirements for the degree of doctor of philosophy in education, George Mason University, Fairfax, Virginia. Retrieved December 3, 2009, from http://digilib .gmu.edu:8080/xmlui/handle/1920/3078

This dissertation incorporates self-study methods in *Project Science Inquiry*, a professional development course developed by the researcher for science teachers' professional development.

Summary

This dissertation examines elementary teachers' beliefs and perceptions of effective science instruction and documents how these teachers interpret and implement a model for Inquiry-Based (I-B) science in their classrooms. The study chronicles a group of teachers working in a large public school division and documents how these teachers interpret and implement reform-based science methods after participating in a professional development course on I-B science methods administered by the researcher. I-B science teaching and its implementation is discussed as an example of one potential method to address the current call for national education reform to meet the increasing needs of all students to achieve scientific literacy and the role of teachers in that effort. The conviction in science reform efforts is that all students are able to learn science and consequently must be given the crucial opportunities in the right environment that permits optimal science learning in our nation's schools. Following this group of teachers as they attempted to deliver I-B science teaching revealed challenges elementary science teachers face and the professional supports necessary for them to effectively meet science standards.

Administrators, Reading Specialists, Research and
Policy Analysts, School and Community Counselors, and
Teachers Engage in Collective Self-Study

Breslin, D., Mittapalli, K., Samaras, A. P., Adams-Legge, M., Infranco, J., Johri, A. K., et al. (2008). Embarking on an adventure while drawing the map: Journeys through critical friend work in self-study methodology. In M. Heston, D. Tidwell,

K. East, & L. M. Fitzgerald (Eds.), *Pathways to change in teacher education: Dialogue, diversity and self-study.* Proceedings of the Seventh International Conference on the Self-Study of Teacher Education Practices, Herstmonceux Castle, East Sussex, England (pp. 31–35). Cedar Falls: University of Northern Iowa. Retrieved December 3, 2009, from http://sites.google.com/site/castleconference2010/Home/proceedings-of-the-seventh-international-conference-2008

Abstract

Smith (1998), exploring the development of collective knowledge, notes the importance of relationships among individuals engaged in self-study projects as a group. Although there has been research about the role of critical friends, or trusted colleagues who seek support and validation of their research in faculty self-study (Bass, Anderson-Patton, & Allender, 2002; Kosnik, Samaras, & Freese, 2006; Russell & Schuck, 2004; Samaras et al., 2006; Schuck & Segal, 2002), there has been less attention on doctoral students' study and application of being and having a critical friend. In this paper, we present a collective exploration of 10 female doctoral candidates and their experiences in critical friend work after they completed a course in self-study research. The course was designed to teach about critical friends through participation and application. We share our perceptions of learning about critical friend work through our engagement in that very process. We asked ourselves what it is like to have and be a critical friend and what difference it makes in a doctoral-level research course.

Glossary

Arts-based data: artifacts from a classroom and/or school (e.g., books, bulletin boards, school mission, school newsletters); also include art projects completed by researcher (e.g., self-portraits, haiku poems, classroom portraits), which provide an alternative format to uncover something that more traditional formats of data collection may not afford

Arts-based self-study method: a self-study method that "promotes and provokes self-reflection, critical analysis, and dialogue about improving one's teaching through the arts" (Samaras & Freese, 2006, p. 73)

Castle Conference: termed affectionately due to its presence at an English castle, this biannual conference is a professional venue that brings together self-study teacher educators from a wide range of countries from both research-intensive and teaching-focused universities; formally known as *International Conference on the Self-Study of Teacher Education Practices*

Cataloguing: a data-gathering technique the self-study researcher uses to memo and document developments and insights of his or her research in a metaconversation with him- or herself and with critical friends

Category: relationships and connections among and between codes create a category that represents "a unit of information composed of events, happenings, and instances" (Creswell, 2007, p. 64)

Check coding: "when two researchers code the same data set and discuss their initial difficulties; aids definitional clarity and also is a good reliability check" (Miles & Huberman, 1994, p. 64)

Codes: "tags or labels for assigning units of meaning to the descriptive or inferential information compiled during a study" (Miles & Huberman, 1994, p. 56)

Coding categories: inductive method used to sort descriptive data by topic; "terms and phrases developed to be used to sort and analyze qualitative data" (Bogdan & Biklen, 2007, p. 271)

Collaborative: "the communion" (Gadamer, 1975/2004) that occurs through the dialogue of critical friend inquiries with mutual benefits

Collective self-study method: a self-study method, interactive examination of an issue and implementation of a team or group project with exploration of individual roles within and across the collaborative (Samaras & Freese, 2006); also called a team-based approach (Davey & Ham, 2009)

Concept maps: a technique for visualizing the relationships and complex ideas among the big ideas or concepts and the dynamics and connections between them (Novak & Gowin, 1984)

Conceptual framework: an integrated mapping of the theories and phenomena that frame and shape a study and are informed by the literature reviewed

Constant comparative method: an inductive research method to generate theory over time in the research process through a constant comparison of incoming data against data previously collected and analyzed (Glaser & Strauss, 1967; Strauss & Corbin, 1990)

Critical collaborative inquiry: a methodological component of self-study that requires that personal insights be documented, shared, and critiqued to validate the researcher's interpretations (Loughran & Northfield, 1998); *critical* here means how a researcher's action might be considered ethically in terms of social justice and equity or "what ought to be" (van Manen, 1977)

Critical friend research memos: letters you write to your critical friend as a way to more naturally discuss and present your research while also deeply thinking about it; critical friend research memos can spark new ideas and promote dialogue to gain another's interpretations of and perspectives on your research

Critical friends: trusted colleagues who seek support and validation of their research to gain new perspectives in understanding and reframing their interpretations

Critical Friends Portfolio (CFP): a specifically designed pedagogical approach to provide opportunities to learn from, and about, one's teaching; entails an anthology of a teacher's work and engagement in a series of critical collaborative inquiries with peer interchange

Critical pedagogy: the work of teachers "grounded on a social and educational vision of justice and equality" (Kincheloe, 2005, p. 6); self-study "is designed to lead to the reconceptualization of the role of the teacher" (Samaras & Freese, 2006, p. 29) despite, and within, the constraints of the politics and practices of schooling

Crystallization: a postmodern analytic approach to explore data and extend data gathering, validity, and analysis through a multidimensional approach such as through the aesthetics to elucidate different angles and invite dialogue, of seemingly similar facets of data (Richardson, 2000)

Data: "the rough materials researchers collect from the world they are studying . . . [which] include materials the people doing the study actively record . . . [and] what others have created and the researcher finds" (Bogdan & Biklen, 2007, p. 117); in self-study, the researcher creates, actively records, and catalogues

Developmental portfolio self-study method: a self-study method that catalogues the research process and enables a teacher to uncover new and not always apparent dimensions of teaching (Samaras & Freese, 2006); provides a structure to scaffold, manage, and make meaning of a personal inquiry and make it public and open to the feedback and critique of peers

Dilemma: a situation that does not have a "right" or "wrong" answer but requires one to make a decision informed by research

Emic coding: a participant's own words used in data analysis; emic codes represent a researcher's first level of analysis

Etic coding: a researcher's interpretation of others' words during data analysis

Exemplars: "concrete models of research practice" (Mishler, 1990, p. 415)

Five Foci Framework: a manageable and definitional framework of five methodological components of self-study research: (1) personal situated inquiry, (2) critical collaborative inquiry, (3) improved learning, (4) transparent research process, and (5) knowledge generation and presentation; gleaned, refined, and extended from almost two decades of work by self-study scholars; includes guideposts for those interested in applying self-study in teacher research

Formal self-study approach: "a systematic research approach to explore one's practice" (Samaras & Freese, 2006, p. 61)

Grounded theory: researchers "set aside, as much as possible, theoretical ideas or notions so that the analytic, substantive theory can emerge" (Creswell, 2007, pp. 67–68); theory is generated and grounded in the data

Hermeneutic: "a research process whereby the researcher shifts forward and backward through the data with no predetermined assumptions to allow for the emergence of seemingly unrelated ideas and part-whole relationships" (Samaras & Freese, 2006, p. 12)

Improved learning: a methodological component of self-study that involves teachers' research efforts to impact and improve learning for themselves, their students, and the education field; is not limited to the cognitive domain

Informal self-study approach: "includes activities that provide practice in exploring one's teaching and learning using reflection as a critical dimension; it does not necessarily involve formal data gathering" (Samaras & Freese, 2006, p. 62)

Informed consent: an agreement by the participants, parent, or legal guardian to allow you to use information collected for stated research purposes in a study before you begin conducting research

Institutional review board (IRB): the federal government required that an institutional review board be established for any organization that receives federal funding for research involving human subjects for review of the proposed research

International Conference on the Self-Study of Teacher Education Practices: provides an international biannual forum for teacher educators to share examples of self-study in teacher education, to discuss methods and issues in self-study, and to consider the role of self-study in the reform of teacher education; also known as the Castle Conference

Interviews: notes and/or transcripts from meetings with students, peers, families, or school administrators through various formats: *in person*—formal or informal interviews with structured or semistructured prompts, audiotaped or videotaped interviews; *written formats*—questionnaires, surveys, checklists; useful for gaining perspectives of participants and obtaining information on questions related to research; journalist's prompts—*who, where, when, what, why,* and *how* are useful

Knowledge generation and presentation: a self-study methodological component indicating that self-study researchers can generate knowledge and make their research public through presentation and publication

Learning zones (LZ): adapted from Vygotsky's notion of the zone of proximal development (ZPD); "organic and diverse communities of diverse communities of expertise where learners co-mediate, negotiate, and socially construct an understanding of a shared task" (Samaras & Freese, 2006, p. 51)

Living contradiction: recognizing a contradiction between what you say you believe and what you actually do in practice, which may occur from personal or external constraints (Whitehead, 1989)

Living educational theory: descriptions and explanations and personal theory making produced from practitioners' accounts of their learning and practice and an exploration of living their values; teaching is based not in propositional theories but in teachers' reconceptualization of practice and with practical implications (McNiff, Lomax, & Whitehead, 2003; McNiff & Whitehead, 2006)

Member checks: examining and validating a researcher's interpretation of pieces of data to check interpretations

Memory work self-study method: serves to "uncover the ways in which individuals build their identities . . . what we remember and how we remember the events in our lives to form the basis of whom [sic] and what we are today" (O'Reilly-Scanlon, 2002, p. 74)

Multiplism: "refers not only to multiple methods but also to multiple triangulation, multiple stakeholders, multiple studies, and multiple paradigms and perspectives" (Miller & Crabtree, 2000, p. 615)

Narratives: stories, journaling of your ongoing record, essays, or other reflections about your study; can include education-related life history, interpretations of visual data, and story of your research process

Observations: an ongoing record of classroom events, student behavior, or school events; useful for noting any repeated behaviors, common occurrences and patterns, and also anomalies or things that break away from a usual pattern, outliers, or unique events; the researcher can be a participant while he or she conducts the observation and/or be a nonintrusive nonparticipant in the observations

Paradigm: a philosophical framework and way of knowing research, which includes an interrelated set of assumptions about how things are and must be (Kuhn, 1962)

Personal history self-study method: a self-study method to explore how personal experience, culture, history, and learning experiences can inform one's teaching (Samaras, Hicks, & Garvey Berger, 2004); this approach has also been called the personal experiences method (Russell, 2009) and education-related life history (Bullough, 1994; Bullough, Knowles, & Crow, 1991)

Personal situated inquiry: a self-study methodological component that emphasizes that personal experience is a valued source of knowledge; personal inquiry or questioning and conducting research about one's teaching is situated, or takes place, within your practical context

Positionality: involves your position and influence within the institutional hierarchy of schooling, and especially in your role as teacher of the students you are studying; should be carefully considered for purpose rather than for the convenience of student to study

Positivist: knowledge is based on natural phenomena that can be observed, measured, and verified; a positivist approach ignores the subjective experience and seeks an objective explanation of phenomena

Poster presentation: "a visual display—including printed text, maps, diagrams, photos, and artifacts—that summarizes the problem addressed, how it was researched, and the outcomes of the investigation" (Wolcott, 2001, p. 153)

Postmodern: postmodernists question that there is a single truth to guide one's research

Prism effect: critical friends work as a prism effect to allow the self-study researcher to alter his or her view through a different medium; critical friends, like the faces of a prism, are not parallel to each other, so the differing angle may unveil something that neither critical friend can see alone

Quadrangulation: includes multiple participants working to coanalyze data; for example, external researchers, participants, and project teams each working with the teacher researcher with the goal "to make a thorough appraisal of the problem, bringing all those with a role into the evaluation process" (McKernan, 1996, p. 188)

Self-study methodology: "a stance that a researcher takes towards understanding or explaining the physical or social world" rather than a way of knowing or doing research (LaBoskey, 2004b, p. 1173)

Self-study methods: *method* refers to "specific techniques" (Wolcott, 2001); *self-study* employs a variety of methods (developmental portfolio, personal history, living educational theory, collective self-study, arts-based self-study, memory work self-study, etc.) to capture the essence of the question being studied

Self-Study of Teacher Education Practices (S-STEP): a special interest group (SIG) of the American Educational Research Association (AERA); a forum for educators who work in a wide variety of settings and who are seeking to make substantial contributions related to the theory and practice of teacher education, self-study research design/practice, and the professional development of teacher educators; see http://sstep.soe.ku.edu/

Self-study research: a personal, systematic inquiry situated within one's teaching context that requires critical and collaborative reflection in order to generate knowledge, as well as inform the broader educational field (Sell, 2009a)

Self-Study School: "a popular research movement that began in the early 1990s by teacher educators studying their practice and through member research, presentation, and publication was formalized and came of age a decade later" (Samaras & Freese, 2006, p. 38)

Self-studyship: the extension of self-study to other practitioners such as administrators, librarians, occupational therapists, psychotherapists, school and community counselors, and other community educators working for social justice and educational reform (Samaras & Freese, 2006)

Self-study teacher researcher log: the researcher's notebook of sorting, meaning making, and documenting of insights, questions, and reflections about research

Student records: records of students' academic progress, transcripts, attendance, promotion and retention records, and discipline referrals; enable you to compare students' performance before and after your study

Themes: interpretation of the links between and across categories or a thematic analysis that is presented in the findings

Transparent and systematic research process: a self-study research component emphasizing the need for a clear and accurate documentation of the research process through dialogue and critique with critical friends

Triangulation: includes examining or triangulating of information or a phenomenon from multiple and independent sources and/or theories and methods (Denzin, 1978); can include more than three data sources

Trustworthiness: "the degree to which we can rely on the concepts, methods, and inferences of a study, or tradition of inquiry, as the basis for our own theorizing and empirical research" (Mishler, 1990, p. 419)

Utilitarian ethics: self-study research is not something you do to others, but something you do with your students to the benefit of all; "the right course of action should be what satisfies all, or the largest number of people" (Taylor, 1982, p. 131)

Validation team: provides feedback on the quality and legitimacy of a researcher's claims as team members examine the researcher's analysis and evidence (McNiff & Whitehead, 2005)

Visual memos: visual display of data (e.g., sketches, painting, objects); incorporate the arts to assist the researcher in thinking about the research and sorting out relationships and concepts in data

Zone of possibility (ZOP): where instructor and students are learners open to new understandings generated through dialogue (Kravtsova, 2006); critical friends extend each other's zone of possibility in understanding their practice

References

Adams-Legge, M. (2006). *"Juggling hats": A self-study of an English department chair.* Paper submitted in partial fulfillment of course requirements in Advanced Research Methods in Self-Study. George Mason University, Virginia.

Aiona, A. M. (2006, August). *Learning to facilitate mathematical discourse: A sixth-grade teacher's journey of self-discovery.* A thesis submitted to the graduate division of the University of Hawai'i in partial fulfillment of the requirements for the degree of master of education in curriculum studies.

Allen, J. (1999). *Words, words, words: Teaching vocabulary in grades 4–12.* York, ME: Stenhouse Publishers.

Allender, D. (2004). What happens to the self in self-study? In D. Tidwell, L. Fitzgerald, & M. Heston (Eds.), *Journeys of hope: Risking self-study in a diverse world.* Proceedings of the Fifth International Conference on Self-Study of Teacher Education Practices, Herstmonceux Castle, East Sussex, England (pp. 17–19). Cedar Falls: University of Northern Iowa.

Allender, J., & Manke, M. P. (2004). Evoking self in self-study: The analysis of artifacts. In D. Tidwell, L. Fitzgerald, & M. Heston (Eds.), *Journeys of hope: Risking self-study in a diverse world.* Proceedings of the Fifth International Conference on Self-Study of Teacher Education Practices, Herstmonceux Castle, East Sussex, England (pp. 20–23). Cedar Falls: University of Northern Iowa.

Allsopp, D., Lovin, L., Green, G., & Savage-Davis, E. (2003, February 1). Why students with special needs have difficulty learning mathematics and what teachers can do to help. *Mathematics Teaching in the Middle School, 8*(6), 308–314. Retrieved February 22, 2009, from ERIC database.

American Educational Research Association. (2001). Annual Meeting of the American Educational Research Association, Business Meeting of the Self-Study of Teacher Education Practices SIG, Seattle, WA.

American Educational Research Association. (2004, November 30). *Ethical standards.* Retrieved November 22, 2009, from http://www.aera.net/AboutAERA/Default.aspx?menu_id = 90&id = 174

American Psychological Association. (2003, June 1). *Ethical principles of psychologists and code of conduct.* Retrieved November 22, 2009, from http://www.apa.org/ethics/code2002.html

American Psychological Association. (2009). *Publication manual of the American Psychological Association* (6th ed.). Washington, DC: Author.

Anderson, G. L., Herr, K., & Nihlen, A. S. (2007). *Studying your own school: An educator's guide to practitioner action research.* Thousand Oaks, CA: Corwin Press.

Anderson, L. (2009). *Cultivating the cultivator: Are teaching and researching mutually exclusive careers?* Paper submitted in partial fulfillment of course requirements in Advanced Research Methods in Self-Study. George Mason University, Virginia.

Associated Content. (2008). *How an interactive notebook engages learners.* Retrieved September 8, 2008, from http://www.associatedcontent.com/

Austin, T., & Senese, J. C. (2004). Self-study in school teaching: Teachers' perspectives. In J. Loughran, M. L. Hamilton, V. K. LaBoskey, & T. Russell (Eds.), *International handbook of self-study of teaching and teacher education practices* (Vol. 2, pp. 1231–1258). Dordrecht, The Netherlands: Kluwer Academic Publishers.

Baker, S., Gersten, R., & Lee, D. (2002, September). A synthesis of empirical research on teaching mathematics to low-achieving students. *The Elementary School Journal, 103*(1), 51–73.

Bandura, A. (1997). *Self-efficacy: The exercise of control.* New York: Freeman.

Barnes, D. (1998). Looking forward: The concluding remarks at the Castle Conference. In M. L. Hamilton, with S. Pinnegar, T. Russell, J. Loughran, & V. LaBoskey (Eds.), *Reconceptualizing teaching practice: Self-study in teacher education* (pp. ix–xiv). London: Falmer Press.

Barone, T. (1995). The purposes of arts-based educational research. *International Journal of Educational Research, 23*(2), 169–180.

Barone, T., & Eisner, E. (1997). Arts-based educational research. In R. M. Jaeger (Ed.), *Complementary methods for research in education* (pp. 73–103). Washington, DC: American Educational Research Association.

Bass, L., Anderson-Patton, V., & Allender, J. (2002). Self-study as a way of teaching and learning: A research collaborative re-analysis of self-study teaching portfolios. In J. Loughran & T. Russell (Eds.), *Improving teacher education practices through self-study* (pp. 56–69). London: RoutledgeFalmer.

Beck, C., Kosnik, C., & Cleovoulou, Y. (2008). A whole-school approach to urban educational renewal: Community, collaboration, and leadership. In A. P. Samaras, A. R. Freese, C. Kosnik, & C. Beck (Eds.), *Learning communities in practice* (pp. 73–84). Dordrecht, The Netherlands: Springer.

Becker, H. S. (2007). *Writing for social scientists: How to start and finish your thesis, book, or article* (2nd ed.). Chicago: The University of Chicago Press.

Bell-Angus, B., Davis, G., Donoahue, Z., Kowal, M., & McGlynn-Stewart, M. (2008). DICEP: Promoting collaborative inquiry in diverse educational settings. In A. P. Samaras, A. R. Freese, C. Kosnik, & C. Beck (Eds.), *Learning communities in practice* (pp. 19–30). Dordrecht, The Netherlands: Springer.

Berlak, A., & Berlak, H. (1981). *Dilemmas of schooling.* London: Methuen.

Berry, A. (2004). Self-study in teaching about teaching. In J. J. Loughran, M. L. Hamilton, V. K. LaBoskey, & T. Russell (Eds.), *International handbook of self-study of teaching and teacher education practices* (Vol. 2, pp. 1295–1332). Dordrecht, The Netherlands: Kluwer Academic Publishers.

Berry, A. (2007). *Tensions in teaching about teaching: Understanding practice as a teacher educator.* Dordrecht, The Netherlands: Springer.

Berry, A., & Crowe, A. R. (2009). Many miles and many emails: Using electronic technologies in self-study to think about, refine, and reframe practice. In D. L. Tidwell, M. L. Heston & L. M. Fitzgerald (Eds.), *Research methods for the self-study practice* (pp. 83–98). Dordrecht, The Netherlands: Springer.

Bilgisayarh, G., & Egitim ve Erisi, D. (2007). Traditional education, computer assisted education, systematic learning and achievement. *Eurasian Journal of Education Research*, 29, 13–24.

Blumer, H. (1986). *Symbolic interactionism: Perspective and method.* New Jersey: Prentice Hall.

Bodone, F., Guðjónsdóttir, H., & Dalmau, M. C. (2004). Revisioning and recreating practice: Collaboration in self-study. In J. J. Loughran, M. L. Hamilton, V. K. LaBoskey, & T. Russell (Eds.), *International handbook of self-study of teaching and teacher education practices* (Vol. 1, pp. 743–784). Dordrecht, The Netherlands: Kluwer Academic Publishers.

Bogdan, R. C., & Biklen, S. K. (2007). *Qualitative research for education: An introduction to theory and methods* (5th ed.). Boston: Pearson.

Boice, R. (1990). *Professors as writers: A self-help guide to productive writing.* Stillwater, OK: New Forums Press.

Boice, R. (1994). Conclusion. In *How writers journey to comfort and fluency: A psychological adventure* (pp. 235–246). Westport, CT: Praeger.

Boice, R. (1996). *Procrastination and blocking: A novel, practical approach.* Westport, CT: Praeger.

Booth, W., Colomb, G. G., & Williams, J. M. (2003). *The craft of research.* Chicago: University of Chicago Press.

Borko, H., Cone, R., Atwood Russo, N., & Shavelson, R. J. (1979). Teachers' decision making. In P. L. Peterson & C. M. P. H. J. Walberg (Eds.), *Research on teaching: Concepts, findings, and implications* (pp. 136–160). Berkeley, CA: McCutchan.

Boyer, E. L. (1990). *Scholarship reconsidered: Priorities of the professoriate*. Princeton, NJ: Princeton University Press, The Carnegie Foundation for the Advancement of Teaching.

Breslin, D. (2006). *Exploring collaboration through self-study in a research firm*. Paper submitted in partial fulfillment of course requirements in Advanced Research Methods in Self-Study. George Mason University, Virginia.

Breslin, D., Mittapalli, K., Samaras, A. P., Adams-Legge, M., Infranco, J., Johri, A. K., et al. (2008). Embarking on an adventure while drawing the map: Journeys through critical friend work in self-study methodology. In M. Heston, D. Tidwell, K. East, & L. M. Fitzgerald (Eds.), *Pathways to change in teacher education: Dialogue, diversity and self-study*. Proceedings of the Seventh International Conference on the Self-Study of Teacher Education Practices, Herstmonceux Castle, East Sussex, England (pp. 31–35). Cedar Falls: University of Northern Iowa.

Brodkey, L. (1996). *Writing permitted in designated areas only*. Minneapolis: University of Minnesota Press.

Brown, E. R. (2002). The (in)visibility of race in narrative constructions of the self. In J. J. Loughran & T. Russell (Eds.), *Improving teacher education practices through self-study* (pp. 145–160). London: Falmer Press.

Brown, E. R. (2004). The significance of race and social class for self-study and the professional knowledge base of teacher education. In J. J. Loughran, M. L. Hamilton, V. LaBoskey, & T. Russell (Eds.), *International handbook of self-study of teaching and teacher education practices* (Vol. 1, pp. 517–574). Dordrecht, The Netherlands: Kluwer Academic Publishers.

Brown, K. M. (2008). *Blogging towards science literacy*. Paper submitted to the Secondary Education Program, Graduate School of Education, College of Education and Human Development, George Mason University, Virginia, in partial fulfillment of the requirements for the degree of master of education.

Bullough, R. V., Jr. (1994). Personal history and teaching metaphors: A self-study of teaching as conversation. *Teacher Education Quarterly, 21*(1), 107–120.

Bullough, R. V., Jr., & Gitlin, A. (1995). *Becoming a student of teaching: Methodologies for exploring self and school context*. New York: Garland Publishers.

Bullough, R. V., Jr., Knowles, J. G., & Crow, N. A. (1991). *Emerging as a teacher*. London: Routledge.

Bullough, R. V., Jr., & Pinnegar, S. (2001). Guidelines for quality in autobiographical forms of self-study research. *Educational Researcher, 30*(3), 13–21.

Bullough, R. V., Jr., & Pinnegar, S. (2004). Thinking about the thinking about self-study: An analysis of eight chapters. In J. J. Loughran, M. L. Hamilton, V. K. LaBoskey, & T. Russell (Eds.), *International handbook of self-study of teaching and teacher education practices* (Vol. 1, pp. 313–342). Dordrecht, The Netherlands: Kluwer Academic Publishers.

Caine, R. N., & Caine, R. (1994). *Making connections: Teaching and the human brain*. Menlo Park, CA: Innovative Learning Publications.

Carrier, K. (2005, Summer). Supporting science learning through science literacy objectives for English language learners. *Science Activities, 42*(2), 5–11. Retrieved April 10, 2009, from Education Research Complete database.

Carroll, L. (1998). *Alice's adventures in wonderland*. London: Penguin Books.

Cerbin, W. (1993). University of Wisconsin–LaCrosse. In E. Anderson (Ed.), *Campus use of the teaching portfolio: Twenty-five profiles* (pp. 88–96). Washington, DC: American Association for Higher Education.

Chan, P., & Harris, C. (2002). Enhancement of self-study of teaching practice via creation of video ethnographies. In C. Crawford et al. (Eds.), *Proceedings of Society for Information Technology and Teacher Education International Conference 2002* (pp. 955–957).

Charmaz, K. (2006). *Constructing grounded theory: A practical guide through qualitative analysis.* Los Angeles: Sage.

Chenail, R. J. (2008). "But is it research?": A review of Patricia Leavy's *Method meets art: Arts-based research practice. The Weekly Qualitative Report, 1*(2), 7–12. Retrieved October 13, 2008, from http://www.nova.edu/ssss/QR/WQR/wqr1_2.html

Cherednichenko, B., Gay, J., Hooley, N., Kruger, T., & Mulraney, R. (1998). Case writing: Making teachers' knowledge public. In B. Down, C. Hogan, & P. Swan (Eds.), *Reclaiming professional knowledge: New ways of thinking about teachers' learning.* Perth, Australia: Murdoch University, Centre for Curriculum and Professional Development.

Chiu-Ching, R. R., & Yim-mei Chan, E. (2008). Teaching and learning through narrative inquiry. In D. L. Tidwell, M. L. Heston, & L. M. Fitzgerald (Eds.), *Research methods for the self-study practice* (pp. 17–33). Dordrecht, The Netherlands: Springer.

Christians, C. G. (2000). Ethics and politics in qualitative research. In N. K. Denzin & Y. S. Lincoln (Eds.), *Handbook of qualitative research* (pp. 133–155). Thousand Oaks, CA: Sage.

Church, M. J., & Wright, J. L. (1986). Creative thinking with the microcomputer. In P. F. Campbell & G. G. Fein (Eds.), *Young children and microcomputers* (pp. 131–143). Englewood Cliffs, NJ: Prentice-Hall.

Ciriello, M. J., Valli, L., & Taylor, N. (1992). Problem solving is not enough: Reflective teacher education at the Catholic University of America. In L. Valli (Ed.), *Reflective teacher education: Cases and critiques* (pp. 99–115). New York: State University of New York Press.

Clandinin, D. J., & Connelly, F. M. (1992). The teacher as curriculum maker. In P. W. Jackson (Ed.), *Handbook of research on curriculum* (pp. 363–401). New York: Macmillan.

Clark, C. M., & Yinger, R. J. (1979). Teachers' thinking. In P. L. Peterson & H. J. Walberg (Eds.), *Research on teaching: Concepts, findings, and implications* (pp. 231–263). Berkeley, CA: McCutchan.

Clarke, A., & Erickson, G. (2003). Teacher inquiry: A defining feature of professional practice. In A. Clarke & G. Erickson (Eds.), *Teacher inquiry: Living the research in everyday practice* (pp. 1–6). London: RoutledgeFalmer.

Clarke, A., & Erickson, G. (2004a). The nature of teaching and learning in self-study. In J. J. Loughran, M. L. Hamilton, V. K. LaBoskey, & T. Russell (Eds.), *International handbook of self-study of teaching and teacher education practices* (Vol. 1, pp. 41–67). Dordrecht, The Netherlands: Kluwer Academic Publishers.

Clarke, A., & Erickson, G. (2004b). Self-study: The fifth commonplace. *Australian Journal of Education, 48*(2), 199–211.

Clift, R. T., Houston, W. R., & Pugach, M. C. (Eds.). (1990). *Encouraging reflective practice in education: Analysis of issues and programs.* New York: Teachers College Press.

Cochran-Smith, M., & Lytle, S. L. (1993). *Inside/outside: Teacher research and knowledge.* New York: Teachers College Press.

Cochran-Smith, M., & Lytle, S. L. (1996). Communities for teacher research: Fringe or forefront? In M. W. McLaughlin & I. Oberman (Eds.), *Teacher learning: New policies, new practices* (pp. 92–112). New York: Teachers College Press.

Cochran-Smith, M., & Lytle, S. L. (2004). Practitioner inquiry, knowledge, and university culture. In J. J. Loughran, M. L. Hamilton, V. K. LaBoskey, & T. Russell (Eds.), *International handbook of self-study of teaching and teacher education practices* (Vol. 1, pp. 601–649). Dordrecht, The Netherlands: Kluwer Academic Publishers.

Cole, A. L., & Finley, S. (Eds.). (1998). *Conversations in community.* Proceedings of the Second International Conference on Self-Study of Teacher Education Practices, Herstmonceux Castle, East Sussex, England. Kingston, ON, Canada: Queen's University.

Cole, A. L., & Knowles, J. G. (1995). Methods and issues in a life history approach to self-study. In T. Russell & F. Korthagen (Eds.), *Teachers who teach teachers: Reflections on teacher education* (pp. 130–151). Bristol, PA: Falmer Press.

Cole, A. L., & Knowles, J. G. (1998). Reforming teacher education through self-study. In A. L. Cole, R. Elijah, & J. G. Knowles (Eds.), *The heart of the matter: Teacher educators and teacher education reform* (pp. 41–54). San Francisco: Caddo Gap Press.

Cole, A. L., & Knowles, J. G. (Eds.). (2000). *Researching teaching: Exploring teacher development through reflexive inquiry.* Boston: Allyn & Bacon.

Cole, M. L., & Cole, S. R. (1996). *The development of children* (3rd ed). New York: W. H. Freeman and Company.

Cole, M., Cole, S. R., & Lightfoot, C. (2004). *The development of children.* New York: W. H. Freeman and Company.

Common, D. (1994). Conversation as pedagogy of reform for public education. *Journal of General Education, 43*(4), 241–272.

Connelly, F., & Clandinin, D. J. (1990). Stories of experience and narrative inquiry. *Educational Researcher, 19*(5), 2–11.

Corbin, J., & Strauss, A. (2008). *Basics of qualitative research: Techniques and procedures for developed grounded theory* (3rd ed.). Los Angeles: Sage.

Corey, S. M. (1953). *Action research to improve school practices.* New York: Teachers College Press.

Costa, A. L., & Kallick, B. (1993). Through the lens of a critical friend. *Educational Leadership, 51*(2), 49–51.

Craig, C. J. (2009). Trustworthiness in self-study research. In C. A. Lassonde, S, Galman, & C. Kosnik (Eds.), *Self-study research methodologies for teacher educators* (pp. 21–34). Rotterdam, The Netherlands: Sense Publishers.

Craig, S. (2008). *Student choice in vocabulary study.* Paper submitted to the Secondary Education Program, Graduate School of Education, College of Education and Human Development, George Mason University, Virginia, in partial fulfillment of the requirements for the degree of master of education.

Creswell, J. W. (2007). *Qualitative inquiry & research design: Choosing among the five approaches* (2nd ed.). Thousand Oaks, CA: Sage.

Cuban, L. (1993). *How teachers taught: Constancy and change in American classrooms 1800–1990.* New York: Teachers College Press.

Curry, M. (2008). Critical friend groups: The possibilities and limitations embedded in teacher professional communities aimed at instructional improvement and school reform. *Teachers College Record, 110*(4), 733–744.

Dalmau, M. C. (2007). Reflections on writing a self-study. Retrieved July 3, 2009, from http://www.ku.edu/ ~ sstep/

Dalmau, M. C. & Guðjónsdóttir, H. (2008). *Learning to find the future together: Distilling public educational knowledge through focused self-study.* A conference inquiry project presented at the Seventh International Conference on the Self-Study of Teacher Education Practices, Herstmonceux Castle, East Sussex, England.

Davey, R., & Ham, V. (2009). Collective wisdom: Team-based approaches to self-study in teacher education. In C. A. Lassonde, S. Galman, & C. Kosnik (Eds.), *Self-study research methodologies for teacher educators* (pp. 187–203). Rotterdam, The Netherlands: Sense Publishers.

DeAngelis, T. (Nov 2008). Crafting a winning manuscript. *GradPSYCH, 6*(4), 38–41.

Demitry, P. (2009). *Frustrated and flunking: The adolescent male struggle with reading in the curriculum.* Paper submitted to the Secondary Education Program, Graduate School of Education, College of Education and Human Development, George Mason University, Virginia, in partial fulfillment of the requirements for the degree of master of education.

Denzin, N. K. (1978). *The research act: A theoretical introduction to sociological methods* (2nd ed.). New York: McGraw-Hill.

Denzin, N. K., & Lincoln, Y. S. (2005). *Handbook of qualitative research.* Thousand Oaks, CA: Sage.

Dewey, J. (1933). *How we think: A restatement of the relation of reflective thinking to the reflective process.* New York: Heath and Company.

Dewey, J. (1938). *Experience and education*. New York: Macmillan.

Dinkelman, T. (2003). Self-study in teacher education: A means and ends tool for promoting reflective teaching. *Journal of Teacher Education, 54*(1), 6–18.

Dumaresq, S. (2009). *Improving vocabulary comprehension in ESOL students*. Paper submitted to the Secondary Education Program, Graduate School of Education, College of Education and Human Development, George Mason University, Virginia, in partial fulfillment of the requirements for the degree of master of education.

Durrant, C., & Green, B. (2000, June). Literacy and the new technologies in school education: Meeting the l(IT)eracy challenge. *Australian Journal of Language and Literacy, 23*(2), 89.

East, K., Fitzgerald, L. M., & Heston, M. L. (2009). Talking teaching and learning: Using dialogue in self-study. In D. L. Tidwell, M. L. Heston, & L. M. Fitzgerald (Eds.), *Research methods for the self-study practice* (pp. 55–72). Dordrecht, The Netherlands: Springer.

Educational Researcher. (2008). Conference News, p. 220.

Eisner, E. W. (1991). *The enlightened eye: Qualitative inquiry and the enhancement of educational practice*. New York: Macmillan.

Eisner, E. W. (1993). Forms of understanding and the future of educational research. *Educational Researcher, 22*(7), 5–11.

Eisner, E. W. (1995). What artistically crafted research can help us understand about schools. *Educational Theory, 45,* 1–6.

Elbow, P. (2000). *Everyone can write: Essays toward a hopeful theory of writing and teaching writing*. New York: Oxford University Press.

Ellingson, L. L. (2009). *Engaging crystallization in qualitative research*. Thousand Oaks, CA: Sage.

Elliott, J. (1991). *Action research for educational change*. Bristol, PA: Open University Press.

Feldman, A. (2003). Validity and quality in self-study. *Educational Researcher, 32*(3), 26–28.

Feldman, A., Paugh, P., & Mills, G. (2004). Self-study through action research. In J. Loughran, M. L. Hamilton, V. K. LaBoskey, & J. Russell (Eds.), *International handbook of self-study of teaching and teacher education practices* (Vol. 2, pp. 943–977). Dordrecht, The Netherlands: Kluwer Academic Publishers.

Fine, M., Weis, L., Weseen, S., & Wong, L. (2000). For whom? Qualitative research, representations, and social responsibilities. In N. K. Denzin & Y. S. Lincoln (Eds.), *Handbook of qualitative research* (pp. 107–131). Thousand Oaks, CA: Sage.

Fisher, D., & Frey, N. (2004). *Improving adolescent literacy: Strategies at work*. Upper Saddle River, NJ: Pearson Education.

Fitzgerald, L., Heston, M., & Tidwell, D. (Eds.). (2006). *Collaboration and community: Pushing boundaries through self-study*. Proceedings of the Sixth International Conference on Self-Study of Teacher Education Practices, Herstmonceux Castle, East Sussex, England. Cedar Falls: University of Northern Iowa.

Fontana, A., & Frey, J. (2000). The interview: From structured questions to negotiated text. In N. K. Denzin & Y. S. Lincoln (Eds.), *Handbook of qualitative research* (2nd ed., pp. 645–672). Thousand Oaks, CA: Sage.

Frattini, K. (2008). *Differentiation of instruction within a geosystems science classroom*. Paper submitted to the Secondary Education Program, Graduate School of Education, College of Education and Human Development, George Mason University, Virginia, in partial fulfillment of the requirements for the degree of master of education.

Freeman, M., deMarrais, K., Preissle, J., Roulston, K., & St. Pierre, E. A. (2007). Standards of evidence in qualitative research: An incitement to discourse. *Educational Researcher, 36*(1), 25–32.

Freese, A. R. (1999). The role of reflection on preservice teachers' development in the context of a professional development school. *Teaching and Teacher Education, 15*(8), 895–910.

Freese, A. R. (2005). Innovation and change in teacher education: An inquiring, reflective, collaborative approach. In G. Hoban (Ed.), *The missing links in teacher education design: Developing a multi-linked conceptual framework* (pp. 117–133). Dordrecht, The Netherlands: Springer.

Gadamer, H.-G. (2004). *Truth and method.* London: Continuum. (Original work published 1975)

Galman, S. (2009). Trading in fables: Literacy and artistic methods in self-study research. In C. A. Lassonde, S. Galman, & C. Kosnik (Eds.), *Self-study research methodologies for teacher educators* (pp. 129–149). Rotterdam, The Netherlands: Sense Publishers.

Gersten, R., & Clarke, B. (2007a, March). *Research brief: Effective strategies for teaching students with difficulties in mathematics.* National Council of Teachers of Mathematics. Retrieved February 22, 2009, from http://www.nctm.org/news/content.aspx?id=8452

Gersten, R., & Clarke, B. (2007b, May). *Research brief: What are the characteristics of students with learning difficulties in mathematics?* National Council of Teachers of Mathematics. Retrieved February 22, 2009, from http://www.nctm.org/news/content.aspx?id=11478

Ginn, W. (2008). *Jean Piaget: Intellectual development.* Retrieved October 13, 2008, from http://www.sk.com.br/sk-piage.html

Gipe, J. P. (1998). Self-study of teacher education practices through the use of the faculty course portfolio. In M. L. Hamilton, with S. Pinnegar, T. Russell, J. Loughran, & V. K. LaBoskey (Eds.), *Reconceptualizing teacher practice: Self-study in teacher education* (pp. 140–150). London: Falmer.

Glaser, B. G. (1978). *Theoretical sensitivity.* Mill Valley, CA: The Sociology Press.

Glaser, B. G., & Strauss, A. L. (1967). *The discovery of grounded theory.* Dallas: Houghton Mifflin.

Glesne, C. (2006). *Becoming qualitative researchers: An introduction* (3rd ed.). Boston: Pearson Education.

Goodson, I. F. (1980–1981). Life histories and the study of schooling. *Interchange, 11*(4), 62–76.

Goodson, I., & Lin Choi, P. (2008). Life history and collective memory as methodological strategies: Studying teacher professionalism. *Teacher Education Quarterly, 35*(2), 5–28.

Graue, B. (2006, December). The transformative power of reviewing. *Educational Researcher, 35*(9), 36–41.

Gray, T. (2005). *Publish and flourish: Become a prolific scholar.* Las Cruces: Teaching Academy, New Mexico State University.

Griffin, S. (2007). Early intervention for children at risk of developing mathematical learning difficulties. In D. Berch & M. Mazzocco (Eds.), *Why is math so hard for some children? The nature and origins of mathematical learning difficulties and disabilities* (pp. 373–395). Baltimore: Paul H. Brookes Publishing.

Griffiths, M. (2002). "Nothing grand": Small tales and working for social justice. In J. J. Loughran & T. Russell (Eds.), *Improving teacher education practices through self-study* (pp. 161–175). London: RoutledgeFalmer.

Griffiths, M., Malcom, H., & Williamson, Z. (2009). Faces and spaces and doing research. In D. L. Tidwell, M. L. Heston, & L. M. Fitzgerald (Eds.), *Research methods for the self-study practice* (pp. 101–118). Dordrecht, The Netherlands: Springer.

Grimmett, P. P. (1998). Reconceptualizing the practice of teacher education: On not throwing out the concurrent model with the reform bathwater. *Alberta Journal of Educational Research, 44,* 251–267.

Grossman, P. (2005). Research on pedagogical approaches in teacher education. In M. Cochran-Smith & K. Zeichner (Eds.), *Studying teacher education: The report of the AERA panel on research and teacher education* (pp. 425–456). Washington, DC: American Educational Research Association & Mahwah, NJ: Lawrence Erlbaum.

Guilfoyle, K. (1992, April). *Communicating with students: The impact of interactive dialogue journals on the thinking and teaching of a teacher educator.* Paper presented at the Annual Meeting of the American Education Research Association, San Francisco.

Guilfoyle, K., Hamilton, M. L., Pinnegar, S., & Placier, M. (1998). Negotiating balance between reforming teacher education and reforming self as teacher educators. In A. L. Cole, R. Elijah, & J. G. Knowles, *The heart of the matter: Teacher educators and teacher education reform* (pp. 171–192). San Francisco: Caddo Gap Press.

Ham, V., & Davey, R. (2006). Is virtual teaching, real teaching? Learnings from two self-studies. In. C. Kosnik, C. Beck, A. R. Freese, & A. P. Samaras (Eds.), *Making a difference in teacher education through self-study: Studies of personal, professional, and program renewal* (pp. 101–116). Dordrecht, The Netherlands: Springer.

Ham, V., & Kane, R. (2004). Finding a way through the swamp: A case for self-study as research. In J. J. Loughran, M. L. Hamilton, V. K. LaBoskey, & T. Russell (Eds.), *International handbook of self-study of teaching and teacher education practices* (Vol. 1, pp. 103–150). Dordrecht, The Netherlands: Kluwer Academic Publishers.

Hamilton, M. L. (1992, April). *Making public the private voice of a teacher educator.* Paper presented at the Annual Meeting of the American Education Research Association, San Francisco.

Hamilton, M. L. (2002). Change, social justice, and reliability: Reflections of a secret (change) agent. In J. J. Loughran & T. Russell (Eds.), *Improving teacher education practices through self-study* (pp. 176–189). London: RoutledgeFalmer.

Hamilton, M. L. (2005). Using pictures at an exhibition to explore my teaching practices. In C. Mitchell, S. Weber, & K. O'Reilly-Scanlon (Eds.), *Just who do we think we are? Methodologies for self-study in education* (pp. 58–68). London: Routledge.

Hamilton, M. L., & Pinnegar, S. (1998). Conclusion. In M. L. Hamilton, S. Pinnegar, T. Russell, J. Loughran, & V. K. LaBoskey (Eds.), *Reconceptualizing teaching practice: Self-study in teacher education* (pp. 235–246). London: Falmer.

Hamilton, M. L., & Pinnegar, S. (2000). On the threshold of a new century: Trustworthiness, integrity, and self-study in teacher education. *Journal of Teacher Education, 51,* 234–240.

Hamilton, M. L., & Pinnegar, S. (2009). Creating representations: Using collage in self-study. In D. L. Tidwell, M. L. Heston, & L. M. Fitzgerald (Eds.), *Research methods for the self-study practice* (pp. 155–170). Dordrecht, The Netherlands: Springer.

Hamilton, M. L., Pinnegar, S., Russell, T., Loughran, J., &. LaBoskey, V. K. (Eds.). (1998). *Reconceptualizing teaching practice: Self-study in teacher education.* London: Falmer.

Haury, D., & Rillero, P. (1994). *Perspectives of hands-on science teaching.* Retrieved September 29, 2008, from http://www.ncrel.org/sdrs/areas/issues/content/cntareas/science/eric/eric-toc.htm

Hendricks, C. (2006). *Improving schools through action research.* Boston: Pearson/Allyn & Bacon.

Heston, M., Tidwell, D., East, K., & Fitzgerald, L. (Eds.). (2008). *Pathways to change in teacher education: Dialogue, diversity and self-study.* Proceedings of the Seventh International Conference on the Self-Study of Teacher Education Practices, Herstmonceux Castle, East Sussex, England. Cedar Falls: University of Northern Iowa.

Heston, M. L., Tidwell, D. L., & Fitzgerald, L. M. (2008). Creating an international learning community for teacher education scholars. In A. P. Samaras, A. R. Freese, C. Kosnik, & C. Beck (Eds.), *Learning communities in practice* (pp. 165–177). Dordrecht, The Netherlands: Springer.

Hiles, J. B. (2008). *Second chance assessment: An assessment for learning?* Paper submitted to the Secondary Education Program, Graduate School of Education, College of Education and Human Development, George Mason University, Virginia, in partial fulfillment of the requirements for the degree of master of education.

Hinde, E. (2003, August 3). Reflections on reform: A former teacher looks at school change and the factors that shape it. *Teachers College Record.* Retrieved August 22, 2003, from http://www.tcrecord.org/content.asp?contentid = 11183

Hoban, G. (2003). Using the World Wide Web for researching teaching-learning relationships. In A. Clarke & G. Erickson (Eds.), *Teacher inquiry* (pp. 129–140). London and New York: RoutledgeFalmer.

Hoban, G. (2008). Lights, camera, action! Using slowmation as a common teaching approach to promote a school learning community. In A. P. Samaras, A. R. Freese, C. Kosnik, & C. Beck (Eds.), *Learning communities in practice* (pp. 45–58). Dordrecht, The Netherlands: Springer.

Hoban, G., & Brickell, G. (2006). Using diagrams as reflective tools to represent the dynamics of classroom interactions. In P. Aubusson & S. Schuck (Eds.), *Teacher learning and development* (pp. 237–250). Dordrecht, The Netherlands: Springer.

Holt-Reynolds, D. (1992). Personal history-based beliefs as relevant prior knowledge in course work. *American Educational Research Journal, 29*(2), 325–349.

Hopper, T., & Sanford, K. (2008). Using poetic representation to support the development of teachers' knowledge. *Studying Teaching, 4*(1), 29–45.

Hubbard, R. S., & Power, B. (1999). *Living the questions: A guide for teacher-researchers.* Portland, ME: Stenhouse.

Infranco. J. (2007). *Integrating the counselor and client roles: Self-study of a therapist's journey.* Paper submitted in partial fulfillment of course requirements in Advanced Research Methods in Self-Study. George Mason University, Virginia.

Jacob, E. (n.d.). *Cultural inquiry process Web site.* Retrieved November 22, 2009, from http://classweb.gmu.edu/cip/cip-ind.htm

Janesick, V. J. (2000). The choreography of qualitative research design. In N. K. Denzin & Y. S. Lincoln (Eds.), *Handbook of qualitative research* (2nd ed., pp. 379–399). Thousand Oaks, CA: Sage.

Janesick, V. J. (2004). *"Stretching" exercises for qualitative researchers.* Thousand Oaks, CA: Sage.

John-Steiner, V. (2000). *Creative collaboration.* New York: Oxford University Press.

Johri, A. K. (2007). *Professional identity: Mapping of the self for a no-audience celebration.* Paper submitted in partial fulfillment of course requirements in Advanced Research Methods in Self-Study. George Mason University, Virginia.

Johri, A. K., & Mittapalli, K. (2008, April). *A self-reflective journey of a researcher and a teacher-administrator seeking answers through arts-based self-study.* Paper presented at the Annual Meeting of the American Educational Research Association.

Johri, A. K., & Ritter, J. K. (2009). *What does it mean to join the self-study community?* Poem authored and presented at Samaras, A. P., Guðjónsdóttir, H., & Dalmau, M. C. (with S-STEP members). (2009, April). *A sociocultural perspective on the outgrowth and development of the Self-Study School.* Symposium, Annual Meeting of the American Educational Research Association (AERA), Self-Study of Teacher Education Practices SIG (S-STEP), San Diego, CA.

Kalmbach Phillips, D., & Carr, K. (2006). *Becoming a teacher through action research: Process, context, and self-study.* New York: Routledge.

Kemmis, S. (Ed.). (1982). *Action research reader.* Geelong, Victoria: Deakin University Press.

Kemmis, S., & McTaggart, R. (1988). *The action research planner.* Geelong, Victoria: Deakin University Press. (Original work published 1981)

Kessler, C., & Wong, C. S. (2008). Growing our own: A learning community partnership between a university and a public middle school. In A. P. Samaras, A. R. Freese, C. Kosnik, & C. Beck (Eds.), *Learning communities in practice* (pp. 59–72). Dordrecht, The Netherlands: Springer.

Kiel, M. (2009). *Evaluating an after-school mathematics program for middle school students.* Paper submitted to the Secondary Education Program, Graduate School of Education, College of Education and Human Development, George Mason University, Virginia, in partial fulfillment of the requirements for the degree of master of education.

Kincheloe, J. (1991). *Teachers as researchers: Qualitative inquiry as a path to empowerment.* London: Falmer.

Kincheloe, J. L. (2005). *Critical pedagogy.* New York: Peter Lang.

King, K., & Gurian, M. (2006). Teaching to the minds of boys. *Educational Leadership, 64,* 56–61.

Kipling, R. (1902). *The elephant's child.* Retrieved March 28, 2009, from http://www.mycoted.com/Five_Ws_and_H

Kitchen, J. (2009). Passages: Improving teacher education through narrative self-study. In D. L. Tidwell, M. L. Heston, & L. M. Fitzgerald (Eds.), *Research methods for the self-study practice* (pp. 35–51). Dordrecht, The Netherlands: Springer.

Kitchen, J., & Ciuffetelli Parker, D. (2009). Self-study communities of practice: Developing community, critically inquiring as community. In C. A. Lassonde, S. Galman, & C. Kosnik (Eds.), *Self-study research methodologies for teacher educators* (pp. 107–128). Rotterdam, The Netherlands: Sense Publishers.

Kitchen, J., Ciuffetelli Parker, D., & Gallagher, T. (2008). Authentic conversation as faculty development: Establishing a self-study group in an education college. *Studying Teacher Education, 4*(2), 157–177.

Klein, E. J., Riordian, M., Schwartz, A., & Sotirhos, S. (2008). *Dissertation support groups: Building a community of practice using Noddings' ethic of care.* In A. P. Samaras, A. R. Freese, C. Kosnik, & C. Beck (Eds.), *Learning communities in practice* (pp. 117–131). Dordrecht, The Netherlands: Springer.

Knowles, J. G., & Cole, A. L. (2008) *Handbook of the arts in qualitative research.* Los Angeles: Sage.

Korthagen, F. A. J. (1995). A reflection on five reflective accounts. Theme issue self-study and living educational theory. *Teacher Educational Quarterly, 22*(3), 99–105.

Kosnik, C. (2008). Funny, this does not look like a community: Working collaboratively across borders and institutions. In A. P. Samaras, A. R. Freese, C. Kosnik, & C. Beck (Eds.), *Learning communities in practice* (pp. 219–239). Dordrecht, The Netherlands: Springer.

Kosnik, C., Beck, C., Freese, A. R., & Samaras, A. P. (Eds.). (2006). *Making a difference in teacher education through self-study: Studies of personal, professional, and program renewal.* Dordrecht, The Netherlands: Springer.

Kosnik, C., Cleovoulou, Y., & Fletcher, T. (2009). The use of interviews in self-study research. In C. A. Lassonde, S. Galman, & C. Kosnik (Eds.), *Self-study research methodologies for teacher educators* (pp. 53–69). Rotterdam, The Netherlands: Sense Publishers.

Kosnik, C., Freese, A., & Samaras, A. P. (Eds.). (2002a). *Making a difference in teacher education through self-study.* Proceedings of the Fourth International Conference on Self-study of Teacher Education Practices, Herstmonceux Castle, East Sussex, England (Vols. 1 & 2). Toronto, ON, Canada: OISE, University of Toronto.

Kosnik, C., Freese, A. R., & Samaras, A. P. (2002b). Searching for integrity of our research to our practices in three teacher education programs. In C. Kosnik, A. Freese, & A. P. Samaras (Eds.), *Proceedings of the Fourth International Conference on the Self-Study of Teacher Education Practices, East Sussex, England* (pp. 48–53). Toronto, ON, Canada: OISE, University of Toronto.

Kosnik, C., Lassonde, C., & Galman, S. (2009). What does self-study research offer teacher educators? In C. A. Lassonde, S. Galman, & C. Kosnik (Eds.). *Self-study research methodologies for teacher educators* (pp. 225–239). Rotterdam, The Netherlands: Sense Publishers.

Kosnik, C., Samaras, A. P., & Freese, A. R. (2006). Beginning with trusted friends: Venturing out to work collaboratively in our institutions. In L. Fitzgerald, M. Heston, & D. Tidwell, (Eds.), *Collaboration and community: Pushing boundaries through self-study.* Proceedings of the Sixth International Conference on Self-Study of Teacher Education Practices, Herstmonceux Castle, East Sussex, England (pp. 152–156). Cedar Falls: University of Northern Iowa.

Kravtsova, E. (November 2006). The tasks and prospects of cultural-historical psychology. Keynote lecture, *The Seventh International L. S. Vygotsky Memorial Conference "Cultural-Historical Theory: Prospects of Development."* Russian State University for the Humanities, Moscow.

Kuhn, T. (1962). *The structure of scientific revolutions.* Chicago: Chicago University.

Kuhn, T. (1970). *The structure of scientific revolutions* (2nd ed.). Chicago: Chicago University.

Kuhn, T. (1996). *The structure of scientific revolutions* (3rd ed.). Chicago: Chicago University.

Kvale, S. (1996). *InterViews: An introduction to qualitative research interviewing.* Thousand Oaks, CA: Sage.

LaBoskey, V. K. (1991). *A conceptual framework for reflection in preservice education.* Paper presented at the Conceptualizing Reflection in Teacher Development Conference, Bath, England.

LaBoskey, V. K. (2004a). The methodology of self-study and its theoretical underpinnings. In J. J. Loughran, M. L. Hamilton, V. K. LaBoskey, & T. Russell (Eds.), *International handbook of self-study of teaching and teacher education practices* (Vol. 1, pp. 817–869). Dordrecht, The Netherlands: Kluwer Academic Publishers.

LaBoskey, V. K. (2004b). Moving the methods of self-study research and practice forward: Challenges and opportunities. In J. J. Loughran, M. L. Hamilton, V. K. LaBoskey, & T. Russell (Eds.), *International handbook of self-study of teaching and teacher education practices* (Vol. 2, pp. 1169–1184). Dordrecht, The Netherlands: Kluwer Academic Publishers.

LaBoskey, V. K. (2006). The fragile strengths of self-study: Making bold claims and clear connections. In P. Aubusson & S. Schuck (Eds.), *Teaching learning and development: The mirror maze* (pp. 251–262). Dordrecht, The Netherlands: Springer.

LaBoskey, V. K. (2009). "Name it and claim it": The methodology of self-study as social justice teacher education. In M. L. H. D. L. Tidwell & L. M. Fitzgerald (Eds.), *Research methods for the self-study practice* (pp. 73–82). Dorchrecht, The Netherlands: Springer.

LaBoskey, V. K., Davies-Samway, K., & Garcia, S. (1998). Cross-institutional action research: A collaborative self-study. In M. L. Hamilton, S. Pinnegar, J. Russell, J. Loughran, & V. K. LaBoskey (Eds.), *Reconceptualizing teaching practice: Self-study in teacher education* (pp. 154–166). London: Falmer.

Lassonde, C. A., Galman, S., & Kosnik, C. (Eds.), (2009). *Self-study research methodologies for teacher educators.* Rotterdam, The Netherlands: Sense Publishing.

Lassonde, C., & Strub, D. (2009). Promoting self-study as a habit of mind for preservice teachers In C. A. Lassonde, S. Galman, & C. Kosnik (Eds.), *Self-study research methodologies for teacher educators* (pp. 207–224). Rotterdam, The Netherlands: Sense Publishers.

Lather, P. (1986). Issues of validity in openly ideological research: Between a rock and a soft place. *Interchange, 17*(4), 63–84.

Lave, J., & Wenger, E. (1991). *Situated learning: Legitimate peripheral participation.* New York: Cambridge University Press.

Lawrence-Lightfoot, S. (1983). *The good high school: Portraits of character and culture.* New York: Basic Books, Inc.

Lee, S. S., & van den Berg, O. (2003). Ethical obligations in teacher research. In A. Clarke & G. Erickson (Eds.), *Teacher inquiry: Living the research in everyday practice* (pp. 93–102). London: RoutledgeFalmer.

Lewin, K. (1946). Action research and minority problems. *Journal of Social Issues, 2*(4), 34–46.

Lighthall, F. F. (2004). Fundamental features and approaches of the s-step enterprise. In J. J. Loughran, M. L. Hamilton, V. K. LaBoskey, & T. Russell (Eds.), *International handbook of self-study of teaching and teacher education practices* (Vol. 1, pp. 193–245). Dordrecht, The Netherlands: Kluwer Academic Publishers.

Lincoln, Y. S., & Guba, E. G. (2000). Paradigmatic controversies, contradictions, and emerging confluences. In N. K. Denzin & Y. S. Lincoln (Eds.), *Handbook of qualitative research* (pp. 163–188). Thousand Oaks, CA: Sage.

Lindsey, R. B., Robins, K. N., & Terrell, R. D. (2003). *Cultural proficiency: A manual for school leaders.* Thousand Oaks, CA: Sage.

Loughran, J. J. (1996). *Developing the reflective practitioner: Learning about teaching and learning through modeling.* London: Falmer.

Loughran, J. J. (2004). A history and context of self-study of teaching and teacher education practices. In J. J. Loughran, M. L. Hamilton, V. K. LaBoskey, & T. Russell (Eds.), *International handbook of self-study of teaching and teacher education practices* (Vol. 1, pp. 7–39). Dordrecht, The Netherlands: Kluwer Academic Publishers.

Loughran, J. (2007a). Researching teacher education practices: Responding to the challenges, demands, and expectations of self-study. *Journal of Teacher Education, 58*(1), 12–20.

Loughran, J. J. (2007b). Series editor's forward. In L. Farr Darling, G. Erickson, & A. Clarke (Eds.), *Collective improvisation in a teacher education community* (pp. xv–xvii). Dordrecht, The Netherlands: Springer.

Loughran, J. (2008). Seeking knowledge for teaching: Moving beyond stories. In M. L. Heston, D. L. Tidwell, K. East, & L. M. Fitzgerald (Eds.), *Pathways to change in teacher education: Dialogue, diversity, and self-study.* Proceedings of The Seventh International Conference on the Self-Study of Teacher Education Practices, Herstmonseux Castle, East Sussex, England (pp. 218–221). Cedar Falls: University of Northern Iowa.

Loughran, J. J., Hamilton, M. L., LaBoskey, V. K., & Russell, T. (Eds.). (2004). *International handbook of self-study of teaching and teacher education practices.* Dordrecht, The Netherlands: Kluwer Academic Publishers.

Loughran, J. J., & Northfield, J. (1998). A framework for the development of self-study practice. In M. L. Hamilton, with S. Pinnegar, T. Russell, J. Loughran, & V. K. LaBoskey (Eds.), *Reconceptualizing teaching practice: Self-study in teacher education* (pp. 7–18). London: Falmer.

Loughran, J., & Russell, T. (Eds.). (2000). *Exploring myths and legends of teacher education.* Proceedings of the Third International Conference on Self-Study of Teacher Education Practices, Herstmonceux Castle, East Sussex, England. Kingston, ON, Canada: Queen's University.

Louie, B. Y., Drevdahl, D. J., Purdy, J. M., & Stackman, R. W. (2003). Advancing the scholarship of teaching through collaborative self-study. *The Journal of Higher Education, 74*(2), 150–171.

Lowe, D. (1982). *History of bourgeois perception.* Chicago: University of Chicago Press.

Lyons, N. (1998). Portfolios and their consequences: Developing as a reflective practitioner. In N. Lyons (Ed.), *With portfolio in hand: Validating the new teacher professionalism* (pp. 247–264). New York: Teachers College Press.

Lyons, N., & Freidus, H. (2004). The reflective portfolio in self-study: Inquiring into and representing a knowledge of practice. In J. Loughran, M. L. Hamilton, V. K. LaBoskey, & T. Russell (Eds.), *The international handbook of self-study of teaching and teacher education practices* (pp. 1071–1107). Dordrecht, The Netherlands: Kluwer Academic Publishers.

Lyons, N., & LaBoskey, V. K. (2002). *Narrative inquiry in practice: Advancing the knowledge of teaching.* New York: Teachers College Press.

MacLean, M. S., & Mohr, M. (1999). *Teacher-researchers at work.* Berkeley, CA: National Writing Project.

Mahler, E. G. (1990). Validation in inquiry-guided research: The role of exemplars in narrative research. *Harvard Educational Review, 60*(4), 415–442.

Manke, M. P. (2004). Administrators also do self-study: Issues of power and community, social justice, and teacher education reform. In J. J. Loughran, M. L. Hamilton, V. K. LaBoskey, & T. Russell (Eds.), *International handbook of self-study of teaching and teacher education practices* (Vol. 2, pp.1367–1391). Dordrecht, The Netherlands: Kluwer Academic Publishers.

Manos, M. A. (2006). *Knowing where to draw the line: Ethical and legal standards for best classroom practice.* Westport, CT: Praeger.

Mason, J. (2002). *Researching your own practice: The discipline of noticing.* London: RoutledgeFalmer.

Maxwell, J. (2005). *Qualitative research design: An interactive approach* (2nd ed.). Thousand Oaks, CA: Sage.

Maxwell, J. A., & Miller, B. (2008). *Categorizing and connecting as components in qualitative data analysis.* In P. Leavy & S. Hesse-Biber (Eds.), *Handbook of emerging methods* (pp. 461–475). New York: Guilford.

McIlwain, M. J. (2007). *Discovering phonological awareness through ourselves and others.* Paper submitted in partial fulfillment of course requirements in Advanced Research Methods in Self-Study. George Mason University, Virginia.

McKernan, J. (1996). *Curriculum action research: A handbook of methods and resources for the reflective practitioner* (2nd ed). London: RoutledgeFalmer.

McMurrer, J. M. (2009). *Designing women: Exploring my role as a member of a research team through self-study.* Paper submitted in partial fulfillment of course requirements in Advanced Research Methods in Self-Study. George Mason University, Virginia.

McNiff, J., Lomax, P., & Whitehead, J. (2003). *You and your action research project.* London: RoutledgeFalmer.

McNiff, J., & Whitehead, J. (2005). *Action research for teachers: A practical guide.* London: David Fulton Publishers.

McNiff, J., & Whitehead, J. (2006). *All you need to know about action research.* Thousand Oaks, CA: Sage.

McTighe, J., & Wiggins, G. (2005). *Understanding by design* (Expanded 2nd ed.). Alexandria, VA: Association for Supervision and Curriculum Development.

Mead, G. H. (1934). *Mind, self and society.* Chicago: University of Chicago Press.

Mercer, J. W. (2008). *Motivating students to learn civics at a rigorous level.* Paper submitted to the Secondary Education Program, Graduate School of Education, College of Education and Human Development, George Mason University, Virginia, in partial fulfillment of the requirements for the degree of master of education.

Merriam, S. B. (1998). *Qualitative research and case study applications in education.* San Francisco: Jossey-Bass.

Mertler, C. A. (2009). *Action research: Teachers as researchers in the classroom* (2nd ed). Los Angeles: Sage.

Miles, M. B., & Huberman, A. M. (1994). *Qualitative data analysis.* Thousand Oaks, CA: Sage.

Miller, W. L., & Crabtree, B. F. (2000). Clinical research. In N. K. Denzin & Y. S. Lincoln (Eds.), *Handbook of qualitative research* (2nd ed., pp. 607–631). Thousand Oaks, CA: Sage.

Mills, C. W. (1959). On intellectual craftsmanship. In C. W. Mills (Ed.), *The sociological imagination* (pp. 195–226). New York: Oxford University Press.

Mills, G. E. (2007). *Action research: A guide for the teacher researcher.* Upper Saddle River, NJ: Pearson/Merrill Prentice Hall.

Mishler, E. G. (1990). Validation in inquiry-guided research: The role of exemplars in narrative research. *Harvard Educational Review, 60*(4), 415–442.

Mitchell, C. (2006). In my own handwriting: Textual evidence and self-study. In C. Kosnik, C. Beck, A. R. Freese, & A. P. Samaras (Eds.), *Making a difference in teacher education through self-study: Studies of personal, professional, and program renewal* (pp. 117–130). Dordrecht, The Netherlands: Springer.

Mitchell, C., & Weber, S. (1999). *Reinventing ourselves as teachers: Beyond nostalgia.* London: Falmer.

Mitchell, C., Weber, S., & O'Reilly-Scanlon, K. (2005). *Just who do we think we are? Methodologies for autobiography and self-study.* London: RoutledgeFalmer.

Mitchell, C., Weber, S., & Pithouse, K. (2009). Facing the public: Using photography for self-study and social action. In D. L. Tidwell, M. L. Heston, & L. M. Fitzgerald (Eds.), *Research methods for the self-study practice* (pp. 119–134). Dordrecht, The Netherlands: Springer.

Mitchell, I. (2004). Identifying ethical issues in self-study. In J. J. Loughran, M. L. Hamilton, V. K. LaBoskey, & T. Russell (Eds.), *International handbook of self-study of teaching and teacher education practices* (Vol. 2, pp. 1393–1442). Dordrecht, The Netherlands: Kluwer Academic Publishers.

Mitchell, I., & Mitchell, J. (2008). The project for enhancing effective learning (PEEL). In A. P. Samaras, A. R. Freese, C. Kosnik, & C. Beck (Eds.), *Learning communities in practice* (pp. 7–18). Dordrecht, The Netherlands: Springer.

Mittapalli, K. (2006). Searching for answers: My self-development as a researcher. Paper submitted in partial fulfillment of course requirements in Advanced Research Methods in Self-Study. George Mason University, Virginia.

Mittapalli, K., & Samaras, A. P. (2008). Madhubani art: A journey of an education researcher seeking self-development answers through art and self-study. *The Qualitative Report, 13*(2), 244–261.

Moxley, J. M. (1997). If not now, when? In J. M. Moxley & T. Taylor (Eds.), *Writing and publishing for academic authors* (2nd ed., pp. 3–18). Lanham, MD: Rowman & Littlefield Publishers.

Munby, H., & Russell, T. (1994). The authority of experience in learning to teach: Messages from a physics methods class. *Journal of Teacher Education, 45*(2), 86–95.

Murray, L., & Lawrence, B. (2000). *Practitioner-based enquiry: Principles for postgraduate research.* London: Falmer.

National Council for Accreditation of Teacher Education. (2007, November 13). *NCATE issues call for action: Defines professional dispositions as used in teacher education.* Retrieved November 22, 2009, from http://www.ncate.org/public/102407.asp?ch = 148

National Council of Teachers of Mathematics. (1991). *Professional standards for teaching mathematics.* Reston, VA. Retrieved December 2, 2009, from http://standards.nctm.org/

National Education Association. (n.d.). *Code of ethics.* Retrieved November 22, 2009, from http://www.nea.org/home/30442.htm

Noddings, N. (1984). *Caring: A feminine approach to ethics and moral education.* Berkeley: University of California Press.

Novak, J. D. (1995). Concept mapping: A strategy for organizing knowledge. In S. M. Glynn & R. Duit (Eds.), *Learning science in the schools: Research reforming practice* (pp. 229–245). Mahwah, NJ: Lawrence Erlbaum.

Novak, J., & Gowin, D. (1984). *Learning how to learn.* New York: Cambridge University Press.

Oda, L. K. (1998). Harmony, conflict and respect: An Asian-American educator's self-study. In M. L. Hamilton, S. Pinnegar, J. Russell, J. Loughran, & V. K. LaBoskey (Eds.), *Reconceptualizing teaching practice: Self-study in teacher education* (pp. 113–123). London: Falmer.

O'Looney, J. A. M. (2006). Self-study and the school psychologist: Reflections on changes in current practice. Paper submitted in partial fulfillment of course requirements in Advanced Research Methods in Self-Study. George Mason University, Virginia.

O'Reilly-Scanlon, K. (2002). Muted echoes and lavender shadows: Memory work and self-study. In C. Kosnik, A. R. Freese, & A. P. Samaras (Eds.), *Making a difference in teacher education through self-study.* Proceedings of the Fourth International Conference on Self-Study of Teacher Education Practices, Herstmonceux Castle, East Sussex, England (Vol. 2, pp. 74–78). Toronto, ON, Canada: OISE, University of Toronto.

Ortiz, D. P. (2008). *Exit paper.* Submitted in partial fulfillment of course requirements in Ways of Knowing. George Mason University, Virginia.

Patton, M. Q. (1990). *Qualitative evaluation and research methods* (2nd ed.). Newbury Park, CA: Sage.

Patton, M. Q. (2002). *Qualitative evaluation and research methods* (3rd ed.). Thousand Oaks, CA: Sage.

Paugh, P., & Robinson, E. (2009). Participatory research as self-study. In C. A. Lassonde, S. Galman, & C. Kosnik (Eds.), *Self-study research methodologies for teacher educators* (pp. 87–106). Rotterdam, The Netherlands: Sense Publishers.

Pearson, B. (2009a). *Evaluating others . . . defining myself . . . and identifying multicultural navigators: Personal history self-study method.* Invited presentation in Advanced Research Methods in Self-Study Course, George Mason University, Virginia.

Pearson, B. (2009b). *Multicultural navigators and college-bound high school students' academic achievement, self-efficacy for learning, and perceived task-value.* Unpublished doctoral dissertation, George Mason University, Fairfax, VA.

Pell, T., Galton, M., Steward, S., Page, C., and Hargreaves, L. (2007). Promoting group work at key stage 3: Solving an attitudinal crisis among young adolescents? *Research Papers in Education, 22,* 309–332.

Pine, G. J. (2009). *Teacher action research: Building knowledge democracies.* Los Angeles: Sage.

Pinnegar, S. (1992, April). *Student teaching as a teacher educator.* Paper presented at the Annual Meeting of the American Education Research Association, San Francisco.

Pinnegar, S. (1998). Introduction: Methodological perspectives. In M. L. Hamilton, with S. Pinnegar, T. Russell, J. Loughran, & V. LaBoskey (Eds.), *Reconceptualizing teaching practice: Self-study in teacher education* (pp. 31–33). London: Falmer.

Pinnegar, S., & Erickson, L. B. (2009). Uncovering self-studies in teacher education accreditation review. In C. Lassonde, S. Galman, & C. Kosnik (Eds.), *Self-Study research methodologies for teacher educators* (pp. 151–168). Rotterdam, The Netherlands: Sense Publishers.

Pinnegar, S., & Hamilton, M. L. (2009). *Self-study of practice as a genre of qualitative research: Theory, methodology, and practice.* Dordrecht, The Netherlands: Springer.

Placier, P. (1992, April). *Maintaining practice: a struggle of too little time.* Paper presented at the Annual Meeting of the American Education Research Association, San Francisco.

Placier, P., Cockrell, K. S., Burgoyne, S., Welch, S., Neville, H., & Eferakorho, J. (2006). Theatre of the oppressed as an instructional practice. In C. Kosnik, C. Beck, A. R. Freese, & A. P. Samaras (Eds.), *Making a difference in teacher education through self-study: Studies of personal, professional, and program renewal* (pp. 131–146). Dordrecht, The Netherlands: Springer.

Pratt-Fartro, T. (2007). *Images of me: A self-study proposal of learning, teaching and leading.* Paper submitted in partial fulfillment of course requirements in Advanced Research Methods in Self-Study. George Mason University, Virginia.

Punch, K. (2005). *Introduction to social research: quantitative and qualitative approaches* (2nd ed.). London: Sage.

Ratke, A. (2007, May). *A reflective look at an inclusive classroom through a formal self-study.* A Plan B paper submitted to the Department of Curriculum Studies, College of Education, University of Hawai'i at Manoa in partial fulfillment of the requirements for the degree of master of elementary education.

Richards, J. C. (1998). Turning to the artistic: Developing an enlightened eye by creating teaching self-portraits. In M. L. Hamilton, with S. Pinnegar, T. Russell, J. Loughran, & V. LaBoskey (Eds.), *Reconceptualizing teacher practice: Self-study in teacher education* (pp. 34–44). London: Falmer.

Richards, J., & Russell, T. (Eds.). (1996). *Empowering our future in teacher education.* Proceedings of the First International Conference on Self-study of Teacher Education Practices, Herstmonceux Castle, East Sussex, England. Kingston, ON, Canada: Queen's University.

Richards, P. (2007). *Risk.* An invited chapter in H. S. Becker, *Writing for social scientists: How to start and finish your thesis, book, or article* (pp. 108–120). Chicago: The University of Chicago Press.

Richardson, L. (2000). Writing: A method of inquiry. In N. K. Denzin & Y. S. Lincoln (Eds.), *Handbook of qualitative research* (2nd ed., pp. 923–948). Thousand Oaks, CA: Sage.

Robinson, V., & Kuin Lai, M. (2006). *Practitioner research for educators: A guide to improving classrooms and schools.* Thousand Oaks, CA: Corwin Press, Sage.

Rossman, G. B., & Rallis, S. F. (1998). *Learning in the field: An introduction to qualitative research.* Thousand Oaks, CA: Sage.

Russell, T. (1992). *Holding up the mirror: Teacher educators reflect on their own teaching.* Paper presented at the Annual Meeting of the American Education Research Association, San Francisco.

Russell, T. (2002). Can self-study improve teacher education? In J. J. Loughran & T. Russell (Eds.), *Improving teacher education practices through self-study* (pp. 3–10). London: RoutledgeFalmer.

Russell, T. (2009). Personal-experience methods: Re-experiencing classroom teaching to better understand teacher education. In C. A. Lassonde, S. Galman, & C. Kosnik (Eds.), *Self-study research methodologies for teacher educators* (pp. 71–86). Rotterdam, The Netherlands: Sense.

Russell, T., & Korthagen, F. (1995). *Teachers who teach teachers: Reflections on teacher education.* London: Falmer.

Russell, T., & Munby, H. (Eds.). (1992). *Teachers and teaching: From classroom to reflection.* London: Falmer.

Russell, T., & Schuck, S. (2004). How critical are critical friends and how critical should they be? In D. L. Tidwell, L. M. Fitzgerald, & M. L. Heston (Eds.), *Journeys of hope: Risking the journey of self-study in a diverse world* (pp. 213–216). Proceedings of the Fifth International Conference on Self-Study of Teacher Education Practices, Herstmonceux Castle, East Sussex, England (pp. 213–216). Cedar Falls: University of Northern Iowa.

Samaras, A. P. (1991). Transitions to competence: An investigation of adult mediation in preschoolers' self-regulation with a microcomputer-based problem-solving task. *Early Education and Development, 2*(3), 181–196.

Samaras, A. P. (1998). Finding my way: Teaching methods courses from a sociocultural perspective. In A. L. Cole, R. Elijah, & J. G. Knowles (Eds.), *The heart of the matter: Teacher educators and teacher education reform* (pp. 55–79). San Francisco: Caddo Gap Press.

Samaras, A. P. (with Reed, R. L.). (2000). Transcending traditional boundaries through drama: Interdisciplinary teaching and perspective-taking. In J. Loughran & T. Russell (Eds.), *Exploring myths and legends of teacher education: Proceedings of the Third International Conference on the Self-Study of Teacher Education Practices, East Sussex, England* (pp. 218–222). Kingston, ON, Canada: Queen's University.

Samaras, A. P. (2002). *Self-study for teacher educators: Crafting a pedagogy for educational change.* New York: Peter Lang.

Samaras, A. P. (2008). *Suggestions for assessing your self-study research project.* Presentation at the Annual Meeting of the American Educational Research Association, Business Meeting of the Self-Study of Teacher Education Practices SIG, New York.

Samaras, A. P. (2009). Explorations in using arts-based self-study methods, *International Journal of Qualitative Studies in Education,* First published on: 18 December 2009 (iFirst) To link to this Article: DOI: 10.1080/09518390903426212URL: http://dx.doi.org/10.1080/09518390903426212

Samaras, A. P., Adams-Legge, M., Breslin, D., Mittapalli, K., Magaha O'Looney, J., & Wilcox, D. R. (2007). Building a plane while flying it: Reflections of teaching and learning self-study. *Reflective Practice, 8*(4), 467–481.

Samaras, A. P., Adams-Legge, M., Breslin, D., Mittapalli, K., Magaha O'Looney, J., & Wilcox, D. R. (2008). Collective creativity: A learning community of self-study scholars. In A. P. Samaras, A. R. Freese, C. Kosnik, & C. Beck (Eds.), *Learning communities in practice* (pp. 141–155). Dordrecht, The Netherlands: Springer.

Samaras, A. P., Beck, A., Freese, A. R., & Kosnik, C. (2005). Self-study supports new teachers' professional development. *Focus on Teacher Education Quarterly, 6*(1), 3–5, 7.

Samaras, A. P., DeMulder, E. K., Kayler, M. A., Newton, L., Rigsby, L. C., Weller, K. L., & Wilcox, D. R. (2006). Spheres of learning in teacher collaboration. In C. Kosnik, C. Beck, A. R. Freese, & A. P. Samaras (Eds.), *Making a difference in teacher education through self-study: Studies of personal, professional, and program renewal* (pp. 147–163). Dordrecht, The Netherlands: Springer.

Samaras, A. P., & Freese, A. R. (2006). *Self-study of teaching practices.* New York: Peter Lang.

Samaras, A. P., & Freese, A. R. (2009). Looking back and looking forward: An historical overview of the Self-Study School. In C. Lassonde, S. Galman, & C. Kosnik (Eds.), *Self-study research methodologies for teacher educators* (pp. 3–19). Rotterdam, The Netherlands: Sense Publishers.

Samaras, A. P., Freese, A. R., Kosnik, C., & Beck, C. (Eds.). (2008). *Learning communities in practice.* Dordrecht, The Netherlands: Springer.

Samaras, A. P., & Gismondi, S. (1998). Scaffolds in the field: Vygotskian interpretation in a teacher education program. *Teaching and Teacher Education, 14,* 715–733.

Samaras, A. P., Guðjónsdóttir, H., & Dalmau, M. C. (with S-STEP members). (2009, April). *A sociocultural perspective on the outgrowth and development of the Self-Study School.* Symposium, Annual Meeting of the American Educational Research Association (AERA), Self-Study of Teacher Education Practices SIG (S-STEP), San Diego, CA.

Samaras, A. P., Hicks, M. A., & Garvey Berger, J. (2004). Self-study through personal history. In J. Loughran, M. L. Hamilton, V. K. LaBoskey, & T. Russell (Eds.), *The international handbook of self-study of teaching and teacher education practices* (pp. 905–942). Dordrecht, The Netherlands: Kluwer Academic Publishers.

Samaras, A. P., Howard, B. J., & Wende, C. (2000). Kyoto redoux: Assessment of an environmental science collaborative learning project for undergraduate, non-science majors. *Canadian Journal of Environmental Education, 5,* 1–22.

Samaras, A. P., Kayler, M. A., Rigsby, L.C., Weller, K. L., & Wilcox, D. R. (2006). Self-study of the craft of faculty team teaching in a non-traditional teacher education program. *Studying Teacher Education, 2*(1), 43–57.

Samaras, A. P., Straits, S. A., & Patrick, S. S. (1998). Collaborating through movement across disciplines and schools. *Teaching Education, 9*(2), 11–20.

Samaras, A. P., & Wilson, J. C. (1999). Am I invited? Perspectives of family involvement with technology in inner city schools. *Urban Education, 34,* 499–530.

Schön, D. A. (1983). *The reflective practitioner: How professionals think in action.* New York: Basic Books.

Schön, D. A. (1987). *Educating the reflective practitioner: Toward a new design for teaching and learning in the professions.* San Francisco: Jossey-Bass.

Schuck, S., Aubusson, P., & Buchanan, J. (2008). Enhancing teacher education practice through professional learning conversations. *European Journal of Teacher Education, 31*(2), 215–227.

Schuck, S., & Russell, R. (2005). Self-study, critical friendship, and the complexities of teacher education. *Studying Teacher Education, 1*(2), 107–121.

Schuck, S., & Segal, G. (2002). Learning about our teaching from our graduates, learning about learning with critical friends. In J. Loughran & T. Russell (Eds.), *Improving teacher education practices through self-study* (pp. 88–101). London: RoutledgeFalmer.

Schulte, A. K. (2002). Do as I say. In C. Kosnik, A. R. Freese, & A. P. Samaras (Eds.), *Making a difference in teacher education through self-study.* Proceedings of the Fourth International Conference on Self-Study of Teacher Education Practices, Herstmonceux Castle, East Sussex, England (Vol. 2, pp. 101–105). Toronto, ON, Canada: OISE, University of Toronto.

Schulte, A. K. (2004). Examples of practice: Professional knowledge and self-study in multicultural teacher education. In J. J. Loughran, M. L. Hamilton, V. K. LaBoskey, & T. L. Russell (Eds.), *International handbook of self-study of teaching and teacher education Practices* (Vol. 1, pp. 709–742). Dordrecht, The Netherlands: Kluwer Academic Publishers.

Schwab, J. J. (1973). The practical 3: Translation into curriculum. *School Review, 81*(4), 501–522.

Seidman, I. (2006). *Interviewing in qualitative research.* New York: Teachers College Press.

Sell, C. (2009a). *Exit paper.* Submitted in partial fulfillment of course requirements in Advanced Research Methods in Self-Study. George Mason University, Virginia.

Sell, C. (2009b). *Moving on: What lights our path towards emancipation?* Paper submitted in partial fulfillment of course requirements in Advanced Research Methods in Self-Study. George Mason University, Virginia.

Shaw, M. (2008). *Homework is a drag!* Paper submitted to the Secondary Education Program, Graduate School of Education, College of Education and Human Development, George Mason University, Virginia, in partial fulfillment of the requirements for the degree of master of education.

Shulman, L. S. (1986a). Paradigms and research programs in the study of teaching. In M. C. Whittrock (Ed.), *Handbook of research on teaching* (3rd ed., pp. 3–36). New York: Macmillan.

Shulman, L. S. (1986b). Those who understand: Knowledge growth in teaching. *Educational Researcher, 15*(2), 4–21.

Shulman, L. S. (1998). Course anatomy: The dissection and analysis of knowledge through teaching. In P. Hutchings (Ed.), *The course portfolio: How faculty can examine their teaching to advance practice and improve student learning* (pp. 5–12). Washington, DC: The American Association for Higher Education.

Simms-Smith, A. O. (2009). *In what ways do my beliefs influence my classroom technology use: A self-study.* Paper submitted in partial fulfillment of course requirements in Advanced Research Methods in Self-Study. George Mason University, Virginia.

Smith, A. (2008,). *Creating an active student learning environment.* Paper submitted to the Secondary Education Program, Graduate School of Education, College of Education and Human Development, George Mason University, Virginia, in partial fulfillment of the requirements for the degree of master of education.

Smith, H. A. (1998). Self-study and the development of collective knowledge. In M. L. Hamilton (Ed.), *Reconceptualizing teaching practice.* (pp. 19–29). London: Falmer.

Smith, K. (2003). So, what about the professional development of educators? *European Journal of Teacher Education, 26*(2), 201–215.

Soehnlin, J. (2008). *Enriching student vocabularies.* Paper submitted to the Secondary Education Program, Graduate School of Education, College of Education and Human Development, George Mason University, Virginia, in partial fulfillment of the requirements for the degree of master of education.

Stencel, J. (1998). An interactive lecture notebook: Twelve ways to improve students' grades. *Journal of College Science Teaching, 27,* 343–345.

Stenhouse, L. (1985). *Research as a basis for teaching.* London: Heinemann.

Stevens, F., Lawrenz, F., Sharp, L. J., & Frechling, J. (Eds.). (1997). *User-friendly handbook for project evaluation: Science, mathematics, engineering and technology education.* Division of Research, Evaluation, and Communication. Arlington, VA: National Science Foundation.

Strauss, A., & Corbin, J. (1990). *Basics of qualitative research: Grounded theory procedures and techniques.* Newbury Park, CA: Sage.

Strunk, W., Jr., & White, E. B. (1979). *The elements of style* (3rd ed.). New York: Macmillan.

Taylor, C. (1982). The diversity of goods. In A. Sen & B. Williams (Eds.), *Utilitarianism and beyond* (pp. 129–144). Cambridge: MA: Harvard University Press.

Taylor, M., & Coia, L. (2009). Co/autoethnography: Investigating teachers in relation. In C. A. Lassonde, S. Galman, & C. Kosnik (Eds.), *Self-study research methodologies for teacher educators* (pp. 169–186). Rotterdam, The Netherlands: Sense Publishers.

Tidwell, D. L., & Fitzgerald, L. M. (2006). *Self-study and diversity.* Rotterdam, The Netherlands: Sense Publishers.

Tidwell, D., Fitzgerald, L., & Heston, M. (Eds.). (2004). *Journeys of hope: Risking the journey of self-study in a diverse world.* Proceedings of the Fifth International Conference on Self-Study of Teacher Education Practices, Herstmonceux Castle, East Sussex, England. Cedar Falls: University of Northern Iowa.

Tidwell, D. L., Heston, M. L., & Fitzgerald, L. M. (2009). *Research methods for the self-study of practice.* Dordrecht, The Netherlands: Springer.

Tidwell, D., & Manke, M. (2009). Making meaning of practice through visual metaphor. In D. L. Tidwell, M. L. Heston, & L. M. Fitzgerald (Eds.), *Research methods for the self-study practice* (pp. 135–153). Dordrecht, The Netherlands: Springer.

Tom, A. (1992). Forward. In L. Valli (Ed.), *Reflective teacher education: Cases and critiques* (pp. vii–x). Albany: State University of New York Press.

Tomal, D. R. (2003). *Action research for educators.* Lanham, MD: Scarecrow Press.

Tosun, N., Sucsuz, N., & Yigit, B. (2006). The effect of computer assisted and computer based teaching methods on computer course success and computer using attitudes of students. *The Turkish Journal of Educational Technology,* 5, 46–53.

Turney, J. (1996, April 20). Public understanding of science. *The Lancet,* 347(9008), 1087.

U.S. Department of Health and Human Services. (2007, July 30). *Code of federal regulations.* Retrieved November 22, 2009, from http://www.hhs.gov/ohrp/humansubjects/guidance/45cfr46.htm

Valli, L., & Buese, D. (2007). The changing roles of teachers in an era of high-stakes accountability. *American Educational Research Journal, 44*(3), 519–558.

van den Berg, O. (2001). The ethics of accountability in action research. In J. Zeni (Ed.), *Ethical issues in practitioner research* (pp. 83–91). New York: Teachers College Press.

van Manen, M. (1977). Linking ways of knowing with ways of being practical. *Curriculum Inquiry, 6*(3), 205–228.

Vygotsky, L. S. (1978). *Mind in society: The development of higher psychological processes.* In M. Cole, V. John-Steiner, S. S. Scribner, & E. Souberman (Eds.), Cambridge, MA: Harvard University Press.

Vygotsky, L. S. (1981). The genesis of higher mental functions. In J. V. Wertsch (Ed.), *The concept of activity in Soviet psychology* (pp. 144–188). Armonk, NY: Sharpe. (Original work published 1960)

Vygotsky, L. (1986). *Thought and language.* Massachusetts: The MIT Press.

Wade, S. E., Fauske, J. R., & Thompson, A. (2008). Prospective teachers' problem solving in online peer-led dialogues. *American Educational Research Journal, 45*(2), 398–442.

Weber, S., & Mitchell, C. (1996). Drawing ourselves into teaching: Studying the images that shape and distort teacher education. *Teaching & Teacher Education, 12,* 303–313.

Weber, S., & Mitchell, C. (2002). Academic literacy performance, embodiment, and self-study: When the shoe doesn't fit: Death of a salesman. In C. Kosnik, A. R. Freese, & A. P. Samaras (Eds.), *Making a difference in teacher education through self-study.* Proceedings of the Fourth International Conference on Self-Study of Teacher Education Practices, Herstmonceux Castle, East Sussex, England (Vol. 2, pp. 121–124). Toronto, ON, Canada: OISE, University of Toronto.

Weber, S., & Mitchell, C. (2004). Visual artistic modes of representation for self-study. In J. J. Loughran, M. L. Hamilton, V. K. LaBoskey, & T. Russell (Eds.), *The international handbook of self-study of teaching and teacher education practices* (Vol. 2, pp. 979–1037). Dordrecht, The Netherlands: Kluwer Academic Publishers.

Westerhoff, J. H. (1987). The teacher as pilgrim. In F. S. Bolin & J. M. Falk (Eds.), *Teacher renewal: Professional issues, personal choices* (pp. 190–216). New York: Teachers College Press.

Whitehead, J. (1989). Creating a living educational theory from questions of the kind, "How do I improve my practice?" *Cambridge Journal of Education, 19*(1), 41–52.

Whitehead, J. (1993). *The growth of educational knowledge: Creating your own living educational theories.* Bournemouth, UK: Hyde Productions.

Whitehead, J. (2004). What counts as evidence in self-studies of teacher education practices? In J. J. Loughran, M. L. Hamilton, V. K. LaBoskey, & T. Russell (Eds.), *International handbook of self-study of teaching and teacher education practices* (Vol. 2, pp. 871–903). Dordrecht, The Netherlands: Kluwer Academic Publishers.

Wiggins, G. (1998). *Educative assessment.* San Francisco: Jossey-Bass.

Wilcox, D. R. (2006). *Inspiring wonder: A self-study of a treasure collector's bucket.* Paper submitted in partial fulfillment of course requirements in Advanced Research Methods in Self-Study. George Mason University, Virginia.

Wilcox, D. (2008). *Project science inquiry: An exploration of elementary teachers' beliefs and perceptions about science teaching and learning.* Submitted in partial fulfillment of the requirements for the degree of doctor of philosophy in education, George Mason University, Fairfax, VA.

Wilcox, S., Watson, J., & Paterson, M. (2004). Self-study in professional practice. In J. J. Loughran, M. L. Hamilton, V. K. LaBoskey, & T. Russell (Eds.), *International handbook of self-study of teaching and teacher education practices* (Vol. 1, pp. 273–312). Dordrecht, The Netherlands: Kluwer Academic Publishers.

Williams, J. M. (1994). *Style: Ten lessons in clarity and grace* (4th ed.). New York: HarperCollins College Publishers.

Wolcott, H. F. (2001). *Writing up qualitative research.* Thousand Oaks, CA: Sage.

Woodward, J., & Brown, C. (2006, September). Meeting the curricular needs of academically low-achieving students in middle grade mathematics. *The Journal of Special Education, 40*(3), 151–159.

Wright, J. L., & Samaras, A. S. (1986). Play worlds and microworlds. In P. F. Campbell & G. G. Fein (Eds.), *Young children and microcomputers* (pp. 73–86). Englewood Cliffs, NJ: Prentice-Hall.

Zeichner, K. (1995). Reflections of a teacher educator working for social change. In T. Russell & F. Korthagen (Eds.), *Teachers who teach teachers* (pp. 11–24). London: Routledge.

Zeichner, K. (1999). The new scholarship in teacher education. *Educational Researcher, 28*(9), 4–15.

Zeichner, K. (2005). A research agenda for teacher education. In M. Cochran-Smith & K. Zeichner (Eds.), *Studying teacher education: The Report of the AERA Panel on Research and Teacher Education* (pp. 737–759). Washington, DC: American Educational Research Association & Mahwah, NJ: Lawrence Erlbaum Associates.

Zeichner, K. (2007). Accumulating knowledge across self-studies in teacher education, *Journal of Teacher Education, 58*(1), 36–46.

Zeichner, K. (2009, April). *Discussant comments for Samaras, A. P., Guðjónsdóttir, H., & Dalmau, M. C. (2009, April): A sociocultural perspective on the outgrowth and development of the Self-Study School.* Symposium, AERA, Self-Study of Teacher Education Practices SIG, San Diego, CA.

Zeichner, K., & Melnick, S. (1996). The role of community field experiences in preparing teachers for cultural diversity. In K. Zeichner, M. L. Gomez, & S. Melnick (Eds.), *Currents of reform in preservice teacher education* (pp. 176–198). New York: Teachers College Press.

Zeichner, K., & Noffke, S. (2001). Practitioner research. In V. Richardson (Ed.), *Handbook of research in teaching* (4th ed., pp. 314–330). Washington, DC: American Educational Research Association.

Zeni, J. (2001). Introduction. In J. Zeni (Ed.), *Ethical issues in practitioner research* (pp. xi–xxi). New York: Teachers College Press.

Index

About the Author

Anastasia P. Samaras is an international scholar, collaborator, and innovator in self-study teacher research with an extensive repertoire of teaching, administrative, and research activity directly related to and integrated with her passion for and contributions to self-study scholarship. Professor Samaras is the author, coauthor, or coeditor of numerous publications including *Self-Study for Teacher Educators* (2002), *Self-Study of Teaching Practices* (2006), *Making a Difference in Teacher Education Through Self-Study* (2006), and *Learning Communities in Practice* (2008). A former schoolteacher in pre-K–12 settings and director of several teacher education programs, she has a firsthand understanding of the realities of teaching. Her decades of teaching and research experiences have centered on designing and studying curriculum, instruction, and teachers' professional practices, including her own. She has presented as a visiting self-study scholar nationally and internationally working collaboratively with faculty and students around the world. Professor Samaras has been an active member of and leader in the Self-Study School and is much indebted to her self-study colleagues and her students for their scholarship, which has been foundational to this book and her earlier writings.

She is currently an associate professor in the College of Education and Human Development at the Graduate School of Education at George Mason University in Virginia.